Science on the Witness Stand

Science on the Witness Stand

Evaluating Scientific Evidence in Law, Adjudication, and Policy

TEE L. GUIDOTTI, MD, MPH

SUSAN G. ROSE, MPH, JD

OEM Press
Beverly Farms, MA

ISBN 1-883595-31-2

Library of Congress Cataloging-in-Publication Data

Guidotti, Tee L.
  Science on the Witness Stand / Tee L. Guidotti, Susan G. Rose.
    p. cm.
Includes bibliographical reference and index.
  ISBN 1-883595-31-2 (alk. paper)
1. Evidence, Expert—United States.   2. Medical jurisprudence—United
States.   I. Rose, Susan G., 1950-   II. Title.
  KF8964 .G85 2001
  347.73'67—dc21   2001002346

Printed in the United States of America

OEM Press ® is a registered trademark of OEM Health Information, Inc.

Note: This book contains information relating to general principles of medical care which are considered correct and compatible with the standard generally accepted at the time of publication. However, the authors and publisher disclaim any liability, loss, injury, or damage incurred as a consequence, directly or indirectly, of the use and application of any of the contents of this volume.

Published by OEM Press
8 West Street
Beverly Farms, Massachusetts 01915
1-800-533-8046

This book is dedicated to two pioneers in the modern use of scientific evidence in law. In the nineteenth century, Dr. Eugene Grissom of North Carolina, President of the American Psychiatric Association (1887–1888), advocated the use of psychiatric testimony in court and the development of scientific psychiatry. In the twentieth century (late 1960s and early 1970s), Ward Stephenson, a personal injury attorney from Oragne, Texas, was among the fist to use epidemiologic evidence in the representation of injured asbestos workers.

Contents

Preface

This book is a product of the collective thought and experience of a small group of colleagues and friends who, over the past decade, have shared an interest in the law and science. This informal group consisted of two physicians, Tee Guidotti and Ernie Levister; two lawyers, Susan Rose and Larry Reynolds; and one epidemiologist, David Goldsmith. The ideas of the group were honed in a series of projects and continuing-education sessions, all on a small scale and all self-supporting. The experiences of the group in litigation and adjudication procedures, especially workers' compensation, were invaluable in our education and in shaping the concepts we present here.

We believe that a systematic approach to assessing scientific evidence in the context of law is possible. However, there is no easy formula. The inspiration for what we are attempting to achieve with this approach comes from the developments of clinical epidemiology and critical appraisal, schools of thought that contributed decisively to the development of evidence-based modern clinical practice. Thus we offer a set of principles that may be used by expert witnesses and lawyers to present scientific knowledge and apply it in the courtroom and in claims adjudication. Our intention in this book is to lay a foundation and to initiate discussion that will lead to greater consistency and more accurate representation of scientific knowledge in the courtroom, in the claims office, and among policymakers.

The name we occasionally use for this intellectual approach, evidence-based medical dispute resolution (EBMDR), is not ideal. The qualifier evidence-based is intended to evoke parallels with evidence-based medicine and public health, a concept that is meaningful to health care practitioners and epidemiologists but not necessarily to lawyers. Medical is used here broadly to refer to issues of health and health care, which are our primary concerns, and is not intended to exclude public health or the application of medical knowledge to public policy. Unfortunately, there is no simple and commonly understood inclusive adjective in English for the applied health sciences. Dispute resolution is a term meaningful to lawyers but not necessarily to health practitioners. By putting these words together, we have an inartful description for an intriguing concept—the evaluation of causal evidence from the biomedical and population health sciences in application to law and the resolution of social issues. We have considered alternatives, such as critical appraisal for health law, but none of them are wholly satisfactory. We welcome proposals for better terms; perhaps someone among our readers will propose a suitable alternative.

The culture of science is both conservative and collaborative. Its function is to produce "general truths." On the other hand, the legal system seeks to produce "particularistic truths"—truths about a single set of events in a case before an adjudicating body—and its truths emerge from an adversarial process. Each of these cultures operates within a set of beliefs and values that dictates the nature of the appropriate language. The problem of differing languages often leads to misunderstanding, frustration of purpose, and unintended consequences. We have addressed this book to both the legal community and the public health community in the hope that greater cross-disciplinary communication will lead to a better understanding of the language and professional constraints of both scientific and legal cultures.

Finally, we caution that both the law and science change over time and can change quickly. Every effort has been made to ensure that the factual material in this book was correct as of January 1, 2001. Thereafter, the legal and technical material presented in this book may require revision. Similarly, we discuss these concepts as generalizations and provide specific examples to illustrate general principles. There is great variation among courts and adjudication systems. Readers are cautioned not to rely on this book to provide legal answers: Always obtain a knowledgeable legal opinion relevant to the jurisdiction or the adjudication system of interest.

The editors wish to extend their appreciation and gratitude to all of the contributors to this book for their enthusiasm for the project and the excellence of their work. A special acknowledgment to our administrative assistant, Rebecca Snyder, who managed to keep track of authors from coast-to-coast as well as the numerous revisions of each of the book's chapters. And a special thank you to Rick, Eden, and Andrew who had the courage to be "first cases."

January 1, 2001
Tee L. Guidotti
Susan G. Rose

Foreword

Doctors and lawyers often do not communicate well with each other. In part, this might be because many lawyers are drawn to law from nonscientific or nonmathematical educational backgrounds and experiences. Doctors and lawyers tend to think about problems differently and use different standards to assess the quality of solutions.

Anyone who has seen lawyers questioning doctors—whether on direct or cross-examination in any trial or other contested proceeding—has witnessed a struggle. Legal terms often are foreign to doctors, and medical terms often are poorly understood by lawyers. The questioning often leads to confusion on the part of the decision-maker who is called upon to make sense out of the combination of lawyers' questions and doctors' answers.

Science on the Witness Stand is an important book, potentially breaking new ground. It is a joint product of medical professionals and lawyers. Lo and behold, they can speak a common language! They can understand each other, and this book promises to assist lawyers, doctors, and medical experts in bridging the communication divide that has existed for far too long,

Science on the Witness Stand borrows from developments in clinical medicine and suggests a new approach to assessing medical and scientific evidence in legal settings. The approach, which the authors concede is far from perfectly named, is evidence-based medical dispute resolution or EBMDR. It is an ambitious approach that addresses how medical data and information ought to be used to resolve medical-legal disputes or to make public policy decisions that depend on medical data.

EBMDR posits that, just as evidence-based medicine has transformed clinical practice, an evidence-based analysis can transform the way in which legal and policy issues are resolved by decision-makers. The hope for EBMDR is that lawyers and medical experts can agree on how to frame issues so that each group understands each other and can use the tools of critical appraisal that have been developed in clinical practice to solve legal problems.

Although the concept of EBMDR seems quite sophisticated, the book should be easily accessible to most lawyers and medical experts. Much of the writing suggests an approach that is at least as much practical as it is theoretical. The first chapter, for example, tells medical experts how to form an opinion that will be persuasive, clear, and correct and how to communicate that opinion in written form so that it is most useful in a legal setting. The advice should help lawyers as much as medical experts.

There are a variety of useful perspectives in *Science on the Witness Stand*. One chapter educates doctors on civil litigation procedure and offers useful guidance on complex, mass tort cases. Another chapter offers a view from the bench (Canadian bench) by a former prosecutor who now sits as a trial judge. Lawyers will find the discussions of the nature of science and the difference between technology and applied science especially useful while both lawyers and medical experts will find the discussion of examples of "problematic language" that impedes their communication with one another valuable.

The heart of the book, however, deals with the subject matter that plagues decision-makers faced with medical disputes in a legal or public policy setting. One of the most important is the issue of causation. Chapter 5 addresses the development of criteria for the establishment of causation in epidemiology and medicine and uses as an example the epidemiological evidence leading the International Agency for Research on Cancer to conclude that crystalline silica is a human carcinogen. The chapter presents an analysis of the limits of epidemiological evidence and concludes that the Supreme Court's decision in *Daubert v. Merrell Dow Pharmaceuticals, Inc., 509 U.S.* 579 (1993), may have assumed that such evidence will be more generally available than can reasonably be expected.

Indeed, the next chapter addresses the effect of *Daubert* and argues that trial judges have assumed too much of a gatekeeping role and have tended to act as junior scientists even when it is not necessary. The authors' view is that judges sometimes exclude medical and scientific testimony because they under-value the validity of certain medical judgments based on sound reasoning and sufficient data. They also express concern that parties increasingly feel compelled to offer experts to support the scientific validity of another expert's methodology, a process that increases the costs of litigation unnecessarily. This chapter un-doubtedly will challenge some judges to rethink their approach to medical evidence.

Chapters 8 and 9 return to the subject of causation. Chapter 8 utilizes Bayes' theorem and offers a mathematical understanding of causation issues, while Chapter 9 examines the full range of issues that must be examined when a causation determination is made. The latter chapter sets forth a preferred sequence of causation analysis in the medical-legal setting. It should be very helpful to both lawyers and medical experts in addressing causation issues. Workers' compensation cases receive particular treatment, and Chapter 9 is both clear and helpful as it sets forth five questions that must be asked in every case. Chapter 9 also introduces the concept of apportionment in causation analysis when multiple causes may account for a disease.

Apportionment is further developed in Chapters 10 and 11. Chapter 10 examines the problem of smoking. Smoking poses a number of problems in a causation analysis as it often interacts with other types of occupational or environmental exposures. Smoking, unlike some others, is a risk factor that can be quantified. The end result is that smoking may pull more weight than other factors in an analysis simply because of the ease of quantification. The conclusion is that smoking, while clearly risky, confounds attempts to assess the contribution of other factors to disease. Chapter 11 turns to workers' compensation proceedings. It points out why workers' compensation agencies want to apportion cause (to assure that a disease or condition was caused by work), but find apportionment to be extremely difficult. This chapter also discusses "presumption," the assumption that a given disease is more likely than not due to a particular cause because of a strong association between the disease and an occupation and exposure (an assumption that is analyzed in more detail in Chapter 14).

The causation discussion leads to the case study in Chapter 13 of a patient apparently suffering from cirrhosis of the liver due to hepatitis C. The problem is that there is more than one possible explanation. The chapter suggests how a careful medical expert would develop an opinion on causation and sets forth the details that ought to be included in an expert's report.

The discussion of medical causation leads naturally to a discussion of evidence issues when environmental health questions are presented: in developing occupational health standards under the Occupational Safety and Health Act of 1973, in complying with the 1990 Americans with Disabilities Act, in assessing substance abuse in the workplace and in athletic competitions, with respect to specific worker's compensation issues, and in thinking about mental health issues. The book ends with a discussion of the standard of care expected of medical professionals.

Lawyers who read this book will better understand how medical experts think, talk, and analyze problems. Medical experts who read this book will understand the requirements of the legal system and the expectations of lawyers who rely upon expert assistance. If both lawyers and medical experts read the book, they will learn how to work together to improve the integrity of medical evidence in legal settings. Such learning will make a substantial contribution to both law and medicine.

Stephen A. Saltzburg
Howrey Professor of Trial Advocacy, Litigation
and Professional Responsibility
The George Washington University School of Law
Washington, DC

Contributing Authors

Stephen L. Demeter, MD, MPH
Head, Division of Pulmonary and Critical Care Medicine
Northeastern Ohio Universities College of Medicine
Akron, OH

Ilise L. Feitshans, JD, ScM
Adjunct Faculty
Cornell University School of Industrial and Labor Relations
New York, New York
School of Public Health and Health Sciences
The George Washington University Medical Center
Washington, DC

David F. Goldsmith, MSPH, PhD
Associate Research Professor
Department of Environmental and Occupational Health
School of Public Heath and Health Services
The George Washington University Medical Center
Washington, DC

Tee L. Guidotti, MD, MPH
Chair, Department of Environmental and Occupational Health
School of Public Heath and Health Services
The George Washington University Medical Center
Washington, DC

Harold E. Hoffman, MD
Department of Occupational and Environmental Medicine
University of Alberta
Edmonton, Alberta, Canada

Michael G. Holthouser, MD, MPH
Medical Director
Norton Health at Work
Louisville, KY

William J. Judge, JD, LLM

Workplace Distance Learning USA, Inc.
Oak Park, IL

Ernest C. Levister, Jr., MD

Clinical Assistant Professor
Department of Occupational and Environmental Medicine
University of California Irvine
San Bernardino, CA

Kent W. Peterson, MD

President, Occupational Health Strategies, Inc.
Charlottesville, VA

Karen E. Read, JD

Director, Mass Tort Litigation Department
Poorman-Douglas Corporation
Beaverton, OR

Larry A. Reynolds, LLB, LLM, PhD

Adjunct Professor in Environmental Health
Department of Public Health Sciences
University of Alberta
Edmonton, Alberta, Canada

Gary Rischitelli, MD, JD, MPH

The Center for Research on Occupational and Environmental Toxicology
Oregon Health Sciences University
Portland, OR

Michael D. Roback, MD

Midway Medical Plaza
Los Angeles, CA

Susan G. Rose, MPH, JD

Law Offices of Stanley & Rose
Washington, DC

Sara Rosenbaum, JD

Center for Health Services Research and Policy
The George Washington University Medical Center
Washington, DC

Christina Guerola Sarchio, JD

Associate Attorney
Howrey Simon Arnold & White, LLP
Washington, DC

Sorell L. Schwartz, PhD

Professor Emeritus of Pharmacology
Georgetown University Medical Center
International Center for Toxicology and Medicine
Rockville, MD

Susan Silverman

President, The Silverman Group
Highland Park, IL

Donna R. Smith, PhD

Senior Vice President
Substance Abuse Management, Inc.
Boca Raton, FL

The Honourable Leo Wenden

Judge of the Provincial Court of Alberta
Edmonton, Alberta, Canada

1

Introduction: Evidence-Based Medical Dispute Resolution

TEE L. GUIDOTTI

SUSAN G. ROSE

Evidence-based medical dispute resolution is a systematic approach to evaluating scientific evidence in the particular context of law and other forms of health-related dispute resolution, such as statutory adjudication systems (workers' compensation, etc.). This book explores the groundwork to establish a consensus on what this approach should be and to discuss some of the pitfalls.

This book is not intended to lay down rules, because that would be both impertinent and impossible. Professor Ilise Feitshans, who contributes Chapter 17 of this book, reminds us that the law tries whenever possible to find the natural rules that give logic to the resolution of a dispute—the rules that were, in a sense, always there. A set of arbitrary rules written today will seem as naive in 20 years as the issues over the reliability of lie detector testing that gave us the Frye rule. However, a set of natural rules that make sense may be so fundamental that they stand for centuries, such as the Magna Carta. Our task is to find those natural rules and to argue convincingly that they apply in both science and law.

We intend in these chapters to lay out a general approach and a coherent philosophy as the basis for ongoing discussion and refinement. It is hoped that in coming years a consensus will emerge among health professionals and lawyers on the most reasonable approach to interpreting scientific evidence in health-related disputes. In law, consensus suggests a normative approach to settling disputes, such as legislation. However, in contemporary views of science, consensus plays a much different and more flexible role. In science, consensus is an integral part of the scientific method, moving the scientific community forward by allowing agreement on essential facts and on a working theory. That a working theory may be challenged by falsification (the demonstration of an inconsistent

1

fact) in the next round of research is part of the process of creating the next level of consensus. We hope for a consensus on the rules of evaluating scientific evidence that will be subject to continual review and inspection, as in science, but that will provide a working framework useful in law to separate the wheat from the chaff.

Thirty years ago, a movement toward evidence-based medicine revolutionized clinical practice. Critical appraisal of the medical literature and the reliance on evidence-based principles by managed care organizations and utilization review organizations led to adoption of evidence-based medicine as the dominant mode of clinical practice today. The concept of critical appraisal and evidence-based medicine was not embodied in legislation or enforced as governmental or judicial policy. This movement advanced for many years by education in medical schools, debate, and consensus until it was ready to be institutionalized in practice. It became the accepted norm because it met a need, satisfied a rising demand, and made sense to all participants. Its history is described in greater detail later in this chapter.

It should be possible to develop a similar framework for the evaluation of scientific evidence in legal settings. This framework could be as simple in design, as robust, and as adaptable as the idea of evidence-based medical practice. The rise of evidence-based medicine shows that it is possible for a consensus to emerge despite highly independent practitioners. Its counterpart in the form of evidence-based medical dispute resolution may well become the next consensus, provided that it meets the need of legal systems, satisfies the demand of society for fairness, and makes sense to all participants.

What would constitute evidence-based medical dispute resolution, or EBMDR? A rational approach to evaluating evidence in the health sciences requires both a capacity to generalize, usually on the basis of a population, and a capacity to individualize to the specific case. If the mechanism is known, the explanation enhances the credibility and therefore the persuasiveness of the conclusion. This approach should be useful in the development of a specific case and in guiding the development of the administrative systems in which it is used. Therefore, such an approach should contain these elements:

- Epidemiology and the interpretation of population data.
- Individualization of the evidence to the specific case, using methods of clinical medicine, toxicology, and (in the future) genetics.
- Statistical treatment that does not necessarily rely on conventional assumptions designed for scientific studies.
- An understanding of science that takes into account the social nature of the scientific enterprise, as shown in contemporary studies in the history and philosophy of science.
- Adaptability to a variety of applications, including public policy, statutory adjudication systems, and tort litigation.

There is no formula or easy set of rules that can be derived for the universal application of this approach to scientific evidence. Our intent here is to define and promote the process, not to confine or direct it. In producing this book, we have commissioned chapters by a variety of authors with expertise in all relevant areas, seeking to outline the essentials of a consistent approach. We have not attempted to dictate content or even to resolve disagreements among the chapter authors. This book is the beginning, not the resolution, of a consistent approach we call EBMDR.

Why EBMDR?

Since the 1993 landmark U.S. Supreme Court *Daubert* decision (discussed in greater detail in Chap. 6), U.S. courts have moved toward greater rigor in evaluating scientific evidence [1]. Adjudication systems supported by expert consultants, such as workers' compensation tribunals, have used an evidence-based approach in some form for much longer. Increasingly, courts are required to examine the scientific evidence in pre-trial (Daubert) hearings to determine for themselves whether testimony or evidence is reliable rather than relying solely on the credentials of experts or the opinion of one set of experts about the credibility of another set of experts. Instead, the courts must decide for themselves whether the evidence is based on valid science and whether the scientific methodology is reliable, tasks for which they are ill prepared by legal training.

This expanded requirement for the court to decide issues of the validity of scientific evidence creates two responsibilities for the expert witness that, if not new, are newly emphasized: (1) to provide a clear rationale behind the expert opinion and (2) to articulate it in a manner that is useful to the court or adjudicating body. The expert witness in a lawsuit or an adjudication hearing always has been expected to express a sound opinion in a comprehensible fashion. Now the expert witness is expected to demonstrate solid scientific grounds with ample documentation as well as a coherent chain of logic for the opinion expressed, to communicate in terms the educated layperson can understand, and to place the opinion in a context that assists the judge or jury to arrive at an informed decision.

In civil litigation, the burden of proof rests on the plaintiff, and the standard employed is "more likely than not," which roughly translates to more than 50% likelihood [2]. This raises interesting questions for the evaluation of scientific evidence. Should every link in the evidentiary chain be evaluated as "more likely than not" or only the final conclusion? What should be done with missing but key evidence? Can one system based on a standard of 95% or more probability for scientific certainty communicate effectively with a system that is based on a standard of more than 50% to decide issues of legal liability?

What we can say now is that clearly there is no escaping the broader redistribution of responsibility: Judges must learn enough to apply the standards of a given scientific field to testimony presented in that field, and conversely, lawyers and expert witnesses must learn to frame their arguments in terms the court can understand and deal with. If we can agree on the terms of reference, not as a set of rules but as norms on which we generally agree, perhaps the use of scientific evidence will be harder to abuse and easier to understand, and legal decisions will become more consistent with the current state of scientific knowledge. Our goal with this book is to start a discussion on the critical issues of how science and the law can best work together.

Evidence-Based Medicine

Thirty years ago, a small group of epidemiologists and clinicians established the field of clinical epidemiology. They formed a loose network, independent but heavily influenced by David Sackett of McMaster University and Sir Richard Doll, later Regius Professor of Medicine at Oxford. This movement revolutionized medical practice by codifying rules and methods for the evaluation of medical treatments and diagnostic tests. Clinical epidemiology created a new consensus in medicine for acceptance of the effectiveness of a new treatment or the predictive value of a test. The randomized clinical trial became the "gold standard" for determining the effectiveness of a treatment, despite its considerable expense and the impracticality of conducting such trials on every conceivable treatment and subgroup of patients. Because clinical epidemiology required large amounts of accurate, complete, and systematically collected data, it drove clinical research to new rigor and professionalism. The result was continuous improvement over a number of years in what previously had been a "hit or miss" clinical research enterprise. After years of contention and resistance, eventually consensus was built among clinical investigators as to what was good science and what was not. Much of this consensus arose as a new generation of physicians left medical school and fellowships imbued with the approach and trained to be skeptical of the anecdotal, case-series approach that had dominated the earlier clinical research literature.

The founders of clinical epidemiology had created a movement. This movement developed its own institutions, such as the Cochrane Collaboration at Oxford, and heavily influenced the renaissance of "general" or "primary care" internal medicine in the 1980s. However, evidence-based medicine's approach to the evaluation of scientific literature, called *critical appraisal,* may be its biggest contribution.

Critical appraisal is both a method and a philosophy of lifelong learning. As a method, it requires a critique of individual studies and the scientific literature as a whole. Using this method, physicians would be able to break away from the influence of authority and think independently. They could read the primary literature and come to their own conclusions. No longer would practitioners be unduly influenced by drug company sales representatives, charismatic speakers at medical meetings in exotic locations, and "throw-away" journals. The movement was widely embraced and quickly moved into the mainstream of medicine. Family medicine practitioners saw in it an opportunity to gain the high ground and to establish a systematic standard of care that would distinguish them from general practitioners of the past. General internal medicine practitioners saw it as the science that justified their identification as a primary care specialty. Specialty practitioners saw it as a way to advance their fields and bring into line practitioners who were not up to par. The movement coincided with increasing attention to the minority of physicians who were negligent or who misbehaved. Discipline improved, and medical boards enforced the rules more publicly. Critical appraisal offered a ready-made approach to determining the elusive standard of practice on which such cases often hinged.

This increasing scrutiny lead to the obvious conclusion that medical practice was not, for the most part, grounded on documented experience. Long before the characteristics and prior probability of disease in the subject population were recognized and described by clinical epidemiology, physicians took note of their own experience and that of their local peers to determine what treatments worked on the patients they saw in their own communities. Before they accessed databases with large numbers and found data that came close to the characteristics of their difficult individual cases, they searched out the experience of other practitioners who saw similar subgroups and patients with special circumstances. This was not really folk art based on anecdote, as some have alleged, but an honest effort to adapt medicine to the realities of the local population and individual needs.

Nobody disagreed, however, that compiling such information into databases and systematically analyzing the experience derived from many patients constituted a better approach. Since it was soon evident that no practitioner could afford the time to do this on every relevant topic in his or her practice, critical appraisal transformed into *evidence-based medicine,* in which data were compiled and analyzed by experienced medical analysts and consensus groups, often using advanced statistical methods such as meta-analysis. Judging from the number of disputes and dissensions, evidence-based medicine did not necessarily mean that medical practice was free of controversy or differences in opinion. Data could be interpreted in dramatically different ways, as the dispute over control of cholesterol and the risk of coronary artery disease illustrated. Rather, the controversies continued on a higher plane but on firmer ground, so to speak, over increasingly fine points. Inexorably, the level of detail and refinement in controversial clinical issues exceeded the capacity of individual practitioners to analyze the evidence for themselves. Recently trained physicians had been taught in medical school not to rely on their own unrepresentative experience. Physicians, therefore, increasingly were forced to turn to consensus statements and analyses done for them in review articles and journals specialized in summarizing the mainstream literature, such as *Evidence-Based Medicine* and the *ACP Journal Club*. The unintended result is that medicine has come full circle and again relies on authority, but now there is a check on and a scientific standard for that authority.

The breakthrough for evidence-based medicine, however, occurred when it became the essential technology for health care rationalization. Utilization review organizations, payers, and later health maintenance organizations began to use evidence-based medicine to define the best practices for large groups of patients. Patient care protocols, care maps, and clinical algorithms became ways to improve practice and reduce costs. Physician discretion was curtailed, but the overall result was closer adherence to medical practices that demonstrated clear benefits for the majority of patients. By identifying the best practices for the majority of patients, managed care organizations could reduce their inventory of unneeded drugs, discourage treatments of little or questionable value, and streamline their staffing to concentrate on services that added value. Not coincidentally, individual physicians became interchangeable. When best practices are understood and replicated, individual experience and expertise become less important in the outcome. The method of evidence-based medicine, which had begun in part as a way of breaking the commercial influence of drug companies and other authorities on medical practice, has now become a major tool for business to standardize and commodify medical practice in a new commercial setting.

The next turn of the wheel is likely to be the response by organized medicine to concerns over medical safety. Evidence-based medicine concentrates on effectiveness. Patient care protocols emphasize outcomes and cost-effectiveness. Adverse outcomes that arise from system failures are not dealt with adequately by this approach, however. The risks and costs of therapeutic misadventures and mistakes have emerged as the next major area for systematic medical reform. Again, clinical epidemiology will likely provide the technology for evaluation.

Evidence-based medicine did not end controversy in medical practice, but it confined the scope to the scientific issues and rooted controversy in evidence rather than in unsubstantiated opinion. Its biggest advantage is that the majority of patients treated according to a protocol based on the best evidence probably will have a better outcome than those treated by means of arbitrary, individualized practice based on the personal preference of the health care provider. The biggest drawbacks of evidence-based medicine are that it cannot be used for every conceivable clinical problem that an individual patient presents and that protocols quickly fall apart when there are complications, more than one condition in which treatments are incompatible, or unusual individual circumstances. It is easy to design a protocol for the treatment of gall bladder disease. It is harder to design a protocol for the treatment of diabetes. It is much harder to design a protocol for the management of gall bladder disease in a brittle diabetic with hypertension. At some point, the clinical judgment of an experienced practitioner must prevail.

It can be argued whether evidence-based medicine revolutionized medical practice or whether it conveniently arrived on the scene to provide medicine with a way forward when it needed one. Medicine had already arrived at a point in its history where a change in practice standards was needed. Clinical epidemiology provided the means.

The current state of affairs in the courts is not unlike the situation in medicine at the time clinical epidemiology was "invented." The "practice" of medical expert witnesses is not standardized or governed by a consistent set of principles. Each expert witness is essentially autonomous. An expert witness cannot link to a community of other experts who have a consistent view of how to approach a problem or interpretation. Likewise, 30 years ago medical practitioners were autonomous and kept their own counsel. This all changed for medical practitioners as a result of increasing external demands for consistency and persuasion. It will not be possible to distill a set of rules or protocols for dealing with scientific evidence in legal settings. However, if the broad outlines of reasonable care can be agreed on, we will have advanced much further and can concentrate on the factors of the individual case.

Evidence-based medicine and critical appraisal succeeded in establishing a new framework for medical practice. Similarly, with EBMDR we now hope to introduce a comparable framework for the use of scientific information in law.

The Way Forward

The chapters in this book are intended to begin a discussion and exploration that we hope will result in the broad outlines of a consistent approach to the evaluation of scientific evidence in court cases and adjudication in health issues. The model of evidence-based medicine is not perfect but illustrates what we would like to see achieved.

We seek a robust but rigorous approach that would be the medicolegal counterpart of critical appraisal. EBMDR recasts the elements of critical appraisal into a framework useful for resolving medical disputes. The disputes to which we refer encompass adjudication of individual cases under systems of insurance or entitlement, civil litigation, alternative dispute resolution (such as mediation and arbitration), and public policy for health and health-related issues (e.g., health care disputes, environmental health issues). In other words, legal actions based on a health-related tort, environmental litigation for the protection of an endangered ecosystem, and broad public policy issues such as the standards applied by EPA in setting the proposed standard for fine-particulate air pollution all would come under the umbrella of EBMDR.

We raise the following questions:

- Can a solid consensus be achieved among legal and medical professionals on how disputes related to health and medical management can be *framed* (legal vocabulary) and the essential health and medical issues defined?
- Can both a medical understanding of complexity and a legal ability to parse the issues each be taught to the other profession so that there is mutual understanding concerning the essentials?
- Can the tools of critical appraisal (clinical epidemiology, meta-analysis, and critical evaluation) be applied to the body of evidence admitted in a legal dispute?
- Can the tools of critical appraisal be adapted to apply to the rules of civil law and administrative practice?

This book is the beginning of the exploration of these issues—but by no means the end.

References

1. *Daubert v. Merrell Dow Pharmaceuticals, Inc.,* 509 U.S. 579, 113 S.Ct. 2786 (1993).

2. Boden LI, Miyares JR, Ozonoff D. Science and persuasion: environmental disease in U.S. courts. *Soc Sci Med* 1988;10:1019–1029.

Bibliography

This book would not have been possible without the previous scholarship of others. The individual chapters give references that pertain to their subject matter. The following list is intended to give special credit to important references that have informed the general field of evaluating scientific evidence for law, adjudication, and policy.

American College of Physicians. Guidelines for the physician expert witness. *Ann Intern Med* 1990;113:789.

Black B. Evolving legal standards for the admissibility of scientific evidence. *Science* 1988;239:1508–1512.

Black B, Lilienfeld D. Epidemiologic proof in toxic tort litigation. *Fordham Law Rev* 1984;52:732–785.

Federal Judicial Center. *Reference Manual on Scientific Evidence,* 2d ed. Washington: Federal Judicial Center, 2000.

Jasanoff S. *Science at the Bar: Law, Science and Technology in America.* Cambridge, MA: Harvard University Press, 1995.

Meyer C (ed). *Expert Witnessing: Explaining and Understanding Science.* Boca Raton, FL: CRC Press, 1999.

Muscat JE, Huncharek MS. Causation and disease: Biomedical science in toxic tort litigation. *J Occup Med* 1989;31:997–1002.

Meufeld PJ, Colman N. When science takes the witness stand. *Sci Am* 1990;262:46–53.

Science and Technology Policy Forum. *Science, Technology and the Law* (Science in Society Policy Report). New York: Academy of Sciences, 1998.

"It is my considered opinion that drowning occurred due to a faulty room humidifier."

2

Constructing the Medical Opinion: Elements, Expression, and Logic

GARY RISCHITELLI

Law and Science

The term *science* is used in a variety of ways. It can be used to describe a body of knowledge, a field of study, or a particular method of study. The word *science* is used in so many dissimilar contexts it may defy concise definition.

The term *scientific method* denotes a formal process of inquiry and is regarded as an objective method of study and observation. In the scientific method, data are collected in a controlled environment in order to support or refute an *a priori* hypothesis. The process of collecting data in a controlled environment is called an *experiment*. The experiment seeks to reduce or eliminate the variation in all but the factors of interest, thus permitting the observer to attribute any observed effect to those factors. Scientists and others using scientific data often fail to acknowledge, however, that some subjectivity invades even the most tightly controlled experimental environment. Subjectivity enters the study from the observer's choice of the study aims, methods, subjects, and techniques of data collection, analysis, and interpretation.

Nonscientists often fail to appreciate this fact and are puzzled or even provoked when scientists disagree about the quality, relevance, or conclusions from seemingly objective data. As a result, in a desire for scientific certainty, nonscientists often voluntarily or unknowingly overlook the reservations, qualifications, and/or disclaimers that scientists routinely attach to their work [1].

This need to satisfy the public's desire for authoritative pronouncements of scientific certainty while remaining honest about the inherent subjectivity and uncertainty of the process is a recurring challenge for physicians and scientists who offer expert opinion in legal, legislative, and administrative proceedings.

Standards of Proof

Preparing medical or scientific reports is a type of technical writing, and technical writing requires a consideration of the needs, background, and capabilities of the audience. Preparing medical reports for use in the adjudication of legal or administrative disputes requires this same consideration. Understanding the needs of a legal audience requires an exploration of the fundamental similarities and differences in legal and scientific reasoning and the differing standards of proof in the two disciplines.

Ascertainment of facts is basic to both science and law, and in both disciplines it rests upon proof. In this context, proof is a quantum and quality of evidence or data sufficient to support a conclusion. But criteria for determining what evidence or data are adequate have taken centuries to develop and are still elusive. Science uses quantitative criteria subject to statistical analysis. Law uses categorical criteria that are described verbally. Analytically, both processes rest upon subjective judgments or assumptions. Science, because of the nature of the questions it addresses, has an empirical or pragmatic model of validation that other disciplines lack; but ultimately proof of facts in all disciplines rests upon subjective judgments of probability. The ascertainment of facts lies at the heart of both science and law. But no discipline, or any human process, enables the human mind simply to apprehend raw facts. Lawyers gather data which they call "evidence"; scientists gather evidence which they call "data." Both terms mean the same thing, which is intellectual support for some conclusion or proposition. The sufficiency of evidence or data to support a conclusion or proposition is what we call "proof." Thus, determination of the quantum and quality of evidence or data that amounts to proof is basic to both disciplines [1].

Proof in law or science is ultimately a probability statement. The basic principles and methods of reasoning are similar in law and science. Science, however, focuses primarily on the use of quantitative data and methods of analysis to describe and model observations of the natural world, whereas law uses qualitative and categorical analyses to classify and regulate the social, moral, and political aspects of human behavior.

The applications of these basic principles and methods, however, ultimately are different. Scientists seek to develop universal laws or theories based on consistent observations of repeated phenomena. The data from these repeated observations support or refute an underlying hypothesis, and the hypothesis is revised or rejected based on the data from subsequent observations. These evolving universal laws or theories are used ultimately to make predictions about future phenomena and to develop new technologies.

Law, on the other hand, requires the application of predetermined normative rules to specific individual circumstances and events. The collection of data and ascertainment of the "facts" surrounding these events are nearly always retrospective and represent a reconstruction of an historical event by techniques of logical inference. Frequently, both the facts and the inferences are the subject of dispute, and the parties present their versions urging different conclusions. This *adversarial method* of fact-finding is the cornerstone of the Anglo-American legal system.

Science is, in essence, descriptive. It is based on prospective observation of events under controlled conditions in order to test an *a priori* hypothesis. Law, in contrast, is inferential and attempts, *post hoc*, to portray or reconstruct events that defy reproduction under exactly the same conditions. Another important distinction is that some legal analyses require inferences regarding human motives, intent, and state of mind that cannot be subjected to direct observation or quantitative analysis.

p < *0.5 and Type I and II Errors*

Scientists, respecting the constant evolution of scientific knowledge, seek to avoid the *alpha* or *type I error*. This kind of error occurs when two phenomena are found to be associated when, in fact (i.e., in nature), a true association does not exist. Scientists prefer instead to remain skeptical of new data or theories until the data can be reproduced and assimilated into the current body of knowledge or, when necessary, are used to revise or reject previous theories (see Chap. 7).

Law, on the other hand, must decide individual cases as they are presented. The parties, and society as a whole, demand a timely resolution to a dispute. In fact, having *an* answer may be more important than having the *right* answer. Courts are cognizant of the evolutionary nature of scientific knowledge and are quick to incorporate new findings into future cases. They cannot, however, stop the judicial process for long periods of time while scientists conduct "more studies." Although scientists, when presented with novel or conflicting data, typically will call for "more research," judges, lawmakers, and the public cannot and will not wait when a "ripe" question requires an answer.

Because of the nominative or categorical nature of many legal standards and rules, lawyers must rely on a qualitative description of proof. The standard of proof varies depending on the legal context but usually falls into one of three general categories. Civil suits usually demand a standard of proof for facts that is "more likely than not." Criminal trials usually require that facts be proven "beyond a reasonable doubt." Some other legal contexts may require an intermediate standard of "clear and convincing evidence."

For scientists, the standard of proof is a predetermined level of statistical significance. Usually this represents a less than 1 in 20 ($p < 0.05$) to 1 in 100 ($p < 0.01$) probability that the data are simply the result of random variation (chance). This is certainly a more stringent standard than the legal standard of "more likely than not," and this causes physicians and scientists no small measure of discomfort. The concept of statistical significance may in some ways be more akin to the "beyond a reasonable doubt" standard of the criminal justice system, although few jurors (or scientists) could define and agree on what constitutes a reasonable doubt.

The "more likely than not" standard is sometimes defined as a "greater than 50% probability," but this is inaccurate. Actual legal proof demands more than a simple probability of greater than 50%. It does not correspond directly with a statistical significance level ($p < 0.5$) because statistical significance addresses only the contribution of random variation (chance) and not the likelihood that one hypothesis is more probable than another. This is where scientists and lawyers often believe that they are discussing probabilities in the same fashion when in fact the proof of legal causation requires something more than a simple "more probable than not" pronouncement based on pure mathematical probabilities.

For example, consider the case of the Red Cab:

> Suppose there are two taxicab companies in town which operate cabs that are identical in appearance except that one company's cabs are red and the other's are green. A person who is color blind and cannot distinguish red from green is knocked down on a deserted street by a cab which is driven wildly. Suppose that the only evidence available for identifying the cab company responsible for the accident is the statistical information that 60% of the town's cabs are red and 40% are green. Since the evidence indicates a 60% probability that the Red Cab Company is responsible, it appears that a preponderance of the evidence supports imposing liability on the Red Cab Company. To impose liability on the Red Cab Company based on these bare statistical facts, however, seems grossly unfair [2].

Like the Red Cab case, extrapolating purely statistical or epidemiologic data can be misleading and result in injustice. For example, concluding that an individual's illness arose from an exposure to a workplace chemical based on population studies demonstrating an excess of the disease would be unjust if the worker's exposure was substantially different in dose, duration, or route than the workers in the study or the worker had other personal or lifestyle factors that significantly modified the risk. Likewise, denying the association also would be unjust under the same circumstances. Population data may not be relevant to the specific circumstances of an individual, particularly where there is significant variation in susceptibility, exposure, and effect. The key issue, therefore, is not the rote recitation of published studies suggesting or refuting an association but a particularized application of the available data to the individual circumstances of the case.

Courts traditionally have avoided using mathematical probability as the sole basis for finding a fact true in legal proceedings. This has changed, however, with the advent of complex civil litigation in the areas of toxic tort and product liability, where the issues are heavily laden with science, statistics, and uncertainty [2]. In a toxic tort case, the plaintiff may have no basis for alleging liability other than statistical and epidemiologic data that show an increased incidence of disease in exposed populations. The burden of persuasion, however, should require some particularistic evidence that the plaintiff has experienced an analogous exposure and that other important risk factors are similarly distributed. Without this evidence, application of solely epidemiologic data demonstrating a greater than twofold increase in risk may meet the greater than 50% interpretation of preponderance but does not address the basis of that particular individual's risk of disease. The expert's task, therefore, is to educate and guide the judge and/or jury regarding the significance of the scientific evidence so that they are not improperly swayed as to the relevance or irrelevance of the data in light of the particular circumstances in the case or proceeding.

Law and Logic

Deductive reasoning results from the construction of an argument such that the conclusion must flow from the given premises. For example:

> All men are mortal.
> Socrates is a man.
> Therefore Socrates is a mortal [3].

The validity of this argument is a product of its form, but the "truth" of the argument depends on the content of the premises.

False premises can allow for a "logically sound" but clearly false argument. For example:

> All men are fish.
> Socrates is a man.
> Therefore Socrates is a fish [3].

This argument, although obviously incorrect, is as logically valid as the first. The truth of the premises is essential to the truth of the deduction.

By contrast, induction is an argument suggesting that the conclusion may follow from the premises, but not necessarily. Induction allows us to draw probabilistic inferences from what we have observed about what we have not or cannot observe. It allows for generalization from the observation of particulars. Most conclusions reached by induction, however, defy independent verification—hence the need to employ inductive reasoning. For example:

> Socrates is a man and is mortal.
> Plato is a man and is mortal.
> Aristotle is a man and is mortal.
> Therefore probably all men are mortal [3].

The philosopher John Stuart Mill identified induction as the foundation of scientific and legal reasoning. Mill also believed that the deductive process relied on induction, as its first step, to generate the premises of the deductive argument.

Mill described a series of methods or canons of inductive inference. The "Method of Agreement" states that if two or more observations of the same phenomenon share only one characteristic, then that characteristic is the cause of the phenomenon. The "Method of Difference" states that if a phenomenon occurs in one instance and not in another and the circumstances are the same except for one characteristic, then that characteristic is the cause of the phenomenon. The "Method of Residues" states that by removing the effects of known causes, the remaining effects are the result of the remaining causes. The "Method of Concomitant Variations" states that if a phenomenon is observed to vary when another phenomenon varies, it is either the cause or effect of the other phenomenon or it is connected through some fact of causation [1].

A brief consideration of Mill's methods reveals that these are the foundational techniques of reasoning in many fields of science, including epidemiology and toxicology. These inductive techniques are used to ascertain causes or to develop rules that help to explain or predict observed phenomena. For example, let us consider an epidemiologic investigation of an outbreak of illness among attendees at a church picnic. After interviewing both ill and well members of the congregation, the epidemiologist discovers that all the ill members and none of the well members ate potato salad. By identifying the similar antecedent in all the members who were sick (Method of Agreement) and the absent antecedent in all who were not sick (Method of Difference), the likely cause (eating potato salad) was identified. Although the cause (potato salad) cannot be proved conclusively with this information, a probabilistic inference can be drawn.

Similarly, the discovery of mosquitoes as the vector of yellow fever followed the observation of an astute Army surgeon that illness was associated with the absence of protective screening from mosquitoes [3]. The Methods of Agreement and Difference can be very powerful tools for identifying causes, especially when used in combination.

The Method of Concomitant Variation is the basis of drawing inference from statistical correlation studies; it is also the basis of the canon of dose-response in toxicology and epidemiology. It was the observation of a correlation between smoking and rising lung cancer rates that originally demonstrated the plausibility of a cause-effect relationship.

A contemporary philosopher of science, Karl Popper, denied the validity of inductive reasoning. He believed that science uses deduction to generate hypotheses and then tests them empirically. Empirical testing can disprove or falsify a hypothesis, but it can never verify or prove a hypothesis. A hypothesis that is tested and not falsified is corroborated but not proved. Scientific statements or theories are never established conclusively and are always subject to revision or rejection [1].

The *principle of parsimony* (also known as *Ockham's razor*) holds that simple statements have greater empirical content and are more easily subject to testing than more complex ones. This is significant because the strength of a hypothesis depends on the rigor of the tests it has survived.

Because statistical or probabilistic hypotheses are incapable of proof or definitive falsification, an element of uncertainty persists (see Chap. 7). An expression of inductive logic, *Bayes' theorem*, demonstrates that information that is particularly surprising or unlikely unless some hypothesis is accepted as true supports that hypothesis (see Chap. 8). For example, the discovery of gunpowder residue on the hands and clothing of a murder suspect would be relevant to proof of guilt. The probative value of this evidence would be greater if a suspect claimed never to have owned or fired a gun compared with a suspect who is employed as a firearms instructor. Similarly, the discovery of an increased incidence of tumors in an exposed population compared with nonexposed controls would suggest an association with the exposure. The probative value of this evidence would be greater if a similar effect were observed in other species or perhaps lesser if the exposed species has a high baseline incidence of similar tumors.

In short, the more unexpected or difficult it is to reconcile the new information without assuming the truth of the prior hypothesis, the greater is the support for the hypothesis. Bayesian reasoning is employed widely in both law and science and is the only logical theory that reconciles induction as a tool of the scientific method.

Another particularly powerful technique of inductive reasoning is analogy. It relies on an assumption that if two entities share similar characteristics in some known respects, then they probably share other qualities or characteristics as well. Analogy is fundamental to most scientific reasoning. Outcomes from controlled experiments are used analogously to explain or predict natural phenomena. Sometimes necessity requires the use of analogy, such as the use of animal models to predict human toxicologic effects.

Analogies are strengthened by the number of *confirming instances* (a function of sample size). Analogies are also strengthened by the number of similarities that the entities share. Conversely, many differences between the entities weaken the analogy. The analogy is meaningless, however, despite its apparent strengths if it is not relevant to the argument at hand. For example, assuming that yellow cars are more reliable because your uncle had a yellow car he drove for 20 years would have several potentially fallacious components, including the number of confirming instances, the number of similarities and dissimilarities, and the relevance of the analogy.

Analogy is one of the most widely used and powerful legal reasoning techniques. The legal doctrine of *precedent* is based on the use of prior decisions to determine the outcome of subsequent cases with similar (analogous) facts and issues. Debating the merits of two competing analogies is essentially the heart of all legal arguments [3].

No discussion of logical reasoning in law and science would be complete without some discussion of common logical fallacies [3]. Experts, advocates, judges, and juries can all fall victim to these fallacies and the resulting errors. Experts must be particularly vigilant in avoiding the use of logical fallacies and in detecting the use of logical fallacies by opposing experts.

The *ad hominem fallacy* arises from an attempt to discredit the view of the opponent not by attacking the substance of the argument but by attacking the credibility of the opponent. This is widely employed in law and has some utility in revealing potential sources of bias. However, this technique is frequently abused. Juries of individuals with limited understanding of complex medical and scientific issues are particularly vulnerable. Jurors may equate the message with the messenger and completely disregard sound scientific data because of a perceived bias of the presenting expert following a skillful *ad hominem* attack by the opposing counsel. Use of *ad hominem* by scientific and medical experts is particularly unprofessional and casts a bad light on the community of professionals. Experts should limit their opinions to the scientific merits of the opponent's arguments and should have sufficient expertise to do so without resorting to *ad hominem*.

The *"slippery slope" argument* suggests that although the opponent's argument has merit, accepting the conclusion inevitably will lead to some undesirable effect. This fallacy is frequently invoked to combat a compelling argument by the opponent or to justify maintaining an inequitable or indefensible status quo. It is particularly dangerous because it draws attention away from the issue and leads the audience to consider improbable future consequences that evoke strong emotional responses. It is this appeal to emotional effect in many "slippery slope" arguments that makes this fallacy particularly dangerous and misleading.

Suppressed evidence is not a fallacy per se, but it has the same practical effect of leading the audience to an illogical or ill-informed conclusion. In using the technique of suppressed evidence, the proponent presents an argument and intentionally omits critical or opposing data. The use of half-truths or leaving out key pieces of information is particularly rampant in politics, advertising, and journalism.

Ad misericordium is an "appeal to pity." It is a favorite tool of trial lawyers and is used to draw attention to the sympathetic state of the party and away from the facts of the case. The proponent presents an argument that is not based on the facts at issue but on some other appealing or provocative fact that captures the sympathy of the audience. Again, it is this appeal to the emotions that makes this technique both effective and dangerous.

Finally, taking the position of the opponent and then distorting it can be a very effective technique to combat a compelling argument by the opponent. Appearing to accept the position of the opponent and then extending the argument until it appears ridiculous is one application of the technique. Alternatively, accepting the argument but then simplifying it to the point of absurdity is also effective. For example, distilling the complex issues of forest ecosystem management in the Pacific Northwest to a simple "owls versus people" argument can have a powerful effect on public opinion, particularly among individuals with limited knowledge of the issues. This technique is widely employed in law and politics.

Scrutinizing the content of our own thoughts, the opinions of others, and the media is an effective way to heighten sensitivity to the logical fallacies and thus is the first step in avoiding the use of these fallacies and identifying their use by others.

The Role of the Expert

Expert, Not Advocate

The role of the expert witness is often misunderstood. It is this misunderstanding of the fundamental role that has resulted in the "hired gun" perception of expert witnesses.

It is not the role of an expert to help the attorney win the case. The role of the expert witness is primarily to assist the trier of fact (judge or jury) in understanding complex issues of medicine or science and *thereby* assist the attorney in winning his or her case. Expert witnesses must not become "spin doctors" for either side. They should acquire, analyze, and interpret the data in the same way that they would in a scientific, rather than legal, milieu.

ACOEM Guidelines for Expert Witnesses

In 1997, the American College of Occupational and Environmental Medicine (ACOEM) adopted a code of ethics for its members [4] (Fig. 2-1). These guidelines were developed based on similar statements by other professional medical societies. They were adapted, however, to meet the particular circumstances of physicians practicing in occupational medicine who participate in legal, legislative, and administrative proceedings regarding occupational health (as opposed to the legal proceedings surrounding cases of medical malpractice).

> The testimony of an expert medical witness should be founded on a thorough and critical review of the pertinent medical and scientific facts, available data, and relevant literature. The expert should specify whether his or her opinion is based on personal experience, specific reference to peer-reviewed literature, or generally accepted professional opinion in the specialty field [4].

This indicates that the expert's opinion should be based on a thorough and honest appraisal of all relevant data. Experts are free to critique and disregard data that appear invalid, but they should explain the scientific basis of their rejection of the data.

The expert also must demonstrate honesty in disclosing the basis of his or

Figure 2-1. Ethical guidelines for occupational and environmental medicine expert witnesses.

I. Purpose or goal of expert testimony	As a citizen and a professional with special training and experience, the occupational and environmental physician has an ethical obligation to provide expert assistance in legal, administrative, and legislative proceedings, and to testify in hearings or trials as an expert witness when appropriate. The physician must clearly understand that the role of the medical expert witness is not to be an advocate but to provide credible information that assists the court or other forum in understanding complex medical or scientific issues.
II. Need for ethical and professional guidelines	Often, criteria or guidelines for qualifying medical or other scientific expert witnesses are inadequate, and as a result, any physician can testify as an expert witness regardless of training, experience, or demonstrated competence. It is in the public interest that occupational and environmental medicine expert testimony be competent, readily available, objective, and unbiased. To limit uninformed and possibly misleading testimony, occupational and environmental medicine expert witnesses should be qualified for their role and should follow a clear and consistent set of ethical guidelines. The following guidelines were developed jointly by the Occupational Health Law and Policy Section and the Committee on Ethical Practice in Occupational Medicine of the American College of Occupational and Environmental Medicine in response to the need to define the recommended qualifications for the occupational and environmental physician expert witness and the guidelines for his or her behavior
III. Qualifications of an expert medical witness	A witness who testifies authoritatively should have current experience and ongoing knowledge in the medical or scientific discipline that is the subject of his or her testimony. It should be kept in mind that expert knowledge in one field does not imply or confer expertise in all fields. A physician expert witness who offers testimony regarding issues of clinical medicine should have appropriate knowledge and experience regarding the area of clinical medicine in which he or she offers expert testimony. To ensure that the public obtains the benefit of testimony by medical experts with demonstrated competence, a physician who testifies as a medical expert should be certified by or have satisfactorily completed the equivalent requirements of a relevant specialty board recognized by the American Board of Medical Specialties. In addition, the expert should be qualified by training or experience to testify as an expert in the specific subject matter of the case or proceeding.
IV. Basis of expert medical testimony	The testimony of an expert medical witness should be founded on a thorough and critical review of the pertinent medical and scientific facts, available data, and relevant literature. The expert should specify whether his or her opinion is based on personal experience, specific reference to peer-reviewed literature, or generally accepted professional opinion in the specialty field.
V. Objectivity of expert medical testimony	The medical expert witness is expected to be objective and should not adopt a position as an advocate or partisan in the proceedings. He or she can have no direct personal or pecuniary interest in the outcome of the case, and his or her review of the medical facts should be thorough, fair, and impartial and should not exclude any relevant information in order to create a view favoring any party.

VI. Conduct of the expert medical witness	The physician expert must demonstrate adherence to the strictest of personal and professional ethics. Truthfulness is essential, and misrepresentation of a personal theory or opinion as scientific doctrine may be harmful to individual parties, the profession, and the public. The physician should testify honestly, fully, and impartially to his or her qualifications regarding the medical or other scientific issues involved in the case. The medical expert must strive to avoid even the slightest appearance of impropriety or partiality. The expert must conduct himself or herself with professional decorum and avoid personal attacks, insults, or deprecatory remarks directed at other witnesses or parties.
VII. Peer review and discipline	Medical experts should be aware that transcripts of depositions and courtroom testimony are public records, subject to independent peer review by colleagues and professional organizations, and that testimony in some states may be subject to the jurisdiction and review of appropriate licensing or disciplinary boards.
VIII. Compensation of the expert witness	The acceptance of fees that are disproportionate to those customary for professional services can be misconstrued as influencing the testimony given by the witness. Therefore, fees should be reasonable and commensurate with the time and effort given to reviewing records and pertinent literature, writing reports, and appearing for deposition or testimony. It is always unethical for a physician to accept compensation that is contingent on the outcome of litigation.

These guidelines were drafted by Thomas Weir, MD, JD, and Gary Rischitelli, MD, JD, MPH, and were modeled after similar guidelines prepared by the American Medical Association, American College of Physicians, American College of Surgeons, American Academy of Orthopedic Surgeons, American College of Obstetricians and Gynecologists, and American College of Radiologists. The authors gratefully acknowledge the contributions of the following individuals who supplied comments or acted as reviewers: Ron Teichman, MD, MPH, Susan Cassidy, MD, JD, Rhaja Khuri, MD, from the ACOEM Committee on Ethical Practice in Occupational Medicine; Charles Lucey, MD, JD, MPH, Patrick Joyce, JD, MD, MPH, Marcia Scott, MD, Modesto Fontanez, MD, JD, Gregg Stave, MD, JD, MPH, and Andrew Campbell, MD, from the ACOEM Occupational Health Law and Policy Section.

her opinion and be willing to distinguish between scientifically derived data, consensus opinion, and personal opinion. The expert must be particularly careful where personal hypotheses or methods are touted as accepted scientific dogma. Materials not subjected to peer review, editorial articles, presentations at advocacy meetings, or publication in obscure journals should not be presented as widely accepted scientific contributions.

The medical expert witness is expected to be objective and should not adopt a position as an advocate or partisan in the proceedings. He or she can have no direct personal or pecuniary interest in the outcome of the case, and their review of the medical facts should be thorough, fair, impartial and should not exclude any relevant information in order to create a view favoring any party [4].

Experts should not benefit personally from the outcome of the proceeding to which they are contributing their expert opinion.

> The physician expert must demonstrate adherence to the strictest of personal and professional ethics. Truthfulness is essential, and misrepresentation of a personal theory or opinion as scientific doctrine may be harmful to individual parties, the profession, and the public. The physician shall testify honestly, fully, and impartially to his or her qualifications regarding the medical or other scientific issues involved in the case.
>   The medical expert must strive to avoid even the slightest appearance of impropriety or partiality. The expert must conduct himself or herself with professional decorum and avoid personal attacks, insults, or deprecatory remarks directed at other witnesses or parties [4].

While giving testimony as an expert, the expert is representing the profession that he or she practices. Considering the personal, financial, social, and political stakes that are often present in legal, administrative, and legislative proceedings, the expert must observe the highest level of personal and professional ethics.

Compelling but Not Persuasive

The expert's opinion should be compelling but not overtly persuasive. The strength of the conclusion should rest on the data and not on the persuasive power of the expert. On reviewing the data that have been presented in an honest, thorough, and unbiased form, the reader should come to the conclusion on his or her own without the need for overt exhortation or subtle persuasion by the writer.

The key to an excellent report is the presentation of a logical argument based on the available evidence that allows only one reasonable conclusion. Of course, rarely can only one reasonable conclusion be reached because the genesis of the expert's report is an underlying dispute between presumably reasonable individuals.

The report, however, should compel the reader to choose among the reasonable conclusions based on the strength of the evidence, and the strength of the logical argument presenting the evidence, in light of all the uncertainties present. Ultimately, the reader should feel the strength of the author's conclusion and be guided to reach the same conclusion.

Writing

Preparation

Preparation is the fundamental step to producing a quality report. Understand fully the issues at hand and the purposes of your report. The expert should have all necessary and relevant information at hand before forming an opinion.

Nothing can be worse than having your report discredited because you failed to obtain or carefully review important data.

Careful research and data abstraction followed by the development of comparison tables, timelines, or other graphic methods of tabulating, summarizing, and analyzing data can be invaluable when preparing or dictating the final report. It helps to organize your thoughts, strengthen your conclusions, and makes your report much easier to prepare and read. Time spent in this stage of preparation is amply rewarded later.

Organization

A compelling report leads the reader to one inescapable conclusion—yours. It must guide the reader to this conclusion firmly and clearly. It must be concise, clear, and well-organized. It must cause the reader to believe that you are well-informed, authoritative, and unbiased. For this reason, the report must be logical, methodical, and precise. Emotional statements, derogatory remarks, or comments not directly related to the scientific and medical issues should be avoided. When the physician makes a conclusion or inference, the reason "why" should be explained carefully.

A high-quality report presents, analyzes, and synthesizes the scientific or medical data surrounding an issue and applies that information to the specific facts of the claim or case. The report should be an objective, exploratory document that thoroughly addresses the issues, evaluates the strengths and weaknesses of the data, and reaches a conclusion based on the analysis. The report should not be an advocacy paper; its persuasive power should arise from the soundness of its medical and scientific conclusions [5].

LARGE-SCALE ORGANIZATION. Medical and scientific opinions often can be organized effectively in the form of a deductive argument. A generally accepted rule regarding a condition or exposure is stated first (major premise), and then the facts in the specific case or circumstances are presented similarly (minor premise). If the facts of the specific case meet the criteria outlined in the general rule, the rule is applied to reach a conclusion [3].

Analyzing a complex case usually involves breaking it down into component parts (issues) that have relevance to the final opinion. Begin by identifying each relevant issue, explain its relevance, and proceed to discuss it in turn. At the conclusion of the discussion, again explain the relevance of each issue to the determination of the final analysis. The summary of the report should synthesize the individual analyses of the subissues into a coherent and compelling conclusion.

One of the most effective ways to achieve this organization and to prepare a cogent and well-reasoned report is to employ the following adaptation of a legal outlining technique. The outline requires that (1) each important diagnostic or treatment *issue* is clearly identified, (2) the medical evidence or diagnostic *rule* regarding that issue is clearly and concisely stated, (3) the *argument* of how the medical evidence is relevant to the issue is presented, (4) any opposing or conflicting evidence supporting a *counterargument* is presented, and finally (5) the expert's *conclusion* regarding the issue is presented. When an expert's opinion is organized using this outlining technique, the product is clear, well-reasoned, and compelling.

For example, analyzing a worker's claim for compensation for occupational asthma would begin with a discussion of the two key issues: (1) whether the worker has asthma and (2) whether it is work-related. First, the issue of the diagnosis of asthma is addressed. The diagnostic criteria for asthma should be stated explicitly, with citation to appropriate sources of authority such as leading articles, consensus statements, or widely recognized textbooks. The historical, physical, and laboratory evidence both supporting and refuting the diagnosis would be discussed. Finally, a conclusion regarding whether or not the worker has asthma would be offered with a discussion of any uncertainties or modifying factors.

Next, the same approach would be employed to discuss the issue of work-relatedness, again discussing the criteria for determining causation with reference to appropriate sources, the evidence for and against work causation, and a conclusion regarding the likelihood that the condition is caused by exposures in the workplace.

The order in which you analyze the issues depends on the larger analysis and the relevance of the issue. If the analysis includes a threshold question on which the analysis turns, then it should be addressed first. In the preceding example, the threshold question of whether the worker has asthma is addressed first because a negative conclusion would moot the remainder of the analysis. If there is no clear logical order, then addressing the issues in order of complexity is a good approach.

SMALL-SCALE ORGANIZATION. Topic paragraphs and topic sentences help the reader to follow the argument and assist with transitions between issues. Begin each section of the analysis with a thesis paragraph. The thesis paragraph should introduce the reader to the issue, the relevance of the issue, the evidence regarding the issue, and your conclusion regarding the issue. The thesis paragraph captures the larger organization of the analysis in a condensed fashion and provides the reader with a map for the remainder of the analysis. The points in the thesis paragraph should then be developed in appropriate sequence in the subsequent paragraphs [5].

Language Techniques

Language is so important to effective presentation of evidence that an entire chapter in this book is devoted to it (see Chap. 15). In general, follow the basic principles of good written English grammar, composition, and style. Avoid jargon, slang, and excessively informal language, but do not use language that is overly formal, antiquated, or stiff. Try not to sound pompous, bureaucratic, or overly poetic and flowery. Your writing should convey the benefit of a professional education but should be written for readers who are not professionals in your field.

Use simple direct words and sentences, employing the active voice as much as possible. Write as you would speak if you were lecturing to a large audience of lay individuals; use vocabulary and syntax that are both natural and comfortable to you and your audience. Use short words, sentences, and paragraphs. Avoid surplus words; try to deliver your message directly and concisely [6].

Introduce new topics, facts, or data at the beginning of a sentence or paragraph. Use tables to present complex or lengthy compilations of data, and use graphs or other pictorial aids where appropriate [6].

The report should be visually appealing and easy to read. Use an easy-to-read type size and font, and provide adequate space between lines and in the margins. Include headers and footers that identify the topic, date, and page numbers.

Guide the reader by placing names and dates at the beginnings of sentences and paragraphs. Use of boldface and italic type can be helpful to provide emphasis and organization, but such typographic distinctions should be used sparingly to preserve effect.

Avoid "legalese," but use substantive legal terms *if* you are comfortable with them and understand their meaning. For example, in discussing an individual's disability and its impact on job performance, it would be appropriate to discuss the impact on "essential functions" and the possibility of a "direct threat" to safety, but only if you are familiar with the precise meanings of these terms.

Document all sources of information, and arrange them in some logical order. Provide a list of references. Carefully proofread the report because grammatical and typographic errors, including errors of spelling and punctuation, can greatly diminish the credibility of the expert and the impact of the report [6].

The Most Important Word Is Because

The most important word in legal writing is *because*. You must explain the basis of your conclusions in a coherent, organized, and compelling format, or it is simply just an "opinion" and not the product of a careful analysis of the data. Every conclusion regarding an ultimate issue in the analysis should be followed by an explanation of why you came to that conclusion.

Cite references as authority, or develop powerful analogies. Use guidelines, position statements, and reports from expert panels and other sources to demonstrate that you are familiar with the body of knowledge surrounding the issue and that your conclusions are based on sound data and reasoning. If these secondary sources of authority do not support your conclusions, then explain why. Make the reader understand why your research has led you to a different interpretation or conclusion or why the conclusions of the other source are faulty or erroneous. Deal with the uncertainties in scientific data explicitly, and explain the impact of missing or ambiguous data.

Content

There are many magic words and incantations in law. The correct use of these words can have a profound influence on the impact or relevance of your report. For example, the U.S. Equal Employment Opportunity Commission (EEOC) defines *direct threat* for the purposes of the Americans with Disabilities Act (ADA) as a "significant risk of substantial harm." Both the terms *significant* and *substantial* have great importance in this context. Although the ultimate definitions of these terms in the ADA are formed gradually through ongoing litigation, these terms do have some basic value to lawyers that may be difficult for nonlawyers to appreciate.

Appropriate use of these terms will lend great impact and credibility to your opinion for all sides in the dispute or proceeding. Appropriate use of the correct terms often will negate the opposing experts' opinions if they do not use these terms or fail to use them properly.

Key Terms

Physicians are often bewildered by the use of legal terms in statutes and administrative rules, which include the frequent use of such terms as *significant, substantial, possible, probable, major,* and *aggravation. Significant* describes any contribution that is weighty, has a notable effect, and is at least in part responsible for an outcome. *Substantial* includes elements that are worthy of note and that may have had an effect which should not be ignored, i.e., more than a *de minimis* contribution. The term *possible* describes a concept or event that is "conceivable." Although broad, *possible* should be used to describe outcomes or events that are reasonably anticipated. The quip that "anything is possible" may be trite but is not very helpful in the determination of medical facts. Physicians should exercise their professional medical judgment in determining whether the connection between an exposure and an illness is possible. *Probable* means "more likely than not" (i.e., a greater than 50% probability). *Major contribution* describes an element that may be more than 50% of the total cause or the largest proportionate share of the cause, depending on a state's definition. Finally, *aggravation* may describe both symptomatic and/or pathologic worsening of the worker's condition, depending on a state's definition [7].

Causation

In the determination of medical causation, the key issue is whether the employment exposure caused or substantially contributed to the worker's illness or injury. If the employment relationship is unclear, vague, or uncertain, then the causal connection has not been established.

Physicians must develop a consistent approach to the medical questions surrounding occupational disease. One model approach involves a four-step analysis specifically determining (1) if there is objective evidence of disease, (2) if there is objective evidence of exposure, (3) if there is credible evidence, in general, supporting a causal connection between the exposure and the disease, and (4) if there is sufficient evidence, in this worker's case, to support a causal connection between his or her exposures and the development of the disease or injury.

The threshold step should be determined using scientifically supported methods and professionally accepted guidelines for arriving at a specific medical diagnosis. Physicians must be prepared to explain the basis of their opinions, particularly with regard to the interpretation of epidemiologic or laboratory data supporting the relationship between the exposure and the illness. Lastly, the expert must be capable of discussing the particular causal and factual issues in an individual worker's claim. For example, the physician may be asked to interpret the relevance of epidemiologic data regarding the risk of lung cancer following asbestos exposure in light of a particular worker's individual lifetime exposure history, including smoking history. Credible history or objective evidence should support each of these determinations before the final conclusion of work causation is offered.

Prognosis, Outcomes, and Natural History

Prognosis should be offered in light of the natural history of a condition, its response to treatment, and the specific individual biological, psychological, and social characteristics of the individual. Potential outcomes as well as an estimate of their probability should be described. Natural history can be helpful when comparing a particular individual's progress, response to treatment, or rehabilitation with other individuals with similar conditions. For example, noting that the natural history of condition A is to improve spontaneously in 6 to 8 weeks may be helpful when discussing an individual who continues to exhibit disability months or even years later.

Fitness to Work

Fitness to work always should be described in terms of the individual's ability to perform the essential functions of the job safely without posing a direct threat to his or her own or others' health and safety. A thorough understanding and discussion of the particular work environment, the work practices performed, the hazards posed by the environment, and relevant health and safety protections are essential to a credible and defensible report.

This process should never be undertaken lightly because of the potential consequences to the worker, coworkers, the employer, and the public. Appropriate use of other professional consultants, laboratory tests and procedures, neurobehavioral performance testing, functional capacity evaluation, and work simulation all may be employed to establish a compelling determination of fitness to work.

Conclusion

Basic Rules

1. *Be prepared.* Make sure that you understand the issues. Do your homework, and have a command of the scientific and medical knowledge surrounding the topic. Make sure that you also have a command of the specific data and facts surrounding the specific event or circumstances.

Try to understand the social, legal, and political environment. Try to determine what are the key legal or policy issues and what burden-of-proof issues may be present. Use this information to place your report in a context that will be most helpful to resolving the questions.

2. *Use plain language.* Avoid jargon. Avoid colloquialisms, clichés, and slang. Avoid overly formal, flowery, or verbose language. Write as though you would speak in normal conversation with a stranger of average intellect and education.

3. *Answer the question.* Unless your report addresses the important issues, it is worthless. Make sure that you understand what these issues are. If the requesting party provides a list of specific questions, then answer them fully, using clear, concise, and definite language. Address uncertainties explicitly, and explain the impact of these uncertainties on your opinions. Do not purposefully hedge or be ambiguous. Do not assume that readers will draw the right conclusions from your premises, and do not expect them to "read between the lines" if you have failed to be explicit regarding your conclusions.

4. *Answer only the question.* Restrict your report to those observations, data, and supporting literature which are relevant to your opinion. Explain why they are relevant. Try not to introduce new issues that may be of academic importance or may be completely irrelevant to the issues at hand. Above all, avoid making observations or comments that are wholly subjective, personal, or inappropriate.

5. *Explain why.* Explain why and how you came to your conclusions. Identify all relevant sources of information and all sources of authority.

6. *Cite authority when possible.* This is really an extension of rule 5. Demon-

strate that your opinion is based on factual data, well-designed valid studies, or the consensus of other experts in the field. The goal, of course, is to demonstrate that this is not simply an unsubstantiated or unsupported opinion and that your conclusions are based on generally accepted premises or data that would survive peer review.

7. *Guide your reader.* Use clear organization to guide your reader. Organizing by topic or issue, with subheadings, helps the reader to follow the report and prepare for transitions. Internally, the use of topic sentences, thesis paragraphs, and summary paragraphs helps readers to follow the steps in the analysis.

References

1. Loevinger L. Standards of proof in science and law. *Jurimetr J* 1992;32:323–329.

2. Dant M. Gambling on the truth: The use of purely statistical evidence as a basis for civil liability. *Columbia J Law Soc Probl* 1988;22:31–70.

3. Landau JL. Logic for lawyers. *Pacific Law J* 1981;13:59–98.

4. Rischitelli DG, Weir T. *Ethical Guidelines for Expert Witnesses in Occupational and Environmental Medicine.* Arlington Heights, IL: American College of Occupational and Environmental Medicine, 1997.

5. Shapo HS, Walter MR, Fajans E. *Writing and Analysis in the Law,* 2d ed. Westbury, NY: Foundation Press, 1991. P 342.

6. Smith GM, Demeter SL, Washington RJ. The disability-oriented medical evaluation and report. In: Demeter SL, Andersson GB, Smith GM (eds), *Disability Evaluation.* St. Louis: Mosby, 1996.

7. Rischitelli DG. A workers' compensation primer. *Ann Allergy Asthma Immunol* 1999;83:614–617.

3

Civil Litigation: Principles and Procedures

SUSAN G. ROSE

KAREN E. READ

The aim of this chapter is to provide a very brief orientation for health profession-als to the substantive principles of tort law and toxic torts in order to furnish a legal background for the issues discussed throughout this book. To further set the stage, the chapter discusses procedural issues and reviews two of the most commonly used management mechanisms in complex litigation—class actions and multidistrict litigations (MDLs). It ends with a discussion of the role of the scientific expert in the courtroom and introduces the issues sur-rounding the admissibility of scientific evidence in the federal court system.

Many books and countless numbers of law review articles have been pub-lished on these topics. The intent of this chapter is to outline broadly today's legal arena in which scientific testimony plays such a vital role.

The Law of Torts

A person who has suffered harm at the hands of another may seek to redress his or her grievance in the courtroom. The law of torts determines when one person (or groups of persons, or corporations, or the government) must pay compensation for civil, noncontractual wrongs caused to others. Tort law in-cludes specific types of intentionally inflicted wrongs (e.g., assault and battery and defamation) as well as injuries inflicted unintentionally through failure to act as an ordinarily prudent person (e.g., negligence).

Recognition of these types of personal harm permits society to compensate with money an individual who has been harmed through no fault of his or her own. While the injury cannot be undone, a negligence lawsuit allows the victim to attempt to shift the cost of the injury to the party responsible for causing the injury. Second, tort law serves to prevent harm through enforced accountabil-ity. By making certain that undesirable and harmful behaviors are costly to the actor, tort law serves to deter such behavior by the defendant and others in the future. "Because individuals can rarely secure either compensation or account-ability outside the legal system, tort law gives the individual citizen a forum in which to complain on a more equal footing against a potentially mightier wrongdoer" [1].

A fundamental premise of tort law is that a plaintiff must have a present injury before he or she can sue for damages. "The threat of future harm, not yet realized, is not enough" [2]. Moreover, a plaintiff who has suffered a present injury is entitled to recover damages for the future consequences of a present injury (e.g., loss of income from wages, etc.). A plaintiff must prove that the defendant's actions were both the "cause in fact" and the "proximate" cause of his or her injuries. Liability will "attach," in legal terms, if the injury would not have occurred *but for* the defendant's conduct, even if that conduct contrib-uted only partially to the plaintiff's injuries. Under the "but for" rule of causa-tion, if the plaintiff would not have suffered damages but for the defendant's act, the act is a cause-in-fact of the injury [3].

An alternative theory of causation is used when there are several factors combining to cause injury and each factor alone would have caused the damage, so the "but for" test fails. Instead, the rule is that if the defendant's conduct was a "substantial factor" in bringing about the plaintiff's injury, liability will attach. (Causation is explored in greater detail in Chap. 9).

Once a court concludes that the defendant's conduct constitutes a cause-in-fact of the plaintiff's injury, it must next determine whether the defendant's conduct is the "proximate cause" of the injuries. "Proximate cause . . . has been defined as any cause which, in a normal and continuous sequence, unbroken by any efficient, intervening cause, produces injury and without which injury would not have occurred" [4].

In general, the plaintiff bears the burden of proving both causation-in-fact and proximate cause. In other words, a plaintiff must establish more than a possibility of causation—a plaintiff must demonstrate that a causal relationship *more likely than not* exists between a defendant's conduct and his or her injuries. In a civil case, the plaintiff's "burden of proof" is sometimes referred to as a "preponderance of the evidence" as opposed to "beyond a reasonable doubt" (the standard in criminal prosecutions).

Toxic Torts

Traditionally, the concerns of tort law are with injuries for which the cause-effect association is evident (e.g., a fall on a slippery floor, a car running into a pedestrian) and for which eyewitness testimony or a physician's opinion is suffi-cient to establish causation. However, over the last 25 years, a new and rapidly growing area of tort law, called *toxic torts,* has emerged with the advent of "mass exposure" or "environmental injury" litigation. The common element in these lawsuits is that some activity or product of the defendant is alleged to be associated with increased rates of a particular type of harm, and the causal relationship between the exposure and the harm cannot be established by eyewitness testimony. Some of the more notorious agents that have been the subject of these lawsuits are dioxin, Agent Orange, low-level radiation, contaminated groundwater, lead paint chips, tampons leading to toxic shock syndrome, asbestos, diethylstilbestrol (DES), and various pharmaceuticals (including polio and flu vaccines as well as Bendectin) [5].

Toxic tort lawsuits do not differ fundamentally from the traditional lawsuit over a motor vehicle accident; however, with a motor vehicle accident, the injuries produced are apparent in a relatively short time period after the event. With toxic tort injuries, there is usually a latency period between exposure and the development of noticeable injury. When the injury or disease manifests 20 or more years after a toxic exposure, the proof of the cause-effect relationship becomes more difficult. Compounding this difficulty is the fact that few toxic tort injuries are limited to a single-cause, single-effect connection. Most can result from several causes, only one of which may involve the defendant. And the plaintiff may have been exposed to more than one noxious agent (e.g., tobacco and asbestos).

Therefore, the plaintiff in a toxic tort case must prove two aspects of causation. The first aspect is the *risk evaluation,* which examines whether the defendant's behavior put the plaintiff at risk of developing the injuries of which he or she complains. The second aspect, the *occurrence analysis,* addresses whether, assuming the defendant's behavior put the plaintiff at risk, the defendant's behavior actually caused the plaintiff's injury [6]. The burden for the toxic tort plaintiff once the defendant has been identified and there is evidence that the plaintiff was exposed to a particular noxious substance by the defendant's actions or inaction is well illustrated by the following hypothetical example:

> While standing in a large crowd at the bus station, a man becomes aware that a bus from the Blue Bus Company is nearing the crowd. The bus pulls into the station, and the crowd moves to stay clear of the bus. The man, although jostled somewhat by the crowd, does not appear to have been injured. Two years later, he develops pain in his lower back, and x-rays reveal a slipped disc. He sues the Blue Bus Company. He proves, in addition to the facts stated above, that statistics indicate it is dangerous for buses to drive near crowds because this can cause injuries to those in the crowd. In addition, he proves that there are more back injuries in crowd-related accidents than would be normally expected. Can he win? [7].

In summary, a plaintiff's burden of proof on the issue of causation in the toxic tort context does not differ substantially from his or her burden in more traditional tort litigation. The unique aspect of toxic tort litigation lies in the significant impediments encountered by plaintiffs in attempting to satisfy this burden—impediments made all the more onerous in federal court under the 1993 U.S. Supreme Court's *Daubert* decision (see Chap. 6).

Mass Torts in Practice

Overview of the U.S. Court System

In the United States, a plaintiff has a choice between two court systems to bring his or her lawsuit—the state court system or the federal court system. Certain requirements must be met to bring a case in federal court, but most cases arrive there because the dispute is between "citizens" of different states. The federal court will look to the law of the state in which it sits for guidance on any non-federal law matters (e.g., the law of torts). Procedural rules also differ between the state and federal court systems, the most notable being that the U.S. Supreme Court's ruling on the admissibility of scientific evidence in the *Daubert* case (1993) only applies to the federal court system (except where certain states have adopted the same standards).

The federal court system consists of three levels: the district courts, the circuit courts of appeal, and the U.S. Supreme Court. The district courts hear criminal cases arising under federal statutes and civil actions arising under the federal statutes or the federal constitution. In addition, they serve as trial courts in matters of civil litigation between citizens of different states (diversity actions).

The 13 circuit courts of appeal hear appeals from the decisions of the federal district courts. Appeals from the circuit courts of appeal are heard by the U.S. Supreme Court. The Supreme Court also may hear appeals from state supreme courts where the cases involve federal statutes, treaties, or the federal constitution.

The system of state courts differs depending on the state. Generally, however, there are three levels of courts: (1) a lesser court of general jurisdiction, which often hears misdemeanor cases and civil cases in which damages sought are below a threshold amount, and a major court of general jurisdiction, which may hear felony cases or civil actions in which the damages claimed are above a specified amount, (2) a state appellate court to which the parties have an "appeal of right" (which means this court must accept all appeals filed), and (3) a state supreme court, which selects and hears certain appeals from the appellate court. A party does not have an appeal of right to the state supreme court.

There are specialized courts within both systems for specific subjects, including bankruptcy (federal), probate, family, and juvenile (state).

Management of Complex Cases

Courts, both state and federal, are charged, in one form or another, with ensuring the "just, speedy, and inexpensive determination of every action" [8]. As a direct result of the advent and rise of "mass exposure" and "environmental injury" litigation and the court's mandates, new forms and new uses of existing forms of global dispute resolution have emerged in the civil litigation system, including class action suits and MDLs. The overriding goal of all these mechanisms is to aggregate multiple claims. While aggregating claims in one fashion or another serves the goals of efficiency, cost-effectiveness, and global resolution of similar proceedings, there is an inherent conflict with individual autonomy. The U.S. civil justice system has always been devoted to securing equity for the individual, but in the mass tort system the courts must balance the need to redress individual yet collective wrongs while reducing transactional costs and expediting the resolution of tort claims with these aggregate procedures. What follows is a brief review of the most commonly used procedures.

CLASS ACTIONS. A class action suit can be filed at the choice of a plaintiff and his or her attorney in state or federal court. Here, one or more injured parties are named as plaintiffs in a suit against a defendant on behalf of an entire class of injured parties similarly situated to the named plaintiff(s). This procedure constitutes an exception to the rule that a person cannot be bound to a judgment in a particular case if that person was not joined as a named party [9].

Federal Rule of Civil Procedure 23, which applies to class action suits, requires that the claims and/or defenses of the named plaintiff(s) must be typical of those to be asserted by the unnamed class members. A class action suit can be brought when the following prerequisites are fulfilled: (1) the case involves so many plaintiffs that it is impracticable to join all in a single lawsuit, (2) there exist common questions of law and/or fact to the class of plaintiffs, and (3) the named plaintiff(s) can adequately and fairly protect the interests of the class [10]. In addition, the court must determine that a class action "is superior to other available methods for the fair and efficient adjudication of the controversy" at hand [11]. The purpose of filing a class action suit is to effectively consolidate and streamline as many matters as possible, including discovery [12], expert depositions, etc. In some cases, trials are undertaken on behalf of the class, although this has been fairly rare in the mass tort context (liability and other truly common legal or factual issues usually can be addressed easily in a class setting).

Historically, class action suits were used in commercial and business litigation, where all the damages suffered by the class of plaintiffs were substantially similar, usually economic in nature, and easily quantified. Justifications, still used today, for developing this method of claim aggregation include protecting defendants from inconsistent verdicts and obligations, protecting absent class members' interests, convenient and economic method for resolving similar claims, and the ability to spread litigation costs among litigants with similar claims [13].

However, class action suits are now being brought in toxic tort cases where, as stated previously, there is a single legal cause of plaintiffs' injuries, but the injuries manifest differently or there are different confounding factors for each of the different plaintiffs. Therefore, proof of actual causation must be presented for each and every class member [14].

Over the last 10 years, there has been growing criticism of the use of class actions in toxic tort or "mass exposure" litigation, and the courts are showing the same hesitancy that was apparent in the early years after the promulgation of Rule 23, where courts routinely denied requests for class certification. In fact, Rule 23 was never intended to be used in the mass tort context. As noted by the Advisory Committee in its 1996 revisions to Rule 23:

> A "mass accident" resulting in injuries to numerous persons is ordinarily not appropriate for a class action because of the likelihood that significant questions, not only of damages but of liability and defenses of liability, would be present, affecting the individuals in different ways. In these circumstances an action conducted nominally as a class action would degenerate in practice into multiple lawsuits separately tried [15].

Admittedly, class action litigations can promote efficiency and cost-effective dispute resolution when used in appropriate circumstances. However, they also can undercut an individual litigant's autonomy [16]. The scale of a mass tort case and the millions, if not billions, of dollars in claims give the term *cost-effectiveness* a new meaning. As recognized by the Seventh Circuit Court of Appeals, "with the aggregate stakes in the tens or hundreds of millions of dollars, or even in the billions, it is not a waste of judicial resources to conduct more than one trial, before more than six jurors, to determine whether a major segment of the international pharmaceutical industry is to follow the asbestos manufacturers into Chapter 11 [bankruptcy]" [17]. Further, defendant companies are using (and some say "abusing") the class action laws to shelter their assets by threatening to file for bankruptcy if the court refuses to approve a mandatory class settlement, including the resolution of rights of future victims [18].

Mandatory or non-opt-out class actions are the most restrictive type of class actions allowed under Rule 23. In a mandatory class, the class members do not have the option to "opt out" of the class and pursue their individual cases, even if an individual plaintiff had a preexisting case filed in state or federal court. Settlements usually are confined to a limited fund, which is inadequate to provide full compensation for all injured class members. Once the defendant pays out its lump sum, it is free to go forward conducting its business without any future liability to any of the class.

Justification for approving mandatory class settlements generally follows this line of reasoning: Absent the court's approval of the mandatory class action settlement, defendant will have no choice but to seek protection under the bankruptcy code. This in turn will delay, complicate, and potentially preclude the payment of any unliquidated tort claims to the settlement-class members, who would become defendant's bankruptcy creditors. For example, in an effort to control the floodgates opened in breast implant litigation around the country,

Dow Corning filed for bankruptcy in the summer of 1995. As of August 2000, Dow Corning was still conducting a healthy business while the class members and individual litigants (called *claimants* in the bankruptcy court) had not yet seen one dime in settlement.

MULTIDISTRICT LITIGATION. Another device available solely in the federal court system to efficiently and inexpensively handle mass tort cases is multidistrict litigations (MDLs). In an MDL, similar federal civil cases pending all over the country can be transferred to a single court for consolidation for pretrial proceedings. The Judicial Panel on Multidistrict Litigation, located in Washington, DC, can order the transfer of cases pending in more than one federal court to a single court if it determines that the transfer "will be for the convenience of the parties and witnesses and will promote the just and efficient conduct of such actions" and if the cases involve one or more common questions of fact [19]. Once pretrial proceedings are completed (e.g., discovery, including production of documents and depositions of the relevant defense witnesses/employees), the cases are returned to the originating court for further proceedings, including trial if the case is not otherwise dismissed or settled.

It should be noted that there is no "right" or "standard" approach to handling or managing these cases. The express and inherent authority given to judges allows them great latitude in litigation management decisions. In fact, in any "mass exposure" or "environmental injury" litigation, both individual and class action suits may be filed in state and federal courts that frequently are not coordinated. Although federal "mass exposure" cases often are sent to an MDL court, the state court cases can be pursued at the same time in the local state courts, resulting in duplication of much of the pretrial work in the various jurisdictions. A prime example is the breast implant litigation. While all the federal cases were consolidated in the Northern District of Alabama (MDL-926), other states were proceeding locally, such as Harris County (Houston), Texas. Ultimately, defendants were required to produce many of the same documents in two different places, and depositions of the same employees of defendants were taken on numerous occasions.

An MDL's sole purpose is to streamline the pretrial proceedings. Once pretrial matters have been resolved and discovery completed, the cases transferred to the MDL court that have not otherwise been settled or resolved will be sent back to the originating court for resolution (i.e., settlement or trial). This distinguishes an MDL from a class action litigation. As stated previously, a class action is a single case brought on behalf of numerous plaintiffs that can be pursued all the way to and through a trial. Generally, most cases are settled before remand, but this trend may be changing. For example, tens of thousands of cases were remanded by the MDL court in the national breast implant litigation, after which most settled. However, several went to trial, and at present, there are still hundreds of cases pending, waiting for trial.

JUDICIAL POWERS. A court has both express and inherent powers that give it broad, although not limitless, authority to supervise and control a case or cases, be they individual, multidistrict, or class-wide litigation, notwithstanding what may be taking place in similar cases in other jurisdictions. In addition to the usual duties and responsibilities a judge may have in a simple personal injury case, a judge managing complex litigation has the authority to "adopt special procedures for managing potentially difficult or protracted actions that may involve complex issues, multiple parties, difficult legal questions, or unusual proof problems [20]. This rule, in effect, gives a judge managing a complex litigation the right to implement procedures that might otherwise be (1) objectionable to the parties or even (2) inconsistent with other federal procedural rules. Such procedures can include (to name just a few)

- Special notification/service rules (e.g., requiring all parties that have Internet access to regularly check a certain Web site for notification of case activity).
- Extensive latitude in developing pretrial case management and scheduling orders.
- Limitations on depositions (including number and length or restricting the use of supplemental depositions).
- Special techniques to encourage settlement (e.g., settlement conferences with parties, trials of selected representative cases, approval of a class for the sole purpose of settlement, or referral to another judge, magistrate, or special master).
- Technology requirements that can apply to all aspects of a case: filing court documents (via e-mail), document production (scanning and indexing all documents produced), expert depositions (videotaping and/or digitizing of videotaped depositions), and courtroom presentations.

Science on the Witness Stand

The Role of Scientific Testimony in the Courtroom

Expert testimony, scientific or other, can be presented in a case "if scientific, technical, or other specialized knowledge will assist the trier of fact [usually a jury, sometimes a judge] to understand the evidence or to determine a fact in issue" in the case [21]. If an untrained layperson can intelligently determine a particular issue in a case without testimony from an expert, then any proffered testimony would be a waste of time and hence properly kept out of the proceeding [22]. For example, in a simple "slip and fall" case, a jury would not need to have some specialist explain that if a person unknowingly stepped into a pool of melted butter on a grocery store floor, he or she could slip and fall.

However, with the rapid rate of technological and scientific advances (and the unfortunate resulting injuries), plaintiffs often cannot satisfy their burden of proof with regard to liability, causation, and/or damages without scientific evidence and/or expert testimony. This is often true in individual personal injury cases (e.g., medical malpractice) and almost always true in "mass exposure" and "environmental injury" litigations. No one would expect a lay juror to understand even basic principles of immunology or epidemiology without the assistance of an expert in the relevant field.

Standards for Admissibility of Scientific Evidence in Federal Court

The key admissibility issues under the *Federal Rules of Evidence* are (1) analysis of an expert's conclusion under Rule 201(b), (2) analysis of an expert's qualifications under Rule 702, (3) analysis of an expert's methodology under Rule 702, (4) analysis of an expert's data under Rule 703, and (5) analysis of probative versus prejudicial balance under Rule 403. The U.S. Supreme Court has had several opportunities to clarify how these rules apply to the admissibility of scientific and other evidence, the seminal case being *Daubert v. Merrell Dow Pharmaceuticals, Inc.*, 509 U.S. 579, 113 S. Ct. 2786 (1993).

With expert testimony (or other scientific or technical evidence), the judge must ensure the relevance, admissibility, reliability, and probative value of the evidence in question. Evidence is relevant if it can "make the existence of any fact that is of consequence to the determination of the action more probable or less probable than it would be without the evidence" [23]. Although relevant evidence and testimony are presumed admissible [24], their reliability must still be examined [25]. The relevance and reliability of all evidence and testimony must be ensured by the court, including evidence that is scientific, medical, or technical in nature [26].

To satisfy the reliability of the evidence, the court must make an inquiry into (1) the expert's qualifications and methodology used to reach his or her opinion [27] and (2) the expert's data [28]. The judge also must determine that the probative value is greater than the prejudicial effect of admitting that particular piece of testimony [29].

The issues potentially raised by the expert testimony presented by defendants and plaintiffs in any case fall into three well-recognized categories: *admissibility* (discussed briefly above and in further detail in Chap. 6), *weight* (referring to the persuasive weight to be given to a particular piece of evidence or testimony by the jury or finder of fact), and *sufficiency* (referring to whether all the evidence presented by the plaintiff is sufficient to meet his or her burden of proof, discussed above). This would appear to be a straightforward task, as courts are used to handling evidence questions on a routine basis. However, the practice of applying these rules to technical and scientific evidence and testimony has resulted in wildly inconsistent and convoluted judicial outcomes.

Until *Daubert* and its progeny appeared on the legal scene [30], all admissibility issues were preliminary factual issues to be decided by the court, whereas actual findings of fact and the persuasive weight to be given to any piece of testimony—i.e., the plausibility or persuasiveness of an expert's conclusion—or evidence were solely in the jury's domain, unless plaintiff waived his or her right to trial by jury and the trial proceeded in front of the judge as the finder of fact [31]. Under federal law, a court has the authority to consider the persuasiveness of the experts' conclusions only after a post-trial motion is brought by the loser at trial seeking a new trial on the ground that the jury's verdict is against the great weight of the evidence.

The Roles for Experts in Complex Litigation

An expert may be asked to testify in any of several capacities. The most common is as an expert for one of the parties, either for the plaintiff or for the defendant. Here, the expert is asked to offer an opinion for one side that will be most vigorously attacked by the other. It may be attacked on paper prior to trial in a series of motions (e.g., in a motion for "summary judgment" alleging a lack of admissible evidence or in a motion *"in limine"* to exclude the allegedly inadmissible testimony) or during the course of the trial with the expert on the witness stand, most commonly during cross-examination by the opposing party. Occasionally, an expert's testimony may be challenged at the time of trial (whether it was challenged previously through motion practice or not), and the judge will be asked to determine the testimony's relevance and scientific validity before the testimony can be presented to the jury. Not only can this drastically increase the cost of trying a case to verdict, but it also can leave a party unable to satisfy his or her burden of proof if the expert's testimony is excluded, effectively closing down the case. If it is the plaintiff's causation expert's testimony that is excluded, the plaintiff is thus denied his or her day in court [32].

An expert also may be brought into a case as an objective third party on the motion of any party or even the court's own motion under Federal Rule of Evidence 706 [33]. This rule was enacted by Congress in response to concerns (1) that parties were participating in "expert shopping" or paying for the presentation of a particular piece of evidence rather than the impartial opinion of an expert in a relevant field and (2) that experts willing to testify for a particular party in a case were susceptible to corruption. Under Rule 706, a scientist may be asked to serve as a "neutral" expert in a case in which the court has determined that the traditional "battle of the experts" may not sufficiently clarify the relevant issues or yield the necessary information for a reasoned resolution. Relying on its broad inherent and enumerated powers, a court may ask its appointed expert to perform any number of tasks, including

- Testifying in court.
- Educating judges and/or juries on scientific, medical, or technical issues.
- Advising the court on the underlying scientific methodology or reasoning to enable the court to make the necessary pretrial decisions regarding the admissibility of testimony and/or evidence
- Providing commentary on the testimony of the parties' experts and offering an independent assessment of the relevant scientific or technical disputes in a case.
- Assisting in the assessment of damages and/or penalties.

Note that nothing in Rule 706 precludes the parties from offering their own expert witnesses when a court-appointed expert or panel of experts is being used in a case.

While the use of an expert who is not working on behalf of a party in the litigation may appear to be a reasonable approach to getting at the "truth" or scientific "answer," this approach is fraught with problems. For example, more often than not, a court-appointed expert is referred to as a *neutral* expert. However, a scientist is anything but neutral. Although a "neutral" expert may not be biased toward one party or another, he or she certainly has an opinion about the issue at hand, which he or she often has formed prior to being engaged to work on behalf of the court (see Chap. 7). This mistaken impression of neutrality also may lead jurors to put undue weight on the opinion of a court-appointed expert when, in reality, his or her opinion carries no more weight that the opinion of a party expert.

Mass tort actions have their own unique problems with employing court-appointed experts under Rule 706. If a court engages an expert to work on a single case, his or her testimony is heard and evaluated by the finder of fact (usually the jury) at or soon after the time the testimony is proffered. Therefore, the testimony should reflect the state of scientific knowledge at that point in time. In the mass tort context, however, the testimony may become stale or irrelevant because by the time the finder of fact hears the testimony, the state of scientific or medical knowledge has moved forward.

For example, a science panel was formed in the National Breast Implant Litigation in 1996 to evaluate the relevant evidence and testimony being proffered by the plaintiffs and defendants in the fields of immunology, toxicology, rheumatology, and epidemiology. The panel evaluated evidence and testimony presented through July 1998. The panel did not issue its report until November 1998, and panel members were not fully cross-examined by the parties to the litigation until April 1999. Currently (late 2000), plaintiffs with cases still pending in both state and federal courts are facing objections from the defendants alleging that the National Breast Implant Science Panel's report from 1998 precludes the presentation of any new evidence in the areas of immunology, toxicology, rheumatology, and epidemiology, notwithstanding the fact that hundreds of studies, many of which support the plaintiffs' allegations, have been undertaken and published since that time. Scientific knowledge is ever-evolving, and the law should not be permitted to ignore this fact.

Endnotes

1. Christoffel T, Teret SP. Epidemiology and the law: Courts and confidence intervals. *Am J Public Health* 1991;81:1661–1666.

2. Keeton WP, et al. Prosser and Keeton on the law of torts, §30 at 165 (5th ed.) St. Paul MN: West Publishing, 1984.

3. Callahan CL. Establishment of causation in toxic tort litigation. *Arizona State Law J* 1991;23:605–674.

4. *Idem,* p 608.

5. Christoffel and Teret, *op. cit.,* p 1662.

6. Dore M. A commentary on the use of epidemiological evidence in demonstrating cause-in-fact. *Harvard Environ Law Rev* 1983;7:435–437.

7. Thompson MM. Causal inference in epidemiology: Implications for toxic tort litigation. *North Carolina Law Rev* 1992;71:247–291.

8. Rule 1, "Scope and Purpose of Rules," *Federal Rules of Civil Procedure,* 2000 ed. The *Federal Rules of Evidence* similarly advise that the court's goal is to eliminate "unjustifiable expense and delay." *Federal Rules of Evidence* 102.

9. *Hansberry v. Lee,* 311 U.S. 32 (1940).

10. *Federal Rules of Civil Procedure,* Rule 23(a).

11. *Idem,* at 23(b)(3).

12. In litigation, *discovery* describes the various tools that can be used by one party to obtain facts and information about the case from the other party to assist in preparation for trial. These tools may include written interrogatories, production of documents or things, permission to enter on land or other property, physical and/or mental examinations of plaintiff, etc.

13. *United States Parole Commission v. Geraghty,* 445 U.S. 388, 423 (1980).

14. Although this book is a beginning exploration into the use of evidence-based medicine in the resolution of legal disputes, the appropriateness of evidence-based medicine in individual causation must be analyzed carefully. It certainly assists in clinical judgments, but one should not ignore the problems of using generalized information or data to assess a particular patient, plaintiff, or situation. Admittedly, the goals of public health may be fulfilled by the "direct application of knowledge derived from population-based studies," but "application of the same knowledge to the individual . . . is problematic." Tonelli, M. The philosophical limits of evidence-based medicine. *Academic Med* 1998;72:1234, 1236. The author concludes that "[m]isunderstanding EMB [evidence-based medicine] or failing to acknowledge its limitations . . . impedes the efforts to expand our understanding of clinical medicine." *Idem,* at 1239. Equally, the misapplication of evidence-based medicine also may impede the civil justice system's goal of individual justice and compensation.

15. *Federal Rules of Civil Procedure,* Rule 23, 1966 Advisory Committee Note.

16. Androgué S. Mass tort class actions in the new millennium. *Rev Litig* 1998; 17:427–432.

17. *In the Matter of Rhone-Poulenc Rorer,* 51 F.3d 1293, 1300 (7th Cir. 1995).

18. See *Amchem Products, Inc. v. Windsor,* 521 U.S. 591 (1977).

19. 28 U.S.C. §1407.

20. *Federal Rules of Civil Procedure,* Rule 16(c)(12).

21. *Joiner v. General Electric,* 78 F.3d, at 524, 530 (11th Cir. 1996), rev'd on other grounds, 522 U.S. 136 (1997).

22. 7 Wigmore, Evidence §1918 (Chadbourne rev. 1972).

23. *Federal Rules of Evidence,* Rule 401.

24. Berger MA. Procedural paradigms for applying the *Daubert* test. *Minn Law Rev* 1994;78:1345–1365.

25. It should be noted at the outset that the *Federal Rules of Evidence* relating to expert testimony assume that "the expert's opinion will have a reliable basis in the knowledge and experience of his discipline."

26. *Kuhmo Tire Co. v. Carmichael,* 526 U.S. 137, 148, 119 S. Ct. 1167 (1999).

27. *Federal Rules of Evidence,* Rule 702. A witness must be found to be "qualified as an expert by knowledge, skill, experience, training, or education." Note that the rule "contemplates a broad conception of expert qualifications." *Thomas v. Newton Int'l Enterprises,* 42 F.3d 1266, 1269 (9th Cir. 1994); see also *Wood v. Stihl, Inc.,* 705 F.2d 1101, 1104–1105 (9th Cir. 1983).

28. *Federal Rules of Evidence,* Rule 703, provides that an expert may base his or her testimony on facts or data "of a type reasonably relied upon by experts in the particular field in forming opinions or inferences upon the subject." It further states that "the facts or data need not be admissible in evidence."

29. Under *Federal Rules of Evidence,* Rule 403, relevant "evidence may be excluded if its probative value is substantially outweighed by the danger of unfair prejudice, confusion of the issues, or misleading the jury or by considerations of undue delay, waste of time, or needless presentation of cumulative evidence."

30. The *Daubert* case and its application to expert testimony are discussed further in Chapter 6.

31. See *Kennedy v. Collagen Corp.,* 161 F.3d 1226, 1228 (9th Cir. 1998).

32. According to one survey of published decisions, plaintiffs lose 70 percent of the *Daubert* motions brought by defendants. See Weimer GA. Expert evidence: What you don't know about *Daubert* can hurt you. *Jun Vt BJ & L Dig* 1998;24:51–53; Woodside FC. *Evidence Problems: Daubert and Beyond.* ALI-ABA Course of Study on Products Liability, CA11 ALI-ABA 101–107, July 28, 1995.

33. *Federal Rules of Evidence,* Rule 706, provides that "[t]he court may appoint any expert witnesses agreed upon by the parties, and may appoint expert witnesses of its own selection."

4

Adjudicating Cases Involving Scientific Evidence: The View from the Bench

LEO WENDEN

Science versus Law

The observations contained in this chapter are the result of my more than 17 years of personal experience first as a prosecutor, whose primary duty was to prosecute infractions of environmental and occupational health legislation, and now as a judge, tasked with adjudicating these infractions when they are tried in the Canadian courts.

Years ago, while I was working as a prosecutor, the issue of the use of scientific evidence first arose. The scientific evidence required was different from the scientific content of previous cases. There was more detail, different terminology, and less definitiveness. Working closely with the scientists, and struggling to come to grips with different fields of scientific evidence, I noted that the same difficulties surfaced in each case and the same mistakes were being repeated. Discussions with the lawyers on both sides of the cases and the scientists who testified in the trials disclosed that they, too, had a sense that not all had gone according to plan. On the one hand, some of the lawyers expressed the view that the scientists, when testifying, had forgotten or abandoned the strategy that had been devised when the briefing took place. In addition, many lawyers admitted to having some difficulty with the scientific concepts and understood only dimly the research methods and terminology used by the scientists. In their minds, science was synonymous with certainty. On the other hand, many of the scientists who testified at the trials were left with the distinct impression that their testimony had not developed the way they had conceived it would. The entire process of testifying, particularly cross-examination, left them feeling that they had been the unwitting victims of a strange and sometimes savage process. They were, for example, unable to understand why procedures and terminology used and accepted in their profession were objected to at every turn by the lawyers.

In retrospect, these problems were fundamentally those of miscommunication. All parties involved had only the most basic understanding of what the other did; the manner in which they carried out their respective occupations, including the research methods used, the terminology employed, and accepted procedures and conventions, were foreign to each of the parties involved. Little, if any, thought was given to or analysis done about problems that might arise when scientific evidence, resting on complicated and sometimes uncertain science, was imported into a legal system designed to resolve and finalize disputes.

The trial process is rife with uncertainties. Witnesses may disappear or not show up when they are required to do so. Evidence may not be entered as originally planned because a witness forgot much of his or her testimony or a crucial part of it. Some evidence may be ruled inadmissible. Cross-examination can and does wreak havoc with well-presented testimony. Any lawyer or judge knows that such events are constants in any trial.

Scientific evidence has its own uncertainties as well. It may be that the evidence required by a scientist to give an opinion is deficient, thus necessitating reliance on weak assumptions. Or it may be that the general principles cannot be applied to the specific fact situation without the use of still more assumptions. Indeed, the very scientific concepts themselves may be topics of honest controversy within the scientific community.

When the uncertainties of both disciplines are forced together in the context of a long, complicated trial, it is little wonder that problems arise. Perhaps, given the nature of the two disciplines, this will always be the case. However, one need not accept the situation as it presently exists. The repetitive nature of the problems that arise may offer some clues for crafting solutions. Clearly, this will not resolve all the problems that arise, given the nature of both disciplines, but a first step is worth the effort.

Science in the Courtroom

The appearance of science in the courtroom is, of course, not a new phenomenon, and its presence in criminal trials and medicolegal disputes is not a recent development. Forensic evidence, such as the identification and typing of blood and other bodily fluids, fingerprint identification, and alcohol analysis, to mention but a few, all have a long history in the courtroom. In criminal trials, the medical sciences are represented by forensic pathology and psychiatry. The presence of these disciplines in court, as contributors to the proceedings, is no cause for concern. Witnesses who appear on behalf of the prosecution are usually civilian members of laboratories that are an integral part of or dedicated to assisting the prosecuting governmental agency. As such, these witnesses are intended to be impartial. Their opinions have a solid factual basis and usually are not based on complex or uncertain scientific evidence. With experience, these witnesses gain an understanding of the trial process, how it works, and their role in it because they appear in court on a regular basis. The last two decades have seen an increasing use of a wider range of scientific expertise in the courtroom. For example, there are more and more environmental cases, both civil and criminal. In addition, class actions are being brought against large corporations, alleging that their course of conduct was detrimental to the health of the litigants. Many of the scientists who are involved in the litigation, either as advisors or as witnesses, are preeminent in their fields. Much of the research used in court may still be subject to ongoing debate among scientists, with criticisms that the methodology is flawed or the results misinterpreted. Conclusions are presented as probabilities or risk estimates. Inferences to be drawn are supported by statistics, which in turn are buttressed by estimates of correctness. Symbols used in statistics or mathematics abound. Trials, on the other hand, are intended to provide answers to single issue topics, no matter how broad a field. The litigants seek answers and closure on these issues. Additionally, the answers provided by the judicial system carry certain legal consequences. Introducing scientific uncertainty into the uncertainty of the legal process only leads to still more uncertainty and a dissonance in court proceedings.

The problems encountered with scientific evidence are different depending on whether one is acting as the prosecutor or sitting as the judge. The presentation of evidence at a trial is solely in the hands of counsel. It matters not whether it is a criminal prosecution, where proof must be established beyond a reasonable doubt, or a civil trial, where the standard of proof is to be made on a balance of probabilities. The standard of proof beyond a reasonable doubt places a heavy load on the prosecutor to ensure that the evidence presented is very persuasive (more so than in a civil trial, where the balance of probability standard is employed). Unfortunately, there is no easy way to determine when the evidence surpasses the required standard. Hence the question of "how much evidence is enough" is another uncertainty and issue of concern.

The Use of Scientific Evidence

The nature of the scientific evidence to be presented, the scientists who will testify, what will be said, and how it will be said are the exclusive domain of the lawyers. One limiting factor—and one that should be taken seriously—is the initial collection of evidence. In Canada, the people who enforce the legislation do the initial investigation of alleged infractions of environmental or occupational health legislation. Although some of them have a background in science, they are by no means trained scientific investigators. Their investigation is not focused solely on gathering evidence that will provide a base for an expert scientific opinion. Rather, they must gather a whole array of evidence that will support a prosecution. Thus their time and attention are divided among finding and interviewing witnesses, taking statements and photographs, collecting documents, and generally trying to get a picture of what happened. Inevitably, some evidence that is necessary to establish a sound scientific opinion is missed. It may or may not be discovered later on. This can have serious consequences as the prosecutor uses the results of the investigation to formulate a "theory of the case." This theory is then presented to a scientist whom the prosecutor intends to use as an expert witness. The absence of critical evidence can skew the expert opinion and set the scientist off on a "false trail" in constructing the opinion(s).

On the other hand, the role played by the judge during the trial is minimal. Aside from ruling on objections as to the admissibility of evidence and other legal objections made by counsel, the function of the judge (when there is no jury) is to listen to the evidence. From time to time, a judge may ask questions if some of the evidence is not clear. Once all the evidence has been heard and arguments have been made by counsel, then the judge is required to consider what has been presented and decide the matter.

There are two basic problems to be solved by lawyers in presenting science in the courtroom. The first is to develop a theory of the case, and the second is to obtain the proper expert. Developing a theory is no more than an effort to determine what happened, a piecing together of the evidence available to counsel. It is an important first step in any litigation process. The theory developed, although tentative and subject to revision, gives counsel a framework on which evidence may be attached and tested. Its usefulness at this stage is to identify the field of science involved and the type of expert needed. Retaining the proper expert may pose some difficulty because most lawyers do not have the necessary background to identify the precise area of scientific expertise required. It is very much a matter of "trial and error." Ideally, the expert retained is well versed in the scientific issues in question. Too often, however, one finds that the expert has at best a peripheral understanding of the problem and lacks the required in-depth experience. In my experience, this obvious lack of expertise becomes evident at the time the expert testifies, especially during cross-examination, when all deficiencies are laid bare. Thus a lawyer dealing with scientific evidence is well advised to hire someone whose expertise is directly relevant.

Once the proper expert has been retained, it is critical that some time be spent setting out mutual professional expectations. Very frequently, scientists only have a vague notion of the role that scientific evidence will play in the case. The part to be played by the scientist as expert witness never seems to be discussed fully. Because the scientist does not know precisely what is required, he or she, in turn, is unable to tell the lawyer exactly what his or her needs and expectations are. It is at this point that if care is not taken, matters may start to unravel; communication is critically important. All too often counsel does not clearly explain the reason or reasons why an expert is required. Very little time, if any, is spent in explaining the forum in which the evidence may be used.

Moreover, many of the difficulties that crop up while an expert is testifying can be avoided if an explanation of what will happen while the expert is testifying is made clear. One of the immediate benefits is that the expert will become accustomed to discussing the scientific evidence in the simple, clear terms that will be required in court. On the other hand, the expert also must ensure that the lawyer has a thorough understanding of the science involved and its complexities, limitations, and jargon.

Assuming that one finds a suitable expert and that the expectations of both have been discussed, the next task is to explain the theory and supporting evidence to the expert and solicit a tentative opinion. It is critical to keep in mind that the theory forms a basis for preliminary discussion and is subject to modification. Too often the approach to discussing the theory is to treat it as if it were virtually immutable, the one that must prevail. This is understandable, because by the time the lawyer has made contact with an expert, a substantial amount of time and energy have gone into formulating the theory, and "tunnel vision" has developed.

Many of the problems caused by scientific evidence, whether they are uncertain, complex, or both, are the result of too inflexible an approach to the scientific legal problem as articulated by the theory. The position should not to be taken that because the evidence is scientific, it must be complicated and can only be understood after a long and arduous explanation. This is not so, and if science is presented in a way that emphasizes its complexity or uncertainty, there is a real risk that it will be rejected out of hand. Too often practitioners overlook the fact that all evidence, scientific or otherwise, must be presented in a cogent, compelling, and lucid manner. Regrettably, there are some who apparently believe the opposite; i.e., if the scientific evidence to be presented is complex and difficult to understand, it will be perceived as being more compelling and worthy of belief. This is not so. The danger is that it might not be understood, and the reality is that the judge (not to mention the jury) will not be impressed. Thus, when the lawyer and scientist get together to discuss the theory of the case, they must keep in mind the need for lucidity and simplicity.

Another point that bears repeating is the fact that the theory, as conceived by the lawyer, is (1) not immutable, (2) should not to be viewed as such, and (3) need not be the one that prevails. Unfortunately, this often happens because the lawyer has already developed the theory, the evidence available has already been examined and structured in such a way that it "fits" the theory, and evidence that does not fit is ignored and/or forgotten. The theory is then presented to a scientist who is asked to provide an opinion based on the theory. However, the scientist is restricted in the practice of his or her profession when the theory is presented as the one that must prevail. Such an approach may be acceptable in a laboratory, for if the theory fails, the scientist can start anew, with a different or changed set of assumptions or a totally new theory. In court, this luxury is not available to the parties.

When a scientist is asked to testify in court, he or she is being asked to provide an explanation about an event that is supported by the evidence and authenticated by demonstrable scientific principles. In other words, scientific experts are expected to give a logical and science-based answer to a set of proven facts. To the extent that these facts are not proven, the scientific explanation fails. It sometimes happens that in order to make up for the missing evidence, the scientist makes certain assumptions or relies on basic scientific principles, all with the intention of establishing a basis for the opinion. Such attempts are too easily apparent to opposing counsel. Once the question is asked regarding what assumptions were used in arriving at the opinion, the process of unraveling the opinion is under way.

I once participated in such a cross-examination. The expert admitted that he had relied heavily on a piece of published research in arriving at his opinion. It was evident that he had assumed that the general principles found therein were applicable to the specific facts of the case, without any need for qualification. However, it was evident by the abundance of footnotes that explained and qualified the research paper that general principles were not applicable to the specific facts of the case. On cross-examination, each of the points that the expert had made were revisited with the added proviso that this time he incorporate the information contained in the footnotes. Each new answer resulted in a progressive weakening of his testimony. The end result was that he abandoned his opinion, with the gratuitous comment that the opposing expert's opinion was probably correct.

Many of the problems caused by reliance on assumptions can be avoided by taking a more flexible approach to the theory postulated by the lawyer. An important first step should be a discussion of the evidence that the lawyer rejected when the theory was formulated. Such evidence is normally put aside because including it might change the theory somewhat or render it untenable. However, this same evidence, viewed from the scientist's perspective, may take on a different meaning. Filtered through the experience and training of the scientist, the initially cast aside evidence may have some value. After all, this is why the scientist has been consulted—to use all of his or her expertise and experience in examining the facts of the case. On proper considered reflection, it may be that the theory can be altered to include the evidence. If this is not possible and the evidence must be discarded, there is still some value to the exercise. The presence of adverse or conflicting data has been noted, considered, and finally rejected. If the scientist is then asked, on cross-examination, to consider this evidence and try to factor it into the opinion, he or she has a prepared and reasoned answer why it will not fit. Too many scientists are caught short in the courtroom as a result of not having reflected on all the evidence, both supportive and adverse.

A secondary benefit to the above-mentioned exercise is that in considering whether or not such evidence can be included, other evidence may yet be discovered. It is the rare case indeed about which it can be said that there is "enough evidence" or "too much evidence." Evidence gathering is an ongoing process that never stops. Crucial relevant evidence is sometimes missed or overlooked. Perhaps the initial investigator is unaware of the importance of the evidence or does not know where or how to look. The scientist, on the other hand, brings a different perspective to the value of evidence and the search for it. An expert scientific opinion can be very helpful at this phase of case preparation. It is important that the expert has an overview of the entire case and can see where and how the scientific evidence fits into the case. Too often scientific evidence is offered without any real thought as to how it fits in with the case. If scientific evidence is just "dropped" into the case, it will defeat the entire purpose in presenting it. Scientific evidence should be used to either explain an event that took place or render comprehensible a chain of events that resulted in harm to the environment, human health, or both. It is intended to clarify and explain a problem, not to dazzle or confuse the judge.

The Experience of a Trial

Many of the problems encountered by complicated scientific evidence are caused by the nature of the litigation process, which is adversarial and confrontational. Scientific evidence brought in by one side will be countered by the scientific evidence of the opposing party. In some cases, there will be room for validly held differences of opinion. In other cases, the science will clash, for the simple reason that it is being presented to support a legal proposition in order to obtain a certain result. Science in the courtroom is intended to assist in resolving some pressing legal issue with finality because the law is a method of resolving disputes in those situations where the parties themselves are not able to do so. Trials follow a certain definable procedure; there are the rules about the questioning of witnesses and the admissibility of evidence that govern what evidence is presented. Standards of proof are different. Scientists, for the most part, are unaware of these rules and procedures, let alone the subtleties involved in appearing as an expert witness. Legal procedure is as foreign to them as scientific research is to lawyers. Indeed, many scientists probably have never been in a courtroom, let alone testified. The courtroom is neither the place nor the time to learn about the process. The unfortunate reality is that many experts do get their "education" in courtroom procedure when they are on the stand testifying. Obviously, the results can vary from barely satisfactory to disastrous.

This situation can be avoided by taking time to educate the expert witness in the legal process. This will give the expert a frame of reference when preparing for the trial in which he or she will testify. To a certain extent, the mystery surrounding the entire event will be dispelled. Experience has shown that one of the best ways to achieve this education is to have an expert witness watch someone else undergoing examination in chief, as well as cross-examination. In my experience, this is a much superior method to rehearsals, which, while valuable, can never satisfactorily reproduce the dynamics of a trial. In the court-room, the expert will be able to see what happens when testimony is interrupted by opposing counsel's objections or rulings from the trial judge. On the other hand, lawyers also would benefit from visiting the laboratory where the scientist carries out the research. I had the opportunity once to see a mass spectrometer in use and obtain a very basic amount of hands-on experience. This was a real benefit because it allowed me to visualize the process when witnesses were testifying about the procedure.

When preparing for the trial, the scientist must not forget that neither the lawyers nor the judge (or jury) has the same degree of familiarity with scientific concepts and terminology as he or she has. Thus it is important, to the extent possible, that scientific evidence be explained and presented in a way that can be understood clearly. Scientific evidence that is presented in a way that empha-sizes its complexity more often than not will be firmly but politely rejected. Furthermore, evidence that is overly complex is difficult to present in court, notwithstanding the use of charts, photographs, and models. Interesting as it may be, scientific evidence that does not explain or assist the judge (or jury) is of little value. A lawyer must ensure that all the evidence needed to support the scientific opinion must be put on the record.

The more complex the science, the greater are the number of evidentiary facts needed to support and sustain it. If some of the critical facts do not make it on the record, the scientific opinion suffers. The significance of these missing facts is that the scientific evidence must be adjusted to meet the new situation. The other reason for avoiding an unnecessarily complicated scientific explanation is that it will not be understood, notwithstanding efforts to make it simple. I once observed such an examination that concerned the chemical composition of a substance said to be harmful to aquatic life after having undergone a certain chemical procedure. The expert was a very learned individual and had spent virtually all his professional life in this particular field. Counsel who was doing the examination had more than a passing familiarity with the subject. The examination that followed was a wonderful exposition of the Socratic method. The questions were short and precise. Not one of them was postulated on some long, drawn-out explanation, and the answers all were given in a similar manner. It was evident that both witness and lawyer were very much at home with the topic. What was equally evident was that they were the only two in the courtroom who knew what they were talking about. The judge, the person who ought to have benefited from the testimony, had clearly been transported beyond his scientific depths and thus was having none of it. This was clear by the slow, yet deliberate manner in which he ceased to make notes. Of greater concern is the situation where the lawyer does not have more than a passing familiarity with the subject matter, and it is abundantly clear that counsel is out of his or her depth. This undoubtedly will fail to impress the judge.

Complicated scientific testimony usually includes *jargon*—the use of scientific or technical terms, brief descriptors to indicate a procedure, or ordinary or conventional words or phrases that have a unique and specific meaning to the person using them or the field in which they are employed. When jargon is used without an accompanying explanation, confusion results. For example, the phrase "personal communication with . . . " simply describes the manner in which a scientist obtained certain information; in other words, the matter was discussed with a colleague, and the information was used in formulating an opinion. While this is a perfectly legitimate procedure in the scientific domain, its legitimacy is brought into question in the setting of a trial. In legal terms, such a procedure is classified as "hearsay." *Hearsay* is a rule of evidence that prohibits the introduction of information obtained from someone who is not a witness when the information is intended to be used and relied on as true. The way around the problem is to have the expert give a brief description of what is meant by "personal communication" and explain that it is an accepted way to communicate research findings in the scientific community. This explanation, accompanied by the argument that the expert should not to be held to a higher standard than that demanded in the field, is usually sufficient to deal successfully with a hearsay objection. Undoubtedly on some occasions it is necessary to use jargon, but this ought to be the exception rather than the rule. When jargon is overused, the result is that the evidence becomes difficult to grasp, and other subtleties in the evidence often are overlooked. If it is absolutely necessary to use technical terms, providing the court with a glossary defining the terms that will be employed will go a long way toward clearing up any confusion.

The problems of dealing with complicated scientific evidence are not confined to those just mentioned. Of course, there are others, but these problems are not unique to the presentation of scientific evidence. They are problems faced by all who appear as witnesses in any trial. How to act and not to act while testifying, how to address the judge, and a myriad of other details are matters with which all witnesses must contend. It is the nature of the scientific evidence that can make it problematic. It is always important evidence and often determinative of the issues before the court. In litigation, there are very few second chances, which is why it is crucial that the evidence be clear and understandable the first time around.

The Importance of Preparation

The preparation and presentation of scientific evidence are keys to success in the courtroom. Too many lawyers seem to forget the basic fact that the trial is the first time that the judge hears the evidence. Lawyers, on the other hand, have spent many hours in preparation, and they have an intimate knowledge or should have an intimate knowledge of the case. A tendency exists to overrefine the evidence—to the point where understanding it is possible only if one has an intimate knowledge of all the facts and all the technical procedures. This, of course, is not the case with the judge. Having been on both sides, judging cases that I once prosecuted, I can state with assurance that testimony that seemed so clear when elicited from a witness from the counsel table now sometimes seems incomprehensible as it makes its journey to the bench.

The role of the judge in dealing with scientific evidence is by definition considerably different from that of counsel. It is the judge who must be persuaded. Whereas lawyers only concern themselves with one point of view, the judge not only must contend with the opposing view but also must decide at the end if the required standard has been met. This is easier said than done. The trial is the first time the judge hears the evidence in its entirety. If there is pressure on the lawyers and witnesses to "get it right the first time," there is a corresponding pressure and duty on the judge to "hear it right the first time."

The problems in dealing specifically with scientific evidence occur at the beginning when lawyers first propose having a witness qualified as an expert, during testimony if objections to the evidence surface or where a particular point of evidence is not clear, and at the end of the trial when all the evidence is considered.

The threshold issue is whether or not the witness is an expert in the sense that the legal profession understands the term *expert*. Too many witnesses are put forward as experts when in reality all they possess is a general knowledge or more than a passing familiarity with the subject at hand. This, in my view, does not justify qualifying them as experts. An undergraduate degree in chemistry, for example, does not qualify one to give expert evidence on the chemical changes that take place when a substance undergoes a certain chemical procedure. Moreover, the expertise must relate to the issues that are in dispute. The closer the expertise comes to the issues to be decided, the greater is the likelihood that the proposed evidence will assist the court. Occasionally, people with only a very general expertise are presented as expert witnesses—so-called generic experts. The appearance of a generic witness usually means that the lawyer is not certain what opinion is to be solicited and, as a result, seeks assurance by using an all-purpose expert. This is poor practice because at the same time a lawyer seeks to have a witness qualified as an expert in a certain field, the opinion the witness is expected to give should be communicated to the judge. This information gives the judge a preview, as it were, of the scientific evidence to come. Throughout the course of the trial, there is little a judge can do except listen and try to absorb and understand the evidence. Questioning of the qualifications of an expert witness is one place where a judge may be more actively involved and may seek more of or a better explanation on various points. This questioning and the deciding of questions of admissibility are the sole active functions of the judge in a nonjury trial.

The problems of dealing with the scientific evidence also arise at the end of the trial when all the evidence has been heard and closing arguments made.

Assuming that the judge has a transcript of the trial, the task is to sort through all the evidence. This is no different from what a judge normally does in any case. Initially, the judge must be satisfied that the evidence establishes a *prima facie* case; i.e., there is evidence to establish proof of the basic elements. Then the judge must be satisfied that there is enough evidence of the alleged event not only to give context to the scientific evidence but also to form the basis for the scientific opinions to be given. If, for instance, the allegation is one of violation of the Canadian Fisheries Act, which forbids "the deposit of a deleterious substance . . . in water frequented by fish . . . ," there must be evidence of all three: (1) that a deposit was made into water, (2) that it was deleterious in nature, and (3) that fish were present.

The amount of scientific evidence the judge must sort through depends on the number of scientists who testified, the complexity of their evidence, and the various disciplines involved. It is obvious that the greater the number of witnesses involved, the more difficult is the task. It must be remembered that the scientific testimony that the judge heard was subject to cross-examination, a process that may have left it somewhat less convincing than when it was first tendered on direct examination. Any evidence on the same point from the opposing side also will add to the problem facing the judge, since this evidence will no doubt do nothing to clarify the issue. There will be many inconsistencies to sort out and rationalize. This is not unusual, and it is the rare case indeed that does not have its fair share. Such a situation becomes more problematic in cases dealing with scientific evidence, particularly when there is a measure of complexity to the evidence, since the judge must first ensure that this evidence is understood. At times, this can mean hours spent pouring over the mass of detail to be found in the transcript, comparing bits and pieces of evidence, and seeking all the while the "Rosetta stone" of understanding. Frequently, if the scientific evidence is overly complicated or lacks the requisite degree of certainty, the judge's attention also will be directed toward trying to determine if the facts necessary to support the scientific opinion in question have been proven. This is an area that provides a more certain ground for the judge, because a fact is not a fact until the trial judge says it is.

If more than one type of science is involved, the evidence from each field is examined to see if the facts that support the scientific opinion are in evidence and that the opinion itself is the one that counsel said would be elicited. This allows the judge to determine whether or not the opinion relates to the facts. Thereafter, each subset of the scientific evidence must be examined to see how it relates one to the other.

Conclusion

In arriving at a final decision in a trial involving scientific evidence, it must not be forgotten that scientific evidence is only one part of the evidence that is considered by the judge—one piece of evidence to be weighed with the rest.

The weight that scientific testimony receives is not enhanced by the fact that it is science, with all that this implies. It may be that the scientific evidence will be given little weight or even rejected outright. If this happens, it is not an indictment of the testimony, but rather, it reflects the fact that the totality of the other evidence outweighed the scientific evidence.

Neither the courts, the institution designated to resolve legal disputes, nor science, a valuable tool in assisting to resolve such disputes, is going to disappear from the scene. This being so, both sides have an obligation to examine some of the more repetitive communication problems that occur and work out a solution. At present, there still exists mutual apprehension, at times bordering on distrust. In my view, professional parochialism should be replaced by open communications. In so doing, not only will law and science benefit, but society as a whole will be well served by both disciplines.

5

Establishing Causation with Epidemiology

DAVID F. GOLDSMITH

SUSAN G. ROSE

This chapter briefly reviews the history of the development of criteria for the establishment of causation in epidemiology and medicine. As a current example of this process, we discuss the epidemiology evidence leading to the International Agency for Research on Cancer's evaluation of crystalline silica as a human carcinogen. We introduce two gradients for assessing causal evidence in medicine/epidemiology and in litigation and suggest that both attorneys and experts must understand their relative positions in order to best argue their scientific/medical cases. We examine the circumstances surrounding the development of the Bendectin epidemiology, which was the foundation for the U.S. Supreme Court's *Daubert* decision. Finally, we conclude that meritorious cases are being wrongly dismissed due to the judiciary's misunderstanding of the incremental process of determining causation in science.

Determining Cause and Effect in Medicine and Public Health

The profession of medicine has struggled to identify the causes of diseases throughout human history. As medicine grew more sophisticated and reliant on scientific advances over the past 150 years, knowledge about cause-effect relationships became crucial to the development of appropriate treatments and prevention strategies. For example, cholera, an infectious disease with high mortality rates, caused nineteenth-century physicians grave concern. The most prevalent view or theory in the first half of the 1800s was that *miasmas* (meaning "bad airs") close to the ground caused cholera and other infectious diseases. When comparing cholera mortality rates in cities at various elevations above sea level, it was noted that death rates for cholera declined as the distance from sea level rose. These data seemed to support the prevailing miasma theory.

Dr. John Snow (1813–1858), a London physician noted for his work in anesthesia, had a lifelong interest in the study of cholera [1]. He rejected the miasma theory for transmission of cholera and instead hypothesized that cholera was spread via water, not by air. His early observations of cholera suggested that the causal agent entered by the mouth, multiplied within the gastrointestinal tract, and then was spread to others by the fecal-oral route. He further deduced that the transmission of the disease was due to drinking water contaminated with raw sewage containing cholera in some form.

When a severe cholera epidemic broke out in 1854 in London, Snow saw an opportunity to test his hypotheses concerning water and cholera when he was asked to investigate the cause of the epidemic. Snow, relying on logic and his previous study of earlier cholera epidemics, deduced that the sharp localized outbreak pointed to a contaminated pump or well. Snow investigated 83 cholera deaths in the Golden Square area of London, found a leaking sewer pipe within a few feet of the well, and discovered "that there [has] been no particular outbreak or prevalence of cholera in this part of London except among the persons who were in the habit of drinking the water of the [Broad Street] pump well."

All these facts provided strong circumstantial evidence for water transmission of the cholera vibrio. Snow persuaded the authorities of the local parish to "take the handle off the [Broad Street] pump," thus preventing more cholera cases by stopping the public from using contaminated water. A scientist ahead of his time, Snow was able to argue persuasively for causal intervention (regulation) without knowing the exact organism (*Vibrio cholerae*), without knowing the precise way it was transmitted (from person to person via contaminated drinking water), without understanding the discipline of bacteriology, and without a detailed knowledge of modern water and sewer systems.

Following the example of Dr. Edward Jenner's successful use of cowpox virus to convey immunity to smallpox, first published in 1798 [2], Henle (1840) and Koch (1882) developed a set of postulates to demonstrate infectious disease causation (specifically tuberculosis) [3,4]. The Henle-Koch postulates set forth the following criteria (modified by Lilienfeld and Stolley in 1994) to be met before an agent could be considered the cause of a disease:

1. The organism (bacteria, virus) must be found in all cases of disease.
2. One must isolate the organism from patients with disease and success-
    fully culture it.
3. When the purified culture is inoculated into susceptible animal or human
    subjects, it must reproduce the disease [5].

While the Henle-Koch postulates brought a certain rigor and discipline to the study of infectious diseases, these postulates were problematic in their requirement that a particular disease must have only one cause and that a particular cause should result in only one disease. However, they did enable the germ theory of disease in the nineteenth century to achieve dominance in medicine over other theories, such as humors and miasmas.

Evans expanded the Henle-Koch postulates to cover questions of multicausal and noninfectious diseases as well as infectious diseases [6]. Each of Evans's criteria contributes a different amount of strength to the likelihood that a relationship between a potential risk factor and a disease is causal. The entire set constitutes very strong evidence of causality when fulfilled.

1. Incidence of disease needs to be significantly greater in those exposed to likely or presumed causal factors than among unexposed controls.
2. Exposure to hypothesized cause(s) should be more frequent among patients with the illness of concern than among healthy controls, when controlling for all other risk factors.
3. The disease must follow exposure to the hypothesized cause; the disease must never precede it or be coincidental to first exposure.
4. A variety of host responses should follow exposure to the putative agent(s) along a biological gradient from none/mild to moderate to severe.
5. Measurable host response(s) following exposure to the cause should appear in those unaffected by past exposure (i.e., those who were healthy should have biomarkers or distinct symptoms), or clinical responses should increase if present before exposure and should not be observed among (healthy) controls.
6. Reproduction or production of disease should occur more frequently among exposed persons than among unexposed persons and be observed in exposed laboratory animals or demonstrated after workplace or environmental exposures.
7. Elimination or control of causal exposures should decrease or eliminate the disease.
8. Modification of host response to the hypothesized cause should reduce or eliminate risk, such as development of immunity from either prior exposure to the agent or from vaccination.
9. All the observed relationships should be rational biologically and epidemiologically [6].

Causation in Chronic Diseases

In the 1950s and 1960s, medical evidence established the role of tobacco smoking in the causation of lung cancer. In order to develop defensible public health policies, it was necessary to measure or quantify the evidence to assess the sufficiency of data on which those policies were based. Building on the Henle-Koch postulates, a new set of criteria emerged that placed much more emphasis on epidemiology findings concerning chronic latent illnesses, such as cancer and heart disease, instead of the traditional reliance on bacteriology and the transmissibility of infectious agents to uninfected hosts. With the release of the U.S. Surgeon General's first report on smoking and health in 1964 [7] and the publication of Sir Austin Bradford Hill's paper on the criteria for causation in environmental medicine in 1965 [8], a synthesis of these criteria soon developed.

The criteria for judging causation for chronic diseases, particularly for cancer, are listed below [5,7–9]. It is critical to be aware that neither a case series nor a single epidemiology study will provide a sufficient body of evidence to determine causation for use in public health. Multiple studies are needed before scientific consensus is obtained and the etiologic links between exposure and disease can be established. However, from a public health perspective, causation can be inferred and action can be taken regarding such issues as water or food sanitation *even if all the criteria are not fully met.* This precautionary approach reinforces the necessity for careful and cautious application of professional judgment to causal assessments rather than blind adherence to a checklist of requirements for causal sufficiency.

As a discipline, the practice of epidemiology is conservative in its nature because of the insistence that consideration of scientific evidence be undertaken without haste. Epidemiologists strive to avoid a premature conclusion that causation exists. Moreover, they are equally concerned not to be misled by false-positive results (an erroneous conclusion that cause-effect exists when it does not, referred to in statistics as a *type I error*).

The criteria below are the usual evidentiary basis by which causation is currently judged in public health.

* *Strength of the association or high relative risk (RR).* The strength of the association is the first indication of a biological effect following a workplace or environmental exposure. There is no clear consensus in the epidemiology community regarding what constitutes a "strong" relative risk, although, at minimum, it is likely to be one where the RR is greater than 2.0, i.e., one in which the risk among the exposed is at least twice as great as among the unexposed. A relative risk greater than 2.0 produces an attributable risk (sometimes called *attributable risk percent* [10]) or an attributable fraction that exceeds 50%. An attributable risk of greater than 50% also means that "it is more likely than not" or, in other words, there is a greater than 50% probability that the exposure to a risk factor is associated with disease. This is the linchpin in the definition of legal causation, although it is not treated as such in public health practice.

* *Dose-response (sometimes called exposure-response) relationship.* In conjunction with an elevated relative risk, there should be a demonstrable exposure response effect showing a positive correlation between the degree of exposure (or dose) and the risk of disease. For example,

increasing smoking rates have led to increasing risks for lung (and other) cancers, respiratory diseases, and cardiovascular effects [12–14].

- *Consistency of findings.* As is the case in all scientific endeavors, consistent findings of adverse effects in multiple studies from different investigators, employing different research methods, add to the weight of evidence. Consistency of findings in epidemiologic studies carries the same positive weight as similar findings in experimental animal research studies. The consistent finding of an excess risk of leukemia among benzene-exposed workers throughout the world is very strong evidence of benzene's causal association with leukemia [15].

- *Biological plausibility, including experimental evidence.* Epidemiology observations must be biologically relevant and consistent with the latest advances in the disciplines of chemistry, toxicology, experimental oncology, and medicine. The U.S. Environmental Protection Agency and the International Agency for Research on Cancer are two agencies that focus on experimental animal evidence to predict human risks. Animal evidence is critical when there are no (or extremely limited) data on exposed humans. It is well known that there is a very high correlation between substances known to cause human cancers and tumor findings in laboratory animals [11]. For example, it makes biological sense that toxic substances that respectively produce sterility and angiosarcoma of the liver in laboratory animals (such as the chemicals dibromochloropropane and vinyl chloride) are also likely to do so among workers.

- *Temporal cogency.* Along with strong relative risk, this criterion is essential for deriving causation in medicine because disease cannot precede (or be coincidental with) exposure. For chronic diseases such as cancer, latency is likely to be a minimum of 10 to 15 years after initiation of exposure. For example, pleural or peritoneal mesothelioma from asbestos exposure has latent periods ranging from 20 to 40 years from first exposure. A corollary of this criterion is that risk should decline after cessation of exposure. A good example is the well-documented reduction in lung cancer risk among people who remain ex-smokers for 10 years or more compared with people who continue to smoke [12].

- *Control of confounding and bias.* Occupational epidemiologists cannot ethically conduct randomized clinical trials. Thus the determination of causal linkages must be based on research that has been controlled for possible confounding and bias. For example, when the Scandinavian findings of soft tissue sarcomas and exposure to phenoxyacetic acid herbicides were reported, there was an extensive debate as to whether there was possible recall bias due to the subjects' prior knowledge from press coverage of the putative link between exposure to defoliants and cancer. When other cancers (excluding soft tissue sarcomas) known not to be related to herbicides were assessed using the same questionnaire, these cancers were not found to be associated with elevated risks of exposure to defoliants. Therefore, it was evident that there was no recall bias and that the press publicity was not the reason for the finding of an association between exposure to herbicides and soft tissue sarcomas [16].

• *Specificity.* The exposure or industrial process and the concomitant disease(s) must be described with specificity. This includes pathognomonic findings of unique exposures producing single types of pathology, such as mesotheliomas in workers with past exposure to asbestos or hepatic angiosarcoma among vinyl chloride monomer–exposed workers. In 1994, Lilienfeld and Stolley included "specificity of the association" as part of the criteria of causation, although they admitted that restricting the focus to "one exposure producing only one disease" is contrary to what epidemiologists have learned about well-researched toxins such as tobacco smoking, where exposure to tobacco smoke alone is known to produce many diseases [5]. Health scientists have learned that a disease can have many potential causal factors, each independent and all necessary (or none sufficient) for producing etiologic links [17]. For example, combining exposure to aflatoxin with a positive history of hepatitis B infection produces a synergistically high risk for liver cancer, higher than the risk from each of these two factors separately [18].

• *Overall coherence.* Finally, one must ask whether all the evidence taken together is coherent. In the practice of epidemiology and public health, one must be careful not to indict innocent exposures or industries. A false-positive determination threatens the credibility of epidemiologists if public health policy changes are based on exposure and disease associations that are not tested thoroughly. Thus the evaluation of coherence becomes useful in looking backward at the overall strength of the evidence as well as in looking forward to the effectiveness of risk assessment and risk control policies, including regulations derived therefrom. For example, it is valid to conclude that exposure to respirable asbestos fibers is the cause of many diseases, e.g., asbestosis, mesothelioma, lung malignancies, and other cancers [19]. However, this causal connection may not justify a policy to remove all sealed (nonfriable) asbestos from every public school building in America. Such a policy would fail to consider both the excessive cost *and* the scientific knowledge that the risk of asbestos-related disease applies to workers and has not been linked with general or public use of buildings. That is, we know that neither school students nor the public have been sufficiently exposed to friable asbestos to produce a real excess disease risk. In fact, health risks *may be raised* by the removal process, where a more prudent course would be to wait for the asbestos to be removed during planned building renovation or demolition.

These criteria are used by epidemiologists to determine if there is sufficient evidence to conclude or to strongly suspect that an occupational or environmental exposure is causally linked to a disease or a specific set of risk factors for a disease.

Classification of Carcinogenicity by the International Agency for Research on Cancer

Over the last 25 years, the International Agency for Research on Cancer (IARC) has developed a methodology to evaluate drugs, environmental exposures, and industrial chemicals for carcinogenicity. The IARC's review process goes beyond the usual causation assessment criteria to classify substances by degree of carcinogenicity based on a rigorous evaluation of both animal and human studies. The IARC's open review process and invited expert panels representing the international scientific community have given its work a high degree of public health credibility.

The purpose of the IARC carcinogen classification system is to evaluate all data on many different chemicals, drugs, and industrial processes to identify likely risks to humans from exposure to these substances. The IARC explicitly considers evidence from experimental tumor biology in its evaluation process for humans and states in every review that ". . . in the absence of adequate data on humans, it is biologically plausible and prudent to regard agents and mixtures for which there is sufficient evidence of carcinogenicity in experimental animals as if they presented a carcinogenic risk to humans."

For humans, there are four IARC categories of carcinogenesis: (1) sufficient, (2) limited, (3) inadequate, and (4) lack of evidence. These categories are defined in the preamble to each monograph as follows:

1. The *sufficient* category is identical to the causal criteria defined earlier, i.e., strength of association, dose-response, consistency, biological plausibility, temporal cogency, control of confounding and bias, specificity, and coherence.
2. The *limited* category is used when "a positive association has been observed between exposure to the agent, mixture or exposure circumstance and cancer for which a causal interpretation is considered to be credible, but chance, bias or confounding could not be ruled out with reasonable confidence."
3. The *inadequate* category is used when "the available studies are of insufficient quality, consistency or statistical power to permit a conclusion regarding the presence or absence of a causal association, or no data on cancer on humans are available."
4. The *lack of evidence* category is used when "there are several adequate studies . . . which are mutually consistent in not showing a positive

association between exposure to the agent, mixture or exposure circumstance and any studied cancer or at any observed level of exposure. . . . '[L]ack of carcinogenicity' is inevitably limited to the cancer sites, conditions and levels of exposure and length of observation covered by the available studies. In addition, the possibility of a very small risk at the levels of exposure studied can never be excluded."

The IARC classifies carcinogenicity in animal studies into four categories: (1) sufficient, (2) limited, (3) inadequate, and (4) evidence suggesting a lack of carcinogenicity.

1. *Sufficient* evidence exists when "a causal relationship has been established between the agent or mixture and an increased incidence of malignant neoplasms . . . in (a) two or more species of animals or (b) in two or more independent studies in one species carried out at different times or in different laboratories or under different protocols."

2. *Limited* evidence exists when there are "data [that] suggest a carcinogenic effect but are limited for making a definitive evaluation because (a) the evidence of carcinogenicity is restricted to a single experiment; or (b) there are unresolved questions regarding . . . dosing, conduct or interpretation of the study; or (c) the agent or mixture increases the incidence only of benign neoplasms . . . or of certain neoplasms which may occur spontaneously in high incidence in certain strains [of animals]."

3. *Inadequate* evidence exists when there are "studies [that] cannot be interpreted as showing either the presence or absence of a carcinogenic effect because of major qualitative or quantitative limitations, or no data on cancer in experimental animals are available."

4. *Lack of carcinogenicity* exists when there are "adequate studies involving at least two species are available which show that . . . the agent or mixture is not carcinogenic. . . ."

When an IARC scientific panel perceives ambiguity in the data, or when the evidence does not fall into a clear-cut classification, the panel will determine if there is other evidence of mutagenicity, or positive short-term bioassay tests, or effects in other biological systems that may move the evidence in one direction or another. For example, the fact that triazine herbicides produced mammary tumors in laboratory animals outside the hormonal pathway necessary for breast cancer led IARC scientists to lower the classification for triazine from Group 2B to Group 3 [20,21].

Table 5-1 contains the synthesis of human and animal data used by the IARC to judge or label the evidence of carcinogenicity. The determination of human evidence is listed in the left margin, and the evaluation of animal evidence is on the top margin. Thus a Group 1 carcinogen, where there is sufficient evidence of carcinogenicity (e.g., tobacco, asbestos, and radiation), is a human carcinogen regardless of the category of animal evidence. Group 2A carcinogens (referred to as *probable* human carcinogens) are those with limited human evidence and sufficient animal evidence (e.g., pesticide chemicals such as captafol or ethylene dibromide). Group 2B (referred to as *possible* human carcinogens) are those with either sufficient animal evidence with any lesser level of human evidence or limited human evidence with any other degree of animal carcinogenicity (e.g., pesticide chemicals such as DDT or heptachlor with some carcinogenicity data but no clear-cut human evidence). (*Note:* Because the U.S. Environmental Protection Agency tends to place more weight on animal data, some chemicals may be listed as "probable" by EPA but labeled "possible" by the IARC.) Group 3 includes materials, chemicals, or industrial processes with inadequate human data to determine carcinogenicity and below all levels of animal evidence or less than sufficient. Group 4 includes materials in which there is evidence of negative carcinogenicity in human studies and below all levels of animal evidence less than sufficient. Group 4 classifications are very rare because IARC monographs primarily consider drugs or chemical processes for which there is some carcinogenic evidence [5], and they do not usually evaluate substances for which the risk of cancer is less than expected.

A Case Study: The IARC Reviews of Crystalline Silica

Crystalline silica exposure has been reviewed by IARC scientific panels for carcinogenicity twice in the past 15 years [22,23]. The history of the evaluation is illustrative of how IARC experts approach the problem of assessing carcinogenicity and the importance of epidemiology findings to this process. Because IARC monographs are relied on routinely in various legal settings, including environmental and occupational standard setting, it is useful to understand the IARC evaluation process.

Table 5-1. IARC Classification Scheme for Human and Animal Evidence of Carcinogenesis

Human Evidence	Animal Evidence			
	Sufficient	Limited	Inadequate	(−) Carcinogenicity
Sufficient	Group 1	Group 1	Group 1	Group 1
Limited	Group 2A	Group 2B	Group 2B	Group 2B
Inadequate	Group 2B	Group 3	Group 3	Group 3
(−) Carcinogenicity	Group 2B	Group 4	Group 4	Group 4

Prior to the IARC's first review of silica in 1986, there was general consensus in the scientific and occupational medical communities that inhalation of crystalline silica dust produced silicosis, silicotuberculosis, and cor pulmonale (enlargement of one of the chambers of the heart). Throughout the first three-quarters of the twentieth century, case studies occasionally appeared in the medical literature suggesting that inhalation of silica also was associated with autoimmune diseases, kidney diseases, and cancer (mostly lung cancer). Although these case reports had existed in the published medical literature beginning as early as the mid-1930s [24], raising the issue that silica might be a carcinogen, it was not until the early 1980s that the literature was examined critically by Goldsmith et al. [25]. These authors presented three types of data suggesting that silica exposure was carcinogenic: (1) rat studies finding lymphatic and lung tumors, (2) epidemiology studies of lung cancer risk among occupations and industries characterized by silica exposures, and (3) epidemiology follow-up studies of workers with silicosis, focusing on lung cancer risks.

This was the evidence the IARC monograph panel had when it first met [22]. To summarize, the animal evidence was as follows: There were two studies in rats showing that inhalation of silica produced significantly more lung tumors than in unexposed controls [26–28]. In addition, injected silica had been shown to produce histiocytic lymphomas in several species of rats [29–31].

The epidemiology evidence was examined using the evidentiary criteria set forth in the left column in Table 5-2 [22,32]. The IARC reviewers found that for silica-exposed workers there was a modest increased relative risk, little information about exposure response, and some consistency of elevated relative risk among workers in dusty trades exposed to silica. There was, however, possible confounding of most studies related to a lack of adjustment for smoking. Nevertheless, there was biological plausibility with the animal evidence and support for temporal cogency and for specificity. When the association was examined among silicotics, there was a stronger relative risk for lung cancer compared with silica-exposed workers, no apparent exposure response, yet consistency of lung cancer risks for most industries. Again, adjustment for confounding by smoking was missing, and there was concern about possible bias by those patients with silicosis who had been selected from compensation records. However, there was biological plausibility and temporal cogency in that lung cancer occurred after silicosis was diagnosed, and there was evidence for specificity. Even though the association was stronger for silicosis than for silica-exposed workers, the evidence in 1986 was more consistent with an assessment of limited support for carcinogenicity because of the lack of exposure response and possible confounding by smoking. With the animal evidence judged to be "sufficient" and the human evidence found to be "limited," the first IARC panel classified inhaled crystalline silica as Group 2A or as a "probable" human carcinogen [22].

When the second monograph panel met in 1996, it reexamined the evidence, which is shown in the right column of Table 5-2. Since there was no change

Table 5-2. Criteria for Lung Cancer Causation for Silica Exposure and for Silicosis Between First and Second IARC Reports

Point of Evidence	Silica-Exposed Workers, IARC 1986	Silica-Exposed Workers, IARC 1997	Workers with Silicosis, IARC 1986	Workers with Silicosis, IARC 1997
Strong relative risk	±	*	***	***
Dose-response gradient	±	**	±	**
Consistent findings	*	**	***	***
Controlled confounding	±	*	±	*
Biological plausibility	*	**	±	*
Temporal cogency	**	**	**	**
Specificity	**	**	**	**
Overall coherence	*	**	***	***

Note: * = criteria met; ** = more than minimal criteria met; *** = large body of evidence; ± = incomplete evidence.

in the animal findings, the experimental evidence was still considered sufficient, but it now included new and confirmatory studies by Muhle et al. [33], Spietoff et al. [34], Saffiotti et al. [35], and Daniel et al. [36]. This new research work confirmed the prior findings and added more information on the biological activity of different forms of silica, the genetic responses, and silica surface effects and thus expanded the toxicologic information of the earlier studies. New epidemiology studies by Checkoway et al. [37,38], Hnizdo et al. [39], Cherry et al. [40,41], and McDonald et al. [42] contained adjustments for smoking and other confounders (such as radon [39] and asbestos [38]) among silica-exposed workers, although the relative risks appeared to group around 2.0. There were key differences from the prior IARC review, including new dose-response findings using high-quality industrial hygiene data from the Checkoway, Hnizdo, Cherry, and McDonald studies. Many of the newer studies included assessments of exposure response indicating that lung cancer risk appeared to increase as the severity of silicosis increased [43]. The lung cancer and silicosis link was demonstrated in occupations or industries where there was little confounding by exposure to other occupational carcinogens. Despite a lack of unanimity of lung cancer risk for all silica-exposed occupations, the evidence was judged sufficient among the newest studies (which were adjusted for smoking) showing dose-response findings for silica-exposed workers and for silicotics as well. In addition, there were no new data (among the animal studies and/or experimental research) to offer a credible alternative explanation for the findings. Furthermore, none of the newer studies with industrial hygiene exposure data demonstrated decreased risk for silica-exposed workers. Thus the IARC upgraded the classification of crystalline silica from Group 2A to a Group 1 carcinogen [23]. The IARC's new findings and assessment were consistent with another independent review of silica dust exposure and cancer made by the American Thoracic Society in the same year [44].

In reviewing the scientific evidence, it is clear that the second IARC monograph panel did not deviate from the agency's methodology in drawing its conclusion. Furthermore, the panel made an evaluation based on what data were considered missing or not addressed in the first assessment—lack of adjustment for smoking and absence of exposure-response data. The IARC's assessments of the scientific evidence of silica's carcinogenicity offer useful case studies with which to demonstrate the process of determination of a causal judgment about a known hazardous exposure and cancer impacts on human health.

Epidemiology and the Law

When allegations of injury from toxic exposure are litigated or debated in workers' compensation hearings, lawyers, judges, and (sometimes) juries must deal with the problem of interpreting scientific links between exposure and disease and fitting the data into the framework of legal causation. Epidemiology findings can be classified into three categories: (1) those showing a positive relationship with exposure (such as the well-known link between smoking and lung cancer), (2) those showing a negative association (such as the benefits of fluorides in toothpaste and reduction in tooth decay), and (3) those showing no relationship between exposure and disease (such as water consumption and IQ score).

In most product liability cases, usually three types of expert scientific evidence are presented: experimental, clinical, and epidemiologic. Experimental research, conducted by toxicologists, pharmacologists, and tumor biologists, is weighted more heavily when there are modest or no human research results or when the epidemiology study results are equivocal. Experimental research is also useful to demonstrate biochemical linkages as well as elucidate exposure-disease mechanisms. Clinical evidence includes case studies and medical opinions based on differential diagnoses in which the disease is linked by deductive logic with exposure [45,46]. This type of expert testimony is key when there is no epidemiology research on the litigated issue or when epidemiology data cannot suggest an evidentiary direction. Finally, epidemiology evidence is essential for interpreting a body of scientific information, particularly when studies indicating different findings have been presented that lack consistency. While epidemiology experts, by their training, can testify that a causation conclusion is (or is not) demonstrable from the scientific evidence, they usually do not testify regarding individual causation. The opinion of the treating physician is determinative on the question of whether an *individual* plaintiff or claimant has suffered injury due to a toxic exposure [46].

Assessing the Degrees of Scientific and Legal Evidence

Figures 5-1 and 5-2 depict medical/epidemiology and legal gradients essential for understanding the degrees for scientific and legal evidence. It is vital for both attorneys and experts to recognize where the relevant scientific evidence is on both gradients to represent clients effectively. We will describe these two gradients and show how this knowledge can assist all actors involved in litigation: attorneys, experts, judges, and juries.

Figure 5-1 shows the medical/epidemiology gradient that rises by accumulation of evidence from case series, through modest epidemiology associations, to clear-cut causal findings. A case series, such as the first three patients with rare hepatic angiosarcoma who were employed in a vinyl chloride plant, reported by pathologists in Louisville, Kentucky (in 1974), may strongly suggest causation because of the rarity of the disease and the fact all three were employed doing the same job at the same plant [47]. However, a case series by itself usually does not constitute sufficient scientific evidence for a causal association, and more supportive findings must be accumulated before reaching such a conclusion. An initial case series, called to the attention of the scientific community by an "alert

Figure 5-1. Medical/epidemiology gradient for causation.

Case series	Some epidemiology	Clear epidemiology
First cases	RR < 2.0	RR > 2.0
"Signature" exposures and diseases:	Smoking and CVD RR = ~1.7	Adjusted for confounding
Vinyl chloride and angiosarcoma of liver	SBI and chronic autoimmune diseases	Smoking and lung cancer: RR = ~15

clinician," is usually the trigger for more extensive research, including controlled epidemiology and toxicology studies.

The next step is the collection of the early controlled epidemiology data that better refine the initial hunch suggested by the case series. The associations from these studies may produce relative risks greater than 1.0 but less than 2.0, and are consistent with evidence such as that used by the Institute of Medicine to describe the relationship between U.S. veterans and Agent Orange: sufficient evidence of an association or limited suggested evidence of association [54]. Thus, for legal purposes, this evidence may be considered supportive of the "significant factor" test but not sufficiently strong for public health experts to conclude "more likely than not" in the absence of other supportive evidence. [Recall that the definition of *more likely than not* is derived from the attributable risk percentage in which a risk factor must produce a relative risk greater than 2.0 to exceed 50% (see ref. 10).] However, it is crucial for both attorneys and experts to examine *all* the evidence for associations when the evidence falls into this category because other scientific findings may strongly support causal

Figure 5-2. Legal decision-making gradient and degree of causal evidence.

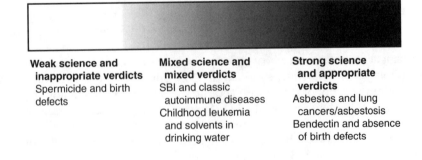

Weak science and inappropriate verdicts	Mixed science and mixed verdicts	Strong science and appropriate verdicts
Spermicide and birth defects	SBI and classic autoimmune diseases	Asbestos and lung cancers/asbestosis
	Childhood leukemia and solvents in drinking water	Bendectin and absence of birth defects

conclusions. An excellent example is the well-known relative risk of smoking and cardiovascular disease, which is approximately 1.7 times greater in smokers than in nonsmokers [14]. The reasons are many why the association is not as great as 2.0: Smoking is a common habit and cardiovascular disease is a common illness (with many risk factors) among both smokers and nonsmokers. Because tobacco smoking is known to produce many adverse clinically significant circulatory effects on humans, the causation argument must include clinical and toxicologic sources of evidence and not rely solely on epidemiology. What is clear from a public health perspective is that there is little doubt of the causal link between cigarette smoking and cardiovascular disease, despite the overall risk being less than 2.0.

The highest category, where there is public health consensus on causation, consists of an extensive body of scientific evidence producing relative risks above 2.0. Examples include smoking and lung cancer, radioactive exposures and many types of cancer, asbestos and respiratory diseases and cancer, and lead and adverse neurologic effects. There is also evidence for causation for such beneficial exposures as fluoridated water and decrease in dental caries, childhood vaccinations and control of pediatric infectious diseases, and adequate vitamin and mineral intake for normal growth and development.

Figure 5-2 shows the legal gradient related to causation, which also flows from weak to strong. From this viewpoint, there have been issues in which lawsuits favored the plaintiffs and where there was strong scientific consensus, e.g., tobacco smoking and asbestos. On the other hand, the Bendectin litigation favored defendants and was based on a large body of epidemiology data (see discussion below). Examples of cases falling in the middle of the gradient are silicone breast implants (SBI) and leukemia related to solvent-contaminated drinking water. Exposure to spermicide and birth defects is an example of a scientifically weak argument. During the twentieth century, tobacco has slowly moved from left to right on the gradient as cigarette makers, while disclaiming any legal liability, have acknowledged that their products are hazardous in the face of the vast amount of epidemiology and toxicology evidence.

In toxic tort litigation, there have been cases where scientific evidence preceded lawsuits (e.g., asbestos, tobacco), and there have been cases where litigation was pursued before scientific consensus occurred (e.g., breast implants, "Fen-phen"). These "first cases" are lawsuits that are brought before full medical and epidemiology evidence can be developed. They are filed because plaintiffs who recognize or believe that they have been injured have a limited amount of time to file a lawsuit (known as the *Statute of Limitations,* generally 1 to 3 years). A plaintiff cannot file a lawsuit after his or her Statute of Limitations has run out. In most jurisdictions, the statute begins to run the moment the plaintiff subjectively believes he or she has been injured and he or she knows what or who injured him or her. In these cases, plaintiffs cannot wait for the full body of health research evidence to accumulate before taking some legal action; failure to file a lawsuit within the prescribed time means they will not have the option to do so when more mature scientific evidence develops.

Since *Daubert*, the problem of the "first case" has become highly troublesome. Under *Daubert*, every "first case" is belittled by the defense as "junk science" because of its anecdotal nature. Thus, if the defendant's motions are successful, the case will never be heard by a jury. This definition of what is admissible in court presents all "first case" plaintiffs with an unfair burden. If plaintiffs can only seek redress for their injuries if they have a body of epidemiologic research showing a relative risk greater than 2.0 at their fingertips or when scientific evidence is fully mature, then they have been denied due process and the right to have their complaints against the defendants adjudicated by a jury of their peers.

Therefore, it is mandatory for experts and attorneys to know where on the scientific and legal gradients their cases fall, especially in jurisdictions that follow the *Daubert* rules of evidence. Attorneys and experts must be aware that if cases are novel—if they devolve on complex toxicologic evidence with little epidemiology data—they will face challenges on admissibility.

Bendectin—An Anomaly in Epidemiology

Bendectin was an antinausea drug used by pregnant women worldwide from 1956 until 1983, when it was voluntarily removed from the market by the manufacturer, Merrell Dow Pharmaceuticals, Inc., under the pressure of numerous product liability lawsuits. The drug has been studied extensively by epidemiologists to ascertain whether it is associated with limb-reduction birth defects [48]. One of every 2000 American babies born each year has a limb defect, and about 2.5 percent of all babies have birth defects. In the wake of the 1960s thalidomide disaster, drugs used during pregnancy, such as Bendectin, were under careful scrutiny.

It is *extremely rare* that so much scientific data, particularly human epidemiology research, is available for purposes of analysis during litigation. Studies attempting to discover a link between Bendectin and birth defects began in 1963 and over time were conducted in Australia, Britain, Germany, and the United States. By 1990, approximately 40 prospective and retrospective epidemiology studies of Bendectin had been conducted in over 130,000 patients. None has showed a statistically significant association between ingestion of the drug and all malformations. When the data were pooled, there was no summary relative risk exceeding 1.15 [48]. Because there was a huge amount of safety data on Bendectin, many physicians felt it was the best-studied pregnancy medication ever [49].

Nevertheless, during the 1980s, there was also a huge amount of litigation concerning the drug. Plaintiffs relied on case reports and some research findings on the pharmacology and toxicology of Bendectin. Experimental data suggested some laboratory evidence for impaired limb development when the drug's active ingredient (doxylamine dicyclomine pyridoxine) was applied to limb bud cells in chickens and mice and some teratology evidence in laboratory animals at doses 50 to 100 times the recommended human dose. Both medical and epidemiology experts for plaintiffs argued that the epidemiologic studies showing either low-ered risk of limb defects among users or no difference in risk were methodologi-cally flawed and that a reanalysis demonstrated a risk that ranged from 0.7 to 1.8 [50]. Therefore, plaintiffs' causation experts opined that Bendectin more likely than not caused birth defects in offspring whose mothers took the drug. The manufacturer, Merrell Dow, spent over $100 million in dealing with thou-sands of lawsuits, always ultimately prevailed in court, and yet decided to remove Bendectin from the market due to the expense of defending itself and the projected cost of insurance [49].

It was this litigation with these unusual epidemiology findings that made legal history by becoming the basis of the *Daubert* decision by the Supreme Court in 1993 (and the *Havner* case in Texas in 1994) on the proper role of the Court in ruling on the admissibility of scientific evidence [50,51].

The Supreme Court's use of a Bendectin case to develop criteria for judging causation evidence in legal disputes unfortunately has placed highly unrealistic expectations on the uses and availability of epidemiology to settle scientific arguments. The question before the Supreme Court was one of the admissibility of expert evidence; it was sheer happenstance that the case involved the Bendectin epidemiology evidence.

The numerous studies of Bendectin that provided scientific evidence for the parties' experts were unprecedented in the field of epidemiology. With the exception of tobacco, the abundance of studies on Bendectin was an anomaly for which there is no parallel in epidemiology or public health, nor is there likely to be again. As stated earlier, Bendectin was under such intense scientific scrutiny because it came on the scene after the thalidomide tragedy. In addition, Bendec-tin's risks were relatively easy and cost-efficient to study because the time from initial exposure to outcome (latency) was less than 9 months (obviously, the appearance of any limb reduction birth defects was immediately discernible on delivery). In contrast, epidemiologic studies of chronic diseases must deal with latencies that last decades or diseases that are slow to become differentiated or to be defined clinically. Therefore, following the *Daubert* decision, judges and lawyers were left with the erroneous impression and, even worse, the expectation that there is, or will be, a significant body of epidemiology evidence to answer any question on causation.

The unfortunate result of selecting this particular body of data as the norm on which all other scientific evidence is measured is that plaintiffs' options have been truncated in bringing cases that are based on novel ideas or methods. As discussed earlier, with a "first case" or toxic tort case scenario, plaintiffs who rely on differential diagnosis and experimental evidence to prove causation are often told that they are espousing "junk science," and their cases are dismissed.

The Consequences of the Daubert Decision

As discussed in Chapter 6 it is now customary in federal cases for the defense to challenge *any* scientific expert who is to offer an opinion about causation. When there is serious debate on the cause of health outcomes related to toxic chemical or drug exposures or when the clinical, experimental, or epidemiology research differs or lacks consensus on either methods and/or findings, *Daubert* challenges are the norm. As pointed out by Finley, *Daubert* and its progeny (*General Electric v. Joiner* and *Kumho Tire Co. v. Carmichael*) are raising the normative bar of scientific evidence to a point not contemplated when the decision was handed down [52]. By so doing, federal courts exceed their gate-keeping role; judges are now making legal rules that require twice as many adverse effects as expected (compared with the unexposed or with the general population) before evidence can be heard in court. In other words, the federal courts are allowing considerable harm (at least twice as much) to occur to consumers or workers exposed to hazardous drugs or chemical products before their cases can be heard. This means that corporations or other responsible parties are being held to a much *lower* standard than society finds acceptable in responding to common public health hazards, such as water or food contamination. For example, if a sanitizing chemical were found at any concentration in the finished products of a meat plant, public health authorities could stop production and recall all contaminated products. However, if a worker at that same plant were exposed to that same chemical and developed asthma, the defense would argue that his or her case could not be heard under *Daubert* until the medical literature showed that exposure to this chemical produced more than twice the risk of asthma compared with unexposed individuals.

This misplaced reliance on a finding of a relative risk that exceeds 2.0 is a consequence of the judiciary's attempt to find a "bright line" test to comply with the *Daubert* requirements. It is also illustrative of the fact that judges are poorly trained in science and do not properly understand what it can and cannot do. Finley states that ". . . epidemiologists, and many other . . . scientists understand the numerous reasons why it is invalid to equate the increase in relative risk in the population being studied with the probability of causation in any individual case. But these reasons seem to have eluded the comprehension of those judges who have made the misleadingly simple equation of legal relevance and the burden of proof on . . . causation with epidemiology [findings] that demonstrate[s] a relative risk of 2.0 or greater" [52].

As Greenlick points out [53], the causation issue in a toxic tort case is more like the individual clinical medical judgment than the population-wide statistical risk estimates of epidemiology. Futhermore, just as "the physician or other expert must draw some working causal model in the case of a single patient, even in the face of a great deal of uncertainty," courts, like clinicians, must make concrete decisions about what has caused a particular person's illness and often must do so in the face of less than definitive science [52]. There is no shortcut to this process. "[T]he only way [to] assess the significance of. . . epidemiological data . . . is through relatively complex integration of that information with [all] the scientific testimony from . . . other fields" [53].

Conclusion

In legal settings, epidemiology's role is to provide a scientific basis for assessing causation. In general, the typical process will require critical assessment of the risk evidence, with particular attention to the criteria for causality: strong relative risk, dose response, consistency, control for confounding, biological plausibility, temporal cogency, specificity, and coherence.

Since *Daubert*, it is apparent that the bar for plaintiffs has been raised in cases where either novel clinical findings emerge ("first cases") or where no epidemiology yet exists. Although *Daubert* was crafted to improve the standards for the review of scientific evidence, in its application, it has been turned 180 degrees to *prevent* the review of new scientific information unless it reaches a nearly unattainable level of certainty. Both lawyers and scientific experts must be able to educate judges and juries that the totality of scientific research may provide strong evidence of causation and that, in almost every case, a "full body" of epidemiology research is a rare occurrence.

References

1. Snow J. *On the Mode of Communication of Cholera,* 2d ed. London: John Churchill 1855.

2. Jenner E. *An Inquiry into the Causes and Effects of the Variolae Vaccinae, a Disease Discovered in Some of the Western Counties of England, Particularly Gloucestershire, and Known by the Name of the Cow-pox,* 1st ed. London: John Churchill, 1798.

3. Henle FGJ. *Pathologiste Untersuchungen von den Miasmen und Contagien und von den miasmatisch-contagiösen Krankheiten (On Miasmas and Contagions and on the Miasmatic-Contagious Diseases)* (privately published) 1840. Translated and reprinted in Henle J. *On Miasmata and Contagia.* Rosen Q (trans). Baltimore: Johns Hopkins Press, 1938.

4. Koch R. The etiology of tuberculosis. *Klin Woschenr* 1882;19:221. Translated and reprinted in the *Aetology of Tuberculosis.* Translated by M. Pinner. New York: National Tuberculosis Association, 1932.

5. Lilienfeld DE, Stolley PD. *Foundations of Epidemiology,* 3d ed. London: Oxford University Press, 1994.

6. Evans AS. Causation and disease: The Henle-Koch postulates revisited. *Yale J Biol Med* 1976;49:175–195.

7. U.S. Department of Health, Education and Welfare. *Smoking and Health.* Washington, DC: U.S. Public Health Service, Office of the Surgeon General, 1964.

8. Hill AB. The environment and disease: Association or causation? *Proc R Soc Med* 1965;58:295–300.

9. Goldsmith DF. Importance of causation for interpreting occupational epidemiology research: A case study of quartz and cancer. *Occup Med State of the Art Reviews* 1996;11:433–449.

10. Gordis L. *Epidemiology,* 2d ed. Philadelphia: Saunders, 2000.

11. McDonald J, Saracci R. Metals and chemicals. In: McDonald JC (ed), *Epidemiology of Work Related Diseases.* London: BMJ Publishing Group, 1995. Pp 7–37.

12. U.S. Department of Health and Human Services. *The Health Consequences of Smoking: Cancer. A Report of the Surgeon General.* Rockville, MD: U.S. Public Health Service, Office of the Assistant Secretary for Health, Office of Smoking and Health, 1982.

13. U.S. Department of Health and Human Services. *The Health Consequences of Smoking: Cancer and Chronic Lung Disease in the Workplace. A Report of the Surgeon General.* Rockville, MD: U.S. Public Health Service, Office of the Assistant Secretary for Health, Office of Smoking and Health, 1986.

14. U.S. Department of Health and Human Services. *The Health Consequences of Smoking: Cardiovascular Disease. A Report of the Surgeon General.* Rockville, MD: U.S. Public Health Service, Office of the Assistant Secretary for Health, Office of Smoking and Health, 1983.

15. International Agency for Research on Cancer (IARC), *IARC Monographs on the Evaluation of the Carcinogenic Risk of Chemicals to Humans: Some Industrial Chemicals and Dyestuffs,* Vol 29. Lyon, France: International Agency for Research on Cancer, 1982. Pp 93–148.

16. Hardell L, Eriksson M. The association between soft tissue sarcoma and exposure to phenoxyacetic acids. *Cancer* 1988;62:652–656.

17. Rothman KJ, Poole C. Causation and causal inference. In: Schottenfeld D, Fraumeni JF Jr (eds), *Cancer Epidemiology and Prevention,* 2d ed. London: Oxford University Press, 1996. Pp 3–10.

18. Qian G-S, Ross RK, Yu MC, et al. A follow-up study of urinary markers of aflatoxin exposure and liver cancer risk in Shanghai, Peoples' Republic of China. *Cancer Epidemiol Biomark Prev* 1994;3:3–10.

19. Morgan WKC, Gee JBL. Asbestos-related diseases. In: Morgan WAC, Seaton A (eds), *Occupational Lung Diseases,* 3d ed. Philadelphia: Saunders, 1995. Pp 308–373.

20. International Agency for Research on Cancer (IARC). *IARC Monographs on the Evaluation of the Carcinogenic Risk of Chemicals to Humans: Occupational Exposure to Insecticide Applications and Some Pesticides,* Vol 53. Lyon, France: International Agency for Research on Cancer, 1991.

21. International Agency for Research on Cancer (IARC). *IARC Monographs on the Evaluation of the Carcinogenic Risk of Chemicals to Humans: Some Chemicals that Cause Tumours of the Kidney or Urinary Bladder in Rodents and Some Other Substances,* Vol 73. Lyon, France: International Agency for Research on Cancer, 1999.

22. International Agency for Research on Cancer (IARC). *IARC Monographs on the Evaluation of the Carcinogenic Risk of Chemicals to Humans: Silica and Some Silicates,* Vol 42. Lyon, France: International Agency for Research on Cancer, 1986.

23. International Agency for Research on Cancer (IARC). *IARC Monographs on the Evaluation of the Carcinogenic Risk of Chemicals to Humans: Silica, Some Silicates, Coal Dust and Para-Aramid Fibrils,* Vol 68. Lyon, France: International Agency for Research on Cancer, 1997.

24. Dible JH. Silicosis and malignant disease. *Lancet* 1934;2:982–983.

25. Goldsmith DF, Guidotti TL, Johnston DR. Does occupational exposure to silica cause lung cancer? *Am J Ind Med* 1982;3:423–440.

26. Holland LM, Gonzales M, Wilson JS, Tillery MI. Pulmonary effects of shale dust in experimental animals. In: Wagner WL, Rom WN, Merchant JA (eds), *Health Issues Related to Metal and Nonmental Mining.* Boston: Butterworth, 1983. Pp 485–496.

27. Holland LM, Wilson JS, Tillery MI, Smith DM. Lung cancer in rats exposed to fibrogenic dusts. In: Goldsmith DF, Winn DM, Shy CM (eds), *Silica, Silicosis, and Cancer: Controversy in Occupational Cancer.* New York: Praeger, 1986. Pp 267–279.

28. Dagle GE, Wehner AP, Clark ML, Buschbom RL. Chronic inhalation exposure of rats to quartz. In: Goldsmith DF, Winn DM, Shy CM (eds), *Silica, Silicosis, and Cancer: Controversy in Occupational Cancer.* New York: Praeger, 1986. Pp 255–266.

29. Wagner MMF. Pathogenesis of malignant histicytic lymphatic induced by silica in a colony of specific-pathogen-free Wistar rats. *J Natl Cancer Inst* 1976;57:509–518.

30. Wagner MMF, Wagner JC. Lymphomas in the Wistar rat after intrapleural inoculation of silica. *J Natl Cancer Inst* 1972;49:81–91.

31. Wagner MMF, Wagner JC, Davies R, Griffiths DM. Silica-induced malignant histiocytic lymphoma: Incidence linked with strain of rat and type of silica. *Br J Cancer* 1980;41:908–917.

32. Goldsmith DF. Silica and pulmonary cancer. In: Samet JM (ed), *Epidemiology of Lung Cancer.* New York: Marcel Decker, 1994. Pp 245–298.

33. Muhle H, Takenaka S, Mohr U, et al. Lung tumor induction upon long-term low-level inhalation of crystalline silica. *Am J Ind Med* 1989;15:343–346.

34. Spietoff A, Wesch H, Wegener K, Klimisch H. The effects of thoratrast and quartz on the induction of lung tumors in rats. *Health Phys* 1992;63:101–110.

35. Saffiotti U, Williams AO, Daniel LN, et al. Carcinogenesis by crystalline silica: Animal, cellular and molecular studies. In: Castranova V, Vallaythan V, Wallace WE (eds), *Silica and Silica-Induced Diseases.* Boca Raton, FL: CRC Press, 1995. Pp 345–381.

36. Daniel LN, Mao Y, Williams AO, Saffiotti U. Direct interaction between crystalline silica and DNA: Proposed model for silica carcinogenesis. *Scand J Work Environ Health* 1995;21(suppl 2):22–26.

37. Checkoway H, Heyer NJ, Demers PA, Breslow NE. Mortality among workers in the diatomaceous earth industry. *Br J Ind Med* 1993;50:586–597.

38. Checkoway H, Heyer NJ, Demers PA, Gibbs GW. Reanalysis of mortality from lung cancer among diatomaceous earth industry workers, with consideration of potential confounding by asbestos exposure. *Occup Environ Med* 1996;53:645–647.

39. Hnizdo E, Murray J, Klempman S. Lung cancer in relation to exposure to silica dust, silicosis and uranium production in South African gold miners. *Thorax* 1997;52:271–275.

40. Cherry NM, Burgess GL, Turner S, McDonald JC. Cohort study of Staffordshire pottery workers: II. Nested case referent analysis of lung cancer. *Ann Occup Hyg* 1997;41(suppl 1):408–411.

41. Cherry NM, Burgess GL, Turner S, McDonald JC. Crystalline silica and risk of lung cancer in the potteries. *Occup Environ Med* 1998;55:779–785.

42. McDonald JC, Burgess GL, Turner S, Cherry NM. Cohort study of Staffordshire pottery workers: III. Lung cancer, radiographic changes, silica exposure and smoking habit. *Ann Occup Hyg* 1997;41(suppl 1):412–414.

43. Goldsmith DF. Uses of workers' compensation data in epidemiology research. *Occup Med State of the Art Reviews* 1998;13:389–415.

44. American Thoracic Society (ATS). Adverse effects of crystalline silica exposure. *Am J Respir Crit Care Med* 1997;155:761–768.

45. *Jennings v. Baxter Healthcare Corporation et al.*, Oregon State Appellate Court No. A92690 (SLIP OP, Feb. 11, 1998).

46. *Jennings v. Baxter Healthcare Corporation et al.*, Supreme Court of the State of Oregon No. A9405-03148 (152 OR App., Nov. 17, 2000).

47. Creech JL Jr, Johnson MN. Angiosarcoma of the liver in the manufacture of polyvinyl chloride. *J Occup Med* 1974;16:150–151.

48. McKeigue PM, Lamm SH, Linn S, Kutcher JS. Bendectin and birth defects: I. A meta-analysis of the epidemiologic studies. *Teratology* 1994;50:27–37.

49. Kolata G. Controversial drug makes a comeback. *New York Times*, September 26, 2000.

50. *Merrell Dow Pharmaceuticals v. Havner*, 953 S.W.2d 706; 40 Tex. Sup. J. 846 (1997).

51. *Daubert v. Merrell Dow Pharmaceuticals, Inc.*, 509 U.S. 579, 113 S. Ct. 2786 (1993).

52. Finley LM. Guarding the gate to the courthouse: How trial judges are using their evidentiary screening role to remake tort causation rules. *De Paul Law Rev* 1999; 49:335–376.

53. *Hall v. Baxter Healthcare Corp.*, 947 F. Supp. 1387, 1446–1451 (App B, Greenlick report) (D. Or., 1996).

54. Institute of Medicine (IOM). Veterans and agent orange: health effects of herbicides used in Vietnam. Committee to review the health effects in Vietnam veterans of exposure to herbicides. Division of Health Promotion and Disease Prevention, IOM, Washington, DC: National Academy Press, 1994. Pp 1–22.

"In the interest of streamlining the judicial process, we'll skip your experts and arguments because the defendant has more money than you."

6

The Daubert *Decision: Effects on the Admissibility of Scientific Evidence and Testimony*

KAREN E. READ

SUSAN G. ROSE

No one will deny that the law should in some way effectively use expert knowledge wherever it will aid in settling disputes. The only question is as to how it can do so best.

Learned Hand, "Historical and Practical Considerations Regarding Expert Testimony," Harvard Law Review, *1901*

Few cases have been as widely misunderstood and misapplied as *Daubert v. Merrell Dow Pharmaceuticals, Inc.,* and its progeny. In *Daubert,* the U.S. Supreme Court reminded federal trial courts that under the relevant Rules of Evidence they should "ensure that any and all scientific testimony or evidence admitted is not only relevant, but reliable" [1]. The Court gave a nonexclusive list of factors to guide judges in determining whether there was reliable and objective support when a "novel" scientific theory or methodology underlay the opinions of a party's expert(s). The factors listed include (1) testability, (2) peer review, (3) known error rate, (4) operational standards and controls, and (5) general acceptance of method or theory in the profession [2]. The court must analyze the reliability of any and all expert testimony [3], and its decision will only be overturned if the appellate court finds that the trial court has abused its discretion in admitting or excluding the evidence [4]. While trial courts have a very wide license in this area, their discretion is not boundless [5].

It is clear that the Supreme Court intended to liberalize the standards to be applied in determining the admissibility of scientific testimony and evidence [6] and that the suggested guidelines are to be used whenever an expert's testimony is based on a "novel" methodology or presents "novel" theories.

However, it has now become standard operating procedure for a defendant to ask the trial court to use *Daubert's* suggested analysis on any and all expert testimony, even when the experts in question are using the classic methodology in their fields (e.g., doctors using differential diagnosis along with other reliable factors to determine the cause of a patient's injuries; discussed further below).

Challenges to all the causation evidence, whether there is a basis under the *Federal Rules of Evidence* or not, are now *de rigueur* in most toxic and/or occupational exposure cases and other mass tort cases and have spread to other individual suits (e.g., medical malpractice or traditional product liability cases).

Unfortunately, trial courts have taken their "gatekeeper" charge as requiring them to act as sentries and even "junior scientists," whose job is to analyze and scrutinize all expert evidence in all cases to prevent "junk science" from sneaking into the courtroom. This is fast becoming standard federal judicial practice as trial courts, eager to clear their dockets, ignore the Supreme Court's caution that (1) these were "general observations" and not "a definitive checklist" to be followed [7] and (2) that it is not necessary to apply this analysis to every expert or even every case [8].

Almost prescient in his dissent from the "general observations" of the majority in *Daubert*, Chief Judge Rehnquist wrote:

> [T]he Court speaks of its confidence that federal judges can make a "preliminary assessment of whether the reasoning or methodology underlying the testimony is scientifically valid and of whether that reasoning or methodology properly can be applied to the facts in issue." *Ante*, at 12. The Court then states that a "key question" to be answered in deciding whether something is "scientific knowledge" "will be whether it can be (and has been) tested." *Ante*, at 12. Following this sentence are three quotations from treatises, which speak not only of empirical testing, but one of which states that "the criterion of the scientific status of a theory is its falsifiability, or refutability, or testability." *Ante*, pp 12–13. I defer to no one in my confidence in federal judges; but I am at a loss to know what is meant when it is said that the scientific status of a theory depends on its "falsifiability," and I suspect some of them will be, too. [See Chap. 7 for the answer!]. I do not doubt that Rule 702 confides to the judge some gatekeeping responsibility in deciding questions of the admissibility of proffered expert testimony. But I do not think it imposes on them either the obligation or the authority to become amateur scientists in order to perform that role. I think the Court would be far better advised in this case to decide only the questions presented, and to leave the further development of this important area of the law to future cases [9].

The result has been that many post-*Daubert* cases have too rigidly applied the *Daubert* factors as threshold criteria for admissibility [10]. The consequence is that the trial court ends up striking relevant and instructive testimony of well-known and respected experts in their fields of expertise, even when the evidence is methodologically sound and meets the two-pronged *Daubert* test of relevance and reliability. Sadly, many deserving plaintiffs are thus denied their day in court.

The Proper Framework for Assessing Admissibility of Expert Testimony

Admissibility issues under *Federal Rule of Evidence,* Rule 104(a) [11], include analysis of the expert's qualifications and methodology under Rule 702, analysis of the expert's data under Rule 703 [12], and analysis of the probative versus prejudicial balance under Rule 403 [13]. Amendments to Rules 702 and 703 were to go into effect on December 1, 2000. These amendments and potential problems with the amendments will be discussed below after the basic framework for assessing the admissibility of expert testimony is explored.

It should be noted at the outset that Rules 702 and 703 of the *Federal Rules of Evidence* are "premised on an assumption that the expert's opinion will have a reliable basis in the knowledge and experience of his discipline" [14]. Only one of these admissibility issues was discussed at any length in the Supreme Court's decision in *Daubert*: the definition of *scientific knowledge* under Rule 702, requiring that the methodology used by a scientific expert be valid.

Analysis of Expert's Qualifications under Rule 702

Under Rule 702, before being permitted to testify as an expert, a witness must be found to be "qualified as an expert by knowledge, skill, experience, training, or education." Rule 702 "contemplates a broad conception of expert qualifications" [15].

Analysis of Expert's Methodology under Rule 702

The Eleventh Circuit provided a historical perspective on Rule 702 that governs the admissibility of scientific evidence. In *Joiner v. General Electric Co.* [16], the court noted that it was the *Federal Rules of Evidence* enacted in 1975, rather than *Daubert,* that overruled the "general acceptance" test established by *Frye v. United States* [17]. Under this general acceptance test [also known in California as the *Kelly test* after *People v. Kelly,* 549 P. 2d 1240, 1244 (Cal. 1976)], no theory can be admitted into evidence unless it has been approved by a loosely defined consensus among a "relevant community" of scientists. Unlike *Daubert,* this inquiry only applies to a very limited category of evidence. As explained by the California Supreme Court,

> . . . *Kelly/Frye* only applies to that limited class of expert testimony which is based, in whole or part, on a technique, process, or theory which is new to science and, even more so, the law. . . .
> The second theme in cases applying *Kelly/Frye* is that the unproven technique or procedure [is one that] appears in both name and description to provide some definitive truth which the expert need only accurately recognize and relay to the jury. The most obvious examples are machines or procedures that analyze physical

data. Lay minds might easily, but erroneously, assume that such procedures are objective and infallible [18].

Therefore, "absent some special feature which effectively blindsides the jury, expert opinion testimony is not subject to *Kelly/Frye*" [19].

Rule 702 introduced a "more liberal approach" to the question of the admissibility of scientific evidence by providing that

> If scientific, technical, or other specialized knowledge will assist the trier of fact to understand the evidence or to determine a fact in issue, a witness qualified as an expert by knowledge, skill, experience, training, or education, may testify thereto in the form of an opinion or otherwise [20].

Notwithstanding Rule 702, most courts continued to adhere to the general acceptance test until 1993 when *Daubert* specifically rejected the concept of general acceptance as the sole test for admissibility of scientific evidence [21]. It should be noted here that although some state courts have adopted *Daubert* as their litmus test for admitting scientific evidence and others have modeled their admissibility inquiries after the guidance given by the U.S. Supreme Court in *Daubert,* 17 states still follow the older standard called the *general acceptance test,* as outlined in *Frye v. United States,* including some of the country's most populous states, e.g., California, New York, Florida, Illinois, Pennsylvania, Michigan, New Jersey, Arizona, Colorado, North Carolina, Maryland, and Virginia.

UNDER RULE 702 AND *DAUBERT,* THE FOCUS MUST BE SOLELY ON THE METHODOLOGY USED BY THE EXPERT. The Supreme Court made clear in *Daubert* that the focus of an admissibility analysis of expert testimony under Rule 702 must be solely on whether the methodology used by the expert is scientifically valid [22]. The validity of the expert's methodology is the key under Rule 702, the court explained, because science is defined by its process, not its product. Science is not "an encyclopedic body of knowledge about the universe" but rather "a process for proposing and refining theoretical explanations about the world" [23]. Thus, "to qualify as 'scientific knowledge,' an inference or assertion must be derived by the scientific method" [24].

The Supreme Court also made clear in *Daubert* that once the Court determines that the scientific expert witness is employing a valid methodology, the inquiry under Rule 702 ends. "The focus . . . must be solely on principles and methodology, not on the conclusions they generate" [25]. Unfortunately, in the Supreme Court's first post-*Daubert* opinion (*G.E. Co. v. Joiner*), the issue became further clouded.

In *Joiner,* the Eleventh Circuit Court stated that trial courts "must examine the reasoning or methodology underlying the expert opinion to determine whether it utilizes valid methods and procedures" but must "be careful not to cross the line between deciding whether the expert's testimony is based on 'scientifically valid principles' and deciding upon the correctness of the expert's conclusions. The latter inquiry is for the jury and, therefore, judges may not implicitly factor it into their assessment of reliability" [26]. While not reversing the appellate court's opinion on this ground, the Supreme Court noted that an expert's "conclusions and methodology are not entirely distinct from one another" [27] with little additional explanation. Although findings of fact and evaluating and weighing an expert's opinions/conclusions historically have been tasks for the jury, this discussion in *Joiner* hints at a possible departure from *Daubert* and may prove to be just the foothold that those who want to stay away from juries (almost always corporate and insurance defendants in civil cases) have long been seeking. As was noted in the dissenting portion of Justice Stevens's opinion in *G.E. Co. v. Joiner*:

> [E]ven though I fully agree with both the District Court's and this Court's explanation of why each of the studies on which the experts relied was by itself unpersuasive, a critical question remains unanswered: When qualified experts have reached relevant conclusions on the basis of an acceptable methodology, why are their opinions inadmissible?
>
> Daubert quite clearly forbids trial judges from assessing the validity or strength of an expert's scientific conclusions, which is a matter for the jury. Because I am persuaded that the difference between methodology and conclusions is just as categorical as the distinction between means and ends, I do not think the statement that "conclusions and methodology are not entirely distinct from one another," . . . , is either accurate or helps us answer the difficult admissibility question presented by this record [28].

This uncertain language in the *Joiner* case will no doubt cause more confusion regarding the boundaries of the trial court's gatekeeper role.

UNDER RULE 702 AND *DAUBERT*, EVEN THE METHODOLOGY DOES NOT REQUIRE GENERAL ACCEPTANCE. To the extent that the general acceptance test has survived after *Daubert*, the courts may look only to general acceptance of the methodology employed [29]. The methodology does not need to be accepted by a majority of the relevant scientific community. As stated in the Ninth Circuit's post-*Daubert* opinion [30]:

> [T]he focus . . . is on the reliability of the methodology and in addressing that question the court and the parties are not limited to what is generally accepted; methods accepted by a minority in the scientific community may well be sufficient.

Stated differently, "the opinion evidence of reputable scientists is admissible in evidence in a federal trial even if the particular methods they used in arriving at their opinion are not yet accepted as canonical in their branch of the scientific community" [31].

Furthermore, an opinion cannot be excluded just because it is in conflict with the opinion of another expert in the case, including that of a court-appointed expert, so long as proper methodology is followed. For example, in the case of *EFCO Corp. v. Symons Corporation* [32], the court allowed the damages testimony of both the plaintiff's and defendant's experts, notwithstanding the fact that defendant's expert disputed the methodology used by plaintiff's expert. The trial court recognized the parties' conflicting theories but allowed both experts to testify regarding damages, leaving the ultimate decision as to which theory was sounder to the jury [33]. The Court of Appeals affirmed the trial court's decision [34].

UNDER RULE 702 AND *DAUBERT,* EVEN ERRORS IN APPLYING THE METHODOLOGY GO TO THE WEIGHT OF THE EVIDENCE. As long as the methodology employed by the expert is scientifically valid, claims that the expert made errors in applying the methodology and thereby reached the wrong conclusion simply go to the weight of the evidence to be assessed by the jury [35].

UNDER RULE 702 AND *DAUBERT,* THE METHODOLOGY "FITS" IF THE PROFFERED TESTIMONY IS PROBATIVE OF A FACT ISSUE IN THE CASE. The second prong of a *Daubert* admissibility analysis under Rule 702 involves the relevance of an expert's methodology to the issues in the particular case. It is not enough under Rule 702 that the methodology used by the expert is valid for *some* scientific purpose; rather, the methodology must "fit" the type of scientific inquiry at hand [36].

There is a strong presumption of admissibility for any evidence that may assist the trier of fact [37]. Accordingly, the "fit standard" is not considered a high standard, requiring only that the proffered scientific testimony or evidence be probative of the "particular factual issues in the case" [38]. For example, in *Paoli II,* the court found that testimony that a substance can cause one type of cancer can "fit" the case, even though plaintiffs were not suffering from that type of cancer, if the expert can reasonably suggest that an increased risk of this one type of cancer is probative of increased risk of cancers from which plaintiffs were suffering [39].

Therefore, the burden on the defendant in challenging the relevance of a piece of evidence under Rule 703 or testimony under Rule 702 is necessarily a heavy one. However, in practice, it is often plaintiffs who bear the burden. Time and again, courts have required plaintiffs to put on their whole medical causation case weeks or months before the trial, at great cost to the plaintiffs. Courts often have ordered such a presentation (known as a *Daubert hearing*) on a mere request from defendants, before the defendants have offered any evidence at all, let alone sufficient evidence to put the burden back on plaintiffs to prove the relevance or reliability of their causation evidence.

A new trend should be noted briefly. With increasing frequency, parties will call experts to testify, not for an opinion on the ultimate issue of causation, but rather in support of the scientific validity of a particular methodology. Because of the turn that case law has taken in the last decade (discussed below in further detail), parties may find themselves out of luck if they do not proffer testimony to support the methodology underlying the testimony of the main causation witness/expert [40]. To a knowledgeable scientist (e.g., an epidemiologist), it may seem insulting to have a second epidemiologist or statistician appear to explain how the previous interpretation of a particular set of data is correct. Unfortunately, it is becoming an expensive necessity because well-qualified, reputable, and extremely knowledgeable experts are being challenged at every turn, notwithstanding the fact that they are properly using techniques generally relied on in their field of expertise to come to their opinions. Too often the result is that these well-qualified experts are excluded from testifying. This trend is also somewhat ironic considering the fact that parties may be prohibited from presenting testimony that the court could consider redundant [41].

Into the Unknown: Amended Rules 702 and 703

Although not yet in effect at the time of this writing, the rules applying to the admissibility of expert testimony have been changed. They were adopted by the U.S. Supreme Court on April 17, 2000, and were scheduled to go into effect December 1, 2000. The modified rules are set forth below with the new material italicized [42].

> Rule 702. Testimony by Experts
> If scientific, technical, or other specialized knowledge will assist the trier of fact to understand the evidence or to determine a fact in issue, a witness qualified as an expert by knowledge, skill, experience, training, or education, may testify thereto in the form of an opinion or otherwise, *if (1) the testimony is sufficiently based upon reliable facts or data, (2) the testimony is the product of reliable principles and methods, and (3) the witness has applied the principles and methods reliably to the facts of the case* [43].

Although it was the framers' intent to (1) generally clarify and codify the flexible guidelines discussed in *Daubert* and (2) reiterate that the trial court's gatekeeping function applies to all testimony, as affirmed by the U.S. Supreme Court in *Kuhmo Tire*, they have actually gone much further. In order to codify *Daubert*'s "fit standard," Amended Rule 702 states that the court must ensure that the witness "appl[y] the principles and methods reliably to the facts of the case." However, the wording also could be interpreted as giving the trial court the authority to look to the expert's conclusions, which historically has solely been the duty of the finder of fact or jury. Thus Justice Stevens's caveat in the dissenting portion of his opinion in *G.E. Co. v. Joiner* (discussed previously) will be even more important when the amended rule goes into effect and as the appellate courts grapple with this issue in the future.

Rule 703. Bases of Opinion Testimony by Experts
    The facts or data in the particular case upon which an expert bases an opinion or inference may be those perceived by or made known to the expert at or before the hearing. If of a type reasonably relied upon by experts in the particular field in forming opinions or inferences upon the subject, the facts or data need not be admissible in evidence *in order for the opinion or inference to be admitted. Facts or data that are otherwise inadmissible shall not be disclosed to the jury by the proponent of the opinion or inference unless the court determines that their probative value in assisting the jury to evaluate the expert's opinion substantially outweighs their prejudicial impact* [44].

The history of the *Federal Rules of Evidence* aids in understanding why this amendment was made. Prior to the enactment of the *Federal Rules of Evidence* in 1975, under common law principles, when analyzing the data underlying an expert's opinion, the court focused on the admissibility of the underlying data, thus drastically limiting information on which an expert could rely, even if it was such that he or she would use in the normal course of business. With the promulgation of the *Federal Rules of Evidence,* experts were allowed to rely on not only the facts already admitted into evidence but also facts that may not be admissible even if offered, so long as those facts were the type of information on which other experts in the same field would rely in coming to an opinion. Thus courts moved from assessing admissibility of this underlying data to assessing their reliability.

Concern was raised that proponents of certain evidence were attempting to bootstrap the underlying facts, data, or other information into evidence when it otherwise would not be admissible in court. Thus this amendment is intended to clarify that although an expert can rely on otherwise inadmissible evidence if it is sufficiently reliable, it cannot come into evidence or be presented to a jury just because the expert has relied on it.

Admissibility of Scientific Evidence in Practice

Now armed with an understanding of how a court should analyze the admissibility of scientific evidence and testimony, we can explore how, in actual practice, these principles have been misapplied. Since the *Federal Rules of Evidence* were enacted in 1975, courts have been evaluating scientific evidence for relevance and reliability. What is new since *Daubert* is the use of a scientific evidence analysis to evaluate expert opinions on medical causation. The trouble comes with the struggle to decide whether the question concerns the sufficiency of the evidence presented versus the admissibility of a particular piece of evidence.

Statistical Evidence Is Not Required for a Differential Diagnosis

In *Hopkins v. Dow Corning Corp.*, 33 F.3d 1116, 1125 (9th Cir. 1994), a breast implant case, the Ninth Circuit concluded that the "reasoning or methodology underlying the [expert] testimony is scientifically valid," despite the absence of a solid body of epidemiologic evidence (citing *Daubert*). Even before *Daubert*, courts recognized that

> [A] cause-effect relationship need not be clearly established by animal or epidemiological studies before a doctor can testify that, in his opinion, such a relationship exists. As long as the basic methodology employed to reach such a conclusion is sound, such as use of tissue samples, standard tests, and patient examination, products liability law does not preclude recovery until a "statistically significant" number of people have been injured or until science has had the time and resources to complete sophisticated laboratory studies of the chemical [45].

The guidance given to the federal courts on scientific evidence, consistent with *Hopkins*, does not support the position maintained by many defendants; i.e., epidemiology is required to show causation, either generally or specifically for a given individual. Epidemiology is one tool—where available, relevant, and reliable, it "focuses on the question of general causation (i.e., is the agent capable of causing disease?) rather than that of specific causation (i.e., did it cause disease in this individual?)" [46]. The reason epidemiology does not focus on specific causation is that "[a]pplying population-based results to an individual plaintiff is generally beyond the limits of epidemiology. Measurements of error and risk, the hallmarks of epidemiology, lose their meaning when they are applied to an individual" [47]. For questions of general causation, scientific models are available besides epidemiology, including "toxicology models based on animal studies (in vivo), . . . [which] [o]ften . . . are the only or best available evidence of toxicity" [48], and differential diagnosis [49].

However, there are a disturbing and growing number of cases, both state and federal, that now require the presence of some sort of studies with statistically significant findings before allowing medical causation evidence and/or testimony to go to the jury [50]. This effectively prevents a plaintiff from bringing a novel theory of causation to a jury, thus turning all new scientific ideas into so-called junk science until those ideas have been approved by the scientific community. Obviously, this approach is antithetical to good scientific practice. If the average patient can benefit from the observations of an "alert clinician," there is no reason why a plaintiff in a lawsuit should be prevented from using those same medical observations to help prove his or her case. A plaintiff bringing a "first case" to court now may have many new obstacles set in his or her way. Some courts, however, recognize that clinical medicine is sufficiently reliable to be admissible into evidence absent any statistical or epidemiologic data

An Example of the Incorrect Use of Daubert Analysis

An example of a judicial misunderstanding of the basic principles of causation and science, and one that illustrates the problem of a "first case," is the California case of *Javor v. Hoffmann-La Roche Inc., et al.* [51]. Although the court initially made a very concise and correct analysis of the use of differential diagnosis and the appropriateness of this methodology for identifying the cause of a medical problem, the court was later led astray by defendant's red herrings, which is too often the case.

RELIABILITY OF DIFFERENTIAL DIAGNOSIS AS A MATTER OF LAW. The most extensive discussion of the application of *Daubert* to the methodology of differential diagnosis is found in *Paoli II*. The *Paoli II* court recognized that the factors enumerated in *Daubert* are not especially helpful in analyzing the methodology of differential diagnosis, with the exception of the final factor of "existence of standards controlling the technique's operation," which is only "slightly more helpful" [52]. The court did, however, review the four factors listed in *Daubert* and make the following findings concerning the methodology of differential diagnosis:

1. *Testing.* "Differential diagnosis can be considered to involve the testing of a falsifiable hypotheses . . . through an attempt to rule out alternative causes" (although this process involves more judgment than other scientific methods, it does not turn it into unreliable science).
2. *General acceptance.* "[D]ifferential diagnosis generally is a technique that has widespread acceptance in the medical community."
3. *Peer review.* Differential diagnosis "has been subject to peer review."
4. *Rate of error.* Differential diagnosis "does not frequently lead to incorrect results" [53].

Techniques that support the finding of a reliable differential diagnosis include performance of physical examinations, taking of medical histories, use of reliable laboratory tests, and consideration of alternative causes [54]. "A doctor only needs one reliable source of information showing that the plaintiff is ill, and either a physical examination or medical records will suffice" [55]. This also applies to physicians who evaluate patients for litigation purposes [56].

THE *JAVOR* CASE—UNDERLYING FACTS. In May 1995, plaintiff Rick Javor (age 24 and a college athlete) traveled to West Africa to do volunteer work in a small hospital in Ghana for 2 years. Following medical instructions, he took Lariam (mefloquine), manufactured by the defendant in the case, for malaria chemoprophylaxis. After taking the second Lariam tablet, he felt very strange and dizzy. From that moment to the present time, he has never felt well. Over the next several weeks, he suffered from dizziness and blurry eyes, and he felt as if he could not stand up straight and that he was off balance. In addition, he felt confused and disoriented, and it was difficult from him to listen to and follow group conversation. He also was profoundly fatigued. He continued to take the Lariam tablets for 3 more weeks.

Following the advice of the physicians in Africa with whom he worked, he switched to another malaria prophylaxis regime—a combination of the drugs chloroquine and proguanil. However, his condition did not improve. In addition to the dizziness, his symptoms now included fast heartbeat, chest pain, shortness of breath, nausea, stomach pain, diarrhea, ear pain, blurred vision and eye pain, difficulty with concentration, paranoia, anxiety, panic attacks, weakness, headache, loss of short-term memory, depression, and confusion. He had never experienced any of these neuropsychiatric symptoms before. Furthermore, he was not told before he left the United States that any or all of these symptoms might occur and that they were recognized side effects of Lariam.

His continued symptoms were a "mystery" to the doctors in Africa. Ten months later, it was decided that he should go back on Lariam. If his symptoms were due to some form of low-grade malaria, it was believed the Lariam would help. He took another 17 pills, but his condition worsened markedly. He felt so weak and so sick that he was afraid he would die if he did not return to the United States to seek medical attention. Thus he was forced to abandon his African commitment and he returned to the United States.

In deposition, plaintiff's expert neurotologist, Dr. Joseph Roberson, opined that plaintiff had suffered a severe injury to his vestibular (balance) system and that his exposure to Lariam was the cause. Dr. Roberson based his opinion not only on his observation of plaintiff's injuries and clinical tests but also on his knowledge of the ototoxic effects of drugs in the quinine family. He concluded that causation could be found (1) in the close temporal relationship between plaintiff's exposure to Lariam and the onset of his symptoms, (2) in the fact that balance disorders such as plaintiff's do not occur in a healthy 26-year-old person without toxic, traumatic, or postoperative causes, and (3) drugs in the quinine family, of which Lariam is one, are known ototoxicologic agents.

THE COURT REASONED CORRECTLY ON DEFENDANT'S FIRST EVIDEN-TIARY CHALLENGE. When the issue of causation was raised in a defense motion for summary judgment (seeking exclusion of Dr. Roberson's opinion on causation), the court found that Dr. Roberson's testimony was admissible, notwithstanding the fact that Dr. Roberson's opinions were not based on any animal studies or other epidemiologic studies showing a causal relationship between Lariam and plaintiff's symptoms. Citing numerous cases, the court found that Dr. Roberson's methodology was appropriate to support his conclusion that Lariam was the cause of plaintiff's injuries. The court noted that the lack of peer-reviewed articles, clinical trials, or other studies conclusively linking a particular agent to a particular injury does not prevent the evidence or testimony from coming into the case if it is based on objective, verifiable evidence and scientific methodology of the kind traditionally used by the expert in question [57]. The court further discussed the reliability of differential diagnosis, stating, "[d]ifferential diagnosis is a reliable scientific method used by doctors every day in reaching conclusions regarding the cause of patients' illnesses" [58]. This is supported by the advisory committee's note to Rule 703, which states

> [A] physician in his own practice bases his diagnosis on information from numerous sources and of considerable variety. . . . The physician makes life-and-death decisions in reliance upon them. His validation, expertly performed and subject to cross-examination, ought to suffice for judicial purposes [59].

THE COURT STUMBLED BADLY ON DEFENDANT'S SUBSEQUENT CHALLENGE. However, after defendant asked the court to reconsider its original order, the court went badly astray when it issued its subsequent order excluding the testimony of Dr. Roberson [60]. Following a *Daubert* hearing in which Dr. Roberson testified, the court substituted its own judgment (and the reasoning urged by the defendant) instead of relying on the various factors that Dr. Roberson found significant in expressing his opinion. The court found as a matter of law that the plaintiff's exposure to other drugs in the quinine family, including quinine, primaquine, and chloroquine, made Dr. Roberson's testimony untenable. The court did not believe Dr. Roberson could "scientifically" determine which drug in the quinine family had the ototoxicologic effect on the plaintiff. While it is a given in medical practice to rely on temporal association to establish cause and effect, the court decided that the temporal association was not sufficient. This holding is directly contrary to well-established and widely cited law from *In re Paoil R.R. Yard P.C.B. Litig.*, where the court found that "[a] medical expert's causation conclusion should not be excluded because he or she has failed to rule out every possible alternative cause of a plaintiff's illness" [61]. In fact, the failure to rule out alleged alternative causes should only affect the weight given by the jury to an expert's testimony rather than the admissibility of the testimony [62].

This final ruling was issued notwithstanding the Court's previous ruling that "where a differential diagnosis is combined, as here, with a temporal relationship between the exposure and the onset of symptoms, it can provide a valid foundation for an expert opinion" [63]. The law certainly did not change in the intervening 8 months. Many cases have found that evidence of a temporal relationship between an exposure to a substance and the onset of a set of symptoms or disease or the worsening of the symptoms or disease "can provide compelling evidence of causation" [64]. In fact, one court found that "there may be instances where the temporal connection between exposure to a given chemical and subsequent injury is so compelling as to dispense with the need for reliance on standard methods of toxicology" [65].

Although the plaintiff took the other drugs in the quinine family in between his ingestion of the second Lariam tablet and his subsequent exposure 10 months later, he reported no change in symptomatology until he underwent a self-administered rechallenge test. Thus his exposure to these other drugs was irrelevant, and Dr. Roberson's reliance on the temporal relationship between the onset of plaintiff's symptoms and his ingestion of the second Lariam tablet and the worsening of his symptoms when he restarted his treatment with Lariam 10 months later was appropriate, as a matter of proper scientific methodology and supported by ample case law. But here the court decided that a temporal relationship was not sufficient to allow Dr. Roberson's testimony to go to the jury. In coming to this conclusion, the court failed to recognize the scientific significance of plaintiff's rechallenge experience with Lariam. The fact that plaintiff's symptoms grew markedly worse on rechallenge is highly significant to medical experts, as it was to Dr. Roberson. Unfortunately, the court, in its scientific ignorance, failed to comprehend the totality of all the facts presented and made the wrong decision.

Whether or not Lariam caused Rick Javor's permanent vestibular injury was a question for the jury to decide. By dismissing plaintiff's case (by ruling Dr. Roberson's opinion on causation was inadmissible) and incorrectly substituting its own flawed and scientifically unsophisticated judgment, the court usurped plaintiff's right to confront the defendant over the cause of his injury.

Conclusion

To summarize, the issues potentially raised by expert scientific testimony fall into three well-recognized categories: admissibility, weight, and sufficiency. The issue of admissibility now includes, but is not limited to, an analysis of an expert's methodology under *Daubert* and the new Rules 702 and 703 of the *Federal Rules of Evidence*. As long as the scientific methodology underlying the conclusion is valid, the opinion must be admitted—even if the court feels that the conclusion is totally implausible and/or other experts (the other party's) strongly disagree. Similarly, when analyzing the legal sufficiency of an expert's conclusion, the court may consider only the logical force of the expert's conclusion, if believed, and may not consider whether the expert's conclusion is plausible. Only time will tell if the newly amended Rule 702 will cause judges to increasingly encroach on the jury's role to weigh the evidence, including an expert's opinions.

It is imperative for lawyers and scientific experts to help the court understand that *absolute* scientific truths are very rare creatures. Courts often equate epidemiology with this mythical beast, not understanding that 40 epidemiologic studies on a single topic are not the norm. However, even if some modest epidemiology exists, and certainly in the absence of a solid body of epidemiology, a court can and should admit reliable expert opinions that are based on medical information, differential diagnosis, and other valid scientific techniques.

Endnotes

1. 509 U.S. 579, 113 S. Ct. 2786 (1993).

2. *Idem,* at 592–594.

3. *Kuhmo Tire v. Carmichael,* 526 U.S. 137, 119 S. Ct. 1167, 1174 (1999).

4. *General Electric Co. v. Joiner,* 522 U.S. 136, 139, 118 S. Ct. 512 (1997).

5. *Wilson v. Volkswagon of Am., Inc.,* 561 F.2d 494, 506 (4th Cir. 1977), "an appellate court would be remiss in [its] duties if [it] chose only to rubber stamp . . . orders of lower courts." *Idem.*

6. *Idem,* at 142, citing *Daubert,* 113 S. Ct. at 2794.

7. *Idem,* at 593.

8. *Kuhmo Tire Co.,* 526 U.S. 137 (1999).

9. *Daubert,* 509 U.S. at 600–601.

10. See, e.g., *United States v. 14.38 Acres of Land,* 80 F.3d 1074, 1078 (5th Cir. 1996), reversing trial court for using "too stringent a reliability test."

11. Rule 104. Preliminary Questions. (a) Questions of admissibility generally. Preliminary questions concerning the qualification of a person to be a witness, the existence of a privilege, or the admissibility of evidence shall be determined by the court, subject to the provisions of subdivision.

12. Rule 703. Bases of Opinion Testimony by Experts. The facts or data in the particular case upon which an expert bases an opinion or inference may be those perceived by or made known to the expert at or before the hearing. If of a type reasonably relied upon by experts in the particular field in forming opinions or inferences upon the subject, the facts or data need not be admissible in evidence.

13. Rule 403. Exclusion of Relevant Evidence on Grounds of Prejudice, Confusion, or Waste of Time. Although relevant, evidence may be excluded if its probative value is substantially outweighed by the danger of unfair prejudice, confusion of the issues, or misleading the jury, or by considerations of undue delay, waste of time, or needless presentation of cumulative evidence.

14. *Daubert,* 509 U.S. at 592.

15. *Thomas v. Newton Int'l Enterprises,* 42 F.3d 1266, 1269 (9th Cir. 1994); see also *Wood v. Stihl, Inc.,* 705 F.2d 1101, 1104–1105 (9th Cir. 1983).

16. 78 F.3d 524 (11th Cir. 1996), reversed on other grounds, 522 U.S. 136, 118 S. Ct. 512 (1997).

17. 293 F. 1013 (D.C. Cir. 1923).

18. *People v. Stoll,* 783 F.2d 698, 710 (Cal. 1989).

19. *Idem.* Although attorneys have historically viewed *Frye*'s "general acceptance" test as too rigid and initially welcomed *Daubert,* believing the Supreme Court when it said that the *Federal Rules of Evidence* were to be construed liberally, "at least *Frye* courts tend not to play amateur scientists and tend not to devise ever-more numerous hurdles to be placed in front of expert witnesses. It may be difficult to win the 'general acceptance' of the scientific community, as is required under *Frye,* but it is even more difficult to

win general acceptance (which is still a *Daubert* 'factor') and meet the dozens of other tests thrown up by inventive and hostile Judges." Ned Miltenberg, Out of the Fryeing Pan and into the Fire, and Out Back Again—or "Back to the Future," Association of Trial Lawyers of America Summer 2000 Convention Papers (July 2000).

20. 78 F.3d at 529.

21. *Idem.*

22. 509 U.S. at 595.

23. *Idem,* at 593.

24. *Idem.*

25. *Idem,* at 595.

26. *Joiner* at 78 F.3d 530.

27. *G.E. Co. v. Joiner,* 522 U.S. at 146. It should be noted that this statement was made in the context of there being "too great an analytical gap between the data and the opinion proffered." *Idem,* at 142.

28. *Idem,* at 153 (citation omitted).

29. *United States v. Bonds,* 12 F.3d 540, 563 (6th Cir. 1993).

30. 43 F.3d at 1319, n.11.

31. *Braun v. Lorillard, Inc.,* 84 F.3d 230, 234 (7th Cir. 1996).

32. 2000 U.S. App. LEXIS 17235 (8th Cir. 2000).

33. *Idem,* at p 8.

34. *Idem,* at p 12.

35. *United States v. Chischilly,* 30 F.3d 1144, 1154 (9th Cir. 1994), cert. denied 115 S. Ct. 946 (1995). See also, *In Re Paoli Railroad Yard PCB Litigation,* 35 F.3d 717 (3d Cir. 1994) (*Paoli II*) ("[T]he judge should not exclude evidence simply because he or she thinks that there is a flaw in the expert's investigative process which renders the expert's conclusions incorrect. The judge should only exclude the evidence if the flaw is large to negate the methodology as the basis for his or her conclusions.") *Idem,* at 1154. See also *G.E. Co. v. Joiner,* 522 U.S. at 146 and *United States v. Shea,* 211 F.3d 658, 2000 U.S. App. LEXIS 8770 (1st Cir. 2000), where the appellate court noted that "most circuits that have spoken have agreed with this approach [citation omitted], relying on the view that 'cross-examination, presentation of contrary evidence, and careful instruction on the burden of proof' are the proper challenge to 'shaky but admissible evidence.'" *Idem,* at p. 19 (quoting *Daubert,* 509 U.S. at 596).

36. *Daubert,* 509 U.S. at 591.

37. *Kannankeril v. Terminix Int'l, Inc.,* 128 F.3d 802, 806 (3d Cir. 1997).

38. *Paoli II,* 35 F.3d at 743, 745 (quoting, in part, *United States v. Downing,* 753 F.2d 1224, 1237 (3d Cir. 1985), whose definition of *fit* was expressly adopted by the Supreme Court in *Daubert.*

39. *Idem,* at 743.

40. See *Weisgram v. Marley Co.,* 528 U.S. 440.

41. "Although relevant, evidence may be excluded if its probative value is substantially outweighted by . . . considerations of undue delay, waste of time, or needless presentation of cumulative evidence." *Federal Rules of Evidence,* Rule 403.

42. Chief Justice, The Supreme Court of the United States, *Communication Transmitting*

Amendments to the Federal Rules of Evidence That Have Been Adopted by the Court, Pursuant to 28 U.S.C. 2072 (hereinafter "*Communication Transmitting Amendments*"), House Document 106–225 (2000).

43. *Idem*, at 9.

44. *Communication Transmitting Amendments,* at 9.

45. *Ferebee v. Chevron Chemical Co.,* 736 F.2d 1529, 1535–1536 (D.C. Cir. 1984); quoted with approval in *Wells v. Ortho Pharmaceutical Corp.,* 788 F.2d 741, 745 (11th Cir. 1986), cert. denied, 479 U.S. 950 (1986); *Quinton v. Farmland Industries, Inc.,* 928 F.2d 335, 337 (9th Cir. 1991). *Ferebee* also was cited with approval in *Mendes-Silva v. United States,* 980 F.2d 1482, 1486 (D.C. Cir. 1993) after the *Daubert* decision.

46. *Reference Manual,* at 126.

47. *Idem*, at 127–128.

48. *Idem*.

49. See, e.g., *Ferebee*, 736 F.2d at 1535.

50. See, e.g., *Berry v. CSX Transportation, Inc.,* 709 So. 2d 552, 570 (Fla. App. 1998); *Kelley v. American Heyer-Schulte Corp.,* 957 F. Supp. 843 (W.D. Tex. 1997), dismissed by *Kelley v. American Heyer-Schulte Corp.,* 139 F.3d 899 (5th Cir. 1998).

51. Recently decided in the United States District Court for the Northern District of California, Civil Case Number C 98-20044 RMW (April 2000).

52. 35 F.3d at 758.

53. *Idem*.

54. *Idem*, at 758–759.

55. *Idem*, at 762.

56. *Idem*. See also *Hose v. Chicago Northwestern Transp. Co.,* 70 F.3d 968, 973 (8th Cir. 1995): "In determining the cause of a person's injuries, it is relevant that other possible sources of injuries . . . have been ruled out by his treating physicians. . . . [R]uling out alternative explanations for injuries is a valid medical method."

57. Order Denying Defendants' Motion for Summary Judgment, filed August 3, 1999, p 3, in part citing *Kennedy v. Collagen Corp.,* 161 F.3d 1226, 1230 (9th Cir. 1998).

58. *Idem*, at p 8.

59. *Federal Rules of Evidence,* Rule 703, Notes of Advisory Committee on Rules (last updated in March 1987), citing Rheingold P, The basis of medical testimony, *Vanderbilt Law Rev* 1962;15:473, 531.

60. Order Excluding the Testimony of Dr. Roberson, filed on May 17, 2000.

61. 35 F.3d at 758–761.

62. *Heller v. Shaw Industries,* 167 F.3d 146, 156 (3d Cir. 1999).

63. Order Denying Defendants' Motion for Summary Judgment, p 8 [citing Forth Circuit Court of Appeals opinion (improperly identified in the Court's order as a Third Circuit opinion), *Westberry v. Gislaved Gummi AB,* 178 F.3d 257, 262 (4th Cir. 1999)].

64. *Westberry*, 178 F.3d at 265. See also *Anderson v. Quality Stores, Inc.,* 1999 U.S. App. LEXIS 13207, pp 7–8 (4th Cir. 1999). "Because the expert opinions proffered by Anderson [the plaintiff] were based on a reliable differential diagnosis and a strong temporal relationship between a substantial exposure to the paint fumes and the onset of Anderson's symptoms, the district court abused its discretion in rejecting the opinions as unreliable." See also *Curtis v. M & S Petroleum, Inc.,* 174 F.3d 661, 670 (5th Cir.

1999). "A temporal connection standing alone is entitled to little weight in determining causation. However, a temporal connection is entitled to greater weight when there is an established scientific connection between exposure and illness or other circumstantial evidence supporting the causal link. In the present case, both scientific literature and strong circumstantial evidence support the causal connection" (citations omitted).
65. *Cavallo v. Star Enter.*, 892 F. Supp. 756, 774 (E.D. Va. 1995).

"The proof was in the pudding, but the pudding was ruled inadmissible as evidence."

7

The Nature of Science

TEE L. GUIDOTTI

This book proposes a systematic approach to evaluating scientific evidence in the particular contexts of law, adjudication, and/or public policy. The approach adapts methods of evidence-based medicine and *critical appraisal* that are now well accepted in health care to assist a court or an adjudicating body (e.g., workers' compensation) to weigh evidence in disputes involving health risks. We have examined these issues primarily from the point of view of the expert witness or consultant, the one person who has the least procedural influence on the process but the biggest job when it comes to interpreting scientific data in context. Expert witnesses giving scientific testimony as well as expert technical consultants are part of a larger professional scientific community. In order to better understand the expert's role, capacity, and constraints, it is critical to understand this broader scientific community and the way in which science actually works.

In this chapter we will go more deeply into the sociology of science, drawing from many fields, especially the history and philosophy of science. We will discuss the images of science and the nature of the scientific process and present the concepts of revolutionary versus normal science.

Law and Science

It is commonly assumed that there is a fundamental difference between the patterns of logic employed in law and in science. The conventional view is that the law is highly deductive, drawing logical conclusions from precedent and legislation. It is certainly true that lawyers work by deduction within the context of statutory and case law. However, the initial framing of a case for litigation is highly inferential or inductive, much like the construction of a scientific theory. Given the importance of identifying and properly assembling the legal elements of a case from a confusing mix of circumstantial evidence, an argument can be made that the law is at least as inferential as science and that both disciplines are primarily inductive in nature. It is the anomaly (or the falsified hypothesis; see discussion below) that ultimately overturns the comprehensive explanation in either case. Legal reasoning is, by this interpretation, much more like scientific reasoning than has been recognized commonly.

The law needs science to determine what is probably correct in technical cases. Science needs the law to protect it and to maintain the civil society in which it thrives. Beyond this, the two may as well be on different planets for all that they interact and influence one another. It has been said that law (and humanities) and science reflect two cultures or two "solitudes," speaking to one another only when they are forced to do so [1].

This is not necessarily bad. The law must be conservative, deliberative, and consistent in order to play its essential role as a permanent mechanism for resolving society's problems. Its role as an arbiter of public knowledge is to be deliberate and slow. Science, on the other hand, must be quick to adapt and capable of rapid reversals in direction if it is to play its essential role as finder of fact and assembler of theory. At the same time, science must be cautious not to be "hijacked" by every novel idea that comes around before this idea has demonstrated its worth. In our modern society, which is both litigious and technology-driven, the two worlds of law and science intersect often but not always well.

Images of Science

In recent years, science itself has become an object of intensive study [2–4]. Traditionally, science has been viewed as a logical, coherent, comprehensive, and dispassionate process of gathering facts and generalizing from them, in which emotion and belief played little role except to motivate the scientist. We now know it to be all those things at times but also frequently messy, contentious, subjective, and counterintuitive. Science is, at its heart, a human endeavor, and its success lies less in excluding the human element than in harnessing it by the creative use of consensus. In this sense, it bears a remarkable resemblance to law.

Scientists usually have little personal insight into the nature of science as a process. C. P. Snow, the British writer, achieved these insights because he had been a writer, a public official, and a practicing scientist himself. In a series of novels and essays, he explored the world views of science and public policy as well as their conflict and interplay [1]. Before Snow, most writings about scientists were hagiography, the biography of saintlike figures, or epic studies of discovery. Snow's work reflected a new willingness to place scientists and the scientific process under close scrutiny [1,5]. He saw scientists as people and, for the first time, treated science as a social phenomenon.

There are two prevalent "naive" views of science among professionals, the *heroic theory* and the *team effort*. Lawyers and judges may believe one or the other to be true, depending on their experience with scientific professionals.

Scientists tend to prefer the heroic theory of science, that it is advanced by the stout-hearted genius engaged out of personal commitment to seek the truth, who by imagination and technical skill achieves a series of breakthrough investigations that bring new facts to light. The highest personal value among scientists is integrity and the second is autonomy. The investigator-initiated proposal, in which a scientist proposes new work that he or she would like to do, without aiming at a preordained outcome, is the preferred norm. The highest value is on individual imagination; thus, to be effective, collaboration must be voluntary and arise naturally out of the work.

Politicians and administrators of scientific agencies tend to believe in the opposite theory, or the team approach. In their view, science is a team effort in which networks of investigators with common interests pool their knowledge, through the literature and at structured meetings, in order to build on the accumulation of facts. Directed research, in which scientists are working toward a common goal and their efforts are guided by incentives, research management, and requests for proposals in a particular field, is the preferred norm. Individual work in isolation is perceived as wasteful; cooperation is expected, and often forced, in the interests of efficiency. Duplication is discouraged in the interest of rational use of resources.

Both naive views have certain characteristics in common. They both assume that the individual unit of scientific progress is the discovery and that progress is incremental and builds on an accumulation of facts. They both assume that science is unitary in nature and that its primary function is to add to a world databank of common knowledge. They both assume that the scientific literature is the place where all this is written down and that if one can only find the right reference, any question that has been asked previously in scientific research can be answered. If there is no answer, it is because the right experiment may not have been done or cannot be found. Science perceives objective truth as immutable and the scientific method as a progression toward increasing certainty in describing this reality.

Unfortunately, these naive views of science have led to an overly simplistic view of the scientific process in litigation and adjudication. In the legal process, it is commonly (and erroneously) assumed that science is progressing toward an objective or end and that facts are being accumulated to "prove" a particular truth or to validate a theory. A *breakthrough* is a new discovery or observation that leads to new understanding by making known a previously unknown fact. The legal system also assumes that the scientific community is grounded in these facts and should demonstrate consensus on important principles. Combined with this naive view of science is the notion that scientific research is a comprehensive process and that if the literature is silent on a particular point, it is due to either an oversight or a problem that will be resolved in the future. These naive views of science are far removed from the reality of how scientists conduct their work.

Modes of Science

Scientists make a critical distinction between two *modes* of sciences—basic and applied science. *Basic,* in this sense, does not mean "simple"; it means "fundamental." Basic science is often thought of as science for its own sake. *Applied* science is the application of science to achieve an intended goal. It builds on basic science and contributes to technology and engineering.

Basic science is the mode of science that pursues the development of new knowledge and is driven internally by problems and issues that arise from the discipline. For example, a biomedical scientist may investigate the structure of an enzyme in order to determine how a particular biochemical reaction takes place and what determines its rate. In order to understand this, it may be necessary to solve various problems related to the physical properties of the active site and its three-dimensional configuration. The scientist is not necessarily interested in the particular reaction for its own sake, although there may be useful applications of this knowledge, for example, in designing new drugs. More important to the basic scientist, however, is how this reaction fits into the numerous reactions of metabolism in general, what the products of the reaction do, and how it may affect those reactions and effects that come after it. The intention is to understand the entire sequence of events, and ultimately, the big picture, through achieving an understanding of the most important processes and structures at the molecular level. Basic science is not just a matter of making discoveries and piecing together bits of information. Basic science accumulates facts and builds models of the universe as a means to an end, which is a broader understanding of the material world. Practical applications certainly arise in abundance from basic science, but attempts to channel basic science tend to impede the freedom to explore that results in new insights.

In contrast, applied science builds on the insights of basic science and lays the groundwork for technology. It is the mode of science that operates toward a goal, such as cure for a disease or an advance in biotechnology. The objective may not be a product, but applied science is always oriented toward an external goal or a useful application. Because applied science is narrowly channeled and directed toward an objective, it is not very good at achieving new insights, although occasionally there is an unexpected discovery. Applied science is concerned primarily with accumulating facts and building practical theories of how things work and can be made to work. The power of applied science is that it can pursue a certain line of investigation to completion and then turn over to technologists a product, such as a promising drug, for development. The difference between technology and applied science is somewhat arbitrary, but in general, applied science achieves a foundation for developing a new technology, and engineering builds on the applied science to make the technology work.

These two modes of science are well recognized by scientists. However, other modes are possible. A prominent philosopher of science, J. R. Ravetz

(1990), described a new and then-emerging mode of science in the 1960s that he called *critical science* [6].

Critical science is the mode of science that acts for the public interest. It provides a critique of technology and society and functions as a "feedback" loop to document problems and to suggest correctives [7]. It is applied science in the sense that it serves a useful purpose, but it is not narrowly channeled and directed for an economic or technological purpose. Critical science is more like solving a puzzle. The scientists who engage in it behave much like basic scientists in that they pursue a particular issue through the internal logic of the problem, such as an ecological disturbance or the effects of exposure to a toxic hazard. What defines critical science is that the problem under study is of human origin and the findings are directly applicable to public policy and law.

Ecological research, which began as a basic science, is the prototype for critical science because it is engaged in documenting the results of social and technological change. However, the principles of critical science are not restricted to any one movement, issue, or point of view. This mode of science easily covers many forensic investigations, research undertaken to resolve a social issue, investigations of problems of technological origin, and documentation of the impact of social change.

Understanding the Scientific Process

Since the 1950s, when Karl Popper (1959) first published critical studies on the philosophy of science [8], new views of scientific thought and the idea of science as a social enterprise have challenged conventional views [9]. Science begins with a set of facts and an individual looking at them. He or she ideally formulates a theory to explain them completely, coherently, and as efficiently as possible [4]. This is the process of induction, reasoning from the particular to the general. How one sees the world shapes this process of induction [10]. For example, if one is a positivist or a materialist and believes that there exists an objective truth that can be verified by human senses, one may be more likely to accept experimental findings on their face. If one is a relativist or is unsure that truth always can be verified, one may be more likely to accept that an outcome may have occurred by chance or the possibility that data have error. If one thinks of a medication as safe, one may overlook the side effects. If one is used to thinking of chemicals as causing risk, one is more likely to be persuaded that a certain chemical may be a cause of cancer.

The formulation of a theory is a creative act that may go far beyond the facts available. Induction is not necessarily a rational process. Induction is often guided by irrational processes such as inspiration, intuition, analogy, and hunches. It can be inspired by images, such as the famous incident in which the German chemist Kekulé dreamed of a snake biting its own tail and saw a model for the chemical structure of benzene. It can be inspired by analogy, such as when one chemical structure is seen to resemble another. It can come as a flash of insight, such as when Watson and Crick realized that the structure of DNA had to contain two strands in a double-helix configuration. Often, it is simply a matter of "seeing" a logical explanation in a set of facts that cannot be explained easily otherwise.

The theory must lend itself to specific predictions or hypotheses. A *hypothesis* is a discrete prediction of what will occur or be observed based on the principles laid out in the theory. The hypothesis is both the link between theory and experiment and the true test of a coherent and satisfactory theory.

The theory must yield "testable" hypotheses, or it is not an acceptable theory. A theory that is completely self-contained and self-referential cannot be a scientific theory. A proper scientific theory allows the prediction of a result that can be searched for and measured. A theory that does not predict an outcome or which predicts an outcome that is vague, subjective, or ambiguous is not a scientific theory. Examples of systems of thought that could not qualify as scientific theories include solipsism (the idea that nothing is real and that everything is imagined), religious faiths, and New Age beliefs where the end points are vague, such as self-awareness.

The hypothesis to be tested is a concrete, specific prediction that is a specific case of the general theory. It is a conclusion elaborated from the general theory by deduction that then becomes a statement to be compared with what is observed in the field or in an experiment. If the hypothesis is in agreement with what is observed, a new set of facts may have been added to scientific knowledge, but what science truly cares about is that the theory has not been falsified. If the hypothesis does not agree with what is observed, the theory must be changed or reexamined. If a theory cannot be reconciled with the facts, it is disproved. A competing theory may be brought in to explain the phenomenon, but more often the theory is modified to explain the anomalous result. Science progresses by degrees by elaborating on an existing theory and then modifying it to account for observed deviations from the data.

Replication

An experimental finding must be *replicable*. In other words, the same investigators repeating their first study and other laboratories and investigators, anywhere in the world, should find the same result under the same conditions. If they do not, the findings are either incorrect or not *generalizable* to other conditions and situations. If a finding appears in one place and at one time but not another, then it is not generalizable. It may be influenced by local conditions, which may lead to a new line of investigation. In either case, the findings are invalidated as support for the hypothesis. Precise replication, by duplicating the original study in every particular, is possible in experimental laboratory settings but is very difficult in observational field studies, especially in human studies where numerous factors influence the results, as is the case in epidemiology. More common is replication under slightly different conditions and converging results from studies that are similar but not identical. Facts are therefore established by replication and by the generalizability of facts by convergence.

Theories cannot be proven definitively by replication, although consistent and convergent findings may give scientists confidence in the theory. Moreover, theories cannot be proven definitively even by the accumulation of positive findings that are consistent with or "support" the hypotheses. It very well may be, and often is, the case that a theory that is fundamentally incorrect predicts hypotheses that continue to be supported by observed data for some time, until an anomaly is discovered. (This has been true for successive theories of atomic structure and chemistry, for example.)

Falsification (and an Explanation for Chief Justice William Rehnquist)

As discussed previously, science does not accumulate facts to prove a theory. Popper [8] has emphasized that science as an enterprise actually tests theories by searching for anomalies and that investigators, scientists whose primary purpose is to advance knowledge, seek to disprove predictions in an effort to disprove the dominant theory. This is called the *doctrine of falsification,* and it is fundamental to scientific research. Under this doctrine, unexpected and unpredicted observations are more important than validation because much useful information is thereby accumulated. These so-called anomalies are failures of the theory to predict reality; they would not be formulated as hypotheses because the theory did not envision their existence in the first place. At first, the number of falsifications and anomalies is usually small, and they relate mostly to marginal aspects of the theory. Indeed, they may be perceived initially as minor inconsistencies or as experimental errors. When the weight of falsifications and anomalies becomes overwhelming, however, it forces a reexamination of the theory and provokes a schism in the scientific community between defenders of the old theory and proponents of a new, comprehensive explanation.

Falsification operates at the level of specific prediction or hypothesis. Hypotheses must be structured in such a way that there is a true-false dichotomy to the answer so that the hypothesis can be flatly disproved. It is not enough to suggest that "exposure to x must cause cancer" and then to count the cases. It is necessary to hypothesize that if exposure to x causes cancer, then "the rate of cancer in this particular group of people exposed to x that will be studied by counting cases in a tumor registry will be greater than in those not exposed, stipulating a specific reference population studied in the same way." Statistics is then used to make a rigorous evaluation of what *greater than* means in practice.

Confusingly to nonscientists, scientists find it useful to invert hypotheses into negative statements whenever possible. These are called *null hypotheses,* and they take the form "the rate of cancer in this exposed group is *not* elevated compared with this reference group." Inferential statistics are used to reach conclusions on the likelihood of a finding arising by chance and therefore being a random error. Because of the technical structure of inferential statistics, the null hypothesis is disproven when there is a positive finding. This counterintuitive way of structuring the problem is a convenient way of expressing the doctrine of falsification in probabilistic terms.

The doctrine of falsification leads to fundamental differences in expectation between scientists and lawyers. The lawyer wants to know if a theory is proven. The scientist can only say that it has not been falsified and that it acceptably explains the observations. The lawyer wants to accumulate facts in support of a theory for the case. The scientist is looking for the fact that is inconsistent. The lawyer or decision maker wants a straight answer—yes or no. The scientist speaks in terms of confidence in a theory. Unfortunately, these differences of expectations lead to much frustration in communication.

Revolutionary Science

Science, in the view of Kuhn [11] and many others [3], progresses when the conventional theoretical framework, the received view or *paradigm,* is no longer sufficient to explain the facts that are observed. A paradigm is one way of thinking about a problem and may include a comprehensive theory or a set of related theories that provide what seemed to be a comprehensive explanation for the facts as they were observed. Over time, scientific research uncovers more and more facts, and some of them, the *anomalies,* do not fit the theory. Anomalies accumulate among the facts and force a reconsideration of the theory. This is the task of a small group of investigators in the vanguard of research. Their theories and observations eventually lead to a new way of looking at the entire problem—in other words, a new paradigm.

This is called *revolutionary science,* and it is the way in which science makes major leaps. However, in this context, the essential "breakthrough" is not the discovery of a new fact but the acceptance of a new paradigm. An essential premise of this contemporary view is that theories are crafted by scientists who are conditioned to think in a certain way because of the society in which they live and the culture of science in which they work. Because it is very difficult to think beyond accepted patterns of thought, even for highly innovative thinkers, all theories are subject to *paradigm blindness.* This blindness to ways of looking at the problem beyond the paradigm is a major reason why no scientific theory is ever complete or adequate and why succession theories are always possible. New and potentially more useful formulations to explain the facts are nearly impossible to visualize when one is working within the field. New ideas require the detachment of an outside observer without a stake in the field as it is currently constituted. When this community mind set changes because of new and highly persuasive information, new cultural trends in looking at problems, new theories with greater explanatory power, or the passage of a generation with fixed views, the change is called a *paradigm shift*.

For centuries, people knew of variations between the observed behavior of celestial bodies and Ptolemy's theory that the earth was the center of the universe. Until Copernicus, these deviations were handled by adding more and more layers of complexity (such as elliptical and off-center orbits) until the basic theory became illogical and ultimately was replaced by the theory of a sun-centered universe. The paradigm shifted again when gravity was identified by Newton as a force in the universe that could keep planets in their orbit by a pulling action, casting aside the assumption that there were fixed planetary tracks in the heavens.

Although in principle it only takes one anomaly to invalidate a theory in question, in practice it requires an accumulation of evidence. Scientists, particularly those on the vanguard of new research, identify and document anomalies, unexplained deviations, or misfit findings that have the potential to falsify the particular theory and even the paradigm of which the theory is a part. The contemporary view of science places a new emphasis on the consensus among scientists on what is true and what is insufficient. In this more sophisticated view, revolutionary science is seen to advance science as an enterprise, and *normal science* is seen to fill in the details between revolutions.

Eventually, the proponents of the new paradigm usually prevail when the evidence is convincing. This is so, in part, because they win over some defenders of the old theory but mostly because the defenders of the old theory quit defending it, retire, or play a diminished role in the scientific debate. In other words, new theories tend to win out because of a generational shift among scientists rather than the conversion of committed scientists away from the point of view they held originally. Over time, often in one generation of scholars, the new paradigm supplants the old and becomes the new received view.

Normal Science

If scientific revolutions are the normal process of paradigmatic shifts, then *normal science* is the process of what Kuhn calls "mopping up," solving the remaining puzzles, elaborating on the framework, and accumulating facts that fit within the conventional paradigm [11]. By this definition, most scientists are engaged in normal science. This is the variety of science appreciated by the politicians and agency managers referred to earlier. It is an incremental process that adds information and understanding, and it is indispensable. Not only does it accumulate facts, which are the principally useful by-products of science, but over time it will uncover the anomalies that lead to the revolutions discussed previously.

Most scientists serving as expert witnesses are engaged in normal science in their "day jobs." However, the work of testing substances for carcinogenicity, documenting elevated disease rates in a population, and assessing the distribution and severity of hazards in the workplace or the environment is not revolutionary science because it rarely involves a new paradigm.

There are exceptions. The identification of a new class of carcinogens or toxic hazards is a paradigm shift in the world of manufacturers, users, and regulators and also may be to scientists if a new mechanism of action is involved.

The work of normal science progresses by the same process of hypothesis testing as revolutionary science. There is no threshold to identify when an investigation moves from normal science to revolutionary science, only the compounding of uncertainty and a realization that discovery of the unexpected can no longer be rationalized. In normal science, however, there is little expectation of uncovering a significant anomaly. It is a progressive elaboration on the fundamental theory, advancing it in those areas in which it is lacking and confirming the utility of its principles in areas previously overlooked or unexplored.

Although this exploration is systematic, it is not comprehensive. Although certain fields may appear to be comprehensive within their scope, such as surveys of plants and animals in an ecosystem, the actual subject matter, which requires such an inventory, is their interrelationship and how they may be changing over time in this example through evolution or after an ecological disruption. To complete the example, this is why there is no global inventory of species—the scientific problem previously did not require such an expensive and tedious study. The problems that scientists work on are defined by the prevailing theory and limited by what the scientist, who is constrained by the existing paradigm, sees. If a scientist cannot think of the problem, he or she will not investigate it. If an experiment is not suggested by the theory, why would one choose to do it? Scientists have limited tolerance for fooling around; there is no reason to conduct research that does not appear to have a point.

Scientists make research a career because they are interested in the subject matter, not because they are committed to a comprehensive exploration of the world. They are led into particular areas of research by incentives such as grant programs. They are often motivated to find a cure or contribute a useful product. Mostly, however, they are motivated to work out a problem or, using Kuhn's term, a *puzzle*. The most satisfying of these puzzles are those with technical and intellectual challenges beyond the usual but that are possible to solve with existing technology. However, granting agencies have their own agendas, fund studies selectively, and thus influence the direction of most basic and biomedical research.

Science will always be incomplete because it maps the real world, which is too complex to reduce. Choices, therefore, must be made. Revolutionary science, and even normal science, progresses along definite lines set out by its theoretical base. In between there are wide gaps where little or no work has been done. For example, only a relatively few of the hundreds of thousands of chemical compounds that are known have been tested for toxicity, including carcinogenicity.

Scientists rarely choose to study the obvious or the well accepted unless they are paid to do so in their job. Of course, there are exceptions, as illustrated by a story I was told during medical school. During World War II, two dermatologists were drafted and assigned to perform induction physical examinations on new soldiers. Accustomed to diagnosing skin diseases, they were bored to distraction by the procession of healthy, unremarkable men with normal skin. To keep up their own morale, they designed a research study. They conducted the definitive study of the distribution and morphology of moles in normal young men, which later turned out to be very useful in the detection of melanoma.

Science is as comprehensive as it is for reasons that have little to do with the basic strategy of normal science. It covers a lot of territory because there are so many scientists and their work intersects. Because students have to be trained and new investigators have to "earn their wings," much of the literature consists of simple, practical studies that elaborate on what is known. Much work is applied research sponsored because of its economic value. The reward system of science, such as competition and incentives for grant awards, acts to promote diversity and dispersion but only to a limited degree. Large and important fields, such as occupational health and toxicology, remain underfunded compared with other areas of biomedical science. Behavioral epidemiology and social epidemiology are notoriously undersupported despite their obvious relevance in law. Even in a field that is comparatively richly endowed, such as cardiology and pulmonary science, certain hot topics attract a disproportionate number of investigators, and others are relatively neglected.

A search through the biomedical literature, for example, regularly turns up numerous gaps and deficiencies on topics that many people assume would have been fully investigated. If they are not perceived as interesting or practical issues, however, there is no reason that scientists would have looked at them.

Many topics of abiding interest in law are of little or no intrinsic interest among scientists. For example, there is little interest on the part of epidemiologists in accumulating a cohort of nonsmoking firefighters just to determine whether their lifetime risk of cancer is elevated. This is an issue that comes up repeatedly in workers' compensation and civil litigation, but it does not advance the state of science. Not surprisingly, if there are no targeted research programs to look into the matter, it will never be resolved.

The obvious is seldom explored in the scientific literature in any detail. For example, in one recent case involving workplace conditions, the assertion was made that cold, damp surroundings were uncomfortable to asthmatics recovering from influenza. This unexceptional statement was challenged on the basis that no scientific evidence was presented to support the assertion. It is true that there are virtually no papers in the medical literature that address the point. However, there are also virtually no papers that document the frequency of muscle aches in influenza. Because muscle aches are considered part of the definition of the disease (and therefore part of the paradigm) and are taken for granted, there is no reason for any clinical epidemiologist to investigate the point. Likewise, nobody building a career in scientific investigation is likely to waste precious time researching whether asthma sufferers recovering from influenza are sensitive to cold conditions; moreover, it is unlikely that funding sources would support such a study.

Understanding the Scientific Expert Witness

Medical and scientific experts often do not understand the process of science themselves, in part because they are too close to it. Most scientists are either blind to the process or reject the contemporary view because it does not fit with the heroic image of discovery and independent thinking that pervades the culture of science. However, the contemporary view of science can give us a greater understanding of how the scientific expert can be employed most usefully in the legal process.

One must understand that, to a scientist, scientific evidence that is inconsistent with the outcome may be more important than evidence that "supports" a scientific position. Therefore, shifts of opinion and points of view among medical experts are something to be explored, not evidence of a lamentable lack of consensus on the part of experts presented with the same data. Because science is a profoundly social process, it is important to ascertain where an expert witness may be placed not only with respect to the mainstream opinion but also among important subgroups of their peers and within the momentum of changing opinion.

Experts and their opinions often are challenged on the grounds of presumed motivation. For example, if a theory has been developed solely for the purpose of litigation, the legal system holds it as less reliable than theories developed for scientific investigation. The fact is that many of the questions asked by litigation would never be the subject of investigation unless there were good reasons outside science to determine the answer—in other words, to answer a question in litigation. For example, the many studies done over the years on the putative relationship between silicone breast implants and the risk of connective tissue disorders would never have been conducted without the pressure of litigation, especially after the first few negative studies appeared in the medical literature.

The social theory of science suggests that no single fact is indisputable in science and that it is the consensus eventually achieved among scientists that establishes scientific truth. A new anomalous observation first must be confirmed. Well-established and well-confirmed observations therefore are stronger evidence, in this view, than a new observation that initially seems to trump conventional wisdom. This point of view favors continuity in interpretation and current scientific explanations and works strongly against the "first case" and claims in areas where the science is lacking, even if the underlying theory is plausible.

Dramatic new data or unexpected findings are always meaningful in the context of scientific debate and a challenge to a paradigm, but most courts are very hesitant to accept as evidence new findings that have not been weighed and discussed thoroughly by the scientific community.

Conclusion

Science is not obvious, nor is it a "fact factory" producing comprehensive information. It is a systematic approach to knowledge about the material world that progresses by ruling out what is not true. Contrary to the way most people (and some scientists) think of science, its purpose is not to amass evidence in support of every critical point in an argument in order to prove truth. In some ways, the accumulation of specific facts is a by-product of science. The true objective of the scientific enterprise is understanding, which comes as much from the intellect as from experience.

So-called junk science can be better understood in this context. The concept of junk science goes beyond isolated facts that are wrong; it also may include an incorrect scientific framework. The following four examples illustrate the ways in which science can go astray:

- An aberration in science that occurs when the dissident minority seizes on data and forgets the importance of falsification (e.g., cold fusion).
- An extreme case of the normal process in which a dissident group pushes hard but cannot shift the paradigm, usually because they are wrong (e.g., the safety of chrysotile asbestos).
- Self-deception, which is as common among scientists as anyone else but particularly dangerous because scientists typically have excellent powers of rationalization (e.g., multiple chemical sensitivity as an expression of previously unknown bodily mechanisms).
- Outright fraud and deception of others, which usually is short-lived because science is basically a self-correcting system of knowledge (e.g., quack cures and nostrums).

The corrective for junk science is dispute followed by constructive neglect, when scientists working in the field agree that there is nothing more to be gained by arguing. However, proponents of junk science may claim

- Their new knowledge is threatening to the scientific mainstream/power structure.
- Science has not advanced sufficiently to understand their logic.
- The paradigm is shifting/is starting to shift/will shift in x years.

- Other scientists are not doing the experiments correctly.
- There are plenty of data in support of their theory, but there may be just a few inconsistencies that they can easily explain if given a chance—which never seems to come despite repeated opportunities.
- They are a lone voice raging against a monolithic scientific establishment that seeks to silence them. (Variation: They are persecuted because of their independence and refusal to compromise.)

Most will be wrong, but with a grain of truth sufficient to sustain them and their argument. And in truth, a vanishingly small subset will be right, and from those true geniuses may come the next scientific revolutions: Galileo, Einstein, Bernard, Boyle, and genome-cracker Craig Ventner. It is difficult early in the process to separate the sheep from the goats. This is why scientists meet face to face at conferences, hover obsessively over their graduate students, argue constantly, write lengthy and redundant reviews, and publish papers in journals where their colleagues will criticize them and are merciless in poking holes in one another's data. They want to get it right but know that there are so many ways to get it wrong.

In law, science must be understood to be one way of knowing, a very powerful way to be sure, but not without its limitations and failings. It is an illusion to think that science will have the answer to every question. It is even more of an illusion to think that scientists will always agree on the interpretation of a set of facts. Dispute, leading eventually to the oft-cited paradigm shift, is how science moves forward. This applies equally well to the courtroom.

This is not necessarily what the law wants or expects, but it is the reality that the law must confront when evaluating scientific evidence. The better understanding the community of law has of how the community of science actually works, the more likely it is that scientific evidence be used appropriately to resolve disputes.

References

1. Snow CP. *The Two Cultures, and A Second Look*. Cambridge, England: Cambridge University Press, 1969.

2. Boyd R, Gasper P, Traut JD. *The Philosophy of Science*. Cambridge, MA: MIT Press, 1991.

3. Suppe F (ed). *The Structure of Scientific Theories,* 2d ed. Urbana, IL: University of Illinois Press, 1977.

4. Harré R. *The Principles of Scientific Thinking*. Chicago: University of Chicago Press, 1970.

5. Snow CP. *Science and Government: The Godkin Lectures at Harvard University, 1960*. Cambridge, MA: Harvard University Press, 1961.

6. Ravetz JR. The Merger of Knowledge and Power: Essays in Critical Science. London: Mansell Publishing Ltd., 1990.

7. Guidotti TL. Critical science and the critique of technology. Pub Health Rev 1994; 22: 235–250.

8. Popper K. *The Logic of Scientific Discovery.* London: Hutchinson, 1959.

9. Shapin S. *A Social History of Truth.* Chicago: University of Chicago Press, 1994.

10. Harré R. *Great Scientific Experiments: Twenty Experiments that Changed Our View of the World.* Oxford, England: Oxford University Press, 1981.

11. Kuhn TS. *The Structure of Scientific Revolutions,* 2d ed. Chicago: University of Chicago Press, 1970.

8

Looking Backward: The Bayesian Approach to Assessing Causation

SORELL L. SCHWARTZ

In *Daubert v. Merrell Dow Pharmaceuticals* (1993), the U.S. Supreme Court addressed the centuries-old problem of induction and a particular scientific philosophical response to it. This is evident in the majority opinion:

> Ordinarily, a key question to be answered in determining whether a theory or technique is scientific knowledge that will assist the trier of fact will be whether it can be (and has been) tested. "Scientific methodology today is based on generating hypotheses and testing them to see if they can be falsified; indeed, this methodology is what distinguishes science from other fields of human inquiry" [1]. See also C. Hempel, *Philosophy of Natural Science* 49 (1966): ("[T]he statements constituting a scientific explanation must be capable of empirical test"); K. Popper, *Conjectures and Refutations* 37 (5th ed. 1989): ("[T]he criterion of the scientific status of a theory is its falsifiability, or refutability, or testability").

The specific references to Hempel and Popper allude to a structure for assessing scientific evidence that has significant philosophical foundations. Moreover, the particular reference to falsification (refutation) invokes Popper's critical rationalism and its reliance on conjecture and refutation as a logical device. Critical rationalism is a particularly anti-inductivist viewpoint, in which induction is considered to have no epistemic value. On the other hand, the act of arriving at a decision based on scientific evidence (or any decision, for that matter) is an uncertainty judgment where the uncertainty reflects a probability assessment. This implies a process that must be considered, in part at least, inductive but is not the contradiction it might seem to be.

Legal decisions, scientific or otherwise, also have no epistemic value. Their purpose is to make an evidence-based selection from two or more alternatives at a declared time, not to establish truth in the knowledge sense. Accordingly, there is a distinct difference between attainment of scientific knowledge and the methods by which that knowledge is used to make a decision. This was further recognized in the *Daubert* opinion:

> It is true that open debate is an essential part of both legal and scientific analyses. Yet there are important differences between the quest for truth in the courtroom and the quest for truth in the laboratory. Scientific conclusions are subject to perpetual revision. Law, on the other hand, must resolve disputes finally and quickly. The scientific project is advanced by broad and wide-ranging consideration of a multitude of hypotheses, for those that are incorrect will eventually be shown to be so, and that in itself is an advance. Conjectures that are probably wrong are of little use, however, in the project of reaching a quick, final, and binding legal judgment—often of great consequence—about a particular set of events in the past. . . . [The] Rules of Evidence [are] designed not for the exhaustive search for cosmic understanding but for the particularized resolution of legal disputes[1] [2].

While a legal decision requires final resolution (as does a medical diagnosis, among other types of decisions) and cannot withstand the temporal burden of the hypotheticodeductive process characteristic of a critical rationalist approach to science, the discipline that conjecture and refutation can bring to the decision process is to be acknowledged. It is inarguable that those scientists committed to verification (proving themselves right) usually will succeed in doing so, especially in court.

A decision is the ultimate reflection of the decision maker's degree of belief. Degree of belief is not directly amenable to quantitative assessment. For this reason, probability is used as a surrogate for degree of belief. The case for using probability as a surrogate for belief is based on the argument that the rational individual would not place a wager against unfair odds. Kyberg, citing Ramsey, noted:[2]

> Ramsey's argument is that you should have degrees of belief such that you could accept all bets offered at odds corresponding to your degrees of belief without having . . . a set of bets that entails that you lose whatever happens . . . made against you [3].

If the process of selecting from alternatives based on degree of belief (probability) is not to be an unruly one, some structure must be attached to the endeavor. Bayes' theorem can be useful in this situation. Distinct from classical applications of probability, where probability has a particular frequency connotation, probability in the Bayesian view is used to allocate theorem likelihood (not epistemic truth). Given the appropriate data, Bayesian statistics can involve extensive mathematical treatment of parameter values. However, while the evidence considered can be objective and defined quantitatively, it can just as well be subjective when empirical observations are imprecise or, for that matter, absent. The distinction between the use of objective and subjective prior odds and likelihood ratios is not always obvious.

We discuss Bayes' theorem in this chapter by using both objective and subjective evidentiary examples. For practical reasons, the emphasis will be on subjective or philosophical Bayes. Posner has noted the value of Bayes' theorem in the law of evidence as heuristic, terming it ". . . [t]he most influential model of rational decision making under conditions of ineradicable uncertainty (conditions which require that the decision be based on subjective probabilities) . . ." [4]. Needless to say, *in science especially*, subjective Bayes is noted with significant skepticism, if not outright contempt. Yet, it can be particularly functional in helping with the subjectivism of evidence-based decision resolution. Much of the criticism arises out of the philosophical dissent from the portrayal of Bayes as an approach to scientific reasoning. The process of science is not an inductive one, based on the selection of a hypothesis from a number of alternatives after consideration of a body of evidence. It is a deductive process, one, as noted by Justice Blackman in *Daubert*, of "perpetual revision," i.e., conjecture and refutation. However, as also observed in the *Daubert* opinion, evidence is considered for the purpose of resolving legal disputes, not for the purpose of gaining cosmic understanding. In other words, from the philosophical perspective, it is an inductive process (the brilliant deductions of Sherlock Holmes notwithstanding[3]).

Bayes' Theorem

Bayes' theorem[4] is an eighteenth-century approach to probability that eventually was eclipsed by controversy and by the frequentist methods that evolved into the statistical analytical approaches. However, it eventually received renewed attention, especially in recent decades, to fulfill the needs for rules of rational preference and a formalized treatment of uncertainty.

Consider two events A and B occurring together. What is the conditional probability of A given B, i.e., the probability P of the occurrence of A conditional n the occurrence of B. This is expressed as $P(A|B)$. (The symbol | is read as "conditional on.") According to the axioms of probability theory, this is

$$P(A|B) = \frac{P(A\&B)}{P(B)}$$

where $P(A\&B)$ is the unconditional probability of the conjunction of A and B, and $P(B)$ is the unconditional probability of B. Similarly, the conditional probability of B given A, that is, $P(B|A)$, is

$$P(B|A) = \frac{P(A\&B)}{P(A)}$$

Algebraically,

$$P(A\&B) = P(A) \cdot P(B|A)$$

and substituting,

$$P(A|B) = \frac{P(A) \cdot P(B|A)}{P(B)} \tag{1}$$

This is Bayes' theorem, and it can be used in hypothesis testing. For example, let Hy be the hypothesis and let Obs be an observation that will confirm or not confirm the hypothesis. Using Bayes' theorem,

$$P(Hy|Obs) = \frac{P(Hy) \cdot P(Obs|Hy)}{P(Obs)} \tag{2}$$

$P(Hy|Obs)$ is referred to as the *posterior probability*. It is the probability of the causal hypothesis conditional on the new observation. The *prior probability* of Hy, that is, $P(Hy)$, is the probability of the causal hypothesis prior to considering the new observation. If $P(Hy|Obs)$ is greater than $P(Hy)$, then Obs confirms Hy. $P(Obs|Hy)$ is an expression of the *likelihood* or expectation that Obs would be observed if Hy were correct. $P(Obs)$ is the unconditional probability of making the observation Obs, and from the axioms of probability, it can be derived that

$$P(Obs) = \sum_{i=1}^{n} P(Hy_i) \cdot P(Obs|Hy_i) \tag{3}$$

where n represents the number of possible hypotheses.

As an illustration of the application of Bayes' theorem, consider the following exchange between a professor and one of his students on the matter of intuitions and probability:

Professor: I have here three envelopes labeled X, Y, and Z. In one of the envelopes I have placed a $10 bill as a prize. All you have to do is pick the correct envelope, and the money is yours. We will use the following procedure: You pick an envelope. Then you will have the opportunity to change your mind and choose a different envelope.

Student: I choose envelope Y.

Professor: Here is your envelope. Tell me, what is the probability that you have the envelope containing the prize?

Student: 0.33, of course.

Professor: I am going to open one of the two remaining envelopes. After I open the envelope, you will have the opportunity to exchange yours

for one of mine. I have opened envelope X, and as you can see, there
is no money in it. So the prize is either in Y, which you hold, or Z,
which I hold. Would you like to trade?

Student: What's the use of doing that? You have one and I have one.

Professor: Oh? What is the probability that you have the envelope with the
money in it?

Student: 0.5! You have one, and I have one.

Professor: Not so fast. Before I opened envelope X, I held two envelopes, and
you held one. You correctly said the probability of your having the
envelope with the prize was 0.33. Why did my opening envelope X
change you from 0.33 to 0.5 or, in other words, change my probability of having the prize-containing envelope from 0.67 to 0.5?

Student: Because we went from three to two envelopes.

Professor: But all I did was show you an empty envelope. You already knew
that one of the envelopes was empty.

Student: But the total number of envelopes changed, so the probabilities
change.

Professor: The probabilities would have changed only if I randomly selected
one of the two envelopes. However, because I was committed to
allowing you to exchange envelopes, if envelope Z contained the
money, I would not have opened it.

Student: So what? There are now only two possibilities for the location of the
prize—it is 50–50.

Professor: That is not so. You are ignoring additional evidence. My selection
of envelope X provided you with evidence that you should consider
when making your choice to trade or not. Let's assume that instead
of three envelopes, there were 100, one of which contained the
money. You chose one. Of the remaining 99, I opened 98, leaving
1 unopened. Would you trade yours for mine?

Student: Of course! Now, I get it.

This problem is a variation on the classic "three prisoners" and "Monte
Hall" problems[5] and illustrates the pitfalls of intuitive responses to uncertainty.
It can be analyzed objectively using Bayes' theorem:

$P(Y|x)$ = the probability (posterior probability) of the prize being in envelope Y conditional on the evidence that the professor chose to open
envelope X, which contained no prize.

$P(Z|x)$ = the probability of the prize being in envelope Z conditional on
the evidence that the professor chose to open envelope X, which contained no prize.

$P(X)$ = the probability (prior probability) that the prize was in envelope
X prior to the opening of envelope X.

$P(Y)$ = the probability that the prize was in envelope Y prior to the opening of envelope X.

$P(Z)$ = the probability that the prize was in envelope Z prior to the opening of envelope X.

$P(x|X)$ = the probability (likelihood) that the professor would have opened envelope X if envelope X contained the prize.

$P(x|Y)$ = the probability that the professor would have opened envelope X if envelope Y contained the prize.

$P(x|Z)$ = the probability that the professor would have opened envelope X if envelope Z contained the prize.

$P(x)$ = the unconditional probability of envelope X being opened.

$P(X) = P(Y) = P(Z) = 0.33$.

$P(x|X) = 0$ (The professor would not have opened the envelope containing the prize.); $P(x|Y) = 0.5$ (If the prize were in envelope Y, the student's selection, the professor would have had the choice of opening envelopes X or Z.); $P(x|Z) = 1.0$ (The professor would have had to open X in order not disclose the prize in envelope Z, if the prize was in envelope Z.)

$P(x)$ can be established intuitively as 0.5; i.e., the professor could have chosen either envelope X or Z if he had no knowledge of the location of the prize. This can be computed using Equation (3):

$$P(x) = P(X) \cdot P(x|X) + P(Y) \cdot P(x|Y) + P(Z) \cdot P(x|Z)$$
$$= 0.33 \cdot 0 + 0.33 \cdot 0.5 + 0.33 \cdot 1$$
$$= 0.5$$

Therefore, using Equation (2),

$$P(Y|x) = \frac{0.33 \cdot 0.5}{0.5} = 0.33 \quad \text{and} \quad P(Z|x) = \frac{0.33 \cdot 1}{0.5} = 0.67$$

The student would double his or her chances of capturing the prize by trading his or her envelope Y for the professor's envelope Z.

As illustrated by the foregoing example, Bayes' theorem can be viewed by directly incorporating alternative hypotheses. Where there are n plausible hypotheses and $\sim Hy$ represents the summation of all $n - 1$ alternative hypotheses, then, from Equation (3),

$$P(Obs) = P(Hy) \cdot P(Obs|Hy) + P(\sim Hy) \cdot P(Obs|\sim Hy) \tag{4}$$

and from Equation (2), Bayes' theorem is expressed:

$$P(Hy|Obs) = \frac{P(Hy) \cdot P(Obs|Hy)}{P(Hy) \cdot P(Obs|Hy) + P(\sim Hy) \cdot P(Obs|\sim Hy)} \tag{5}$$

Similarly, the alternatives to *Hy* conditional on the empirical observation *Obs* can be represented as

$$P(\sim Hy|Obs) = \frac{P(\sim Hy) \cdot P(Obs|\sim Hy)}{P(Hy) \cdot P(Obs|Hy) + P(\sim Hy) \cdot P(Obs|\sim Hy)} \tag{6}$$

This is an important representation because it illuminates the role of alternative hypotheses in causal inferential analyses. In a rearranged form,

$$P(\sim Hy|Obs) = \frac{P(\sim Hy)}{P(\sim Hy) + \dfrac{P(Obs|Hy)}{P(Obs|\sim Hy)} \cdot P(Hy)} \tag{7}$$

where $P(Obs|Hy)/P(Obs|\sim Hy)$ is the likelihood ratio.

It can be seen that as the likelihood ratio approaches 0, $P(\sim Hy|Obs)$ approaches 1. This exemplifies the power of hypothesis falsification (refutation) discussed at the outset and reinforces the exhortation that no matter how compelling the evidence for the hypothesis under consideration, it cannot be considered as a rational preference until all other plausible alternatives are considered within the same frame of reference.

Odds Form of Bayes' Theorem

Alternative hypotheses also can be represented in the *odds* form of Bayes' theorem. Dividing the Equation (5) by Equation (6), the odds form of Bayes, theorem is obtained:

$$\frac{P(Hy|Obs)}{P(\sim Hy|Obs)} = \frac{P(Hy)}{P(\sim Hy)} \cdot \frac{P(Obs|Hy)}{P(Obs|\sim Hy)} \tag{8}$$
$$\quad\;\;(a) \qquad\qquad (b) \qquad\quad (c)$$

where (a) represents posterior odds, (b) represents prior odds, and (c) represents the likelihood ratio. This can be expressed in a more concise notation:

$$\Omega(Hy|Obs) = \Omega(Hy) \cdot L \tag{9}$$

where Ω represents the odds favoring the parenthetical expression and L is the likelihood ratio.

Bayesian Evidence Interpretation

The use of the odds form of Bayes' theorem provides an advantage in evidentiary considerations because the likelihood ratio can be a useful tool for the presentation of evidence and the processing of information by an assessor or fact finder. Accordingly, this will be the form discussed below.

Understanding the Implications of Probability Estimation

Lane has cautioned against evidence assessment using "global introspection," which he describes as follows:

> Think about every factor that could possibly make a difference (not forgetting to include possible biases of which most people are not even aware); make a list of all these factors and stare at *it* for a while; screw up your brow, scramble it all around in your brain—and then make your decision [5].

Edwards has pointed out the pitfalls of undisciplined evidence assessment [6]. He found that people tend to be conservative information processors and to underestimate probabilities, and he provided the following example from actual experimental observations:

> Two identically looking book bags each contain 1000 poker chips. One contains 700 red and 300 blue; the other contains 700 blue and 300 red. The test subject picks a bag. At that moment the odds are 1:1 (probability of 0.5) that the subject has chosen the predominantly red bag. The subject now randomly draws 12 chips, with replacement after each chip. In the 12 samples 8 reds and 4 blues are drawn. What are the odds that the subject is drawing from the predominantly red book bag? The odds are obviously higher than 1:1, but by how much?

If H_A is the hypothesis that the book bag contains predominantly red chips, then $\sim H_A = H_B$, the alternative hypothesis that the book bag contains predominantly blue chips. Using standard probability calculus,

$$P(Obs|H_A) = \theta_A^r (1 - \theta_A)^{n-r} \quad \text{and} \quad P(Obs|H_B) = \theta_B^r (1 - \theta_B)^{n-r}$$

where θ_A and θ_B are the proportions of red and blue chips in the bag, respectively, n is the total number of chips drawn, r is the number of red chips drawn, and $n - r$ is the number of blue chips drawn. Accordingly, the likelihood ratio is

$$L = \frac{\theta_A^r (1 - \theta_A)^{n-r}}{\theta_B^r (1 - \theta_B)^{n-r}} = \frac{0.7^8 \cdot 0.3^4}{0.3^8 \cdot 0.7^4} = \frac{29.6}{1}$$

Because $P(H_A)$ and $P(H_B)$ are equal, that is, 0.5, $\Omega(H_A) = 1$. Therefore, according to Equation (9), $\Omega(H_A|Obs)$ is equal to the likelihood ratio, that is, 29.6.

Edwards found the typical subject estimated the probability that the book bag contained the predominantly red chips to be in the range of 0.7 to 0.8 (odds of 7:3 to 4:1) [6]. As demonstrated, the actual probability based on Bayesian analysis is 0.97 (odds of approximately 30:1). This is a rather striking example of the vulnerability of decision to heuristic bias.

While Bayes' theorem can be used with frequentist data, e.g., probability density functions, as has been done with the assessment of DNA analytical data (as opposed to the application of that data), this is not the issue here, which is subjective Bayes. How can Bayes' theorem be used in deciding which hypothesis to select from a group of alternatives?

Application to Causation Problems

Bayes' theorem has been applied with varying degrees of reliability to the assessment of medical diagnostic data and subsequent decision making. A simplified view is to consider clinical manifestation of the patient's presenting symptoms as representing the prior odds of the ith diagnosis from a finite group j of initial diagnostic hypotheses, expressed as $\Omega(D_{ij})$. The clinical testing component of the diagnostic hypothesis can have properties defining the true-positive rate (TPR), false-positive rate (FPR), true-negative rate (TNR), and false-negative rate (FNR). Because the TPR is the probability of a positive clinical test (T_{pos}) in the case of D_{ij}, that is, $P(T_{pos}|D_{ij})$, and the FPR is the probability of T_{pos} in the absence of D_{ij}, that is, $P(T_{pos}|{\sim}D_{ij})$, then the likelihood ratio (L_{pos}) = TPR/FPR. Accordingly,

$$\Omega(D_{ij}|T_{pos}) = \Omega(D_{ij}) \cdot L_{pos}$$

This application of Bayes' theorem for interpreting clinical data is a convenient example of Bayesian evidence assessment. Interestingly, the medical application can be used to illustrate another possible means to assess evidentiary impact, i.e., the absence of a positive response to a test when one is expected. In the medical as well as the legal environment, tests can be supportive of the causal hypothesis and thereby increase posterior odds over the prior odds, thus favoring the hypothesis. It should not be a foregone conclusion, however, that a negative response to the test necessarily reduces the posterior odds below the prior odds. This is another question, as is also the extent to which the posterior odds are reduced below prior odds, if, in fact, such a reduction occurs. Because FNR is the probability of a negative test (T_{neg}) in the case of D_{ij}, that is, $P(T_{neg}|D_{ij})$, and the TNR is the probability of T_{neg} in the absence of D_{ij}, that is, $(T_{neg}|D_{ij})$, then L_{neg} = FNR/TNR, i.e., the odds of the test being negative in the case of D_{ij}. Accordingly,

$$\Omega(D_{ij}|T_{neg}) = \Omega(D_{ij}) \cdot L_{neg}$$

Bayesian approaches to medical decision making, as with nearly all Bayesian methods, are not without criticism. A source of criticism concerns the estimation of prior odds and likelihood ratios. It should be obvious that basing prior odds on presenting symptoms implies that each individual member of the population from which the prior odds were derived is accurately represented by those odds. This issue is discussed below in greater detail with respect to a related matter, namely, attributable risk. Suffice it to say, population background information without case-specific information is a seemingly faulty base for prior odds estimation.

A particular causation problem with significant medicolegal relevance concerns adverse drug reactions (ADRs). Determining whether a health disturbance temporally related to a drug's administration is an ADR influences clinical decisions during routine therapy or investigational drug studies, as well as fact-finding decisions in medical malpractice and product liability litigation. Lane suggested a Bayesian approach that can be (and has been) used in some fashion in all three circumstances [7].

Posterior odds are defined as

$$\frac{P(D \to E|B,C)}{P(D \not\to E|B,C)}$$

where $D \to E$ is the statement that drug (D) caused the event (E); $D \not\to E$ is the statement that D did not cause E, B represents the background information that is not specific to the particular patient, and C represents case-specific information about the patient and attending circumstances of E. Case-specific information includes the patient's history (e.g., patient's previous experience with the drug, prior experience with the health disturbance unrelated to the drug, risk factors for the health disturbance), temporal factors, event characteristics (e.g., body tissue and fluid levels of D, distinctive details in clinical presentation), and dechallenge and rechallenge findings, if any.

The likelihood ratio in the ADR assessment is composed of the likelihood ratios representing all components of the case-specific information C. This can be generalized in a form that is relevant to causation assessments in toxic tort and workers' compensation as well as medical malpractice and product liability disputes. Case-specific details in toxic tort litigation include the patient's occupational, family, social, and medical histories as well as exposure data, including the accuracy of exposure assessments and information regarding exposure to other possible causes of the health disturbance. Thus for the kth case-specific factor among n such factors, the likelihood ratio for the factor L_k is expressed as

$$L_k = \Omega(D \to E|B, C_k)$$

and where $k = 1$ to n, the composite $L = L_1 \cdot L_2 \ldots \cdot L_n$. Thus

$$\Omega(D \to E|B, C) = \Omega(D \to E|B) \cdot L$$

The pitfalls of this analytical process are evident. Where can the probability data be obtained for estimating likelihood ratios or, for that matter, prior odds? This question represents the bases of many objections to using Bayesian methods for both medical and legal causation problems. The efficacy of using Bayesian methods for medical decision making has been questioned on grounds that physicians generally do not have the mathematical sophistication necessary to understand the limitations inherent in Bayesian methods. Feinstein raised a number of these issues in expressing his skepticism of using Bayesian medical decision-making methods [8].

The same issue has been raised with respect to the application of Bayes' theorem to legal fact finding. Finkelstein and Fairley [9] were among the first to propose the use of Bayes' theorem for this purpose. Tribe [10] and later Brilmayer and Kornhauser [11], among others, argued against relying on probability for fact finding; Kaye [12,13] was more receptive and distinguished what was meant by *probability* in the Bayesian sense. A treatise on the matter of Bayes' theorem in law from the legal perspective is *Probability and Inference in the Law of Evidence* [14]. It sets forth ideas and commentary from thoughtful contributors with diverse viewpoints.

Kept within a certain perspective, Bayes' theorem can be a useful tool by which to present "expert" opinions to a jury. It can be a section of the decision-making line that stretches between the stiffness of frequentist statistics and the heuristic biases of Lane's global introspection and accommodates Nesson's view [15] that

> "probability" as we use the term in law, particularly in the civil standard of proof, is not a hard-edged mathematical concept. It is, rather, a concept that incorporates less rigid ideas of justice and reflects the judicial function of resolving disputes in the real world, where values shift and knowledge is uncertain.

Attributable Risk, Individual Causation, and Naked Statistical Evidence

Statistical evidence in court can be misconstrued, if not distorted, when addressing two general problems of causation: (1) for a group and (2) for an individual. Based on the premise that judgment in civil action goes to the plaintiff when "more likely than not" (greater than 50% probability) has been established, contradictions can emerge. The issue can be posed in the form of the "gatecrasher paradox" [12], which has been used on numerous occasions to examine the law's responsiveness to statistical data.

A rodeo sells 499 tickets, yet 1000 people occupy the seats. No paper tickets were issued, and no testimony is available to identify those who paid the admission fee. Thus, for any one individual occupying a seat, there is a greater than 50% probability (i.e., 50.1%) that the occupant is a gatecrasher. Assume that M is one such individual. Are the rodeo organizers entitled to a judgment against M for the admission money based on the probability in their favor? As has been noted by others, the law has been unwilling to rely on such "naked statistical evidence" [16].

Posner [4] recently has addressed the same issue, modifying an oft-cited example:

> Suppose that the plaintiff is hit by a bus, and it is known that fifty-one percent of the buses on the road where the plaintiff was hit are owned by Bus Company A and forty-nine percent by Bus Company B. The plaintiff sues A and asks for judgment on the basis of this statistic alone; he tenders no other evidence. If the defendant also puts in no evidence, should a jury be allowed to award judgment for the plaintiff?

As Posner points out, the answer is intuitively "no," which would appear to undermine the use of Bayes' or any other mathematical probability to guide fact-finding. Part of the rationale for not awarding judgment is that there was no further investigation by the plaintiff. On the other hand, maybe he did investigate, and he found that the bus was owned by Bus Company B. He would be unlikely to report this if he were inclined toward disingenuousness. Perhaps Bus Company B has a worse accident record than Bus Company A. If so, the defendant should have inquired about bus accident records. Can Bayesian considerations help? The 51:49 relationship establishes $\Omega(A) = 1.04$. Consider the evidence that would be necessary to make $\Omega(A|e) \leq 1$ for Bus Company A to prevail. Intuitively, the likelihood ratio, $\Omega(e|A)$, would have to be no larger than the reciprocal of 1.04, that is, 0.96. From Equation (8), it can be seen that $P(e|B) = 0.51 > P(e|A) = 0.49$. Thus it only takes a small or "outside" chance for there to be evidence pointing toward B in order to avoid the problem's paradox.

While the forgoing example has a "straw man" character to it because the fractional differences were so slight, this is the type of situation that can occur in toxic tort and product liability litigation and workers' compensation. An analogy to this concept is found in an epidemiologic measure called the *attributable fraction* (AF), sometimes referred to as *attributable risk*. The attributable fraction is the proportion of a disease in the population attributable to a characteristic, such as the proportion of a particular type of cancer attributable to a particular environmental exposure. This is illustrated by the following example.

Consider an industry where plant workers are exposed to suspected carcinogens. Assume that an epidemiologic study is done by reviewing the health records of persons working in the industry, characterized by such plants, over a 40-year period. Employees of the plants are divided into two groups based on employment records: (1) those whose job descriptions imply exposure to the suspected agents and (2) those whose job descriptions imply no exposure to the suspected agents. The results of the study show (1) that 45% of the employees were in jobs implying exposure to the suspected agent and (2) that the cumulative incidence rate of lymphatic cancer for the exposed group was 3.5 times the rate in the nonexposed group. Furthermore, the relative risk (RR) of lymphatic cancer for the exposed group was 3.5, and this finding was statistically significant.

At this point in the analysis of the study, there is initial evidence of an association between working in the plant and increased incidence of lymphatic cancer. The steps from that point to establishing a credible causal inference are many and steep. For the sake of this example, however, assume that the evidence exists for such a credible inference that exposure in the plant has caused cancer. The proportion of lymphatic cancer among workers in this industry that can be attributed to the characteristic exposure is 0.53, or 53%.[6] Thus 53% of the lymphatic cancer occurring in the industry's worker population is attributable to that exposure $[D \rightarrow E|B$ or $\Omega(D \rightarrow E|B) = 1.12]$.

Now consider an employee who worked in one of the plants in the subject industry for a period of 17 years and developed lymphatic cancer. Can it be assumed legitimately *a priori* from the epidemiologic study that his industry employment is the cause of his lymphatic cancer? On formal grounds, the prior probability of an occupationally related disease is greater that 50%. It would appear, therefore, that in a civil trial, the probability is sufficient to support a verdict for the plaintiff. Here again is the issue of "naked statistical evidence." Certainly, each party in such a civil matter will have the opportunity to present evidence that can modify the *a priori* probability, leading to an adjusted probability, that probability considering case-specific evidence. For example, if the employee's job description placed him outside the exposure area, then the probability of an exposure-caused condition approaches zero.

However, suppose that the employee's job placed him squarely in the exposed group of workers: Can the statistical data from the epidemiologic study sustain his claim? Or consider, for one reason or another, that there is no further evidence from either the plaintiff or the defendant. Will the statistical data from the epidemiologic study suffice? The answer to both questions is no. This answer is not based on a hesitancy to rely solely on background statistical data but is based on the argument that attributable fractions cannot, except under unusual circumstances, be used to reliably assess the probability of causation. Robins and Greenland, in a study [17] directed at the problem of causation within the context of tort litigation, have shown by mathematical definition that probability of causation among exposed cases cannot be ascertained from epidemiologic data:

> [T]he value of the probability of causation depends upon both the degree of hetero-geneity in the background risk and the type and degree of interaction between exposure and other unmeasured environmental and genetic risk factors. Because of our inevitably limited knowledge of interaction of exposure with other risk factors and of the degree of background heterogeneity of risk, we cannot estimate the probability of causation from epidemiological data without making unverifiable assumptions.
>
> We have shown that, even in the absence of bias and misclassification, the average probability of causation . . . [over a period of time] among exposed individuals developing a disease . . . [within that period of time] cannot be estimated from epidemiological data without resorting to nonidentifiable biological assumptions. Furthermore, even in the absence of competing risks, the average probability of causation . . . among all exposed cases cannot be estimated. This is because these probabilities of causation depend on (i) the unknown mechanisms by which exposure affects disease risk and competing risks, (ii) the unknown degree of heterogeneity in the background risks of disease, and (iii) the unknown dependence between risk of disease and competing risk.

These examples showing that prior odds cannot be used as an essential condition for causation judgments have all used prior odds hovering around 1.0, thereby allowing adjustments with some ease. Obviously, the same principles apply irrespective of the prior odds, but adjustments can be more demanding of data reliability. For example, consider the never-smoker waitress working in a smoke-filled bar for 10 years who then develops laryngeal cancer. She pursues an action against her employer, claiming that her laryngeal cancer was due to environmental tobacco smoke exposure. In support of her claim is a report from an oncologist who notes, correctly, that the attributable fraction for tobacco smoke and laryngeal cancer and the population is 0.80. This would represent $\Omega(D \to E|B) = 4.0$, very strong prior odds favoring causation in the employee. The problem is B, the background information. Because of the very strong relationships between tobacco smoke exposure and cancers of the oropharynx and respiratory tract, there is a plethora of epidemiologic data that would allow assessment of the employee's cigarette-equivalent exposure, exposure duration, tumor histology, tumor location, etc. within the context of the background data on which the prior odds are based. In this case, her cigarette-equivalent exposure is likely to be very low compared with the population from which the prior odds were determined. A similar assessment would be necessary for the temporal factors and tumor characteristic, as well as the patient's medical, family, and social histories. Accordingly, attributable risk cannot be used as prior odds in a causation assessment without consideration of the background data.

From these examples and discussion we have established that evaluating the probability of causation requires the assessment of three factors: (1) the general background knowledge concerning the putative causative agent, (2) specific knowledge concerning the exposure to the putative causative agent, and (3) case-specific knowledge concerning the individual being evaluated. All these can be incorporated conveniently into a Bayesian assessment. Bayesian assessment can be an effective method to aid understanding evidence. It is not the *sine qua non* of scientific reasoning, nor even a valid means to test scientific hypotheses. It is a tool that may help decision makers form uncertainty judgments. Whether or not that is accomplished will depend on information quality and the judgment of the assessor.

Endnotes

[1] Also of significance to this discussion is the footnote to the cited statement: "This is not to say that judicial interpretation, as opposed to adjudicative fact-finding, does not share basic characteristics of the scientific endeavor: 'The work of a judge is in one sense enduring and in another ephemeral. . . . In the endless process of testing and retesting, there is a constant rejection of the dross and a constant retention of whatever is pure and sound and fine'" [B. Cardozo, *The Nature of the Judicial Process* 178, 179 (1921)].

[2] While it is generally agreed that belief must satisfy the constraints of the probability calculus, Kyberg makes a disquieting distinction between belief and probability. Any single probability can range from 0 to 1, absolute rejection to absolute certainty, and the cumulative probability of any series of hypothetical propositions cannot exceed 1. If $P(X)$ is the probability of the hypothesis X and $P(\sim)$ is the probability of some hypothesis other than X, then $P(X) + P(\sim X) = 1$. However, Kyberg distinguishes this calculus from that for belief. That is, if $Bel(X)$ is a measure of the belief that the evaluator has that X is true and $Bel(\sim X)$ the belief that X is not true, then $Bel(X) + Bel(\sim X)$ does not have to be equal to 1. That is, it is feasible to have very little belief in X or in its denial.

[3] Holmes speaking: "'We have got to the deductions and the inferences,' said Lestrade, winking at me. 'I find it hard enough to tackle facts, Holmes, without flying away after theories and fancies'" ("The Boscombe Valley Mystery," by A. Conin Doyle).

[4] Bayes theorem is named for Rev. Thomas Bayes (1702–1761), an English clergyman and a mathematician. His "An Essay Toward Solving a Problem in the Doctrine of Chances" was discovered among his papers, after his death, by a friend, Richard Price, who sent the paper to the Royal Society of London. The paper was published in the *Philosophical Transactions* of the Royal Society of London in 1764. (It was reprinted in *Biometrika* 45:293–315, 1958.) Generalization of Bayes' theorem by Laplace in 1814 provided the place for it in probability theory.

[5] The "three prisoners" problem has many iterations and is widely used in classes on probability. The "Monte Hall" problem refers to a 1970's television game show and also is the subject of probability exercises. Both are discussed at a number of Internet sites.

[6] $AF = P(RR - 1)/[P(RR - 1) + 1] = 0.45(35 - 1)/[0.45(35 - 1) + 1] = 0.53$, where P is the proportion of the population exposed to the characteristic agent.

References

1. Green M. Expert witnesses and sufficiency of evidence in toxic substances litigation: The legacy of Agent Orange and Bendectin litigation. *Northwestern University Law Rev* 1992;86:643.

2. *Daubert v. Merrell Dow Pharmaceuticals,* 509 U.S. 579 (1993).

3. Kyberg HE Jr. Uncertainty and the conditioning of belief. In: von Furstenberg GM (ed). *Acting Under Uncertainty: Multidisciplinary Conceptions.* Boston: Kluwer, 1990. Pp 77ff. Citing from Ramsey FP. Probability and partial belief. In: Braithwaite RB (ed). *The Foundations of Mathematics and Other Logical Essays by Frank P. Ramsey.* London: Routelage and Kegan Paul, 1990. Pp 56–257.

4. Posner RA. An economic approach to the law of evidence. *Stanford Law Rev* 1999;51:1477–1546.

5. Lane DA. A probabilist's view of causality assessment. *Drug Info J* 1984;18:323–330.

6. Edwards W. Conservatism in human information processing. In: Kleinmentz B (ed). *Formal Representation of Human Judgement.* New York: Wiley, 1967. Pp 17–52.

7. Lane DA. The Bayesian approach to causality assessment: An introduction. *Drug Info J* 1986;20:455–461.

8. Feinstein AR. Clinical biostatistics: XXXIX. The haze of Bayes, the aerial palaces of decision analysis and the computerized Ouija board. *Clin Pharmacol Ther* 1977; 21:482–496.

9. Finkelstein M, Fairely W. A Bayesian approach to identification evidence. *Harvard Law Rev* 1970;83:489–517.

10. Tribe LH. Trial by mathematics: Precision and ritual in the legal process. *Harvard Law Rev* 1971;84:1329–1393.

11. Brilmayer L, Kornhauser L. Review: Quantitative methods and legal decisions. *University of Chicago Law Rev* 1978;46:116–153.

12. Kaye D. The laws of probability and the law of the land. *University of Chicago Law Rev* 1979;47:34–56.

13. Kaye D. The paradox of the gatecrasher and other stories. *Arizona State University Law J* 1979:101–109.

14. Tillers P, Green D. *Probability and Inference in the Law of Evidence: The Uses and Limits of Bayesianism.* Boston: Kluwer, 1988.

15. Nesson C. Agent Orange meets the blue bus: Fact-finding at the frontier of knowledge. *Boston University Law Rev* 1986;66:521.

16. Brilmayer L. Second-order evidence and Bayesian logic. In: Tillers P, Green ED (eds). *Probability and Inference in the Law of Evidence: The Uses and Limits of Bayesianism.* Boston: Kluwer, 1988. P 147.

17. Robins J, Greenland S. The probability of causation under a stochastic model for individual risk. *Biometrics* 1989;45:1125–1138.

9

Causation

TEE L. GUIDOTTI

Causation is rarely a simple matter of cause and effect. There may be many risk factors or exposures that participate in the process that leads to the health outcome. In the evidence-based medical dispute resolution (EBMDR) approach, causation is a layered concept that includes the responsible agent and circumstances of exposure but also includes other significant factors that may have contributed to the outcome.

A full discussion of causation would include

- Determination of the proximate cause (what was immediately responsible).
- Determination of the underlying causes (what conditions created the situation).
- Liability for the causal situation (who was responsible for allowing it to happen).
- Contributing behavioral factors.
- Apportionment among the various causes that are possible.
- Preexisting conditions (such as atopy) and personal factors (such as host defense or susceptibility states).

The aspect of causation on which the interpretation of the case rests is the one that is emphasized.

Causation is akin to the concept of etiology in clinical medicine but without the implication that there can only be a single cause. In clinical medicine, etiology is usually not as important as diagnosis, because in clinical practice, regardless of what caused the condition, the task at hand is to treat the patient. In law and policy, however, the assessment of causation is critical.

The concept of causation in law has been described as the "occurrence or aggravation of an underlying disorder by the one causative element [in isolation]. . . ." This definition has many features. It requires the fact of contribution to the disorder; it admits, by making an effort to isolate the pertinent cause, that effects may be moderated by complexity; it is deterministic and assumes a proximate cause; and it admits preexisting conditions and permissive factors. This legal concept of causation therefore is remarkably flexible and concordant with the following essential features of the idea of causation in science: strict cause and effect, moderation by complexity and interaction, a chain of events the outcome of which may be unforeseeable (as in chaos theory), contributing causes in deterministic mechanisms, and multifactorial risk factors in stochastic phenomena. Thus perceptions of causation in law and medicine are fundamentally compatible.

Different Concepts of Causation

The concept of causation has different implications in different disciplines. In epidemiology, the concept assumes that the risk factors bear a "causal" relationship to each other in that they either establish a necessary condition or set into motion a process that results in the outcome. This does not necessarily mean, as in common language, that a cause must be "sufficient" in itself to produce an effect. In toxicology, the concept of causation tends to be more mechanistic and assumes that there is a chain of biological causation from first exposure to outcome. However, toxicologists are also accustomed to thinking in terms of complex interactions. In occupational medicine, causation is the determination of the most probable cause of the worker's condition or disability. Finally, in workers' compensation, to establish causation means identifying the factor that created the condition and also demonstrating that it arose out of the work setting or conditions.

In law, there are two elements of causation: cause in fact and proximate cause. *Cause in fact* is the necessary condition, similar to the notion of "underlying cause" on a death certificate. It can be identified by a simple test: Would the adverse outcome have been avoided "but for" the presence of the cause? A cause in fact can be necessary but not sufficient. The *proximate cause* is the particular event or factor that initiated the chain of events leading to injury or damage and is comparable with "immediate cause" on a death certificate. In law, especially in adjudication proceedings, a proximate cause also may be a "substantial factor" that contributes to the outcome even if it is not wholly responsible. Thus, in a heavy cigarette smoker who also was heavily exposed to asbestos and developed asbestosis and who subsequently developed lung cancer, the smoking may be a cause in fact, but the asbestos exposure could be a proximate cause and the basis for a judgment [1] (see Chap. 1).

However, consider the problem of the "first case." By definition, the first case occurs before there is sufficient evidence to decide causation. This obviously places a much greater burden on the plaintiff or claimant. Argument based on plausible mechanisms, analogy, and weak evidence plays a disproportionate role in the first case. Until new data become available and good studies are conducted and published, such cases almost always will appear to be "junk science" at the very beginning (see Chap. 6).

Assessing Causation

Causation analysis must be undertaken on two levels. The individual case must be documented and evaluated thoroughly, and the evidence in the individual case must be linked with the broader body of knowledge in science regarding risk.

The preferred sequence of causation analysis in the medicolegal context should include

- *Confirm the injury.* Occasionally, a lawyer's or other party's second-hand report of the diagnosis will be incorrect.
- *Determine the circumstances of exposure.* Confirm that there is a plausible pathway for exposure. For example, is it likely that an exposure actually took place? Was the person merely in the vicinity and a bystander to the event?
- *Determine other possible exposures that may be causal or significant in the case.*
- *Determine whether the injury is a recognized effect of the exposure.* This is relatively easy to do in the case of carcinogens because the International Agency for Research on Cancer is an authoritative body that provides assessment of the evidence for carcinogenicity of chemicals and industrial processes. It is much more difficult when the scientific literature is scanty, contradictory, or of poor quality.
- *Document the feasibility of causation by comparing the particulars of the individual case to findings in the scientific literature.* If the association is not recognized as causal, is there evidence in the scientific literature to suggest an association between the exposure and the outcome under consideration in circumstances similar to the case?
- *When the findings in the scientific literature fail to apply to the particulars of the case, search for new information or develop a reasonable hypothesis for how such an event might have happened.*
- *Test the strength of each link in the chain of logic against the literature, and compare the exposure factors suggested in the literature with the particulars of the case.*

Levels of Causation in the Individual Case

Causation may be simple if the disorder typically is associated with a single external cause, such as mesothelioma and asbestos exposure. The challenge in such cases is to demonstrate the opportunity for exposure to an agent that is a known cause, requiring a thorough history. Medical records are often poor sources of the exposure history because the first person to take the history is rarely trained for this, is not interested primarily in exposure assessment, and is relying on second-hand information from an anxious and excited party, the patient. Subsequent references to the exposure in the medical history often merely copy the first and occasionally distort it.

Even conditions for which there is a strong or suspected association with occupation on a group basis may be hard to prove on an individual basis. Some workers' compensation systems have schedules of recognized diseases for which claims qualify more or less automatically if there is a history of exposure or if the worker is in an occupation with a demonstrable and accepted risk. This is called a *rebuttable presumption* (see Chap. 14).

Because most types of occupational and environmental diseases have many possible causes, identifying a particular cause in each case is often difficult. The occupational and environmental history certainly narrows down the range of possible exposures and may rule out all but one or a few possibilities, particularly in the case of the pneumoconioses. However, cases of asthma and hypersensitivity pneumonitis are rarely as easy because the disorders may mimic common nondisorders and the number of possible exposures triggering the immunologic responses may be large. Toxic inhalation cases are always associated with a discrete event; there may be uncertainty over which particular chemical exposure caused the injury, but the association with the event in question is rarely a subject for dispute. Obstructive airways disease and cancer are exceedingly difficult and often impossible to tie to a specific occupational and environmental exposure in the presence of other risk factors, such as cigarette smoking.

While the veracity of the history always must be confirmed, a comprehensive work history does not have to be completely accurate to identify a "most likely" cause. A pneumoconiosis identified by appropriate structural markers demands an explanation. It is not easily mistaken in the presence of a compatible occupational history, although other disease may produce a similar x-ray. If the occupational history suggests exposure to one fibrogenic dust, this is enough work-related exposure to cause a simple pneumoconiosis.

In recent years, there has been increasing interests in testing for functional capacity. These tests assess the capacity of a worker for physical activities or for exercise or cognitive functions. They are used to quantify impairment, but baseline testing, e.g., at the time of hire, is performed rarely. The problem with tests of function for assessing causation, therefore, is that they do not allow a quantitative assessment of exacerbation or aggravation. For example, at the present time, it is not possible to determine the relative contribution to airways reactivity of multiple factors: the baseline airways reactivity associated with atopy, occupational asthma in response to a workplace antigen, conventional asthma associated with an antigen in the living environment, or idiosyncratic irritant effects. Exposure to irritants, such as cigarette smoke, welding fumes, solvents, nuisance dusts, and indoor air pollutants, often is superimposed on the many intrinsic and extrinsic factors that contribute to airways reactivity. All one can do at present is to temporarily withdraw the worker from exposure and then assume that the particular factor in question no longer has an effect. That assumption may well be wrong, however, because in a multifactorial model of airways reactivity, there often may be longer-lasting effects.

Assessing Causation in the Individual

In clinical medicine, we concentrate primarily on diagnosis and management of patient care. Assessing causation is not the same as making a diagnosis, although the two are related. The assessment of causation in occupational medicine, for example, is primarily in order to establish the association with work, not to guide treatment. Causation is more central even than diagnosis in initiating compensation and stimulating prevention. It is not at all unusual for a physician to be able to make a diagnosis without knowing the cause. It is usually but not always necessary to know the exact diagnosis to assess causation so long as the pathologic process is known. For example, one can know that a worker has nonallergic airways reactivity following an exposure clearly associated with work without determining for certain whether it is occupational asthma associated with irritant exposure, reactive airways dysfunction syndrome, or an aggravation of preexisting but subclinical airways reactivity in allergic rhinitis.

The medical approach to the worker with suspected occupational disease or the patient with suspected environmental disease must reflect two realities:

- Medical diagnosis and treatment, with which physicians are universally familiar.
- The requirements of adjudication systems for handling disease due to occupation or environmental exposure.

Legal and administrative claims require extensive documentation, which is necessary to fulfill their purposes, which, in turn, affect social concerns, policies, and the interests of all parties. If both these realities are not addressed satisfactorily, the clinical evaluation is insufficient, notwithstanding how well it deals with diagnosis and treatment. A good medical evaluation alone is not enough.

Medical Evaluation

The approach to medical evaluation in occupational or environmental disease preserves the traditional orientation of identification, diagnosis, functional evaluation, treatment, and prognosis but requires further information depending on the case and the criteria of the agency handling compensation or liability:

- Level of causation (direct, proximate, precipitating, underlying).
- Work relationship.
- Apportionment.

- Explanation of the causal circumstances.
- Assessment of impairment.
- Prediction of future impairment.
- Surveillance for sentinel event monitoring.

The evaluation of patients with a disease that arises out of occupational, environmental, or consumer product exposure therefore is similar conceptually to but subtly different from the evaluation of disease from other causes. Accurate diagnosis remains important but is seldom the critical factor in comprehensive management. The primary consideration in stating a prognosis usually is not to predict the natural history of the disorder but instead to predict the capacity to work as well as fitness to return to the worker's usual occupation. Each case of an exposure-related disease is also a "sentinel event" calling for an explanation and consideration of the exposure of others who may share the same risk. This places a duty on the treating physician to consider the significance of the case as a public health indicator and not to restrict attention solely to the individual case.

Causation must be linked to conditions in the workplace or arising out of the work. This may mean identifying not only the likely exposure but also the likely job, employer, or other circumstances, especially if there is a question of which workers' compensation carrier or insurance company is providing coverage. The work history is invaluable in identifying the putative exposure responsible for occupational or environmental disease and the setting in which it may have occurred. This information is also central to prevention because it may identify exposure situations that remain ineffectively controlled. When the work history is backed up by the results of exposure assessment or industrial hygiene reports, however fragmentary, it is even more persuasive.

In individual cases, the following approaches may be used to develop an inventory of exposures and possible causes:

- A thorough occupational history.
- Employer personnel records.
- Industrial hygiene survey records (when available).
- Union records.
- Pay stubs, tax records, and income statements that identify particular employers.
- Medical records.
- Testimony of coworkers.
- Past workers' compensation claims.

Advanced Diagnostic Tests

The evaluation of occupational and environmental disease may be assisted by more advanced diagnostic modalities. Technology has advanced the precision of medical diagnosis but does not necessarily help to the same degree in causation assessment and etiologic determination.

The use of advanced diagnostic tests without guidelines may even bias the system. A claimant who receives a sensitive but not specific test, such as high-resolution computed tomography for fibrotic lung disease, may be more likely to have his or her claim accepted than a claimant whose physician did not use the technology. Likewise, x-rays of the spine that show erosion of the vertebral body and spurring often are accepted as evidence of a structural abnormality for low-back pain alleged to have arisen out of work, yet such lesions are common in people without low-back pain and are not by themselves evidence of an occupational cause.

Surveillance also may be biased when new technology is introduced and as cases are newly identified by different criteria. New tests also often are more difficult to interpret than established tests both because there is less experience and because they are more sensitive, showing positive results even when there may not be evidence of impairment. For example, advanced methods of imaging the lung certainly would increase identification of early occupational lung disease. However, such methods are not readily available everywhere and therefore would introduce inequities in surveillance standards. They are also so sensitive that they detect changes well before manifestations of clinical disease and impairment. The low-tech chart film, on the other hand, is universally available, and on it, the appearance of an abnormality tends to correlate more closely with significant disease. For this reason, evaluations done for purposes of prevention and surveillance in occupational medicine in particular are best based on accepted and generally available technology. Workers' compensation evaluations tend to rely on studies with known and familiar technology. Insurance carriers may not authorize newer or highly sensitive tests that are not easily interpreted. The evaluation of occupational disease may appear very conservative to practitioners who are accustomed to applying the latest medical breakthroughs, but there are reasons for this.

Approach to Evaluation: The Five Questions

Five basic questions must be answered in every case in a systematic manner:

1. What is the nature of the disease process?
2. What exposure in the worker's employment history may have been responsible?
3. What is the natural history of the disorder, and what ultimate level of impairment can be predicted?
4. What can be done to control or limit the disease process?
5. Are other people in the workplace likely to be affected now or in the future?

These five questions refer to the basic elements of disease evaluation:

- Identify the disease process by determining structure, function, and malignant potential.
- Identify proximate causation or the exposure that led to the disorder.
- Prognosis and stability of impairment.
- Treatment and other interventions.
- Prevention.

The first three elements will be discussed in turn. A discussion of treatment and prevention is outside the scope of this particular monograph but is, of course, fundamental to the principal values of occupational and environmental medicine.

Identifying the Disease Process

The first question, on the nature of the disease, requires a description of the structure, function, and possible malignant potential. Many diagnostic modalities are available to assist in the evaluation of disorders, but in practice, only a few are useful in most cases.

Structure

Structure is usually evaluated by a plain posteroanterior chest film. The chest film is a simple test of extraordinary yield that has the merits of being sensitive enough to identify many diseases before they are functionally significant. Most pneumoconioses, for example, are obvious on chest films as 1/1 disease by the ILO Classification (a system of grading changes developed by the International Labor Organization) long before they produce significant functional impairment. The exceptions tend to be disorders, such as hard metal disease and beryllium disease, in which the reaction to the dust is systemic and generalized beyond local fibrosis. Very few pneumoconioses show pathognomonic signs on a chest film, but most fortuitously, the two most common severe ones, asbestosis and silicosis, often do.

Structural change as observed on the chest film may directly characterize the disease process, as in the case of pneumoconioses, hypersensitivity pneumonitis, and pulmonary edema. It may indirectly suggest the process, as in the case of cancer, requiring confirmation through biopsy or testing of tissue. Structural changes also may provide useful markers that point to etiology, such as pleural plaques in the case of asbestosis.

The search for such markers by more sensitive means, such as computed tomography (CT), is a natural extension of medical technology but has limited utility. Although CT scanning may well show plaques where they were not clearly visible on chest film or fibrosis where the image was unclear, it is not likely to uncover a functionally significant lesion not visible on chest film. A CT scan, being much more sensitive than a routine chest film for certain lesions, cannot be correlated with functional abnormalities for most disorders, such as pneumoconioses. As a consequence, CT scanning plays a bigger role in the investigation of diagnostic dilemmas and pleural disease than in the identification of disorders. Similarly, other "high tech" modalities, such as positron-emission tomographic (PET) imaging, are less interesting when applied to disorders than one might expect. They lack standardization, and the level of sensitivity is greater than what is necessary for early detection.

Function

Functional assessment begins with the history, and this history is validated and extended by laboratory studies. Symptoms are a subjective perception reflecting the functional implications of the disease, and each statement of a symptom contains information on how the change in function affects the worker's ability to cope.

Pulmonary function testing, for example, provides a valuable assessment of the process, either by spirometry or bronchoprovocation testing. Exercise testing provides a basis for assessing functional capacity for workers with lung disease. Except for reversible spirometric changes suggesting asthma, however, neither conventional pulmonary function testing nor exercise testing is diagnostic. They provide functional evaluation but rarely point clearly to the disease process. Restrictive changes may be compatible with a pneumoconiosis but also with much else. The impairment of function resulting from severe restriction or moderate to severe obstruction, or desaturation (oxygen depletion) on exercise testing, on the other hand, is valuable quantification of work capacity. It is therefore of greatest value in assessing impairment.

Other functional indicators are confirmatory but not diagnostic and have value as ancillary studies. For example, air trapping in volumes helps to confirm and to some degree quantify the degree of asthma, reduced diffusing capacity suggests possible effacement of the alveolar-capillary bed and therefore is consistent with an interstitial process, and fixed airflow obstruction may suggest a role for either cigarette smoking or other causes of airways disease usually not associated with occupational exposures. However, these findings are only characteristic, not reliable or strong correlates of disease. Their presence (or absence) may give confidence in the diagnosis, but they do not prove it.

Malignancy

Documentation of malignancy usually requires recovery of tissue. This is generally done by biopsy or sputum cytopathology in the case of lung cancer. The indication for documentation is usually a suspicious lesion on chest film. Because screening for lung cancer by either cytopathology or chest film has been shown to be an unproductive exercise, ineffective in improving outcome, most such films will now be taken for other purposes or in the case of chest symptoms. In the occupational or environmental evaluation, therefore, malignant lesions are usually a subset of structural lesions that conform to certain patterns that suggest cancer.

Prognosis and Impairment

Prognosis and impairment assessments are linked because the level of impairment may change over time in many disorders. Impairment assessment for disease is almost always performed at the time that the condition is "stable," or not obviously progressing further. Generally, there is little point in assessing tempo-rary disability for a disease that usually is slow to develop and will not produce significant impairment until later in life, which is usually the case with emphy-sema. The issue of prognosis in most diseases is related either to projections of future impairment and the likelihood of return to work or to permanent impair-ment interfering with the activities of daily living for workers who are not employable.

Unlike apportionment of causation, apportionment of impairment is done routinely. Where baseline pulmonary function studies are not available, deviation from predicted function is a reasonable estimate of loss of function that is unlikely to underestimate the decline by much. When baseline function studies are available, it is possible to track the progression of pulmonary function loss over time to see if it exceeds the usual rate of decline for nonsmokers (about 30 ml/year for healthy adults). Most people who do not smoke stay more or less at the same percentage of predicted performance throughout their lives. If, by using the same prediction values, there is evidence of accelerated loss of function, this becomes evidence that the process is translating into increasing impairment. Theoretically, it might be possible to calculate deviation from the expected decline in pulmonary function for smokers based on how much they smoke. In practice, however, this is not likely to work because smokers vary considerably more in their rate of decline than nonsmokers, and there is a considerable heritable component to susceptibility to cigarette smoke (see Chap. 10 on the problem of smoking).

Although most of the pneumoconioses do not progress after the exposure to dust ceases, asbestosis and silicosis may progress, and the complications associated with them may add to the burden of impairment beyond compromise of pulmonary function. Most of the pneumoconioses, including those two disor-ders, cause relatively little functional abnormality and impairment until they have progressed quite far, well beyond 1/2 or 2/1 in the ILO classification. Occupational asthma, and asthma in general, may be a risk factor for decline in pulmonary function later in life and is, in any event, a special case because there is little or no impairment absent the specific exposure. Hypersensitivity pneumonitides and toxic inhalation may result in chronic sequelae. Occupational cancer carries a generally poor prognosis unrelated to fitness to work in the short term.

The prognosis can be inferred from the natural history of the occupational or environmental disease, but most workers who develop occupational or environmental disorders are older and have other medical problems. As a practical matter, therefore, the question is only occasionally what impairment one might expect in the future from the disease itself. More often, the question is what additional impairment the disease will confer that further impedes the older patient with unrelated cardiac, pulmonary, or musculoskeletal disease, and will the combination interfere with a productive and satisfying life? This, again, is an apportionment question, one that can only be answered by a judgment call combined with a thorough understanding of both the disease process and the individual patient.

Evidence from the Literature in Support of Causation

Causation is a reasonable conclusion when a case conforms to the risk factors that are described in the scientific literature and there is a clear consensus that the exposure is associated with the disease outcome. These are the easier cases. The harder cases are those in which the literature is not clear or scarce. The first step is to review the literature to determine whether the evidence suggests a causal association. The literature may be clinical, toxicologic, or epidemiologic. In general, the clinical literature tells one that something happened, the toxicologic literature tells one that something could happen, and the epidemiologic literature tells one that something does happen—or not.

Clinical studies usually are case series or clinical epidemiologic studies that review the accumulated experience with the disease. Because they tend to concentrate on what happened to the patients and how they were managed, the clinical literature usually gives clues to etiology, not definitive or even persuasive answers. Most of the emphasis is downstream from the causal event and therefore irrelevant to the assessment of causation. Occasionally, however, a case series will suggest a consistent association with a risk factor, such as the early studies of nephritis or rheumatologic disorders among patients with pneumoconiosis. In the absence of an etiologically based epidemiologic study, this is valuable information, but it is only suggestive of causation.

Toxicologic studies may demonstrate that an association between exposure and an outcome in the case exists in animals and may demonstrate a plausible mechanism. The methods, relevance to humans, comparative exposure levels, and species and strain differences then become issues of controversy and contention.

Epidemiologic studies have a great advantage because they reflect the human experience and a great disadvantage because they are generalizations. The science of epidemiology describes patterns in populations, and from this one infers the most likely history or the most likely future risk in an individual case. However, studies on populations are not the same as predictions for individuals. Individuals may or may not conform to the pattern of characteristics in a population or a relevant subgroup. Individuals have life histories and risk factors that exist in combinations in one person but as frequencies in groups, scattered among individuals in a population. Thus it is very important to separate the two roles of epidemiology as a science in providing evidence for a causal association:

1. As observational data that relate the risk factor (putative cause) and effect and provide evidence on a statistical basis from population-based science.
2. As predictions for individuals, based on an estimate derived from the experience of a population from which they were drawn or that they are presumed to resemble.

Chapter 5 addresses establishing causation with epidemiology. Chapter 13 addresses the individualization of risk in EBMDR. Chapter 8 describes an alternative way of assessing individual probabilities that is a little different from classical statistical treatments in epidemiology.

Causation in Epidemiology

Causation is an easy concept when there is a single or predominant cause and the mechanism can be identified or inferred. One of the benefits of toxicologic research is that it gives plausibility to an observed association by providing a reasonable explanation for why an association might occur. This increases our comfort in concluding that it does. Causation is a more elusive concept applied to epidemiology [2]. Human populations are vastly more complex than experimental systems, subject to numerous influences on health, behavior, and social adjustment. Each individual in the population may be subject to numerous other exposures that influence the outcome of interest. Although these are called *confounding* factors, they are often every bit as important in determining the outcome as the risk factor under study; it is a mistake to dismiss them as merely sources of bias. In the presence of numerous confounding factors, clear associations demonstrated in epidemiologic studies are remarkable observations, with three likely explanations: an effect, a statistical chance event, or a bias in the study method. If the latter two "false" outcomes are excluded, the effect that remains is not necessarily causal in nature [3].

A fundamental concept of epidemiology is that main effects will demonstrate consistency in association, whereas other complicating associations will vary in strength. Two corollary problems are that a relatively weak association may be lost among stronger confounding associations and that bias may mimic this consistency in association [4]. Thus a consistent and strong association is fairly persuasive evidence for a causal association, but when the literature is highly variable or contradictory, despite sufficient numbers and power, it either argues against a causal association or demands a plausible explanation of the variability.

Various sets of criteria have been suggested to determine whether a particular agent causes a particular disease. In the early days of microbiology, Koch's postulates frequently were applied:

1. The organism must be found in all cases of the disease.
2. The organism must be isolated from patients with the disease and grown in culture.
3. The cultured organism must produce the disease when inoculated into a susceptible host.

These criteria are still applied to infectious disease.

The most widely accepted set of criteria for assessing the likelihood of causation reflected in epidemiologic data is that proposed by the late Sir Austin Bradford Hill [3]. The criteria are to be applied rigorously and as a group; the more that appear to be satisfied, the more likely it is presumed that the association observed is truly causal. These criteria are as follows:

1. Strength of the association.
2. Consistency among studies, especially by different techniques.
3. Specificity of outcome.
4. Exposure precedes disease outcome.
5. Dose-response relationship (epidemiologic).
6. Plausibility of a biological mechanism.
7. Coherence of chain of evidence.
8. Experimental association, especially dose-response (toxicologic).
9. Analogy to similar effect produced by a similar agent.

Obviously, some of these criteria are stronger than others. In particular, analogy is considered a weak criteria but "temporality" (cause precedes effect) is essential. Early in the investigation of an association there simply may be no evidence to address these criteria (see Chap. 5).

The Multifactorial Model

Causation is a more difficult concept when different risk factors are at play and there is a possible interaction among them. For example, this is manifestly the case in the risk of cardiovascular disease: Male sex, family history, age, obesity, diabetes, hypertension, smoking, serum cholesterol, serum high-density lipoprotein (HDL) levels, serum iron, serum homocystein, and numerous other factors, both known and unknown, interact and play a role in elevating risk.

Similarly, environmental disorders tend to be multifactorial health outcomes. One usually does not see a simple one-to-one relationship between a unitary cause and mechanistic, deterministic progression to effect, as is often the case in physics or biochemistry. There is often not even a relatively well-defined relationship among agent, host defenses, and environment, as there is for most communicable diseases. Rather, the problems we study are akin to cardiovascular disease, in which numerous partial determinants (agents and host factors) converge in a complex structure. Obviously, studies of environmental determinants of cancer follow this model, but it holds true as well for environmental respiratory diseases and undoubtedly will be the operative model for the developing fields of neurotoxicology and immunotoxicology.

In epidemiologic terms, many causal factors may be acting through a defined pathogenetic mechanism, each sufficient, none in itself necessary, and each potentially interacting to increase the probability of a particular outcome [5]. The multifactorial model is not well reflected in legal theory. The law may consider a sufficient but not necessary cause to be a "substantial factor," or a factor aggravating a preexisting condition. A legal requirement of such a cause, however, is that it must "more likely than not" contribute to the risk.

A useful distinction can be made between causes that are risk factors in an epidemiologic sense, in that they increase the probability of an outcome that is not certain, and those few causes which are invisible precisely because they are intrinsic components of the mechanism that produces the effect, e.g., oncogenes and pathways of the metabolism of procarcinogens. These "component causes" are more usefully considered to be a means to the end rather than initiating events [5]. Exposure to these component causes cannot be controlled because they are intrinsic; exposures may be modified, however, in such a way as to slow or prevent the action of the mechanism in producing the outcome. The distinction has obvious relevance to cancer control.

For purposes of this discussion, a cause is a factor that contributes to the likelihood that an outcome will occur. This is a stochastic, or probabilistic, definition, not strictly a mechanistic definition. There is a certain probability, or odds, that a step will occur but no certainty. In daily life, one speaks of "cause and effect" relationships as if there is one cause for every effect and as if an effect necessarily follows the presence of a cause. This is too rigid to be useful in epidemiology and in cancer toxicology, where the mechanisms are complicated and influenced by numerous external and internal factors. It is not even useful, in this context, to speak of a cause as being either necessary or sufficient because causes may be interchangeable in the mechanism or may interact [6,7].

For example, exposure to either cigarette smoking or asbestos alone is known to result in lung cancer in a roughly predictable probability. Exposure to both vastly increases the risk beyond that of the summed probabilities of either alone, suggesting a substantial interaction. However, most workers who have been exposed to either or both do not develop lung cancer, although they might if they lived long enough and were free of other fatal risks. Uncommonly, a few unlucky people who neither smoke nor are exposed to environmental carcinogens such as asbestos develop lung cancer. While neither asbestos exposure nor cigarette smoking is necessary, sufficient, or a predictor in individual cases as a cause of lung cancer, the association is clear, and these factors truly are "causes."

This example also illustrates the difficulty in trying to apportion the contribution of multiple causes in individual cases. Is the interaction in the case of asbestos and cigarette smoking one of asbestos enhancing the effect of cigarette smoking, or vice versa? In several exercises, authoritative investigators have attempted to estimate the proportion of cancer "caused" by various classes of external influences and almost invariably have concluded that smoking and diet are major causes of cancer in the population and that occupational and environmental exposures contribute much less. It may well be true that control of smoking is the single most effective approach to the reduction of cancer incidence now available. However, the apportionment of the relative contribution of causes of cancer to cancer incidence overall or in a single case assumes that their effects on the underlying mechanism are separable and individually discreet when they clearly are not. Therefore, it is useless to attempt to apportion causation on the basis of risk estimates for factors in (relative) isolation because the mechanism is intrinsically always interactive. As Rothman has stated, ". . . it is easy to show that 100 percent of any disease is environmentally caused, and 100 percent is inherited as well. Any other view is based on a naive understanding of causation" [5].

Applying Generalities to the Individual Case

In the past, physicians were asked for their judgment, which was often taken at face value. Today, in both litigation and adjudication, opinions must be based on evidence. While there is still room for clinical judgment and analysis in these opinions, they must now come after and build on the knowledge base. Personal opinion does not substitute for reasoned analysis, but neither is clinical judgment worthless. In any legal setting, cases must be decided on an individual basis and not on generalities. Clinical judgment is mandatory to interpret the evidence taking into account the individual characteristics of the plaintiff/claimant. Further, when applying the scientific literature to a particular case, it is important to know the limitations of the knowledge base available and how the characteristics of the individual match what is known in the knowledge base.

It is important to know whether the profile of the injured party/worker corresponds to the population the study has investigated. It may matter, for example, that the plaintiff/claimant is younger, has worked longer, does or does not satisfy the expected latency period, or belongs to a particular subgroup in the analysis. An important principle in workers' compensation is that we "take the worker(s) as they come," meaning that once they are hired, personal characteristics do not matter. For example, unless there is a policy against hiring people who smoke, an employer cannot argue that an exposure that makes only smokers sick is not work-related. Some claimants, by their family history or some acquired condition, may be more susceptible than others to injury. Such persons are sometimes known as "eggshell plaintiffs" or "eggshell skull plaintiffs" after an early legal case in which a person sustained a skull fracture after a minor blow. The fact that the victim was more susceptible than average did not absolve the person responsible for hitting him on the head from liability and paying damages.

As a practical matter, empirical evidence that can be demonstrated to apply to a given case trumps a mechanistic argument that is based on toxicologic principles, which in turn trumps personal opinion based on clinical experience.

Drawing Conclusions

Aggravational causation occurs when an exposure makes an existing condition worse or brings out symptoms in a previously silent condition. Exposure to an irritant gas, including passive cigarette smoke, may aggravate reactive airways disorders in an individual with atopy, for example, even if he or she has had no previous asthma. This is not the same as *de novo* asthma but may be accepted as permanent impairment in some systems if it persists and interferes with the worker's ability to perform his or her usual occupation.

Substantial contribution is a feature of some legal systems. This doctrine suggests that the condition should be considered to have arisen out of the workplace if the exposure was sufficient to contribute more than trivial risk and would have added enough to the causation of the disorder to tip the balance, all other things being equal. This criterion is particularly common in situations where strict causation is difficult or impossible to prove or in which the job was particularly hazardous or involved national security and the assumption of personal risk. The Black Lung Benefits Program in the United States is such a system, administered under the Department of Labor (with some supplemental benefits from Medicare).

Apportionment of the disorder or the impairment that arises out of it among various possible causes of the condition is desirable, if possible. In a given case, more than one plausible agent or risk factor may be responsible for the condition, such as cigarette smoking, exposure to asbestos, and exposure to other chemical carcinogens. Separation of the nonfactors, as well as attribution of the factors to the correct employer, is an ideal to be sought but rarely feasible in practice. Demonstration of substantial contribution by workplace-associated exposures is usually sufficient to declare the disorder and all associated impairment to be work-related.

In the medical evaluation of disease, some sense of apportionment by cause is needed to explain the history and presentation of the disorder and to sort out the extent of contribution of work-related factors. Only occasionally and for certain disorders that present markers (such as asbestosis) can this apportionment be taken to the next level of rough quantification. The fact that this cannot be done easily for claimants with a number of similar diseases raises questions of fairness and equity if it can be done for only a small subset of claims with usual clinical clarity. On the other hand, a system of apportionment by cause that reflects epidemiologically derived risks as a best estimate of the contribution of work-related causation in the individual case may distort by under- or overestimation the contribution of work-related exposures in the individual case (this is discussed further in Chap. 11).

Communicating Conclusions

In preparing any type of medicolegal report, it is critically important to use the language required by the legal system that has adjudication authority over the case. Chapter 15 describes the problems of language and clear communication in detail. In brief, when one attempts to communicate concepts of causation, specific terms should be used with deliberate consideration.

Words such as *aggravation* have very particular meanings in workers' compensation and in law, meanings that are not always obvious from common usage and may be defined quite differently from what they are in medicine. At the extreme, words such as *and* and *or* can be misconstrued. If one writes, "Asthma is characterized by airways reactivity *and* responsiveness to an airborne sensitizer," this does this mean that *both* are always required and that sensitization is always and invariably a feature of the condition? (For example, where does reactive airways dysfunction syndrome fit in?) However, if one continues the sentence and adds, ". . . *or* an irritant exposure," this implies that any exposure to a known sensitizer or irritant may be responsible in any case, which the writer probably did not intend to say. In a string of items, the word *and*, which is usually inclusive, can become exclusive, requiring that all the items be present before a conditional phrase is true. Likewise, *or* can appear to be inclusive in a list when read as a series of alternatives. These counterintuitive interpretations may significantly complicate full understanding of a medical opinion. Be aware that *possible* is a very weak statement of probability, implying that causation is not necessarily more likely than not. *Probable* is a much stronger word and does imply "more likely than not."

Causation in chronic diseases, and especially diseases with long latencies, always will be difficult to assess. The current state of the art with regard to biomarkers and other indicators of individual etiology is rudimentary and limited to recent exposures. We need a technology that can reconstruct exposures and biological effects in a more distant time and in a manner that allows identification of probable causes on an individual basis, not only generalization by group experience. This will not come easy and may not be possible for many exposures, but any progress that can be made will be valuable.

References

1. Goldstein RL. The twilight zone between scientific certainty and legal sufficiency: Should a jury determine the cause of schizophrenia? *Bull Am Acad Psychiatr Law* 1987;15(1):95–104.

2. Greenland S. *Evolution of Epidemiologic Ideas: Annotated Readings on Concepts and Methods.* Boston: Epidemiology Resources, 1987.

3. Hill AB. Environment and disease: Association or causation? *Proc R Soc Med* 1965;58:295–300.

4. Susser M. What is a cause and how do we know one? A grammar for pragmatic epidemiology. *Am J Epidemiol* 1991;133:635–648.

5. Rothman K. *Modern Epidemiology.* Boston: Little, Brown, 1986. Pp 7–21.

6. Bunge M. *Causality and Modern Science,* 3d ed. New York: Dover, 1979.

7. Blalock HM Jr. *Causal Inferences in Nonexperimental Research.* New York: WW Norton, 1964.

"Love it! 'People of smoke' instead of 'Smokers.'"

10

The Problem of Smoking

TEE L. GUIDOTTI

The harm done by cigarette smoking and by the tobacco industry is now a matter of legal record as well as scientific fact [1]. Cigarette smoking is a classic example of a confounding exposure in toxic tort litigation and workers' compensation. This chapter will not discuss the direct effects of smoking and the class-action litigation that recently breached the defenses of the tobacco industry. Rather, this chapter will examine the issues that are raised by smoking when evaluating medical evidence as an illustration of the gaps in scientific knowledge. A close look at smoking will lay the groundwork that will be explored more fully in the following chapters on apportionment and presumption.

Cigarette smoking is a common habit and therefore often occurs in combination with other exposures that may be harmful to human health [1,2]. As a consequence, it is often difficult to determine how much injury or, for cancer especially, what degree of risk has been contributed by the smoking habit and how much is attributable to the exposure in question.

Smoking is a significant problem in assessing the effect of occupational and environmental exposures for several reasons [1,2]:

- Smoking is a major confounding factor in epidemiologic studies. A *confounder* in epidemiology is a risk factor that is linked both to the risk factor under study and to the outcome so that it interferes with interpretation of the risk factor under study.
- Smoking may be used as a defense against liability for an occupational exposure that may result in the same outcome. It is difficult to refute such rebuttals because smoking is such a major factor in the risk of so many diseases.
- Smoking interacts, often strongly, with other exposures. The interactions are almost always in the direction of increased risk, and it is often difficult to know whether to attribute this increased risk to the cigarette habit or to the occupational exposure.
- Smoking is one of the few risk factors that is easy to quantify in the individual case. The ability to quantify risk precisely by number of cigarettes smoked per day makes it much harder to determine the

contribution of nonsmoking risk factors. As a consequence, smoking almost always emerges as carrying the most weight in analysis.

- Impairment and disability evaluation is more complicated when the claimant smokes. There is a natural tendency to blame most of the impairment in lung function on smoking because the relationship with the cigarette habit is well known and well quantified. Loss of lung function from other exposures is poorly characterized by comparison.
- Smoking carries a great deal of sociological and psychological weight. Smoking cessation is a major target of wellness programs in industry. For many years, nicotine addiction was not properly appreciated, and the smoking habit was considered a matter of personal character, first as an indication of "manliness" or sophistication and later as a test of strength of character necessary to break the habit. The recent societal stigmas against smoking have led to victim blaming, denial of health effects by smokers put on the defensive, and prejudicial attitudes, all of which may bias the assessment of an individual's medical condition.

Overview

Cigarette smoking on a massive scale is a comparatively recent phenomenon [3,4]. In the United States, per capita cigarette consumption climbed precipitously from 1914 to reach a peak of over 4000 cigarettes per adult per year in 1965. This rise was punctuated by dips during the Depression, following publicity on the causal relationship between smoking and lung cancer, and following the ban on broadcasting of tobacco-related advertising. Cigarette smoking has now declined to a level not seen since 1940, a per capita consumption of approximately 2000 cigarettes per adult per year. Women continued to increase their rates of smoking up to the late 1950s, while the rate for men was leveling off, and women's decline in cigarette smoking lagged behind that of men in subsequent decades. Teenage girls were the only demographically defined group in which cigarette smoking was rising during the early 1990s.

This overall picture masks a number of hidden trends. Women have always smoked less than men in the United States but are more susceptible to the effects of smoking-related exposures. Thus, for a given smoking history, women are more likely to develop chronic obstructive pulmonary disease (COPD) or lung cancer. In 1986, lung cancer matched and has since surpassed breast cancer as the leading cause of cancer deaths in women [3].

Cigarette smoking, as an exogenous, self-imposed toxic exposure, affects many of the same organs and causes many of the same diseases as other environmental exposures. Sorting out the contribution of smoking is therefore a very common problem in cases that involve the principal smoking-related cancers (i.e., lung, larynx, pancreas, and bladder), coronary artery disease, COPD, exacerbation of asthma, and peripheral vascular disease. (COPD is a shorthand term that includes emphysema and chronic bronchitis, singly or in combination, often with some degree of airways reactivity, either overt asthma or a less obvious contribution of asthma-like reversible airflow obstruction.)

Because of the long latency of many smoking-related health effects, particularly the cancers and COPD, past history is very important in assessing risk. A smoking-related health condition arising in a claim today easily may have been 20 years or more in the making. For individuals, the usual scale of assessing risk is the smoking history, which is quantified as "packs per day." Assuming 20 cigarettes per pack (there are 30 cigarettes per pack in Canada and the United Kingdom), a smoking history equivalent to 20 years at 1 pack per day is conventionally accepted as an unequivocal risk of chronic health effects. However, it is also accepted that many smokers experience health problems at much lower levels of exposure and that somewhat fewer people are highly resistant to the effects of cigarette smoke. Studies by Cohen et al. [5–7] in the 1970s demonstrated that family history plays a major role in determining individual risk for many health effects, after accounting for differences in smoking habits. In fact, there appears to be a familial constitutional susceptibility to both lung cancer and COPD. The genetic basis for susceptibility and resistance has been explored extensively, and undoubtedly we will have a biochemical explanation soon [8].

Cigarette smoking accelerates the loss of lung function (measured as the amount of air that can be moved in a forced expulsion of breath in 1 second) from the natural decline due to aging (about 30 ml/year after the twenties) and may double or triple this rate of loss. Some individuals lose lung function at a more rapid rate than others and are particularly susceptible to disease after the additional loss due to cigarette smoking pushes their lung function inexorably below normal (80% of predicted by race, age, and height). Reduced lung function may then drop below normal functional capacity, or the physiologic level required to sustain comfort and normal activity, causing impairment, disability, and ultimately, death. Thus every cigarette smoker is in a race against time, in which the loss of lung function is running against the risk of lung cancer or heart disease and both adverse conditions are running against the life span of the person. The winner will survive the length of his or her natural life without developing these outcomes, which would be inevitable if the smoker lived for a century or more. The loser will develop a smoking-related disorder and may die, perhaps prematurely, from it [9].

The pattern of increased risk tends to vary for the smoking-related outcomes. The risk of COPD appears to increase more or less in proportion to the smoking history, whereas the risk of lung cancer increases as a power function, meaning that it increases exponentially [3]. Thus the few persons at the extremes of the smoking habit, such as those who smoke more than 2 packs per day, may have a higher risk of lung cancer than other smoking-related outcomes. Intensive exposure also shortens the latency period of cancer, making it more likely that a cancer will appear in less than the 20 years commonly used as a rule of thumb for plausible latency.

Smoking and Occupation

Cigarette smoking is linked to occupation in highly specific ways:

- Smoking may be related to the duties of the job.
- Smoking is closely associated with socioeconomic status, which in turn is linked with occupation.
- Environmental tobacco smoke may be or may have been present in the workplace.
- Smoking may be a factor in the delivery of toxic substances such as contamination of cigarettes by lead dust.
- Smoking may add to the risk of a disease in addition to the contribution of occupational or environmental exposures.
- Smoking may be biologically interactive with occupational exposures and therefore contribute to the risk of occupational disease.
- Smoking may contribute proportionately to impairment in the individual case.

The National Health Interview Study (NHIS, 1997) provides a snapshot of current prevalence rates of smoking by occupation [4] (Table 10-1). These data have been presented publicly at a National Institute of Occupational Safety

Table 10-1. Prevalence Rates of Smoking for Selected Occupations (National Health Interview Survey, 1997)

Occupation	Percent (rounded)
Teachers (elementary)	8
Physicians	8
Accountants	14
Nurses	17
Secretaries	20
Bookkeepers	22
Sales	23
Managers, administrators	24
Cashiers	31
Nursing aides, orderlies	33
Janitors, cleaning workers	34
Financial managers	34
Cooks	40
Truck drivers	42
Waiters and waitresses	46
Roofers	60

and Health (NIOSH) workshop and are expected to be published in complete form shortly by the Office on Smoking and Health of the National Center for Chronic Disease Prevention and Health Promotion of the Centers for Disease Control and Prevention.

Smoking Related to the Job

Cigarette smoking and exposure to cigarette smoke are conditions of many occupations. Smoking is more than an addictive habit. It is also a complex social ritual in which people engage in reciprocal "gift giving" (lights and cigarette brands), exchange ("bumming" cigarettes), and sharing moments in a common activity. Increasingly, with social pressure against smoking in public, it may be a shared moment of relief (or even rebellion) among smokers who see themselves as stigmatized and oppressed. Smoking may be an integral part of the social networking and personal cultivation in occupations that require bonding and mutual trust, such as sales. Jobs requiring intense concentration or high intensity may have higher smoking rates than those which do not. Jobs that involve frequent exposure to noxious odors may provoke an attempt to mask the odor by smoking, much as nineteenth-century pathologists used to smoke cigars during autopsies. Smoking may reduce perceived discomfort and sensitivity to the odors or to other irritants in the short term. This may be one reason that roofers in the construction industry have such a high prevalence of cigarette smoking (60%) [4].

Cooks, truck drivers, waiters and waitresses, crane and hoist operators, nurse's aides, assemblers, and cashiers all demonstrate a higher prevalence of smoking (over 30%) than secretaries and clerks (less than 20%). This may reflect work organization factors such as the work setting, pace of work, and physical demands, or it may reflect the recruitment of people from a specific social class into these occupations. This dimension of the association between smoking and work requires further study.

Smoking is also part of the job responsibilities or expectations of a small number of occupations: tobacco store personnel often smoke conspicuously in their workplaces, as do bartenders. While smoking may not be part of the job description, it is often part of the expectations for an occupational role. Environmental tobacco smoke (ETS) is enriched in many carcinogens compared with mainstream cigarette smoke and has been associated with an increased rate of both lung cancer and heart disease [10]. Increasingly, public service occupations are being protected from ETS by the growing amount of state and local legislation to prohibit smoking in public places [11].

Smoking Related to Socioeconomic Status

The prevalence of cigarette smoking is clearly concentrated in the lower socioeconomic strata (SES) and is inversely correlated with educational attainment.

However, this is not absolute. Certain higher SES occupations associated with high stress levels, such as financial managers, have high smoking prevalence rates. Overall, however, blue-collar workers smoke more than white-collar workers and laborers more than professionals. NHIS data clearly show that this is the case, with overall percentages at 24% for white-collar workers and 39% for blue-collar workers. The NHIS data in Table 10-1 bear this out, with janitors, cleaners, and other lower SES occupations tending to show higher prevalence rates. There are, of course, other confounding factors such as race and sex. When age, sex, and education are adjusted, the difference is less than the crude rates suggest. Nevertheless, blue-collar workers still smoke as much as 50% more than their white-collar and farm counterparts [4].

In addition to being more likely to smoke, blue-collar workers also smoke more. Workers in lower SES occupations and with less educational attainment consume more cigarettes overall and tend to consume cigarettes with a higher nicotine content. They also have a lower rate of success when they try to quit smoking. In addition, more of them begin smoking at an early age (31% before age 16 compared with 24% for white-collar workers).

These differentials have great practical significance. Hazardous occupations, such as roofing, typically are low in status. Minorities and recent immigrants are disproportionately concentrated in lower SES occupations and often have higher cigarette smoking prevalence rates, depending on the subgroup. Workers in these high-risk groups therefore are at increased risk from both hazardous exposures and smoking. The gap in smoking behavior between blue-collar and white-collar workers also appears to be widening [4].

Smoking Contribution to Risk

Cigarette smoking may play a toxicologic role that modifies or adds to the effect of an occupational exposure because the cigarette is a vehicle for delivery of toxic substances to the mouth and lungs. The smoking habit has been associated with increased exposure to lead in workplaces where lead dust was present simply because of contamination of cigarettes. Polymer fume fever is a short-term, self-limited illness that was associated with contamination of burning cigarettes with particles of a fluorohydrocarbon polymer degraded by the heat. The degradation products inhaled with the cigarette smoke caused a flulike illness. The risk of contamination and exposure is an excellent reason for the prohibition of cigarette smoking in most industrial workplaces.

Smoking may add to the risk imposed by exposure to similar carcinogens and irritants. For example, tobacco smoke contains numerous chemical substances, but certain compounds, particularly the polycyclic aromatic hydrocarbons (PAHs), are produced in common with other products of combustion. These exposures occur in occupations such as firefighting and roofing. Effects that are probably dominated by exposure to this class of chemicals, such as the risk of lung cancer, are likely to show an additive risk when a worker both smokes and sustains exposure to the same substances from an occupational source. This may contribute to the high rate of lung cancer seen among roofers and may, in part, be responsible for obscuring the expected association that has been so difficult to demonstrate between lung cancer and occupation as a firefighter. Compared with cigarette smoking, the exposure to PAHs among roofers is high and may predominate, but the exposure among firefighters to PAHs is less and is more likely to be confounded.

Cigarette smoking is known to interact with a variety of occupational exposures in causing cancer. In toxicology, an *interaction* occurs when the effect of exposure to two substances is not merely the same as the sum of the two. A *positive interaction,* sometimes called *synergy,* occurs when the effect of one enhances the effect of the other out of proportion to what would be predicted by their individual effects. A *negative interaction* occurs when one exposure reduces the effect of another and in combination there is less of an effect than would be predicted.

The best known and best documented of these interactions with occupational exposures are for lung cancer. They include

- Asbestos, in which the interaction is strongly positive and the combination of cigarette smoking and asbestos exposure multiplies the risk disproportionately.
- Radon daughters, which are radionuclides that are produced by decay of radon and uranium. The interaction between radionuclide exposure and smoking is generally positive, but in certain circumstances associated with uranium mining it has been negative (probably because of increased bronchial clearance of radioactive particles).
- Silica, for which there is evidence that smoking disproportionately increases the risk of lung cancer in combination with exposure to silica, but not to the same degree as with asbestos. (Miners who smoke also may be at somewhat more risk for progression of silicosis.)

The interactive effects of smoking lead to several problems of interpretation. One is whether to attribute the interaction to the smoking or to the occupational exposure. Another issue is that in these situations of interaction, the yield of occupational cancers will be much higher among smokers than among nonsmokers. For example, is asbestos a hazard primarily to smokers, or is smoking a personal characteristic that enhances the risk of working with asbestos? Both are true. While occupational health standards in the past have regulated asbestos, tobacco smoke has not been considered an occupational exposure in its own right until recently.

Smoking as a Confounder

As noted earlier, smoking is a frequent confounder that interferes with the interpretation of studies in occupational epidemiology. Because many occupations, such as butchers, have shown an increased risk of lung cancer on the order of 1.5 (150%) in various studies, but do not involve an obvious exposure to a lung carcinogen, it is tempting to dismiss these elevations as a consequence of confounding by smoking [12]. After all, cigarette smoke is such a potent carcinogen and the exposure is so direct in personal smoking that one would expect the effects of smoking to outweigh most exposures in the workplace. While there is no doubt that cigarette smoking is the predominant cause of lung cancer, it can be demonstrated that differences in the prevalence of smoking are unlikely to explain doubled excess risk.

Fletcher and Ades [13] in 1984 were among the first to address this issue in their study of foundry workers by demonstrating that the confounding effect of smoking was not great enough to explain their observation of an increased relative risk for lung cancer greater than 2.0. Exaggerated concern over confounding by smoking continues to be a frequent criticism of studies of occupational exposure.

A simple calculation demonstrates why smoking prevalence alone generally cannot explain an elevation in risk of 2 or more. Consider a population in which the overall prevalence of smoking is 30%. A group of workers drawn from this population has a doubling of risk of lung cancer compared with that expected from rates in the general population. What would be the prevalence of smoking among these workers in order to achieve this result due to confounding alone?

Assuming conservatively that the risk of lung cancer is 10 times greater among smokers than among nonsmokers, that 30% of the population are smokers, and that 70% are not, the problem is as follows:

$$2.0 = \text{observed/expected} = [1(1 - x) + 10x]/[1(0.7) + 10\ (0.3)]$$

where x is the proportion of smokers among the workers. Solving for x, the answer is 71%. Therefore, within this workforce, the prevalence of smoking would have to be more than twice that in the population as a whole. This magnitude of difference in smoking prevalence is highly unlikely and much higher than the prevalences observed in the NHIS survey or in past occupational surveys. A more modest relative risk of 1.5 would require a prevalence of 50%, which is possible but also unlikely. Changing the equation to higher relative risks quickly leads to the absurd conclusion that there are more smokers than there are workers.

Apportioning Smoking Effects

It would be very desirable, for purposes of compensation, to have a standard method to assess the relative contribution of various occupational and avocational exposures of personal cigarette smoking, of other types of smoking (such as pipes and cigars), and of environmental tobacco smoke. Unfortunately, state-of-the-art research tools do not permit more than a crude assessment at this time.

Currently, there is no technology that allows one to assess the contribution of smoking in retrospect. Although biomarkers such as serum and urinary cotinine or nicotine levels and adducts allow the detection and quantification of smoking-related exposures in the recent past, there is nothing on the horizon that will provide a biomarker for distant exposures and health effects in the individual case.

This means that for the foreseeable future, apportionment of the effects of cigarette smoking will require judgment and interpretation of the epidemiologic literature. It will be an inexact art, based as much as possible on generalizations that come as close as possible to the circumstances of the individual case.

Conclusion

Smoking is unique as a confounder in assessing the risk of cancer and other health outcomes because of its strength and prevalence. However, active or passive smoking as a risk factor also may be work-related. Tobacco smoke may independently or interactively contribute to the disease outcome and disability. It is too simple to apportion smoking-associated health effects to smoking alone when significant occupational exposures are involved. Smoking should be treated as an important risk factor among many, not as a reason for automatic exclusion or denial of a claim.

References

1. Gray N. Tobacco products. In: Greenwald P, Kramer BS, Weed DL (eds). *Cancer Prevention and Control*. New York: Marcel Dekker, 1995. Pp 353–370.

2. Pinkerton KE, Grimes SH, Schenker MB. Interaction of tobacco smoking with occupational and environmental factors. In: Harber P, Schenker MB, Balmes JR (eds). *Occupational and Environmental Respiratory Disease*. St. Louis: Mosby, 1996. Pp 827–834.

3. Samet JM. Lung cancer. In: Greenwald P, Kramer BS, Weed DL (eds). *Cancer Prevention and Control*. New York: Marcel Dekker, 1995. Pp 353–370.

4. Pederson LL, Giovino GA, Trosclair A. Prevalence of selected cigarette smoking behaviors by occupation in the United States. Presented at Work, Smoking and Health: A NIOSH Scientific Workshop, Washington, June 15–16, 2000.

5. Cohen BH, Ball WC, Bias WB, et al. A genetic-epidemiologic study of chronic obstructive pulmonary disease: I. Study design and preliminary observations. *Johns Hopkins Med J* 1975;137:95–104.

6. Cohen BH. Is pulmonary dysfunction the common denominator for the multiple effects of cigarette smoking? *Lancet* 1978;2(8098):1024–1027.

7. Cohen CH. Chronic obstructive pulmonary disease: challenge in genetic epidemiology. *Am J Epidemiol* 1980;112:273–288.

8. Cook JT, Crystal RG. The genetic basis of lung cancer. In: Crystal RG, West JB, Weibel ER, Barnes PJ (eds). *The Lung: Scientific Foundations.* Philadelphia: Lippincott-Raven, 1997. Pp 2589–2597.

9. MacNee W. Chronic bronchitis and emphysema. In: Seaton A, Seaton D, Leitch G (eds). *Crofton and Douglas's Respiratory Diseases.* Oxford, England: Blackwell, 2000. Pp 620–621.

10. NIOSH. Environmental Tobacco Smoke in the Workplace: Lung Cancer and Other Health Effects. *Curr Intell Bull* 1991;54:18.

11. National Cancer Institute. *State and Local Legislative Action to Reduce Tobacco Use* (Smoking and Tobacco Control Monograph No.11). Bethesda, MD: U.S. Dept. of Health and Human Services, National Institutes of Health, National Cancer Institute (NIH Publication no. 00-4804), August 2000.

12. Guidotti TL, Baser M, Goldsmith JR. Comparing risk estimates from occupational disease monitoring data. *Public Health Rev* 1987;15:1–27.

13. Fletcher AC, Ades A. Lung cancer mortality in a cohort of English foundry workers. *Scand J Work Environ Health* 1984;10(1):7–16.

11

Apportionment

TEE L. GUIDOTTI

Workers' compensation boards (WCBs) in all jurisdictions have faced an expanding challenge in the management of claims related to occupational disease. The adjudication of occupational diseases is often more difficult than the adjudication of occupational injuries. Questions of causation, the presence of multiple risk factors, and modifications of the characteristic presentation of occupational diseases may greatly complicate adjudication.

The basic tenants of workers' compensation require that there be some effort to discriminate between occupational and nonoccupational causes of disease and injury. Although this can be exceedingly difficult and in some cases impossible in practice, the imperative to consider apportionment is an integral part of the philosophy of workers' compensation.

Confronted continually by such issues, workers' compensation agencies have considered *apportionment by cause* as a means for dealing with these problems. Apportionment by cause is, in essence, an attempt to assess how much of the damage that led to a disease or impairment was caused by one factor compared with others. Ideally, WCBs would like to compensate only that portion of a claim which was likely to reflect work-related causation. In principle, this would be very much like apportioning impairment, except that the underlying cause of the disorder is being considered rather than its expression in functional impairment.

The benefits of apportionment, if it could be quantified accurately and usefully, are obvious: Adjudication may be simpler (especially if formulas could be worked out for relative proportions under certain assumptions), adjudication may be fairer to employers and some injured workers (although not necessarily the case being apportioned), financial resources would not be depleted compensating for nonoccupational disease, incentives might exist for workers to take responsibility for their own health, the burden of disease would be more fairly shared among health care agencies (in Canada, the provincial health insurance programs, the WCBs, and the specialized agencies for cancer and mental health), and the relative contribution to disability benefits for permanent impairment could be divided up and allocated to different payers, such as pension plans and private long-term disability insurance.

Unfortunately, the limitations of apportionment are also readily apparent:

- There is an inherent lack of precision in determining degree of apportionment.
- Unverifiable assumptions are required to determine apportionment.
- Partial benefits based on apportionment may not meet the total needs of individual claimants.
- Agencies may resist cost sharing or may apply their own criteria, allowing some claimants to fall "through the cracks."
- Apportionment performed inaccurately may significantly distort reporting of occupational disease.
- Apportionment based on population estimates may not fit the individual case.
- Inconsistent application of apportionment in some cases and not others may lead to inequities in the management of claims for injured workers.
- Apportionment of many claims for small contributions to risk or impairment may result in numerous small payments that drain available funds and cause administrative difficulties.
- Workers may be subjected to policies that "blame the victim" for health outcomes.
- Compensation benefits are remote and probably inconsequential in motivating health-related behavior.

Thus apportionment, even under the best of circumstances, is not a panacea.

The Concept of Apportionment

Apportionment by Cause

Apportionment by cause is the assignment in an individual case of a relative estimate of the contribution to an outcome, such as a multifactorial disease, of several risk factors or potential causal exposures that are present in the case and are known to be associated with the outcome. This is sometimes called *apportionment of harm* in the legal literature [1].

Basically, apportionment by cause is a process of allocating to each physical cause a relative weight proportional to the contribution of that cause to the sequence of events that led to the outcome, whatever the magnitude of the outcome itself. For example, if exposure to heat, dehydration, lack of worker adaptation, and intense physical activity all contribute to a myocardial infarction in a case of heat stroke, apportionment by cause seeks to determine the degree to which each external cause (occupational demands of the job, occupational requirements to work in heat, occupationally associated access to water or lack thereof, and nonoccupational underlying disease) may have acted on an intrinsic mechanism (the unadapted worker) to produce the outcome (heat stroke), whether or not the heat stroke led to a myocardial infarction.

Apportionment by cause may then be used to assess the relative contribution of each factor to final disability. A particular cause may be "necesssary," "individually sufficient," "substantial and cumulatively sufficient," or "barely substantial but cumulatively sufficient."

Causation is a difficult abstract concept. There are many definitions and degrees of causation. The term *cause* is used here to mean an exposure out of the norm of daily living that initiates or allows to come to completion a sequence of events that produces a disorder. Risk factors may be proximate causes or markers closely linked to proximate causes. Confirmed risk factors are described in various studies as closely linked to the disease outcome. They may be sufficient to produce the outcome either singly or may act in combination with other risk factors. This is, of necessity, a probabilistic (or "stochastic") definition because most such factors associated with disease outcomes are subject to a degree of uncertainty due in part to measurement error, incomplete understanding, variability in individual susceptibility, and the nature of the inherently random process.

At some point, an arbitrary decision must be made with respect to how proximate in the chain of events the risk factor has to be before it is considered too remote to be a *cause*. For example, are advertisements for cigarettes a cause of lung cancer? Historically not, even though they affect smoking behavior, which controls cigarette smoke dosage, and cigarette smoke dosage is a proximate cause of lung cancer. Also, biological mechanisms such as hereditary predispositions are not counted as "causes in the usual sense" [2] but may be considered risk factors because they can be measured by indicators, and their presence or absence affects the means by which other factors operate. However, both factors are clearly *causes* in the general sense because under certain circumstances they may be necessary to cause the outcome.

The concept of apportionment by cause is not the same as assessing the general contribution of different causal factors in a multifactorial disease such as coronary artery disease (e.g., cholesterol, blood pressure, serum high-density lipoproteins, activity level, obesity, family history, and diabetes). This assessment of contribution is abstracted from the findings of epidemiologic studies, with the mechanism of each individual risk factor validated in animal or toxicologic studies. (Laboratory studies of multiple causal factors acting in combination are relatively rare, difficult to perform, and even more difficult to extrapolate to humans.) Apportionment, in contrast, must be performed on the individual case, which may vary greatly or in unknown ways from the population as a whole. Often, the individual differences cannot be determined with certainty, and in such cases, epidemiologic data may be used to derive an estimate of the relative contribution of a risk factor in an individual claim. However, this is a derived estimate, not to be confused with the apportionment of impairment or disability that can be done by specific measurement in the individual case.

Apportionment of Fault (and Damages)

Perhaps the most common use of the term *apportionment* is in assigning an estimate of the blame, fault, or contribution to injury in a tort case for each of the parties that may have contributed to the injury—in other words, the defendants. The concept of fault is the essential key to the assessment of damages in tort litigation. In particular, apportionment for contributory negligence, assessing whether the plaintiff may have contributed to the injury by failing to protect himself or herself, is a subject of legal debate with a history dating to Roman times [3]. Apportionment in this context may be conducted several ways, but the most common approaches are "comparative negligence," in which responsibility for damages is divided between the plaintiff and the defendant, and "joint and several liability," in which the share apportioned to the defendants as a group is distributed among the various defendants according to each one's share of liability.

The essential difference between apportionment of fault and apportionment by cause is that *apportionment of fault* assumes responsibility on the part of a human agency or defendant who had responsibility in the situation. In contrast, apportionment by cause is an estimate of the relative magnitude of contribution of a set of physical causes or conditions, without regard to the intent of or circumstances of exposure. While apportionment of fault is almost entirely an issue of damages, the two types of apportionment are indivisible in practice. In the arena of workers' compensation, apportionment of fault is not relevant because workers' compensation is a "no fault" system that explicitly rejects joint and several liability in favor of a social policy of pooled risk in the common interest of employers and workers [4,5].

Apportionment of Impairment

In the assessment of functional impairment, there may be more than one injury or condition that limits use of a body part or that contributes to total impairment. The most common example in workers' compensation is a work-related injury followed by another nominally unrelated work-related reinjury (sometimes related because of weakness or incomplete recovery) or an injury to an individual who already had an impairment as a result of a pre-existing condition unrelated to work, such as arthritis or nonoccupational back pain. In this situation, the practice is to assess the contribution to impairment of the relevant work-related injury alone, usually by taking total impairment and subtracting the degree of impairment that already existed, if this is known or can be estimated.

The essential difference between apportionment of impairment and apportionment by cause is that *apportionment of impairment* is based on a widely accepted system of impairment rating that relates to functional capacity and therefore outcome, whereas apportionment by cause is an attempt to assign relative weights to those factors which contributed to the outcome, whatever the magnitude of the outcome may be.

Apportionment of impairment is primarily a concern in the assessment of secondary disability following a reinjury or second injury or in the context of an aggravational injury acting on a pre-existing condition.

Apportionment of Disability

Apportionment of disability is the same as apportionment of impairment after the impairment rating is converted into a disability rating. Disability reflects more than lack of functional capacity; it also reflects the social context (e.g., the job market) in which the claimant functions and the implications of the impairment for employment. The apportionment of disability is the same as apportionment of impairment except that these factors are taken into account, and disability is the index rather than impairment rating. Therefore, the relative degrees apportioned to each injury will be the same.

Apportionment of disability is fundamental to managing a series of claims by the same individual. It is dealt with within various workers' compensation systems in one of three ways: through the "full-responsibility rule" (i.e., the last employer bears full responsibility for disability resulting from the last significant injury), through the apportionment of liability between the original and later employers based on history or risk of injury (with obvious implications for repetitive strain injuries), or through second-injury funds [6].

Apportionment by cause and apportionment of disability are intimately connected in cases of total disability or total incapacity for work because the employment market cannot accommodate a partial disability. For instance, the Supreme Court of North Carolina initially argued [7] that the employer must pay disability compensation only for that portion of an employee's ability to work that is caused, accelerated, or aggravated by an occupational disease.

Apportionment by Cause

Basic Concepts

As stated previously, *apportionment* is a process of determining relative contributions to an outcome in an individual case. *Attribution,* as it is typically used in epidemiology, is determination of the magnitude of contribution to risk in a population (measured by the attributable risk). Colloquially, attribution also may be used in reference to an individual case but usually in the same sense as *presumption;* that is, a case of lung cancer is "attributed" to smoking or asbestos but not both. Thus, in usual usage, *attribution* refers to a particular putative cause, and *apportionment* refers to the process of determining the relative contributions of different possible or putative causes.

In theory, apportionment by cause may appear to be simple. Some idea of the relative contribution of various causes to a disease or health outcome should be available through epidemiologic or clinical investigations [1]. Comparing each risk factor with the others, it should be possible to approximate the percentage contribution of each to the final outcome and thereby to apportion by cause. Causes that are occupational may then, in theory, be separated from those due to lifestyle and those due to environmental exposures other than in the workplace. The fraction that is due to occupation then would be the apportioned responsibility for work-related hazards [8].

However, this simple model of risk-based apportionment has been criticized because it apportions risk based on exposure, associating this with probable outcome, rather than cause of actual harm in a particular case [9]. In order to apportion by cause properly, one must progressively refine the risk derived for groups of people as they constitute the best approximation to the individual and then further individualize the estimate to apply to a particular case.

CATEGORIES OF CAUSATION. In order to discuss apportionment clearly, it is necessary to distinguish among different causal relationships [2]. The literature on causation in the disciplines of philosophy, law, and epidemiology is enormous, and no attempt will be made here to survey the principles of causation (see Chap. 9). However, in legal terms it is useful to distinguish among several different types of causal relationships that are significant in apportionment [1,10]:

- *Proximate causes.* These are the immediate factors that directly resulted in the injury. They are distinguished from *remote causes,* in which the sequence of events leading to the injury is too distant or involved to be considered on a practical basis.
- *Necessary causes.* These are causes that are required for the injury to occur. The rule of thumb is that "but for" the cause, the outcome would not have occurred. However, a necessary cause does not inevitably or invariably result in the outcome. It is only a requirement, not an absolute determinant. In apportionment by cause, confusion often arises because an occupational cause may have been necessary to produce a certain degree of disability but not sufficient to explain all the disability. When disability is total or is incapacitating insofar as employment is concerned, "but for" the occupational cause, the degree of disability may not be total, and the injured worker may be able to return to employment. This situation reflects the nature of employability, however, and reflects

rated disability compared with fitness to work. In principle, the cause may still have been necessary but not necessarily sufficient in itself.

- *Sufficient causes.* Sufficient causes are enough in themselves to explain the outcome. They are, by definition, necessary when they occur alone, but when they occur with other substantial causes, they may not then be "necessary." Several sufficient causes may explain the same outcome, and in such a situation, apportionment is particularly attractive.

- *Partial causes.* Partial causes are those which may contribute to the damage but are neither necessary nor sufficient. Partial causes assume some cumulative injury that can be divided among different contributing causes. A subset of partial causes is *successive causes,* in which similar acts or exposures occur over a period of time to create a cumulative injury.

To illustrate these categories of causes, consider a middle-aged carpet cleaner with undetected coronary artery disease who smokes and is exposed to carbon monoxide from a poorly ventilated air compressor and who has a myocardial infarction on the job. Depending on the level of heart disease, this may be necessary, but it obviously was not sufficient, because the worker's heart attack did not occur before. The carbon monoxide exposure may have been sufficient because even people with a low risk of cardiac disease may succumb at very high concentrations, but it may not have been necessary if the carbon monoxide from the cigarette smoke accumulated to levels high enough to trigger myocardial ischemia. The cigarette smoke may or may not have been necessary, depending on whether its contribution of carbon monoxide tipped the balance, and it was certainly not sufficient because the worker had smoked before and had not had the outcome and because the contribution of carbon monoxide would have been marginal compared with the compressor exhaust; thus cigarette smoke was a partial cause. The cigarettes smoked prior to the incident may be considered successive causes to the extent that they may have added to the cumulative risk of heart disease.

LEGAL STANDARDS FOR ACCEPTING APPORTIONMENT BY CAUSE. Legal theory regarding apportionment is driven largely by the feasibility of assessing injury in the particular situation. In the United States, the legal issues surrounding apportionment have been highly refined [1]. Shuter, explaining one key federal decision, describes the general situation: "In cases where there is a single harm, the [appeals court decision] authorizes apportionment only if 'there is a reasonable basis for determining the contribution of each cause to a single harm.' . . . [When] two independent factors cause an indivisible harm, the court can allow apportionment as long as it can be effected without injustice to any of the parties" [11].

Under this legal decision, therefore, the feasibility of apportionment by cause is based on whether the available methods allow it to be done reasonably accurately and on whether the outcome is fair to the parties. In workers' compensation, the need for establishing causation as work-related has pushed the issue of apportionment ahead of the scientific ability to estimate contribution to risk. The epidemiologic approach that has served for establishing causation has been extended naturally to address issues of apportionment in causation. By the legal rule articulated above, this historical fact has pushed workers' compensation ahead of the law in relying on epidemiology and accepting its analysis without assessing fairness to all parties. Because workers' compensation exists as a substitute for the process of litigation but not to eliminate issues of fairness, this is an anomaly that needs to be addressed. While issues of fairness are beyond the scope of this chapter, issues of accuracy in apportionment are sufficiently problematic to call the rigor of apportionment into question.

The alternative to apportionment by cause is to force the adjudicating party (the judge or jury in tort litigation) to allocate all the responsibility to a single party responsible for one contributing cause [11]. In the workers' compensation system, only two candidates are available to assume the full, undivided liability, either the employer or the claimant. In some occupational fields, such as contractor services and the building trades, it may be possible to apportion employers' contributions to the single accepted cause among several employers if the same exposure occurred in the same job category at different times; this is apportionment of successive causes to a cumulative injury [12].

PRACTICAL DIFFICULTIES WITH APPORTIONMENT BY CAUSE. The problem with apportionment by cause is that its effectiveness in practice is determined by both the theoretical and practical limitations of available methods. Available methods are subject to considerable uncertainty for the following reasons: (1) they are blind with respect to hazards that are not yet recognized or that remain controversial, and (2) they are subject to challenge on the basis of which data are selected, data availability, and how data derived from populations can be applied to any one person. These issues are not unique to apportionment—they underlie all of epidemiology, for example—but they are exacerbated in this context because uncertain estimates are being compared with other uncertain estimates, so the uncertainties are compounded.

These limitations might be tolerable, however, if they provided at least a rough guide for apportionment, as crude as halves, quarters, and bits rather than accuracy to the second decimal [9]. As will be described below, the method that seems to do this best is paradoxically the one that is most subjective, not the approach that is most quantitative.

AGGRAVATION AND SUSCEPTIBILITY. A special case of apportionment by cause is assessment of the relative contribution of an occupational cause in situations where there is a pre-existing disorder. In such cases, a disease or condition that does not cause total impairment is made worse by the occupational exposure to the extent that significant additional disability results. The aggravation may be temporary or permanent. Although both may result in lost time from work and impairment, it is obvious that the latter is of most importance in the compensation setting. In at least one important American case, this problem was further divided into two situations [7].

In the first situation, the pre-existing condition was latent or, at least, not incapacitating. The occupational exposure made the condition worse or in some way added to the effects of the condition so that the resulting disability was much greater than would have occurred with the natural history of the pre-existing condition. (For example, a person with well-controlled asthma working in a workplace with solvent or isocyanate exposure may find that the irritant effects or the development of sensitization to isocyanate makes the asthma more difficult to manage, and therefore, the capacity to work at that occupation is lost.) In this situation, the apportionment theory holds that while the pre-existing condition may have contributed to the final disability, it did so because of the effects of the occupational exposure. Apportionment is not considered appropriate in this situation because the workplace exposure acts to "transform latent infirmity into disability" and is thus completely responsible for the disability. (This is the "but for" argument.)

In the second situation, the pre-existing condition contributes independently to the resulting disability. Then the issue becomes one of apportioning the resulting impairment (on which apportionment of disability is subsequently based) because the occupational cause was not the only factor that converted the pre-existing condition into a disabling condition.

These two situations are to be distinguished from the problem of susceptibility. *Susceptibility*, in this context, represents a potential to be injured by an occupational cause, not a pre-existing condition that is already manifest. Under virtually all systems of workers' compensation and employment legislation, the rule is that the employer takes the worker as he or she comes and that, once employed, every worker may expect protection to the degree that he or she requires it. If an injury results in disability in one susceptible worker that would not occur in another, the fact of individual susceptibility does not relieve the employer of responsibility. This is a variant of the "thin skull" or "eggshell skull plaintiff" rule in tort litigation [13]. This common-law rule states that a victim of an injury does not share responsibility with the party responsible for the injury just because the victim was unusually susceptible—the defendant bears all the liability of a tort regardless of whether the magnitude of the consequences could be foreseen.

Thus apportionment cannot be applied to the theoretical contribution of susceptibility states. This exempts consideration of any hereditary or involuntarily acquired personal characteristics as a cause of disability, such as family history or a susceptibility to infection due to compromised immune function. The key here is whether the condition under discussion can be described as an illness, in which case *aggravation* theory applies, or as a latent constitutional condition. One distinguishing factor may be whether the individual is aware of the condition or could have changed it with effort. A test of such awareness could be whether a reasonable person could have gone through life entirely unaware of the susceptibility state if he or she had not been informed. Another test may be whether the susceptibility state reflects a condition that would never result in illness unless acted on by an external factor, such as exposure to a carcinogen or to an infectious agent. For example, a worker with a family history compatible with one of several specific "cancer prone" phenotypes may be more susceptible to the effects of carcinogens than another worker without such a family history. If he or she developed cancer after working with a known carcinogen, the cancer-prone family history would be irrelevant for purposes of apportionment. The presence of a susceptibility state would only serve to make it even more likely that the occupational exposure caused the cancer.

A susceptibility state, in this context, should be differentiated from a subclinical pre-existing condition (one not apparent to the person nor obviously detectable on a medical evaluation). If the condition is likely to lead to a disease or to impairment by itself, without requiring the action of an external agent to progress, it is logically a pre-existing condition in this context. (For example, HIV infection would be considered a pre-existing condition in this sense, not a susceptibility state, even in the absence of clinical AIDS. If, for example, an HIV-positive health care worker were infected with tuberculosis due to exposure in the hospital workplace and subsequently developed tuberculosis within a few years, the case probably would best be dealt with on an aggravational basis. Left to its own natural progression, the pre-existing HIV infection would be expected to cause impairment resulting in disability without the need for an external cause. It is an acquired characteristic that predisposes to impaired host defenses and to tuberculosis. Because most persons with intact immunity do not develop clinical tuberculosis so soon after exposure, it is most likely that it would not have occurred but for the pre-existing condition.

It is not clear that the same logic of susceptibility states can be applied to conditions that reflect lifestyle choices or voluntary exposures, even when they do not result in obvious clinical illness. These are voluntarily assumed, as in the case of smoking, and typically lead to at least some impairment or would as part of the natural history of exposure. Thus a cigarette smoker without overt clinical respiratory disease may not be entitled to argue that his or her cigarette smoking made him or her more constitutionally susceptible to the bronchoconstrictive effects of organic dusts. A claim from a cigarette smoker with a mild cough could, however, be construed as an aggravation of chronic bronchitis. This is unlikely to result in significant disability, except perhaps in a glassblower.

Assuming that voluntarily acquired characteristics represent susceptibility states would in effect lead to absolving claimants from any personal responsibility in which the effect of any occupational exposure could be demonstrated. The theory is that the worker (in this case) was not "whole" at the time of exposure and that the employer is responsible only for the harm that may have been done in the course of employment and has an obligation to the claimant only insofar as required to restore the claimant to whatever functioning state would have occurred without the occupational exposure. The complication in workers' compensation is that the "harm" is measured as loss of capacity to work and that the contribution of the work-related exposure may have turned a partial nonoccupational disability into a total one [7]. However, in this situation, the claimant has already adopted a voluntary risk, and logic compels apportionment because the claimant has contributed to his or her own risk. This interpretation in fact has been adopted by some American courts [13].

The Epidemiologic Approach

A rational approach to apportionment by cause might be to apportion by the contribution of each risk factor to disease outcome using epidemiologic studies. This approach is actually highly complex because risk estimates are uncertain, describe the experience of a population (not the risk of an individual), and do not act in isolation.

Epidemiologic studies measure the risk in a population that is associated with exposure to a risk factor, itself either a presumed determinant of the disease outcome or a marker for some other determinant. These risk estimates are invaluable as an indication of the direction and magnitude of an association between the risk factor and the outcome, but they are not necessarily valid when applied to individual members of the population. In the absence of any information specific to the individual or a well-defined subgroup, the population risk estimate only represents the single best estimate of what the risk would be for members of the group chosen at random. Moreover, although risks derived from populations may provide estimates for an individual, any given individual may not approximate the "average" of a population under study. Additionally, population estimates are dynamic; risk levels in industry change as new technology and methods are introduced, and different populations may show strikingly different risk profiles. For example, Ontario gold miners once showed marked elevations in their risk for lung cancer and silicosis, presumably due to silica exposure, but these findings have not been replicated since the late 1950s. Furthermore, epidemiologic estimates of risk are not consistently accurate or robust. In fact, risk estimates vary greatly and often have wide confidence intervals; they are also unavailable for many chronic morbid outcomes such as chronic nonmalignant respiratory diseases that cannot be determined from mortality statistics.

The best estimate of risk derived from an epidemiologic study applicable to a particular case is the risk associated with the age, sex, and duration of exposure (and level of exposure, if such information is available) that most closely approximates the claimant and his or her experience. Unfortunately, most published studies cannot support analysis at this level of detail because the results are not reported in sufficient detail. Furthermore, the estimates become very uncertain (because of small numbers) when broken down in this manner. Given this limitation, it is common practice, but not strictly correct, for the risk estimate for the total population to be used indiscriminately, applying it to the individual without taking other characteristics into account.

The risk estimate applies to the population as a whole and represents only an estimate for any given member of that population. A member of the population may share the mean or average characteristics of the population, but usually, most will not. A risk estimate derived from the mean for a whole population will not necessarily apply to most of its members, some of whom will be very different from the mean of these characteristics, and the mean itself may be influenced by a few extreme cases. It is known that the best estimate of the absolute risk for one person of developing a disorder is approximately the mean risk for the population as a whole for "rare" diseases, such as cancers, but not necessarily for common diseases [14]. For common disorders, there may be even greater uncertainty surrounding the best estimate.

The risk estimate is usually expressed in terms of relative risk, as a ratio of the risk of the population exposed to a risk factor under study compared with an unexposed population. However, this is not the most useful number in apportioning risk by cause. What one would like to know is the relative contribution of each cause to the total excess risk of the outcome, or what might be called the *proportionate attributable risk*. In epidemiologic terms, this is the fraction represented by the attributable risk of each risk factor over the total excess or attributable risk for the population, which is almost never known. Usually the best one can do is compare relative attributable risks (basically, the relative risk minus 1) for each suspected cause or, more crudely, the relative magnitude of the relative risks for each suspected cause. This is not very satisfactory because every significant risk factor is not always accounted for in any one study, and risk factors are likely to be confounded in any one study. Often, one must use figures from more than one study, presuming that the estimates are reasonably accurate. In short, the proportional attributable risk is not usually available, so instead one must compare risk estimates from known causes, often from different studies.

In addition to these theoretical problems, a number of practical problems are associated with using epidemiologic estimates of risk to apportion risk by cause:

- *Risk estimates are uncertain because of statistical error* (and usually are expressed with confidence intervals). How does one take this uncertainty into account in apportioning risk by cause?

- *Different studies often produce different risk estimates.* How does one decide which to accept?
- *Risk changes over time in most situations.* How does one take into account change, especially when a follow-up study is not available?
- *"Risk factors" are often markers for another exposure that is more important as a cause* (e.g., alcohol is associated with lung cancer risk because people who drink are likely to smoke). How can this be taken into account, especially if there is uncertainty or the problem has not been studied?
- *Because of problems with statistical power, a large number of studies are unable to find an elevated risk that truly exists* (especially for rare diseases). Does one therefore ignore negative studies or count them and risk diluting the estimate of the real risk that is more accurately estimated in positive studies?
- *Meta-analysis gives a summary or average risk estimate for several studies combined* (weighted by the contribution to the overall estimate of their populations). How does one deal with negative studies with low power, outlier studies with exceptional results, and the usual absence of exposure data needed to link exposure and response?

These problems essentially preclude the use of epidemiologic findings to make fine distinctions and careful calculations of apportionment by cause. However useful, they are at best estimates and rough guides. Therefore, epidemiologic estimation of risk cannot go beyond an imprecise ranking of causes.

On the other hand, the value of epidemiologic studies is in the identification of risk factors and the "order of magnitude" of their effect in a population. What is true for the population may be the best guess for the individual but only in the absence of more specific information.

The Individualized Approach

Another approach is to individualize the risk estimate by taking into account all the factors relevant to the individual claimant. This approach can be done in two ways: (1) by attempting to isolate the best applicable epidemiologic risk estimate by breaking down or adjusting the risk estimate based on the claimant's personal characteristics or (2) by identifying personal risk factors and building a case for or against them being sufficiently substantial in magnitude to influence risk.

The approach of adjusting the epidemiologic risk estimate to the profile of the claimant when data are available from relevant studies was described above. The major problem is that risk estimates are often broken down by age and sex and exposure duration but only occasionally by all three or by other factors of interest, such as smokers/nonsmokers. Statistical uncertainty usually results in wide confidence intervals that make acceptance of the risk estimate difficult. A wide confidence interval suggests more than statistical error; it means that there may be wide variability in the underlying distribution as well. Some of this variability may come from characteristics that are unrecognized.

Building a risk profile from individual characteristics of the claimant is more difficult. Usually quantitative estimates of risk are not available, and thus, comparing likely contribution to personal risk requires judgment. The most important personal characteristic is usually age, especially for cancer and heart disease, and age-specific risk estimates are available for most common diseases. The age-specific risks associated with cigarette smoking are also available for many common diseases. Risks associated with occupational exposures may be available from relevant epidemiologic studies but are subject to many of the limitations described earlier.

One must then factor in family history, lifestyle, and other pertinent characteristics for which risk estimates are not knowable. In practice, this means a judgment call in adjusting risk up or down in the individual case and in comparing relative contributions to the outcome.

The result is an uncertain mix of defensible quantitative risk estimates compared with qualitative, sometimes subjective risk patterns. Clinicians may be better able to adjust a risk estimate up or down compared with the epidemiologically derived risk than they are in guessing the absolute risk. At the very least, they are able to individualize the risk profile and to point out how the individual claimant or patient differs from the group mean. Although it is attractive to place greater emphasis on quantitative risk estimates, these may be misleading because of poorly characterized risk factors and wide confidence limits. For example, family history is known to be a major risk factor for lung cancer, particularly in the presence of smoking. However, family history is much more difficult to quantify, and so lung cancer risks are almost always figured on the bases of age and cigarette smoking alone.

Because of all these drawbacks, individualized risk apportionment may be considered an informal, or subjective, approach to the problem. Although it has advantages in flexibility compared with quantitative approaches, it is always subject to challenges of clinical judgment. Its principal drawback is that no systematic verifiable method is available. One cannot confirm or reject the method scientifically, regardless of the subjective confidence one may have in the conclusion. Thus the individualized approach must be considered a belief or a social norm rather than a quantifiable method. As long as the social norm is consistent and different adjudicators reach consistent conclusions, this may have some acceptability.

The Toxicologic Approach

Toxicologic methods using animals or human volunteers help to identify health risks associated with specific exposures and have a great advantage over epidemiologic methods in that they can be performed as controlled experiments. So-called in vitro or test tube methods are very specific and informative in characterizing the potential for certain outcomes such as genotoxicity and carcinogenicity but have little direct relevance to human exposures. Experimental studies on animals are extremely valuable and yield important information on the mechanism of toxicity, but they cannot be extrapolated easily to human effects. They are generally most useful in establishing what may happen, the mechanisms of toxicity, and the rough magnitude of dose required to produce a toxic effect. Experimental clinical toxicologic studies on human beings cannot be conducted at toxic doses and are of little help in assessing contribution to disease outcomes. Anecdotal or descriptive studies of occupational or accidental toxicity in humans are very useful in defining possible health outcomes and give almost the only relevant human information available on toxicity thresholds for most toxic chemicals. However, they are usually incomplete in their documentation and only involve a small number of individuals, often without precise quantification of the exposure level associated with the outcome. Because of these limitations, standard toxicologic methods are of little help in apportioning by cause despite their usefulness in other ways. (Boston [9] presents a perceptive analysis of the strengths and weaknesses of toxicology from a legal perspective.)

Quantitative risk assessment is a method used in environmental studies to estimate the possible risk associated with low levels of exposure to a particular hazard. In theory, it is well suited for apportionment by cause, and calculations have been made for human health risks following exposure to many chemicals and physical hazards. However, quantitative risk assessment is extremely uncertain, and estimates of risk may vary by orders of magnitude. Risk assessments are very dependent on underlying assumptions, on extrapolations from often-limited animal toxicology data, and on estimates of dose. Moreover, the risk estimates are derived from either epidemiologic data or (more often) data from experimental animal populations and are population risk estimates, not individual risk estimates. The correct interpretation of estimates derived from quantitative risk assessment is that these estimates describe the highest risk likely to occur in a population given a certain level of exposure, not the most likely outcome associated with a particular occupation in which an exposure might occur. Thus, despite its apparent promise and its demonstrated utility in environmental policy, quantitative risk assessment is not very well suited to apportionment by cause.

In the future, technology may help refine individual apportionment by cause. Biomarkers of personal susceptibility and of exposure may, separately and together, allow a more precise risk profile of an individual to be derived, even after the disease has occurred. This would allow one to apportion risk more accurately in a complex case. However, no such tests have been validated for this purpose, nor are any available for general use at present. It is probable that the complexity of the problem will defeat efforts to fully characterize risk using biomarkers. Within the foreseeable future, biomarkers are likely to become available individually for selected risk factors. They are not likely to become available any time soon as part of a coherent system that allows apportionment among several causes.

Apportionment by Cause and Presumption

Presumption is the assumption that a given disease is more likely than not due to a particular cause because the association between the disease and an occupation or exposure is consistently large enough to make it "more likely than not." Some diseases, such as silicosis, are never seen without an occupational association, and these diseases are easily dealt with by presumption. Even in these cases, related impairment may be apportioned to nonoccupational causes such as smoking. Others are not unique to occupational causes but occur more often in occupational settings and must be evaluated by epidemiology. The relative risk favoring an association must exceed 2 for presumption to be supported by epidemiologic evidence because this corresponds to greater than even odds in favor of the risk factor and therefore satisfies the criterion of "more likely than not."

A claim that meets this standard of presumption should, all other things being equal, be accepted routinely. There may be rebuttable presumptions and reasons for evaluating individual cases, but the essential logic of presumption is that the association has already been demonstrated. Rebutting the presumption requires showing that the claimant is different in some important way from the majority of such cases. The most frequently encountered grounds for rebuttal are that other exposures that are not occupational have contributed a substantially greater risk than the occupational exposure. The case for rebuttal is strongest when the occupational exposure was unusually weak (e.g., of short duration or in a job classification where the level of exposure was relatively low) and the nonoccupational exposures were unusually strong.

A problem arises when both occupational and nonoccupational exposures are strong enough to contribute a significant risk, as in the case of occupational carbon monoxide exposure and smoking for coronary artery disease and acute myocardial infarction. Then the most conservative policy would be to accept the presumption if the occupational exposure was substantial in absolute terms and would have been sufficient to cause the resulting disease. A more flexible policy would be to apportion the relative contribution of the different risk factors and to determine which predominated. However, this would be challenged easily in the individual case because causal exposures add to risk and often interact in ways that cannot be separated. Most WCBs and commissions have policies that preclude apportionment by cause in such situations and declare that only a substantial contribution must be demonstrated. A "substantial" contribution for a risk factor that is subject to a presumption is hard to distinguish from a contribution sufficient to make the presumption. For this reason, an exposure sufficient to make a presumption in the first place probably should be accepted in all cases, even when there are other risk factors.

Two criteria need to be met:

- Significant magnitude or risk associated with exposure (e.g., studies with relative risk greater than 2)
- Substantial exposure of individual, similar to those in epidemiologic studies.

Even if we can demonstrate the first point, the second can be hard to prove. This is really an issue of attribution, where uncertainty is relatively minimal and the contribution is large enough to be sufficient.

Apportionment by Cause and Significant Contribution

This raises another difficult problem, the definition of a significant or substantial contribution. Presumption can be defined in terms of more likely than not, but *significant* or *substantial* implies that the contribution was (or could have been—in the individual case there is no certainty) necessary but not necessarily sufficient. In terms more familiar in law, "but for" the additional risk conferred by the occupational exposure, the health outcome would never have happened.

In this sense, the terms *significant* and *substantial* take on new meaning compared with use of the terms in the context of presumption. In the context of *significant contribution,* the effect of the exposure must be sufficient to have a demonstrable effect on the body but not necessarily enough to cause impairment in itself. This subtle change in definition rather unexpectedly reopens the argument for toxicologic interpretations because it accepts a "significant contribution" to injury that may be subclinical or not easily detected or quantified in populations. Epidemiology is of little use in such situations, unless one is documenting interactions, but a purely toxicologic or clinical approach would be stronger evidence in this context than in cases where strict causation is the issue. It would be sufficient to demonstrate that the effect of exposure could have tipped the balance into clinical disease by demonstrating that the effects of exposure are real and realistically large enough to affect the body adversely in the presence of greater injury contributed by some other risk factor. Such evidence can be provided by clinical toxicology, and even by laboratory studies if they are highly germane, and can be related clearly to human effects. In the absence of scientific data, the judgment of a clinician may be weighted more strongly in cases where "significant contribution" is an issue than in apportionment generally.

The clinical course of a disorder may vary, but deviations from the expected course are obvious to clinicians and may be the basis for an interpretation of substantial contribution. Elements of a case may include when the disease started

and whether it would be expected to start at that age or under those circumstances in most cases and whether the timing was associated with occupation.
For example, a young man with a cancer of the bowel working in an occupation
associated with an increased risk of bowel cancer might have a case for substantial
contribution, despite a dietary profile and family history consistent with a normal
risk for bowel cancer later in life. The argument may hinge on whether the
worker would have developed the same degree of impairment without the
additional occupational exposure. For example, a coal miner exposed to high
levels of dust might have a strong case for COPD despite cigarette smoking if
he was a very light smoker, lacked a family history, and had a pattern of accelerated
decline in pulmonary function out of proportion to the smoking history. Thus
apportionment by cause in this situation reduces to the need to demonstrate
substantial or significant contribution. The acceptable standard of evidence for
demonstrating this contribution necessarily relaxes and can be based on evidence
that would not otherwise carry much weight in establishing causation or presumption, such as estimates based on the occupational history or by industrial
hygiene consultants.

There is a problem in the logic of this approach. It makes an artificial
distinction between occupational and nonoccupational risk factors and treats
the occupational exposure as the "straw that broke the camel's back," in all
cases the last factor in the chain of causation. In the presence of more than one
risk factor, who is to say that the outcome would not have occurred "but for"
the nonoccupational cause? The treatment of occupational exposures in this way
is similar to the legal endeavor to separate intentional injury from contributory
negligence so that damages resulting from an injury may be apportioned properly.

The idea is that intentional injury and negligence are different categories
of behavior; intentional injury violates a social norm, and negligence is free from
willful intent to cause injury. The degree of injury due to different acts should
not be apportioned strictly on the basis of contribution of each act because the
acts differed in type and are not comparable. It is, however, an extralegal social
policy to punish or deter intentional injury, and therefore, this may outweigh
comparative responsibility in egregious cases. (For example, different contributors to an assault situation may have equal contributions according to current
injury theory but under civil law. For example, one court has apportioned a
disproportionate share of responsibility in an assault case to the person commit-
ting the assault, a significant but much less share to a landlord who allowed
unsafe conditions to exist that permitted the assault, and a strictly nominal share
to a third person whose negligent actions apparently negligently allowed the
assault to happen.) Likewise, in workers' compensation, the idea that employers
who permit occupational exposures must take a greater share of responsibility
is attractive, but what about the employer who is conscientious? Is it fair to
model apportionment by cause on the assumption of intentional injury?

The resolution of this problem ultimately is a policy decision. In Canada, the policies of the WCBs and the legislation that sets these policies have made the decision that the public good requires that any substantial contribution means a presumption in cases where more than one risk factor exists.

Glossary

Cause A term used in the conventional sense [2] of a factor or influence that directly participates in the mechanism of disease or risk of an outcome.

Disorder A term used to mean either a disease or an injury when the concept applies to both.

Exposure Following accepted epidemiologic usage, a term that means a situation in which a person comes into contact with a hazard at some level of intensity. To show that an exposure is directly related to disease, one needs to know the level and duration of exposure.

Outcome A term used to mean a clinical condition or level of impairment that derives from the disorder under discussion. It is used here in its epidemiologic sense and does not necessarily imply a given disease state or result of treatment.

Risk factor A term used in its epidemiologic sense to mean an exposure or characteristic that is associated on a statistical, or probabilistic, basis with the risk of a disorder. Not all risk factors are causes; some are markers for characteristics that predispose to an outcome or substitutes for a real cause.

References

1. Boston GW. Apportionment of harm in tort law: a proposed restatement. *University of Dayton Law Rev* 1996;21:267–378.

2. Rothman KJ. *Modern Epidemiology.* Boston: Little, Brown, 1986. Pp 7–21.

3. White RR III. Comparative responsibility sometimes: The Louisiana approach to comparative apportionment and intentional torts. *Tulane Law Rev* 1996;70:1501–1536.

4. Bachrach BA. Damage apportionment in Maine: A proposal for reform. *Maine Law Rev* 1982;34:367–405.

5. Owen-Conway S. Contributory negligence and apportionment of damages. *Australian Bar Rev* 1990;6:211–218.

6. Kadi M. Workers' compensation law on successive disabilities: An argument for the use of an apportionment statue. *South Dakota Law Rev* 1991;36:640–662.

7. Garrett LR. Workers' compensation: Apportionment of disability compensation: *Morrison v. Burlington Industries. Wake Forest Law Rev* 1982;18:801–821.

8. Robins J, Greenland S. The probability of causation under a stochastic model for individual risk. *Biometrics* 1989;45:1125–1138.

9. Boston GW. Toxic apportionment: A causation and risk contribution model. *Environmental Law* 1995;25:549–649.

10. Fleming JG. *The Law of Torts,* 8th ed. Agincourt, ON: Law Book Co., 1992. Pp 200–204.

11. Shuter RK. Apportionment of damages: Third circuit predicts Pennsylvania courts would not allow jury to apportion liability in a cigarette smoking, asbestos-exposure case: *Borman v. Raymark Industries, Inc.*, 960 F.2d 327 (3d Cir. 1992). *Temple Law Rev* 1993;66:223–238.

12. LaDou J, Mulryan LE, McCarthy KJ. Cumulative injury or disease claims: An attempt to define employers' liability for workers' compensation. *Am J Law Med* 1980;6:1–28.

13. Shubat JG. Apportionment of harm to causes: Asbestos and the smoking plaintiff. *Indiana Law Rev* 1988;21:522–545.

14. Dupont WD, Plummer WD Jr. Understanding the relationship between relative and absolute risk. *Cancer* 1996;77:2193–2199.

12

Impairment

STEPHEN L. DEMETER

Case Study

Chris is involved in an accident. He is rushed to the hospital, and despite all the latest interventions, Chris is paralyzed from the neck down. His ability to breathe is significantly compromised, and he must use a ventilator to prevent death due to insufficient respiratory capacity. He requires complete care to prevent infections and the development of flexion contractures and to enable him to take in nourishment and dispose of bodily wastes. No one would argue that Chris is not significantly impaired and totally disabled. This example raises several medical and legal issues. The medical issues encompass (1) what is impairment, (2) what is disability, (3) who measures them, (4) what criteria are used, (5) what determines the conversion of impairment into disability, and (6) what is the definition and meaning of *maximum medical improvement?* The legal issues include (1) how does a person receive compensation for an injury, (2) how are the medical conditions distilled into a workable legal definition, (3) who makes this conversion, and (4) how reliable are these conversions?

Medical Issues

Any layperson would recognize immediately that Chris is severely impaired and totally disabled. However, a layperson's concept of impairment and disability has little place in the proper handling of Chris's case by the medical and legal professionals involved in assisting Chris. While a layperson will see a paralyzed man in a specialized wheelchair on a breathing machine, a physician will see a patient who needs a variety of special interventions to ensure that all bodily functions are maintained to a sufficient degree to prevent, as much as possible, both short- and long-term complications that could cause significant morbidity and mortality. A lawyer will see a client who needs to be "fit" into some compensation system so that financial reimbursement of medical bills, in addition to the normal costs of living, are paid. An economist will see a series of costs (what is the charge for the ventilator, the nurse's aides, home care, modifications to the house, lost earnings potential), all which can be used to figure the expenses for a quadriplegic patient.

How can these professionals talk with each other so that Chris's needs are addressed properly by all parties and none of his current or future needs "fall through the cracks"?

Definitions

Listed below are some common definitions for medical terms involving disability and impairment.

IMPAIRMENT. *Impairment* is the deviation of anatomy, physiology, intellectual capability, or emotional status from that which the individual possessed prior to some injury or trauma or from that derived from population norms. Thus a person with an IQ of 80 is considered impaired because his or her IQ is 20 points below the population average. A person with an IQ of 100 is not considered impaired unless his or her prior IQ (e.g., before head trauma in an automobile accident) was 120.

DISABILITY. *Disability* is "a medical impairment that prevents an individual from performing specified intellectual, creative, adaptive, social, or physical functions. It is the inability to successfully complete a specific task which the individual was previously capable of completing due to a medical or psychological deviation from an individual's prior health status or from the status expected of most members of a society" [1]. For example, a person who has an amputation of the fifth digit of the right hand has, by definition, a medical impairment. However, he or she is only disabled if loss of that fifth digit prevents him or her from engaging in a desired activity, such as being a concert pianist [1].

HANDICAP. *Handicap* is an impairment or disability that is partially or totally mitigated either by an assistive device or by manipulation of the environment [1]. A person with poor vision may have his or her medical impairment or disability partially or totally corrected by wearing corrective lenses (assistive device) or by using books with large print (modifying the environment).

MEASUREMENT. If an impairment represents a deviation from "normal" of a physical, psychological, or behavioral function of an individual, then the amount of deviation should be amenable to measurement. This seems intuitively obvious. A person with one arm is clearly impaired, and it is plain that the amount of deviation is loss of one arm.

There are three underlying problems involved in the measurement of impairment: (1) what is "normal," (2) how accurate are the measurements, and (3) how much does the measured impairment translate into an impairment of the "whole person"? The issue of who should measure is not a matter of major dispute. Health care professionals are delegated this task. The choice of which health professional is best equipped to perform the measurements is sometimes contested, however. A physician should be able to measure deviations from normalcy. Is a family practitioner the better choice to measure the range of motion (ROM) of the low back instead of a chiropractor or a physical therapist? Both the latter practitioners are better equipped by training and experience to perform the low-back ROM than is a family practitioner, who deals with back examinations as only an incidental part of his or her practice, yet many compensation systems bar these two health professionals from providing these measurements.

Who should perform these examinations? The state of Ohio, for example, sends claimants entered in the Bureau of Workers' Compensation (BWC) Program to qualified physicians for an impairment rating. There are two basic levels of examination: entry level and specialist level. Entry-level examinations are performed by individuals having passed a Board examination in a primary care field (e.g., family practice, internal medicine, general surgery, or anesthesiology), whereas specialist examinations are performed by individuals having certification in the area of concern (e.g., orthopedics, neurology, cardiology, etc.). In the past, Ohio had only two requirements for entry into the BWC Program: a willingness to perform the examination (i.e., register) and the Board certification.

At the end of 1999, only Ohio, Pennsylvania, Nevada, California, and Texas required training in impairment evaluation and use of the American Medical Association's (AMA) *Guides to the Evaluation of Permanent Impairment* [2]. However, this left 45 other states that did not require any specialized training or experience to perform this type of examination. (Note that several organizations are dedicated to teaching this discipline, including the American College of Disability Evaluating Physicians, the American College of Occupational and Environmental Medicine, SEAK, Inc., and others. Specialty components in some medical societies also teach this subject at their meetings, e.g., the American College of Orthopedic Surgeons, the American Academy of Physical Medicine and Rehabilitation, etc.)

The state of Ohio's policy is that family practitioners and orthopedists are capable of performing the same quality of entry level examination, thereby fulfilling the stated goal of the AMA guidelines: "Two physicians, following the methods of the Guides to evaluate the same patient, should report similar results and reach similar conclusions."

Measurements are performed in a number of specified fashions. The specified fashion is sometimes not dictated by the health professional. For example, if the health professional is examining a person for a workers' compensation claim and the injured worker resides in a state that uses the AMA guidelines [2], then the examination is performed with that reference dictating the method of the examination. The issue of which method of evaluation is used is system-specific. For example, many, but not all, states use the AMA guidelines [2]. Some states use the current edition, and some use older editions. Some states (e.g., Minnesota) do not use the AMA guidelines and have their own systems. Still other states use a hybrid of their system and the AMA guidelines (e.g., California) [1]. In addition, some compensation systems have their own criteria. For example, the Social Security Administration has its own guidebook, *Disability Evaluations under Social Security* [3], which specifies which tests can or cannot be used, which tests will or will not be paid for, and specific testing protocols. A brief review of the cardiac chapter of the AMA guidelines [2] and the cardiac section of the Social Security handbook [3] makes this point very clearly.

Given that the examination/evaluation is performed by a nonbiased health professional who, by training and experience, is capable of performing a competent evaluation of the deviations in an examinee's health status using an examination protocol that is system-specific, how does the health professional assess the deviations from normalcy?

How Is a Deviation Measured?

In order for the health professional to "rate" a deviation from normal, some reference is needed to establish what is "normal." As discussed earlier, each system for rating impairment and disability has a specified reference guide to tell the health professional how to perform the examination. The same guide also defines *normal* so that the health professional can rate the deviation. For example, if a person has only 50 degrees flexion of the last joint of the fifth finger as his or her sole abnormality, under the AMA guidelines [2], there is a 10% impairment of the fingers, which yields a 1% impairment of the whole person.

Surprisingly, for most organ systems described in the AMA guidelines, little scientific evidence exists to support the impairment ratings, and the AMA guidelines represent the most "scientific" of all the rating systems! However, there are a few organ systems for which scientific evidence does exist. The pulmonary system is one of these and thus will be presented here as a working model.

Pulmonary Impairment

There are many "normal" values for forced vital capacity (FVC), forced expiratory volume in 1 second (FEV_1), and diffusing capacity (DLCO). The values for pulmonary function testing (PFT) have been available for over 50 years, but more recent values are more accurate because individuals are prescreened for existing cardiopulmonary disease and people testing positive are excluded. (For example, prediction values in the 1950s included, in their sample population, cigarette smokers.) The way "normal" values are usually derived is by taking a large number of people and measuring their lung function. The larger the sample pool, the greater is the scientific validity of the results. Regression formulas are then derived, and tables of "normalcy" are generated. The predicted functions are more valid for people with average anthropomorphic values than for people whose values are outliers. Thus the extrapolations, while necessary, may not accurately predict "normal" lung function for all individuals. The values derived by Crapo et al. [4] were chosen by the AMA guidelines as the values defining normalcy and also were adapted by the American Thoracic Society (ATS) in its official policy statement entitled, "Evaluation of Impairment/Disability Secondary to Respiratory Disorders" (adopted March 1986) [5].

Many variables could have been included in the assessment of pulmonary performance other than height, age, weight, sex, and race. For example, other variables include posture during the test, time of day when the test is performed, smoking history, history of any disease that could have an impact on an individual's respiratory system (e.g., pulmonary, cardiac, neurologic, etc.), environmental exposures, altitude, training (e.g., athletes, professional singers, wind-instrument musicians, etc.), and socioeconomic status [6,7]. Crapo et al. [4] screened 311 subjects, more than 90% of whom were members of the Church of Jesus Christ of Latter-day Saints (126 women and 125 men were chosen for analysis). There was an equal age distribution. All were lifetime nonsmokers and had no signs or symptoms of cardiopulmonary disease. The test was performed at an altitude of 1400 m. Weight, race, and other variables were not specified [4].

Other prediction formulas are different, but as long as one reference system is used consistently, it is assumed that there will be minimal effect on the impairment rating. Harber et al. [8] reviewed the effects of a number of variables on determination of disability, including prediction equations, adjustment factors, cutoff points, and methods of deriving percentage of predicted values. The choice of the prediction formula had a small but noticeable effect on whether or not a person qualified for disability benefits. The variables of age, sex, and race were of greater importance [8].

The AMA guidelines use a conversion formula for the FEV_1, FVC, and DLCO for assessing black versus white examinees. This creates a noticeable change in the whole person impairment (WPI) rating (see Case 1). The AMA guidelines assume that the values for all blacks are equal. However, Ethiopians have an FVC that is 1 liter below that of West Coast Africans. Other racial groups also are found to have spirometric values different from those of whites. Mexican-Americans and Native Americans have values slightly less than whites, with Mexican-Americans having values slightly less than Native Americans, Asians have values below those of Mexican-Americans, and blacks having the lowest values, after adjustment for age, sex, and height. The AMA guidelines adjust for blacks and whites, but not for other races. The Social Security listings adjust only for height and ignore age and race [3].

In 1986, the ATS used the preceding reference values for PFTs and published an "official ATS statement" on their use in the evaluation of impairment and disability [5]. The values of the FVC, FEV_1, FEV_1/FVC, and DLCO were then used to reflect various grades of impairment (Table 12-1). The definition of

Table 12-1. Impairment Classifications by PFT Analysis: A Comparison between the ATS and AMA Classifications

	ATS [5]	AMA [2]
FVC		
Normal	≥80%	≥80%
Mild	60–79%	60–79%
Moderate	51–59%	51–59%
Severe	≤50%	≤50%
FEV$_1$		
Normal	≥80%	≥80%
Mild	60–79%	60–79%
Moderate	41–59%	41–59%
Severe	≤40%	≤40%
FEV$_1$/FVC		
Normal	≥75%	≥70%*
Mild	60–74%	
Moderate	41–59%	
Severe	≤40%	
DL$_{CO}$		
Normal	≥80%	≥70%*
Mild	60–79%	60–69%*
Moderate	41–59%	41–59%
Severe	≤40%	≤40%

*Differences between the ATS and AMA. Note that the AMA guidelines do not use the FEV$_1$/FVC except to define normalcy.

mild impairment was "usually not correlated with diminished ability to perform most jobs," that of moderate impairment was "progressively lower levels of lung function correlated with diminishing ability to meet the physical demands of many jobs," and that of severe impairment was the inability "to meet the physical demands of most jobs including travel to work" [5]. (The reader should take note here of the "blurring" of the concepts of impairment and disability.) The AMA guidelines have used these values with little difference between the two impairment classifications (see Table 12-1).

Categorizing Impairment

How reliable, valid, and accurate are the demarcations for respiratory impairment based on various levels of PFT? To extend the question, are any other variables better equipped to categorize impairment?

The AMA guidelines [2] provide a table on dyspnea (shortness of breath). Would this yield a better categorization of individuals with pulmonary impairment? Some authors believe [1] that a dyspnea index correlates better with measurements of health-related quality-of-life parameters than does the FEV$_1$. If one is attempting to measure impairment, one could use the deviation in health status derived from medical history alone rather than from testing. Ultimately, the deviation in health status is related to the ability of the person to adequately perform the activities of daily living. The AMA guidelines state that an "impairment estimate based on Guide's criteria is intended, among other purposes, to be an estimate of the degree to which an individual's capacity to carry out daily activities has been diminished" [2].

If the dyspnea index is a better reflection of the disease impact on a person, why are PFT values used as a surrogate? It will come as no surprise to anyone in the disability field that claimants sometimes exaggerate symptoms. Thus a verifiable, reliable test result, although less perfect, becomes a better choice for this type of assessment.

Another test of pulmonary function is derived from a cardiopulmonary exercise stress test (CPEST). This test is dynamic, not static, as are PFTs. It provides a number of measurements, including the oxygen uptake. This value ($\dot{V}O_2$) can be translated into work capability. Oxygen uptake also can be described as a metabolic equivalent (MET) level or metabolic equivalent (defined as the oxygen uptake for a given task divided by the resting oxygen uptake). If the resting oxygen uptake is 3.5 ml/kg/min and an activity such as lifting and carrying 20 to 44 lb requires a $\dot{V}O_2$ of 15.7 ml/kg/min, then 4.5 METs are required.

While not measuring impairment per se, the CPEST will provide a measurement of a person's physical capabilities so that the translation to disability becomes easy. The values of METs or $\dot{V}O_2$ for a number of activities are known [9–11]. Further advantages include an indication of other organ system disturbances (either singly or in combination with pulmonary disease) causing exercise intolerance and diminished work ability. Malingering and deconditioning also can be diagnosed reliably [9]. Thus CPEST would appear to be an ideal test of disability, if not impairment.

The AMA guidelines [2] and the ATS statement [5] have both used the $\dot{V}O_{2,max}$ as a measurement of pulmonary impairment. Additionally, in contrast with use of the FVC, FEV_1, or DL_{CO}, the ATS statement provides a justification for use of the $\dot{V}O_{2,max}$ as a means of categorizing and rating impairment. The authors state, "based on the two concepts discussed above: (1) that a worker can perform a job comfortably at 40% of his $\dot{V}O_{2,max}$ and (2) that $\dot{V}O_2$ values can be assigned to specific jobs, the following rating is recommended" [5].

Thus the ATS statement (and by adoption, the AMA guidelines) have justified an impairment scheme. Several points, however, need to be settled before the justification can be accepted.

1. *Is the exercise stress test reliable, valid, and reproducible?* Numerous studies have found this test to be valid and reliable [9,12], although not all job situations have been studied and not all those studied have been studied repeatedly and extensively.

2. *Are these results better than those obtained by other tests?* Wasserman et al. [9] address this issue and state flatly that the maximum work capacity cannot be predicted reliably from resting pulmonary function. Cotes et al. [11] tested the concept using $\dot{V}O_2$ as the dependent variable in a stepwise multiple regression analysis. Sue [13] stated that "although maximum exercise VA is related to FEV_1 in most subjects, there are likely differences in this relationship between those with normal lung function, those with obstruction, patients with restrictive lung disease, and obese subjects."

3. *How do the values derived on a complete CPEST correlate with "normal" values?* The resting values of the FVC, FEV_1, and DL_{CO} are all "normalized" and expressed as a percentage of "normal" based on a number of anthropomorphic discriminators (see above). The values derived from an exercise study are similarly subjected to the same analysis. Healthy subjects were studied, and regression formulas were derived. Thus, in the interpretation of a CPEST, values can be expressed as a percentage of "normal." However, this dilution of the meaning of the test is not used in the AMA guidelines' formula; only the raw data result is used (e.g., the $\dot{V}O_{2,max}$ is 7.9 ml/kg/min, not 46% of normal). This value is then compared with $\dot{V}O_{2,max}$ values derived from a variety of job situations. Thus this question becomes moot.

4. *How well do the values derived on a complete cardiopulmonary exercise stress test predict "normal" for the individual?* Unfortunately, the CPEST can only provide data for a given day and time, and the test is influenced by a number of variables, including the fitness of the person, whether he or she has disease(s) that will influence his or her exercise capacity, the presence of certain medications, obesity, etc. Can "normal" be predicted from prior work capabilities? The answer is "Probably." For example, if a person was known to have been able to perform heavy manual labor (estimated $\dot{V}O_{2,max}$ at 30 ml/kg/min) based on a job description, witnesses, and a perusal of reference tables, and if the measured $\dot{V}O_{2,max}$ is currently only 20 ml/kg/min on a valid CPEST, then we can measure the reduction. The problem is that maximal, sustained exercise is rarely known, even for individuals in heavy manual labor.

5. *Are the objections raised in questions 3 and 4 of concern?* If one is attempting to measure impairment (a deviation in health status) rather than disability, these are very important questions. *Impairment* is defined as a deviation from either a population norm (expressed as a percentage of "normal" or the average value derived from population studies) or from the individual's prior health status. If the question is how much capability did the individual lose due to a medical illness, then the deviation from population norms becomes the surrogate measuring point. For example, when ROM of a previous, now well-healed shoulder injury is assessed, the ROM measured is adjusted to population norms, not the preinjury ROM. Sometimes, the ROM of the opposite shoulder is measured, and the deviation of the injured from the noninjured ROM is used as the impairment measurement. This assumes, however, that the preinjury ROMs of

the two shoulders were equivalent and that the noninjured shoulder has no other restrictions. Obviously, this surrogate function of population norms is not a perfect method of impairment measurement, but it is the best that we can offer in most circumstances.

Other rating schemes also have their problems. The AMA guidelines, as noted earlier, were used as the model for discussion because (1) they appear to have the greatest degree of scientific justification, (2) they have a high degree of sophistication, and (3) they are used widely. The Social Security definitions of pulmonary impairment, on the other hand, base impairment on the following criteria: FEV_1, FVC, and PaO_2 (corrected for altitude and obesity) [3]. The tables for the spirometric values are very simplistic and adjust only for height, ignoring other important variables such as age, race, and sex. As can be seen in Table 12-2, there is a distinct bias against younger white males, with older black females having an "easier" time qualifying for SSA benefits. The bias is unlikely to be intentional, but it does exist (see Cases 2 and 3).

Finally, we look at the timing of testing, specifically with regard to the concept of maximum medical improvement (MMI). The AMA guidelines [2] define *permanent impairment* as "one that has become static or stabilized during a period of time sufficient to allow optimal tissue repair, and one that is unlikely to change in spite of further medical or surgical therapy" [2]. "A permanent impairment is considered to be unlikely to change substantially and by more than 3% in the next year with or without medical treatment. If an impairment is not *permanent*, it is inappropriate to characterize it as such and evaluate it according to Guides' criteria" [2]. However, the guidelines also state that a "patient may decline treatment of an impairment with a surgical procedure, a pharmacologic agent, or other therapeutic approach. The view of the Guides' contributors is that if a patient declines therapy for a permanent impairment, that decision should neither decrease nor increase the estimated percentage of the patient's impairment." The preceding statements are inherently self-

Table 12-2. Differences in Percentage Predicted for FVC and FEV_1 in Men/Women and Caucasians/African-Americans for Meeting the SSA Requirements for Pulmonary Disability [for a man 5 ft, 11 in. (180 cm) tall and a woman 5 ft, 4 in. (162 cm) tall]

	Male		Female	
Age (years)	36	56	36	56
FVC				
Caucasian	32%	35%	40%	46%
African-American	36%	40%	45%	52%
FEV_1				
Caucasian	35%	39%	41%	49%
African-American	40%	45%	46%	56%

contradictory. A person is either at MMI or not. If he or she is not, he or she should not be classified as having attained a "permanency" to his or her impairment.

Recommendations

1. More research is needed to obtain valid impairment and disability ratings. It is estimated that the total cost of disability in the United States in 1980 was $177 billion, or 6.5% of the gross domestic product [1].
2. The AMA guidelines are the best (although far from perfect) system available for categorizing, measuring, and rating impairments. They should be used by all social agencies requiring an impairment rating.
3. The AMA guidelines should be improved so that the ratings are consistent and fair from organ system to organ system. Further, one standard [perhaps the ADL, as measured by the Health-Related Quality of Life Index or an alternate method (the medical literature is rich in tests that can assess the quality of life [14])] should be used to grade impairment. This standard could be correlated with physiologic parameters of impairment to reflect real impairments rather than arbitrary cutoffs. The AMA guidelines have been found to be inaccurate at lower levels of impairment [15], so internal consistency and external validity are important.

Cases

Case 1

Joe is a 34-year-old, 6-ft man (183 cm) who has an FEV_1 of 2.46 liters. From Table 2 of the AMA guidelines [2], he has a predicted FEV_1 of 4.56 liters. Therefore, his FEV_1 is 54% of predicted. He is in a class 3 impairment group ("moderate impairment of the whole person") with a WPI rating of 26% to 50%. However, if Joe is an African-American, his expected FEV_1 is only 4.01 liters (a conversion of 0.88 is used [2]), and his FEV_1 is 61% of predicted. Now he is in a class 2 impairment group ("mild impairment") with a WPI rating of only 10% to 25%.

COMMENT. It can be seen that for the same sex, age, height, and spirometric values, an African-American will rate with less impairment than a white person.

Case 2

Frank is a 24-year-old, 5-ft, 10-in. white man who suffered a chemical burn of his lungs while at home due to excessive chlorine exposure while working on his swimming pool. While on maximal medication and after the administration of a bronchodilator, his FEV_1 was measured at 1.70 liters (37% predicted using the AMA guidelines). He has dyspnea on exertion to one-half flight of stairs and can only perform sedentary work. Despite the severe dyspnea, his PaO_2 after exercise was 67 mmHg (it was 96 mmHg at rest). He applied for but did not qualify for Social Security disability.

COMMENT. Contrast this case with Case 3.

Case 3

Ruth is a 56-year-old African-American woman who is a 2 pack per day smoker. She is 5 ft, 4 in.(163 cm) tall. She complains of shortness of breath and can climb only two flights of stairs. She has been counseled to quit smoking, but she has no interest in doing so. She has applied for disability. Her predicted FEV_1, using the AMA guidelines, is 2.25 liters. Her measured FEV_1 is 1.25 liters after the use of an aerosolized bronchodilator (55% of predicted). She was accepted for Social Security disability because she met the criteria.

COMMENT. Frank's FVC was only 37% of predicted, whereas Ruth's was 55% of predicted. Yet Ruth, despite having potentially reversible disease (if she were to quit smoking and/or take bronchodilators) and fewer symptoms, qualified for Social Security disability, and Frank did not.

References

1. Demeter SL, Andersson GBJ, eds. *Disability Evaluation,* 2d ed. Philadelphia: Saunders, 2001 (in press).

2. Doege TC, Houston TP, eds. *Guides to the Evaluation of Permanent Impairment,* 4th ed. Chicago: American Medical Association, 1993.

3. Social Security Administration, U.S. Department of Health and Human Services. *Disability Evaluation under Social Security.* Publication no. 64-039/ICN 468600. Washington: Social Security Administration, 1998.

4. Crapo RO, Morris AH, Gardner RM. Reference spirometric values using techniques and equipment that meets ATS recommendations. *Am Rev Respir Dis* 1981;123:659–664.

5. American Thoracic Society. Evaluation of impairment/disability secondary to respiratory disorders. *Am Rev Respir Dis* 1986;133:120S–9.

6. Gardner RM, Crapo RO, Nelson SB. Spirometry and flow-volume curves. *Clin Chest Med* 1989;10(2):145–154.

7. Clausen JL. Prediction of normal values in pulmonary function testing. *Clin Chest Med* 1984;10(2):135–143.

8. Harber P, Schnur R, Emery J, et al. Statistical "biases" in respiratory disability determinations. *Am Rev Respir Dis* 1983;128:413–418.

9. Wasserman K, Hansen JE, Sue DY, et al., eds. *Principles of Exercise Testing and Interpretation,* 3d ed. Philadelphia: Lippincott Williams & Wilkins, 1999.

10. Zavala DC. *Manual on Exercise Testing: A Training Handbook,* 3d ed. Iowa City, IA: University of Iowa Press, 1993.

11. Cotes JE, Zejda J, King B. Lung function impairment as a guide to exercise limitation in work-related lung disorders. *Am Rev Respir Dis* 1988;137:1089–1093.

12. British Thoracic Society. BTS guidelines for the management of chronic obstructive pulmonary disease. *Thorax* 1997;52:28.

13. Sue DY. Exercise testing in the evaluation of impairment and disability. *Clin Chest Med* 1994;15:369–387.

14. McDowell I, Newell C. *Measuring Health: A Guide to Rating Scales and Questionnaires,* 2d ed. New York: Oxford University Press, 1996.

15. Sinclair S, Burton JF. A response to the comments by Doege and Hixson. *Workers Compensation Monitor* 1997;10:13–17.

13

Individualized Medical Evaluation and Personal Risk

ERNEST C. LEVISTER, JR.

Case Study

MG is a 42-year-old custodial worker. On presentation to his physician for complaints of fatigue, he had low-grade abnormal liver function tests. MG worked in the Housekeeping Department of Mercy Community Hospital for the past 5 years. He received a puncture wound with an unknown contaminated needle source 3 years ago at Mercy Community Hospital. For 20 years prior to employment at Mercy Hospital, he worked in housekeeping at County Hospital. He denies any alcohol or recreational intravenous drug use. Twenty years ago he received several whole blood transfusions because of gastrointestinal bleeding. Liver function tests demonstrated elevated ALT and AST, which are indicators of damage to liver cells, with a reversed albumin-to-globulin ratio. Hepatitis C antibody was positive, confirmed with HCV RNA. A liver biopsy was performed and yielded pathology that was consistent with cirrhosis. Clinical correlation suggested that the cirrhosis was due to hepatitis C.

Hepatitis C may be associated with occupational exposure among health care workers, but at one time it also was a significant risk of receiving transfusions. In order to interpret this case, the expert witness or medical advisor needs to know certain facts: Epidemiologic studies of hepatitis C have become available only relatively recently because this virus was late to be discovered. "Non A, non B hepatitis virus," as it was called for many years, was a form of hepatitis distinguished only because it appears in the absence of serologic markers of infection by hepatitis A or B. It subsequently turned out that 80% of this unidentifiable form of hepatitis was due to a newly recognized virus, hepatitis C. Hepatitis C frequently was transmitted via multiple blood transfusions until 1990, when methods became available commercially to screen blood donors. Hepatitis C virus also can be introduced into the body via puncture wounds and wound contamination with resulting transfer of body fluids from an infected patient. However, transmission also can take place as a result of sharing of needles with an infected person during intravenous drug use (80% of intravenous drug users show evidence of past infection). As many as 50% of patients infected with hepatitis C virus progress to cirrhosis. Cirrhosis of the liver due to hepatitis C takes 10 or more years to develop. The more common cause of cirrhosis, however, is alcohol abuse. Hepatitis B, which this man did not have, is also a common cause of cirrhosis. There are other causes of cirrhosis, but they are rare. MG worked in the Housekeeping Department at County Hospital for 20 years and subsequently at Mercy Hospital for 5 years but there is no history of a needlestick. The puncture wound from a possibly contaminated needle occurred 3 years ago at Mercy Hospital.

The medical opinion would read something like this:

Specific diagnosis: Cirrhosis of the liver due to hepatitis C.

Adverse outcome: Cirrhosis of the liver and its concomitant disability.

Mechanism of injury: The virus probably accessed the body via whole blood transfusions 20 years ago.

Reason for opinion: The latency period for the development of cirrhosis of the liver due to hepatitis C is 10 + years, making the puncture wound at Mercy Hospital an unlikely cause. The blood transfusion dating 20 to 25 years ago fits the time frame for the natural history of the disease.

The goal of this chapter is to outline a general approach to the evaluation of a patient or injured individual for the purpose of determining causation. For our purposes, an *adverse outcome* is an injury or disease resulting in residual disability or impairment. Asbestos, for example, is a hazard. *Hazards* are exposures that may result in specific adverse outcomes, such as asbestosis or lung cancer.

Evaluations by a physician are requested because of questions concerning how and what caused a specific adverse outcome. In physical trauma, the cause of the adverse outcome is usually obvious. In toxic or environmental exposure cases, the cause of the adverse outcome may be difficult to determine.

The trigger for physician involvement will be a call to apply professional knowledge in the area under question. This is usually a request for evaluation of a patient and/or review of records. The correct role of a physician in a particular case must be determined at the beginning. The request may be for treatment or care of the patient. The physician may be asked to serve as an expert witness or medical advisor to render an opinion concerning issues in dispute, usually focusing on causation. The request in most instances will be on behalf of one side or the other, but occasionally both sides will agree to retain a particular expert. The purpose of the expert witness is to present the truth in the best light on behalf of the requesting party. In addition, there are usually gray areas that allow for individual interpretation.

In many instances, request for evaluations on the behalf of the defense are couched as an *Independent Medical Examination,* requesting the physician to serve as a medical advisor to the insurer or claimant in a workers' compensation case or to the defendant or the plaintiff in a legal action. In some instances in litigation, the judge may make the request, which is truly independent. In the arena of workers' compensation in California, both parties may jointly ask a physician to arbitrate medical aspects of a case in the capacity of an *Agreed Medical Evaluator.*

The treating physician is usually not asked to render an opinion in disputed cases. Treating physicians generally are viewed as the patient's advocate or lacking sophistication in the analysis of the legal aspects of the case. Most have not mastered the "magic language" that is required for truly effective opinions in workers' compensation cases. The treating physician may be called as a factual witness, however. On the other hand, there are some venues in which the treating physician is automatically an expert witness whose opinion is given great weight.

The expert should focus on the assignment as outlined in the cover letter received from the lawyer or claimant's advocate. The expert should strive to answer the questions posed because they are essential to the case. The cover letter may contain the referring party's medical/legal theory concerning causation in this specific case. The expert may be informed of other experts who will be involved in a team approach. However, the expert may not receive the entire picture, in which case the information may be filtered.

The issue of causation will arise in various venues. There may be instances in which the adverse outcome in a workers' compensation case on its own will become a personal injury issue tried in the state or federal system. Federal employee compensation programs, including longshoremen and harbor workers' compensation programs, black lung benefits for coal miners and their families, and postal workers' and state workers' compensation programs, are examples of administrative venues. Each has its own definitions, terminology, and standards for concluding relationship to work, and terminology. The key to the physician's value and participation in the process is an understanding of the requirements of the venue and familiarity with the "magic language" to identify and connect the adverse outcome to the causative factors.

Threshold Question

A specific set of symptoms or an adverse outcome that is being related to a specific causative factor will be presented. The physician must sort through the symptoms and the proposed adverse outcome and arrive at a specific diagnosis. The specific diagnosis remains totally in the domain of the physician. The medical expert should review the diagnosis, and if possible, it should be confirmed with generally accepted diagnostic testing. However, the point of the medical expert's involvement is just not to make a diagnosis. It is to address the *threshold question,* which follows confirmation of the diagnosis.

The threshold question is causation: What caused the adverse outcome, and what was the relationship of that cause to work or the circumstances of exposure? Once a specific diagnosis has been made, the causative issues in question can be examined for biological cohesiveness. This necessitates a more detailed and in-depth evaluation including assembling external and internal factual evidence.

Individualizing Interpretation: External Factual Evidence

Evidence external to the patient must be evaluated, including epidemiologic data, workplace, hobbies, environment, and mechanism of injury. The mechanism of injury is how the event occurred, causing the adverse outcome. The current understanding of the natural history of the disease resulting in the outcome in question will help in organizing a time-line characterization of the mechanism of injury. Then the physician will be able to formulate and discuss issues of causation that are biologically cohesive. Drawing from the workers' compensation arena, we can categorize the mechanism of injury as shown in Table 13-1.

Epidemiologic studies are powerful tools for identifying a hazard that is associated with a risk of a specific adverse outcome. This will alert the physician to potential causative factors. The more unique the adverse outcome, the easier it is to identify a cause-effect relationship. For example, asbestos is a hazard with a risk of causing a mesothelioma in susceptible individuals. Mesothelioma is rarely associated with anything else. Therefore, one can conclude causation with a reasonable degree of medical certainty.

The more common the adverse outcome, the more difficult is the application of epidemiologic studies when applying commonly occurring hazards as a risk to a specific individual. Fine, inhalable particles are a hazard that carries the risk of causing inflammation of the mucous membranes resulting in bronchitis. Bronchitis is a common adverse outcome caused by various hazards. The physician is the only one who can take this general information derived from epidemiologic studies and apply it on a case-by-case basis.

Table 13-1. Determining Mechanism of Injury

Mental-physical	Mental stressors causing a physical adverse outcome
Mental-mental	Mental stressors causing a mental adverse outcome
Physical-physical	Physical stressor or chemical exposure causing a physical adverse outcome
Physical-mental	Physical stressor or chemical exposure causing a mental adverse outcome
Physical-mental-physical	Physical stressors or chemical exposure resulting in a mental stressor causing a physical adverse outcome

Epidemiologic studies, in addition, serve as scientific data to support the expert's opinion. They help to identify specific hazards that are risks for causing an adverse outcome to an individual or group. The studies may identify a unique group of people or a cluster that develops a specific adverse outcome. The physician must match the hazards identified in the epidemiologic study with the salient hazards in the case under study and determine if the study supports that the individual was at increased risk.

The percentage of individuals exposed to the hazard who become ill will assist the medical expert in determining individual or group risk. If the hazard is an allergen, it becomes a specific risk for susceptible individuals who are sensitized to the allergen. If the hazard is hydrogen fluoride, it becomes an indiscriminate risk, one that may affect anyone.

The mechanism of injury will be a characterization of the exposure to the various hazards or risk factor. This may be macro- or microtrauma. It is useful to distinguish between events that cause a single incident of demonstrable injury and those which cause repeated small injuries that add up to an injury great enough to result in an adverse outcome. *Macrotrauma* is intense exposure over a short time frame. This results in a risk to the individual. *Microtrauma* results from chronic, low-dose repetitive or continuous exposure to the hazard in question, which may be occult. This cumulatively results in a risk to the individual. Table 13-2 illustrates the difference by examples.

Exposure assessment rarely can be performed accurately or in detail. The documentation and measurements are almost never available after the fact. Instead, the expert must characterize exposure by the evidence available. The characterization of exposure will take into consideration the method, circumstances, duration, and intensity of exposure. The expert will develop a time-line characterization of the exposure that will lend itself to a dose-response curve.

The characterization of the exposure also will cover location. The emphasis changes as a function of the event. Did the event occur indoors or outdoors? This helps to determine the physical parameters of the environment and whether

Table 13-2. Macrotrauma versus Microtrauma

	Event	Outcome
Macrotrauma		
Energy transfer	A fall from height	A fracture
Chemical exposure	A toxic spill	Lung problem
Psychogenic stress	Holdup with death of a coworker	Posttraumatic stress disorder
Microtrauma		
Repetitive motion	Picking lettuce	Low-back problems
Exposure to particles in the atmosphere	Underground mining	Bronchitis

one is dealing with a closed or an open space. Did the exposure occur in a confined space if it was an inhaled hazard? Is there something in the materials of the structure itself that is causing the problem? For example, is there asbestos lagging on pipes, or is water collecting, allowing for the growth of molds?

What activities occurred within the structure? Various activities that occur within a structure can result in different hazards that can be carried by the ventilation system to distant locations. Was the structure used within designed parameters, or has design conversion occurred? Modification from an engineering point of view can enhance or create hazardous conditions. This helps to answer questions of potential lawsuits. Was it an accident? This helps to determine type of causation and the steps necessary to prevent recurrence.

The method of delivery and access of the defined hazard are of concern. This will help in ascertaining dose and risk. This also will help to mitigate future occurrences. How did it access to the breathing space or the skin? This helps to determine the potential areas of damage.

The physical and chemical characteristics of the hazard are important. The pH of the hazardous substance will determine if it is acidic or basic, which has a major effect at the point of contact on mucous membranes or skin. The further the pH of the substance is from neutral, the greater is the potential damage.

Volatility is a function of environmental temperature and partial pressure. Water-soluble substances will dissolve in the 100% relative humidity of the lungs and have a local impact. Lipid-soluble (organic) chemicals for the most part bypass the lungs and are absorbed. In addition, they have the potential to be absorbed via the intact skin, particularly if they are bipolar, and absorption is increased if the skin is disrupted. Such chemicals also can have an impact on lipid-rich solid organs such as the brain and liver.

Particles are irritants to mucous membranes at the point of contact, resulting in inflammation and leading to bronchitis, airways obstruction, or reactive airways disease. They can have an impact on the lungs and cause lung parenchymal damage. Oxides of various metals may produce a fever or flulike illness called *metal fume fever.*

Infectious agents can be airborne, infect through close contact, penetrate the skin, or be ingested. The time line from contact to onset of acute disease is particularly important in analysis of infection. An appropriate incubation period must occur between the time of initial exposure and development of the infectious disease.

What were the engineering mechanisms available or in use to mitigate the impact of the hazard? Was appropriate personal protection equipment, such as respirators or hearing protection, available and used? Was the personal protection properly maintained? Were the employees provided with adequate training for hazard protection? This helps to quantify the potential individual and/or group exposure. It also helps to determine if the employer was appropriately protecting the worker. This may help in determining the potential exposure and the degree of worker cooperation. In a no-fault venue, such as workers' compensation, this cannot be used to mitigate the award, but it is important in determining what further steps may be necessary to prevent other cases.

Was the dangerous element used in the manner as and for the purpose it was originally designed? Modifications of equipment and process occur by the employer and the worker, and they can be detrimental. This knowledge helps in determining the mechanism of disease or injury. The general risk factors from epidemiologic studies coupled with the mechanism of injury are stratified into an individual risk profile that may be the sole cause or component of the symphony of causes resulting in a specific adverse outcome.

Individualizing Interpretation: Internal Factual Evidence

Internal evidence focuses on characteristics inherent to the individual patient. It requires an in-depth medical, family, and social history that includes emotional stressors, pre-existing physical conditions, and past diagnostic testing. The patient-physician interview environment may not conform to the usual doctor-patient setting. There are various reasons for this. The patient may have been instructed to limit cooperation and not volunteer any information. There may be audio or visual recording devices. There may be a court reporter or a witness to the encounter. Once a diagnosis has been made and the adverse outcome determined, then an individual internal personal risk profile can be stratified.

Individual susceptibility must be considered. People are genetically different. The individual genetic code will play a role in susceptibility (e.g., family history of diabetes). Previous exposures may sensitize the individual to specific substances (e.g., allergens) and may leave the individual more susceptible to current risk factors. The patient may have a particle load, and the current exposure may push the individual over the top.

Latency period helps to identify an association between the hazard in question and the adverse outcome. It determines a time line from exposure to development of various stages of an adverse outcome. Interstitial disease from asbestos particles takes 15 years to develop. Cirrhosis of the liver from hepatitis C takes approximately 10 years to develop.

Cancer has growth characteristics related to the doubling time until the tumor mass is detectable. The medical expert will have to give his or her best judgment on the time necessary for initiation and promotion that lead to alteration of the DNA, causing it to go awry. Once this has occurred, it usually takes 30 to 36 doublings before detection. Each doubling may take from 30 to 90 days as a function of tumor type. This concept is adaptable to a time line for causation.

Incubation periods are required to develop acute infectious disease. Chemical shellfish toxin takes 1 hour or less for intoxication to occur. *Escherichia coli,*

Salmonella, and *Shigella* take 14 hours or more before gastrointestinal complaints occur. The incubation period from time of exposure to symptoms is 100 days (range 28–225 days) for acute hepatitis B. This allows for a time line from causative exposure to the onset of the adverse outcome.

Biological markers can be used to identify prior exposure to a risk. Bilateral calcification, diaphragmatic or pleural, is a marker for exposure to asbestos 15 or more years ago. Scanning electron microscopy (SEM) and energy dispersive x-ray (EDX) spectroscopy of lung tissue can identify specific increased mineral load compared with the normal population. This documents exposure to a risk. The next step: Do epidemiologic data support the fact that the identified risk can cause the adverse outcome in question? This finding demonstrates what can happen. The next step after this is to demonstrate to the satisfaction of the court or adjudicator that it actually did happen.

Patients will vary in terms of how they respond to the emotional aspects of the hazard or the adverse outcome. It is normal to have some symptom magnification because of the inherent human makeup. Humans will try to present the issues more favorably from their own perspective to enhance their position. If this does not occur, it is a red flag. In many instances the individual is seeking empathy. Symptom magnification may result from the inherent emotional makeup of the individual or from a desire for secondary gain.

The adverse outcome may not occur in isolation. The physician must consider modifying factors in terms of treatment or other disease process that may alter the natural history of the adverse outcome.

Remember the general principle, in most venues, that one takes the individual as one finds him or her. Pre-existing situations may require apportionment of ultimate damage as a function of the venue but have no effect on responsibility for treatment.

Confounding Factors

Confounding in epidemiologic studies occurs when the hazard under study and a different hazard operate independently but parallel with respect to exposure and causing the same outcome. They are independent, parallel hazards from the same exposure at risk for causing the same adverse outcome.

Cigarettes are a common culprit. When dealing with an individual, all identifiable and present hazards must be taken into consideration and given a specific weight in the issues of causation or the severity of the outcome. Two or more hazards may work independently or together as additives or multipliers in terms of causing the adverse outcome.

Social and Legislative Priorities

In some venues there are presumptions concerning causation. That is, a specific adverse outcome is presumed to be related to a specific job or risk. These are social decisions, which may have some scientific basis, made by legislative bodies to protect a group of workers or society. For example, safety officers or firefighters are presumed to be exposed to emotional stress resulting in heart disease. These presumptions can be rebutted if the expert expounds a sound scientific basis for disagreement. An example would be a safety officer with heart disease due to an atrial septal defect (a congenital lesion) as compared with coronary artery disease related to the stress concept.

Interpreting Cases on an Individual Basis

Framing the case deals with the factual scenario established, defined, and interpreted with defensible scientific probabilities by the medical expert. Once the adverse outcome has occurred, medical judgment is necessary to determine if sufficient evidence indicates that the defined risk from epidemiology coupled with external and internal evidence increases the probability of the adverse outcome under study. This should fit plausibly into what is known of the natural history of the adverse outcome. This is highly inferential, much like the framing of a scientific theory. The key is identifying and properly assembling the factual scenario, which includes the legal and medical elements of the case gathered from confused circumstances where there may be differences of opinion as to where to place the emphasis. The mechanism of injury (including the identified hazard that puts the patient at risk) must be cohesive in terms of its temporal relationship to the outcome and must have a biological or clinical causal link to the adverse outcome. The defined hazard may be the sole or a contributing cause. It may aggravate or accelerate the adverse outcome. It may be the "straw that broke the camel's back." The legal venue determines whether a sole or contributing cause is sufficient.

The boundaries of medical science are expanded with the "first case." One can stretch the scientific envelope and explore new ground. Other concepts of causation will be accepted more readily if one has the support of articles or case studies in peer-reviewed journals. The absence of such support should not necessarily limit one's conclusions. The question that must be answered ultimately to cross the threshold of causation is, did the hazard arise out of the activity in question, placing the individual at risk, or did the activity the individual was engaged in cause the adverse outcome?

Did the hazard causing the risk arise during the course of the activity in question? But for his or her job requiring him or her to drive to the construction site from the supply depot, the worker would not have been in a vehicle accident. Did the activity in question place the individual at increased jeopardy when compared with other potential causative risks? Backhoe trenching that disturbed the soil in an arid area placed one individual at increased jeopardy for contacting coccidioidomycosis, which is not endemic where that person lives. When was the last injurious exposure to the risk in question? In cumulative trauma or repetitive exposure cases such as silicosis, this becomes important in determining or identifying the party be held responsible. Did the hazard work in symphony with other hazards, causing increased risk for the individual? One may have to prioritize various hazards in terms of their risk in attributing causation of the adverse outcome.

One may be asked to apportion causation as a function of the venue between different insurance companies or hazards. This takes into consideration pre-existing conditions or concurrent exposures. In cumulative hazardous exposures, the expert must decide the weight to be given to the various periods of exposure. What aspect of the event would have occurred when one saw the patient absent the hazard in question?

Once an opinion of causation of an adverse outcome has been made, the foundation for dealing with issues of residual impairment or disability, future medical care, and rehabilitation can follow.

The Report

Evaluation of the facts or evidence usually is presented in a timely, well-articulated report that is an educational, well-reasoned, biological, cohesive, scientific discussion of the mechanism of injury and its relationship to the adverse outcome written for sophisticated nonmedical readers. The internally cohesive report will lead the reader down a cone, arriving at the apex with a full understanding of the case. The report includes the summation of the pertinent factual scenario that has been developed and relied on in support of the expert opinion. The mechanism of injury must be described in an accurate, nonbiased manner. The mechanism of injury may allow for other legal proceedings. The accident occurred while working, driving a personal vehicle, resulting in an adverse outcome, stimulating a workers' compensation case and a personal injury case. The injury occurred as a result of a known design flaw in the equipment. The employer was not notified of the flaw, nor has a recall occurred.

In answering the threshold question of causation, the expert has weighed the pertinent factual information in determining the hazard that resulted in the exposure risk or the last injurious exposure that resulted in the adverse outcome. Did the event in question place the individual at increased jeopardy when compared with the nonexposed population? Except for the event in question, would the adverse outcome have occurred when it did?

The preferred answer is a reasonable medical certainty of 95%. The acceptable answer is a reasonable medical probability of, more likely than not, 50.1%. At times, one may debate the most probable risk among several possibilities, which is weak. Possible is unacceptable. One cannot speculate. Table 13-3 lists information that is particularly useful in providing clues for searching the medical literature.

All reports should be organized in the same fashion with information in the same place. The discussion should answer all direct questions from the

Table 13-3. Information that Provides Clues to Possible Hazards

Chronologic occupational history
  Job titles
  Type of work performed (actual duties performed with duration)
  Dates of employment and worker's age for each job activity
  Geographic and physical location of employment
  Product or service produced
  Description of engineering protection
  Description of personal protection
Name of agents or substances to which worker is or has been exposed, if known; include frequency
and average duration of each exposure situation
  Environmental history
  Distance from an industrial plant
  Use of chemicals at home
Evidence of exposure
  Industrial hygiene reports
  Statements of colleagues or event witnesses
  OSHA reports
  Police reports/accident investigations

referring party and include all information the court or adjudicating body will need.

The general format for a medical report may follow the usual format for a consultation, with the addition of sections for recording documentation reviewed, the opinion, and justification. The usual format is outlined in Table 13-4. Discretion should be used in omitting items of information that are clearly not germane to the clinical evaluation and that may be intrusive, such as the obstetric history and other personal details.

A list of all documents and records reviewed during the course of the evaluation should be provided. Table 13-5 lists various documents that may be used in an evaluation. Examples of records to consider also are summarized in the table.

The parties present during the evaluation should be identified. The role of any member of the physician's staff that participated in the evaluation should be noted in the report of the medical expert. If an interpreter was used, this should be so stated. If a chaperone was present during any aspect of the evaluation, this also should be indicated.

The medical expert should review the original documents and extract pertinent information. The records reviewed and/or relied on in arriving at a conclusion should be listed. Use caution when dealing with HIV results and the diagnosis of AIDS. There are issues of confidentiality. In California, the name of the individual may be removed and a number or "John/Jane Doe" assigned. There are rules to prevent these reports from falling into employers' hands. Articles, journals, and texts relied on should be available. Some venues require signing of the report and specified statements under penalty of perjury.

Table 13-4. Usual Format for a Medical Evaluation

Introduction (description of how subject came to be referred)
Qualification of medical expert (optional, depends on case)
Documents received and reviewed
Description of subject: age, sex, occupation, employer, home location (if relevant)
    Chief complaints
    History of present illness
    Subjective and objective information descriptive of the mechanism of injury
    All previous childhood and adult illnesses (mental and physical)
    Injuries
    Surgical procedures
    Hospital admissions, outpatient procedures, and emergency or urgent care visits
Personal history
    Age, sex, number of marriages, and number of children
    Name and location of all places of residence since birth
    Areas visited prior to onset of symptoms
    Alcohol and tobacco use (how much and how long)
    Allergies (inhalant, oral, or contact)
    Prescription medications (present and past, dosage, reason for and length of use)
    Recreational drug use (present and past), include IV drug use
    Herbs and other nontraditional medication use
    Recreation and hobbies
    Physical exercise
    Use of chemicals in the home (cleaning agents, aerosols, etc.)
    Legal history (multiple claims, similar injuries, encounters with the law)
Family history
    Grandparents, parents, siblings, spouse, and children
    Age, sex, and health status currently (if deceased, cause of death)
    Chronic or occupational disease in the family or in the persons in the individual household
    Medical records
    Hospital records
        Treating physician records
        Prior diagnostic studies
        Clinical evaluation
        System review
        Physical examination
        Appropriate general and specific diagnostic testing
Diagnosis
Opinion
Justification of opinion

Postreport Preparation of an Expert

Postreport preparation is easy if one has practiced the 7 Ps: "Prudent prior planning prevents piss poor performance." Each case should be approached from the perspective that the medical expert very probably will undergo a discovery deposition or court appearance in the future. All reports, therefore, should be organized in the same fashion with information in the same place. The analysis should answer the questions from the referring party and include information the physician will need.

Table 13-5. *Records and Documents that May Yield Useful Information in an Evaluation*

Medical records
Emergency room reports
Clinic notes
Hospital records
Laboratory tests
Work records
Timesheets and pay stubs
Product descriptions
Job description or job analysis
Material Safety Data Sheets
Personal records
   Private investigator reports
   Accident reports
   Personal notes and lists
Legal
   Court records
   Court opinions
   Previous workers' compensation awards
Medicolegal reports
   Reporting physicians

One should have a meeting with the referring attorney to prepare for court appearances and depositions. The attorney should review the expert's file for appropriate content from a legal perspective. The types of questions that will be asked and the questions anticipated from the other side should be discussed. The key issues should be discussed along with the current legal theory of the case. The expert should not carry any extraneous information into the proceedings. The attorneys can inspect the expert's files at any point and may ask for a copy of the file and a copy of any doodling. Be prepared to deal with authoritative texts or articles that may be presented to contradict your opinion. Be cautious in conceding that an entire text or journal is authoritative unless you know what it says on the subject.

14

Presumption

TEE L. GUIDOTTI

Modern presumption developed as a simplifying doctrine within the workers' compensation system. The concept of presumption makes sense when a disorder is well known, and well documented, to be strongly associated with particular workplace or environmental conditions. A claimant who presents with a particular diagnosis or type of injury in the particular setting that is characteristic for the disorder is presumed to be eligible for compensation and benefits as long as the conditions are documented. In other words, if a case walks like a duck and quacks like a duck, it probably is a duck, and the adjudicating agency should not waste time disputing its essential "duck-ness."

The justification for presumption is that the disease is either so common within a particular occupation or so rarely found outside certain occupations that any given claimant almost certainly developed the disorder as a result of work-related exposure. The simplest example is mesothelioma, which in the presence of a work history suggestive of exposure to asbestos is almost universally accepted as work-related. The most controversial presumptions are those for elevations in risk of common disorders. This is the general problem with presumption in the case of most adverse health outcomes relevant to occupations such as firefighting, where lung cancer has been a persistent issue.

Presumption in Practice

In practice, presumption usually takes one of three distinct forms:

1. Scheduled or "prescribed" occupational diseases.
2. Rebuttable presumptions.
3. Legislated entitlement programs.

Schedules of Prescribed Diseases

Occupational disease schedules are lists of disorders that are considered an outcome of occupation in almost every case. The first schedule arose as a supplement to the workers' compensation system in the United Kingdom, which originally covered only injuries but not diseases. In the 1906 amendments to the British Workers' Compensation Act of 1897, six diseases were identified as meriting compensation without argument as long as occupational exposure could be documented: anthrax, lead poisoning, mercury poisoning, phosphorus poisoning, arsenic poisoning, and ankylostomiasis. (Workers' compensation was later replaced in the United Kingdom by a system limited to disability compensation with the advent of National Health Insurance, which provides universal health care regardless of whether the condition requiring treatment is occupational or nonoccupational.) In this early legislation, certain criteria were spelled out. The disorder should be a risk associated with particular occupations and not a universal risk, and the circumstances from which the disorder arose should be documented or obvious. These criteria are fundamental to present-day presumption as well. Today, the Industrial Injuries Disablement Benefit Scheme in the United Kingdom recognizes dozens of specific conditions associated with specified workplace exposures. Claimants who cannot demonstrate that they have one of the prescribed diseases or who cannot document their occupational history to the satisfaction of an adjudication officer are not recognized as having an occupational disease. New diseases are added from time to time by an advisory council (Industrial Injuries Advisory Council) after review of the evidence.

Obviously, a system that rests so completely on the incorporation of occupational diseases into schedules risks denying compensation to workers who have conditions that represent new or previously unrecognized occupational associations. It puts workers at a serious disadvantage who develop, as a result of work exposure, common disorders (such as obstructive lung diseases) that have nonoccupational risk factors and are not characteristic for a particular occupation. The advantages, however, are that such a system can be very quick and responsive to workers who qualify or are "lucky enough" to have simple injuries. The great majority of injury cases are handled satisfactorily, but those with complicated circumstances and occupational disease cases may find the system very slow. A schedule expedites the handling of obvious cases.

Rebuttable Presumptions

A *rebuttable presumption* is a policy that a disease will be considered as arising out of work unless there is a reason to dispute this conclusion. The rebuttal is based on the circumstances of the case and the characteristics of the individual worker. The general association between the disorder and occupation is not itself disputed, only the association in the particular case.

For example, a workers' compensation board or carrier routinely may accept cases of new-onset asthma in workers exposed to isocyanates as being work-related unless there is a challenge to the claim, usually by an employer. The claim may be rebutted with evidence, for example, that the worker was not exposed to sufficient levels or for a sufficient duration, that the particular isocyanate used was not volatile, that the chemical was not used near the workstation in question, that the worker had a prior history of asthma, or that the effect was an irritant effect and not true sensitization, which would limit future employment prospects in the industry for the claimant.

Although a rebuttable presumption may be contested by the employer, the burden of proof is on the insurance carrier or the employer to demonstrate why the claim should not be accepted. Some rebuttable presumptions have been written into law; for example, the states of California and Virginia have rebuttable presumptions enacted for chronic obstructive pulmonary disease or cancer for firefighters and for myocardial infarction for firefighters and police.

Ideally, rebuttable presumptions should be limited to disorders in which the group risk is at least doubled, such that in every case the odds are as or more likely than not the result of work-related factors. However, legislated schedules often are based on notions of risk that cannot be documented scientifically or that are historical but not necessarily current. Once legally established, it is almost impossible to remove such provisions.

Entitlement Programs

Certain occupational groups have received special recognition for their unique occupational health risks in the form of legislated programs. The Black Lung Benefits Program, for example, was established under the Coal Mine Health and Safety Act of 1969 and is financed by a tax on every ton of coal mined. Miners qualify by virtue of the level of impairment from respiratory disease and documentation of their work history. Similar programs exist for nuclear workers who worked with radiation and have been proposed for workers in the nuclear industry who were exposed to chemicals, especially beryllium, but not necessarily radiation.

These programs often are predicated on the role and predicament of the population being served. For example, the Black Lung Benefits Program was in part a political response to the perceived need to alleviate the historical social burden of occupation-related disability in Appalachia. Programs for nuclear workers have been motivated in part by a desire to ensure compensation for workers who took health risks during the Cold War in the interests of national security. However, such programs also can be motivated by a political desire to reduce or manage liability. In 2000, efforts were made to introduce legislation in Congress to manage compensation for asbestos-exposed workers by establishing an adjudication process that would operate by presumption. One of the explicit reasons given by the sponsors for why the legislation was needed was to limit and control civil litigation verdicts, thus ensuring the viability of defendant companies at risk for large punitive damages.

Assumptions Underlying Presumption

Presumption rests on a set of assumptions that rarely are examined in detail. A general presumption of risk rests on the conclusion that any given claim from a particular group (such as workers exposed to lead) for a particular disease (such as lead poisoning) that comes before the adjudication agency is (much) more likely than not to be work-related. The claim can be expedited on this assumption. Presumption requires that the individual case matches circumstances known to give rise to the condition and that the case is drawn from a specific, defined population known to be at risk. As a practical matter, the probability that the injury came about because of any other cause must be so low that assessing causation is not worth the administrative effort.

This level of certainty may be achieved in two ways:

1. Exclusive causation.
2. General presumption of risk.

Certain diseases, such as the pneumoconioses, are rare or nonexistent outside certain occupations. Presumption here is essentially a question of exclusive causation. In contrast, with disorders that are not unique to certain occupations and exposures, there is a general presumption of risk that occurs when a particular disorder is so common in a population that within that population most cases are work-related. For example, asbestos-exposed workers with mesothelioma are not usually challenged because mesothelioma is very rare except among workers handling asbestos.

It is possible to rebut the presumption in an individual case by demonstrating the presence of hazards and risks unrelated to the claimant's stated occupation that are likely to have made a greater contribution to the outcome than the occupational risk. For example, in a police officer with elevated blood lead levels who is also an avid hunter, the exposure to lead from loading ammunition at home may be greater than the exposure to lead on the police firing range. Likewise, if the personal risk profile of the claimant is unusually low, the occupational risk may be negligible. In cases where there is a reasonable presumption, the expert who challenges the presumption must explain why the individual would have contracted the disorder from another cause. These are problems of apportionment, which are discussed in Chapter 11. In general, unless there is a clear and compelling alternative explanation, it is hard to argue against a presumption.

General Presumption of Risk

The analysis of presumptive occupational causation in a disease that is not unique to occupational exposures is a process with multiple steps. First, the association with occupation or, preferably, a specific occupational exposure must be demon-strated. Usually this is done by means of epidemiologic studies, from which a population-specific relative risk (hereinafter *population risk*) is derived. Finally, the criteria have to be shown to apply in the individual case. Then rebuttals are formulated and presented or anticipated. These actual hypothetical rebuttals are addressed in the report on file to ensure that other causes have not been overlooked.

Presumption must satisfy the usual compensation standard of proof that the occupational cause must be "more likely then not" responsible for the outcome (giving the benefit of the doubt to the claimant). Therefore, a general presumption of risk requires demonstration that the risk associated with occupa-tion must be at least as great as the risk in the general population. This can be shown if the usual measure of risk in epidemiologic studies is at least double the expected risk, making allowances for uncertainty in the estimate. Therefore, a general presumption of risk is only justified if there is a consistent and plausible association with occupation and the magnitude of risk is at least double that of the general population.

General presumption of risk, on the basis of population estimates, assumes that all members of the population or occupation share in the pooled risk about equally or randomly and that it is more likely than not, in the individual case, that the cause of the condition is work-related. In terms of epidemiology, pre-sumption reflects an attributable risk that is greater than the expected risk in an unexposed or general population. One cannot know for certain that any individ-ual case drawn from the population is due to this exposure, but the odds are so great that it is a reasonable working assumption.

A general presumption of risk is not the same as identifying an association. In epidemiology, an *association* merely means that there is a relationship between the risk factor and the outcome. A general presumption of risk implies that the elevated risk is sufficient in magnitude to make it more likely than not that in the individual case the cause of the disorder is related to work. A *presumption* means not only that there is a relationship but also that it is strong enough and consistent enough to be caused by and accounts for more than half the cases of the disease. Both assume that some association with the exposure or occupation already has been proven to a reasonable standard of scientific or legal proof.

The magnitude of risk is critical to the plausibility of a general presumption of risk. The odds of a case that arises out of a working population actually being related to that work have to be such that a presumption in the individual case is reasonable and fair. In the interests of public policy, it is acceptable if a small number of individuals are compensated for diseases that actually were not work-related, but the number cannot be so great that the system overdraws its re-sources. It is less acceptable if individuals are not compensated for diseases that actually did arise from work. Because it is not possible to know with diseases that are not unique to occupations which are work-related and which are not, the presumption depends on the probabilities.

Establishing Presumption

There are two separate questions to be considered in evaluating the association between a putatively work-related condition and occupational exposure when population risk data are applied to individual cases: (1) how strong is the evidence for an association, and (2) how strong is the association itself? The Hill criteria (see Chap. 5) address the former but not the latter. For population risk data to be useful as applied to the individual, however, some indication must be given that the individual risk, inferred from the strength of the association in the population, is at least as great as that from other causes not associated with occupation. This criterion must be satisfied before concluding that an occupational cause is likely in an individual case.

The doubling criterion is not necessarily evidence against an association in the individual case. Its value is in evaluating a general presumption that all (or the great majority of) workers in a given occupation are at risk. The specific case still must be evaluated individually. When a general presumption of risk cannot be made, individual assessment of risk should be used to deal with the merits of the case. Unfortunately, in some jurisdictions, such as Texas, risk doubling has been elevated by judicial decision to the exclusive basis for accepting causation in civil litigation. This is a misunderstanding of what it actually means.

A general presumption of risk is not easily justified or defended in situations of weak associations or when diseases are common in the general population. A more productive approach may be to take the claims on a case-by-case basis, examining individual risk factors and overall risk profile. A general presumption of risk is applied more easily to unusual disorders with high relative risks, particularly when they are unique to or characteristic of certain occupations.

Application to the Individual Case

The next step is to apply this population risk to the individual case. A population risk, which conforms to the past experience of the population under study, is only an estimate of the individual risk. Characteristics of the individual, such as age, length of employment, family history, and lifestyle, all may substantially modify the individual risk profile. For an individual with few risk factors for the disorder, the population risk may be an overestimate of total risk but an underestimate of the risk due to occupation. Conversely, for an individual with many nonoccupational risk factors for the disorder (or occupational risk factors unrelated to the claim), the population risk may be an underestimate of total risk but an overestimate of the risk that can be attributed to occupation. Rebuttal rests on assessing personal characteristics on a case-by-case basis. This is covered in Chapter 11.

Appendix

The rationale behind making a doubling in risk a criterion for presumption requires elaboration. A standardized mortality ratio (SMR) of 200 means that the risk due to the exposure is equal to the risk of the general or comparison population. In epidemiologic terms, this corresponds to an attributable risk that is 100% of expected. This corresponds to an overall probability of 50% that the condition was due to the exposure in the population under study and as applied as an estimate of risk due to exposure in the individual. An SMR of 200 or an equivalent risk estimate, therefore, corresponds to equal odds, or 1:1. A formal treatment is as follows:

$$RD = \text{risk difference (Monson) or attributable risk}$$
$$= R_e \text{ (Monson, risk in exposed population)}$$
$$- R_o \text{ (Monson, risk in unexposed population)}$$

Therefore,

$$R_e = R_o + RD > 2$$

If there is a 50% chance that a condition is the result of exposure, in the individual case, the estimate of *attributable fraction* used as an estimate of apportionment when applied to the individual equals or exceeds 50%. For this to occur, one must show a risk difference equal to 50% of the total risk.

$$RD/(RD + R_o) = 0.5 \ (50\%)$$

Therefore,

$$RD = R_o$$

and

$$RR = \text{relative risk (Monson)} = R_e/R_o$$

Therefore,

$$RR = (R_o + RD)/R_o = (R_o + R_o)/R_o = 2$$

In practice, the criterion of a doubling of risk can be applied liberally, as it should be given the uncertainties and the wide confidence intervals surrounding most of the available estimates. This criterion still excludes many disorders for which there is a clear association but for which nonoccupational risk factors appear to be much more important in determining risk.

"The doctor is in court on Tuesdays and Wednesdays."

15

Communication in Medical Dispute Resolution

MICHAEL D. ROBACK

The use of language may be the most important evolutionary skill of humans because it allows the exchange of information among persons—especially those separated by distance and time. Unlike the opposable thumb, which humankind mastered relatively quickly, language daily contributes both clarity and confusion to our lives. The intermingling of Germanic Old English with Latin- and French-influenced Middle English led to a polyglottic Modern English, a language that is difficult to learn and use. Although we receive much pleasure from the allegorical and metaphorical expansion of the meanings of words by the great poets and playwrights, particularly Shakespeare, the singular simple meanings of common words have been lost to us forever. As Shakespeare *might* have said, "Our thoughts are tortured by text and tongue." The word *butterfly* is an excellent example of a confusing modern word that once made sense before transposition of letters changed it from the original word *flutterbye*.

The preceding paragraph could have been written: English is a complex language. Each slightly varied use of a word, such as in a play or poem, makes understanding more difficult.

The latter paragraph is more precise, succinct—and boring. It is so short and lacking of style that it does not capture the reader's interest nor evoke any involvement. The first paragraph is more interesting and captures the reader's attention, particularly with the explanation of the derivation of the word *butterfly*. However, the first paragraph does not relay the information in a clear and precise manner. The sentence that explains the change from Old to Middle and now Modern English is too long and confusing. It probably would work better in rhetoric than in writing. The first paragraph uses a fallacy of logic called *appeal to authority* when it refers to Shakespeare. Furthermore, the term *text and tongue* that was intended to mean "writing and speaking" might be interpreted completely differently by each reader.

During the Renaissance and post-Renaissance period, two major linguistic events occurred: (1) the attempted unification and standardization of the English language, e.g., Samuel Johnson's dictionary, and (2) growth of the middle class as a result of economic power fueled by the advancement of commercially applied knowledge. Each faction of this new economy developed its own vocabulary within the overall framework of standard English. These special forms of the English language became increasingly incomprehensible to the general public and eventually evolved into the written and spoken "legalese" and "medicalese" of lawyers and doctors, making the general public suspicious and distrustful of what they do not comprehend. Pressured by this growing distrust of lawyers and physicians, each profession now has attempted to demystify its language in order to regain the public trust. While doctors have been very willing to give up the dependency on Latinized phraseology—probably due to laziness—our explanations to patients too often lead to such comments as, "I know the doctor is a good doctor and very smart, but I can't understand what he tells me." After a trial, one may hear, "The doctor gave such a complicated explanation that the jury did not understand a single word."

This chapter looks at the use of language as it underlies decision making and judgments in medical dispute resolution. In addition, this chapter attempts to increase the efficient exchange of information through language between the professions of medicine and law by providing examples of problematic language that impedes clear and precise information exchange in writing and speaking. While one chapter—or even one book—is not sufficient to present a full and complete thesis on this subject, I hope that this discussion will help in the journey to improve communication. While we never can truly become linguistic experts, we can all aspire to be scholars of language.

Thoughts or Words, Who's the Boss?

At the core of all knowledge of language is the concept of *ontology,* the study of existence, which in daily life may be best thought of as what is real, correct, or true. Another foundational concept is *epistemology,* or the study of how we gain knowledge, especially with reference to that which is real and valid. In philosophy, these lead to two separate and often conflicting pathways to knowledge called *rationalism* (truth based on internal thought) versus *empiricism* (truth learned by external observation). With society's reliance on science, rationalism has been relegated to discussion of the larger questions, such as "What is the purpose of life?" Empiricism has shaped the pursuit of practical knowledge applied to most medical and scientific situations because empiricism is excellent for describing the current state of a situation. By its nature, it cannot, however, define how a situation may be improved. Nevertheless, it is through rationalism that most progressive social changes occurred, such as the political evolution from feudal hierarchy into the American democratic experience.

Many medicolegal articles have been written by physicians in a hostile tone emphasizing that medical information can never be adapted to use in law because medicine is based on hard facts determined in a scientific manner and law is created at the arbitrary whim of judges and legislators. Antagonistic physicians fail to recognize that rationalism has its own methodology that, in many ways, is more rigid than the pseudoscience of incomplete medical studies with unsubstantiated conclusions, which often forms the basis for medical decisions. The basic problem with empiricism (and rationalism) is that it must depend on the use of language to describe and discuss all ideas and information. In the 1800s, particularly following the work of the Swiss linguist Ferdinand de Saussure [1], it became apparent to scholars that language does not merely describe reality but often defines it. How we speak actually may determine how we think. It also became clear that language does not evolve in an organized, precise manner but expands and reforms in an unpredictable manner in response to social changes. For example, we are now witnessing an increase in the number of new words derived from the development of computers and the Internet.

The paradoxical problem in the study of communication is that we must use language to analyze language. Thus, given the subject of this chapter, the only way one could do it appropriately would be to use pictures without captions. There is no word that is not vulnerable to differences in interpretation. As Nelson Francis said, "Words do not have meanings; people have meanings for words." The most commonly used words have multiple definitions in dictionaries. Yet word meanings in daily conversation often surpass the dictionary discussion.

Linguistics: The "Science of Words"

To improve the use of the language for the purpose of better dispute-resolution management, an understanding of linguistics, the systematic study of language, is required. According to Geoffrey Finch [2], linguistics cannot be considered a "science" because it is not governed by precise laws. It is not developed through the usual scientific procedure of establishment of hypothesis with subsequent verification by testing. However, linguists try to approach language scientifically by using observation, description, and explanation as a way of developing rules for the analysis of human communication.

Semiotics

The basis for linguistics is an understanding of *semiotics*, or the study of signs. Letters are signs for speech sounds, and words are signs for concepts. Even a photograph is only a sign of an object because it relays incomplete visual information, partially because it reduces a three-dimensional object to a two-dimensional representation. By some process, we are able to expand the abstracted information contained in the word to the photograph and in the photograph to the actual object. However, at each level of abstraction, the potential for distortion is introduced. Ultimately, our goal is to improve the use of language to reduce the distortion in medicolegal dispute resolution.

Semantics and Pragmatics

Two fundamental subdivisions in linguistics are *semantics* and *pragmatics*. Semantics, the older of the two subsets, deals with the definitions and arrangements of words. It analyzes parts of language as synonyms, antonyms, homonyms, and other relationships between words. It attempts the systematic analysis of word groups to develop a taxonomy of word relationships that determines specific differences and similarities between words (e.g., the relationship of the different words for physical attractiveness, i.e., *beauty*, compared with other words such as *pretty, sexy, cute,* and *gorgeous*). Semantics also studies different grammatical arrangements of words, for example, *Do I love you?* and *I do love you*. A semanticist would help us understand why one requires a question mark and the other may use an exclamation mark.

Semantics also looks at the difference between synthetic and analytical "truth." A synthetic statement represents an attempt to use language as a representation or documentation of the reality of experience. This is the area of scientific or inductive reasoning. Synthetic discoveries express new concepts as the definitions of new words. Analytical statements are "true" because of the meaning and relationship of words within a statement and do not necessarily reflect the reality of the world of sensory experience. It is analytical statements that are the subject of *logic* (to be discussed later). This is the realm of deductive logic. Often the use of words falls into the vast undefined area between analytical and synthetic truth.

Pragmatics is newer than semantics and deals with the "chaotic" aspects of language. It was developed in response to the recognition that formal logic was inadequate to the task of the complete and final analysis of language. Consider the use of the word *happy* in the following statements. The statement "Michael is happy" is mutually exclusive of the statement "Michael is not happy." However, the fact that "Michael is not happy" is not the same as "Michael is unhappy." This is a semantically developed analytical statement. There are more than two possible statements of emotion between *happy* and *unhappy*. Furthermore, the situation becomes more complicated with the statement "Michael is not unhappy." Now we have four statements conveying four different ideas, yet we are not sure of the precise meaning of *happy*.

Pragmatics studies these types of incompatibilities. Pragmatics considers the practical use of the language beyond the formal semantic development. It deals with certain understandings that are beyond the specific statement, which are called *implicatures*. The study of implicatures is the basis for the pragmatic approach and is the manner by which formal language is often adjusted to fit the needs of common understanding and interpretation. For this reason, the rules of grammar as well as the definitions of the words are mutable and can change. Grammarians now function more in a descriptive rather than a prescriptive manner. This understanding of the use of implicatures was developed by the philosopher H. P. Grice [3]. Grice hypothesized that for communication to occur successfully in natural everyday language, there must be an implied agreement over interpretation of language, either initially or developed through discussion. The successful exchange of information using language requires cooperation of the participants.

The expansion of the semantic approach to language by the pragmatist has resulted in the further development of *deconstructionism*. Its originator, French thinker Jacques Derrida [4], set forth his views that (1) language is actually not as unified and precise as traditionally believed, (2) there are an infinite number of variations of any linguistic statement, and (3) one of the purposes of linguistics is to understand the social and other forces that shape language. Derrida demonstrated that all the rules of linguistics cannot explain how one specific conversation will develop between two specific individuals on a specific day. Deconstructionists assert that the only chance for improving the application of language to thought development is by pointing out that the idol (dictionary-defined language) has clay feet (intrinsic ambiguities in the common use of all words that severely limit the absolute certainty of any statement).

Languid Language

One of the major problems with medical reports in medical dispute-resolution situations is the unintentional use of expressions that are vague or have multiple meanings rather than those which are precise and clearly understood. For example, take the common medical phrase *essentially normal,* which often is used to describe a finding on physical examination or on a diagnostic test. Examples include "The MRI was essentially normal" and "The range of motion was essentially normal." The modifier *essentially* confuses the more absolute term *normal* by suggesting that it was not completely normal without explaining the degree of variation from *absolutely* normal. This language error is compounded when it is introduced to describe tests in the physical examination section of a report, when it should be used in the conclusion section (prognosis) of the report after tests are completed. If a doctor in his or her physical examination report states that the lumbar range of motion is "essentially normal," he or she is not reporting an actual physical finding but the *conclusions* based on the physical finding. If the actual tests performed and their specific results are omitted, this prevents meaningful comparison of the conclusions by other examining physicians (who may interpret the test results differently.) The term *essentially normal* says "essentially nothing."

In understanding how words and sentences relay information, one must be aware of the concepts of denotation and connotation. The *denotation* of a word is its primary meaning, whereas the *connotation* deals with the spectrum of derived secondary meanings and associated feelings/emotional responses that the word commonly suggests or implies. Thus connotation can be thought of as "reading between the lines." Denotation is a semantic subject, whereas connotation is more of a pragmatic or *deconstructionist* concept. The connotations are often unrecognized but are highly influential in how medicolegal language is applied.

For example, the distinction between *denotation* and *connotation* explains the confusion behind such statements as "It is only a soft tissue injury." The term *injury* describes etiology but does not identify the nature of the resulting damage. *Tissue* is redundant because all physical injuries in some manner involve tissue. The word *soft* is an abstract term dealing with a quality of firmness or hardness in a comparative manner. The question always is, "Softer than what?" The general understanding is that it means "softer than bone," but what is the significance of this distinction? The heart, lung, and brain are composed of tissue that is "softer than bone," and yet injuries to these organs can be of a greater life-threatening nature than that of a fractured bone. The primary difficulty is that the connotation of this phrase is used to suggest a type of injury that is (1) poorly defined, (2) less significant, (3) expected to resolve with little or no residuals, and (4) requires minimal to no treatment. Yet this connotation may not be evident, except to those practicing the specialty of orthopedics.

Fallacies of Logic in Language

The word *fallacy* in its original use indicated a quality of intentional deceptiveness or deceitfulness in purposefully giving false information. However, the original meaning has been modified somewhat, and now the word means a false or mistaken idea or opinion based more on an unintentional error rather than an attempt to deceive:

> The term "fallacy" as appears in common usage has a meaning so broad that it defies definition. . . . In its more restricted logical meaning a fallacy is generally taken to be *an argument which, although having some semblance of validity, is actually inconclusive.* Accordingly, a fallacy is not primarily a mistake in judgement but a mistake in reasoning . . . [5].

It is a fallacy to use extraneous methods of persuasion as a substitute for simply giving supportive documentation—even if the final conclusion is the same. While one may criticize the fallacious approach for any information exchange, it becomes more unacceptable when this false appeal is the only basis for a *sales pitch,* i.e., any propagandistic attempt to influence another person's decision, by means other than the application of exact language to accurately describe all pertinent information. However, one may justify the use of analogy to explain medicolegal information to nonmedicolegal persons because unless the highly technical information of medicine is somehow translated into terms of common experience and understanding, the public (e.g., members of a jury, claims adjusters, attorneys, or judges) will not be able to understand the information and use it meaningfully in decision making. However, this substitution of common terms of medical jargon should not result in the dependency on emotionally charged connotations for dialectic advantage. This following section deals with selected examples of some of the more insidious and inappropriate language fallacies found in medicolegal discussions.

The first is the *fallacy of appeal to authority*. This fallacy harks back to the language of feudal Europe. Such phrases as *low morals* and *higher goals* relate to medieval times, e.g., peasants were "low" and nobles were "high." The use of elevated social position has lost its significance for the most part in our democracy, making these types of references somewhat comical. One example still found in medicine is the reference to a test, such as the magnetic resonance imaging (MRI), as the "gold standard." This is an appeal to authority (higher value). At one time, gold probably could be considered an appropriate reference not only because of its elevated value but more so because of the stability of its value. However, the use of any financial standard today would suggest an unpredictable roller coaster. Nevertheless, even if one discards the term *gold standard*, how well does the MRI (and its current descriptive language) rate as a diagnostic test in the determination of lumbar pathology and associated impairment and disability?

Diagnostic Testing and Descriptive Language

Medical testing, as all science, is predicated on certain assumptions: (1) the future will be like the past, (2) individual experience allows the development of general rules, and (3) general rules can be applied to individual situations. The MRI, like any currently available medical test, does not duplicate reality but only gives a representative "sign." Unfortunately, this is overlooked both in the application of MRI-derived information to treatment situations and in medicolegal disputes. When we use absolute language in situations of relative information, we confuse the medical conclusion, which makes medicolegal determinations more difficult. How does one analyze the MRI on a semiotic basis?

As in any photographic system, choices must be made in order to develop visual information in an MRI. These are no different than choosing the speed of a film or the aperture of a camera. The first major "abstraction" is that MRI information represents in gray tones objects that have color in real life. Also, it reduces three-dimensional material to a two-dimensional representation. Looking at lumbar MRIs, there is further distortion as the size is decreased to put more views on a single film (probably for economic reasons). The gray tones can be manipulated to increase the impact of certain tissues by selectively increasing the contrast to allow visual distinction (such as the disk from bone). These photographic choices, however, make it more difficult to distinguish among other tissues, such as the distinction between scar and disk. Even more important than the "photographic decisions" is the fact that this test in no way can duplicate function during life activities because the test currently demands that the patient remain motionless. In order to accomplish this, the patient is placed in the position of maximum relaxation and minimal stress. Therefore, when a radiologist describes a disk bulge as being 2 mm (or less accurately using the descriptive adjective *minimal*), it must be understood that the disk bulge is under the least amount of deforming forces. Therefore, the information reported is probably the bulge at its smallest and not the maximum size of the bulge as if the patient were repeatedly lifting heavy weights in awkward positions. Further obscuring the issue is that the written reports do not indicate any of these limitations of the MRI. This is true for most, if not all, current tests.

One way that a physician can analyze the conceptual limits of any test is to list those structures of potential pathology/abnormal function and determine the efficacy of each of their representations by the test in question. The assumption that MRIs are accurate visual representations of the disk unfortunately does not solve the dilemma. One also must question whether demonstration of the disk deformity is the most important medical factor in determining functional impairment (an important medicolegal determination). For example, nerve root dysfunction is a reason for most lumbar disk surgery. However, the current MRI systems do not allow an uninterrupted mapping of the entire nerve root within the spinal canal. There are sections on an MRI in which the nerve root is not visualized completely, and in some sections it is not visualized at all. Therefore, the MRI test is remarkably deficient in its inability to map out the entire nerve pathway. Finally, reliance on the MRI is problematic because no matter how much the visual representation can be improved (e.g., using color cineradiographic imaging under strenuous conditions), what one sees is just a study of structure, and it cannot give us information concerning pathologic physiology.

This same type of analysis can be applied to most current diagnostic tests, which are presented as having a level of exalted certainty. Each has sufficient value (and limitations) that the term *gold standard* adds nothing.

A further problem impeding understanding of diagnostic test information again relates to language. Most early medical articles used different terminology chosen according to the discretion of each author. As the number of articles increased and the information was disseminated to the general medical community, medical organizations tried to develop common terminology. In the interpretation of MRIs, terms such as *protrusion* (current) versus *herniation* (prior) have added to the confusion. Obviously, this problem with the use of different terms for the same basic subject impedes communication and understanding.

Language Errors

Mistakes in reasoning often lead to the incorrect use of common language. These mistakes have been categorized by scholars of language in an effort to eliminate incorrect usage by increasing the awareness of the misuse.

Equivocation describes the faulty use of a single term. A lawyer may ask, "Doctor, aren't you being unreasonable to question the *facts* in this case?" Because the lawyer is substituting the word *facts* for the word *assumptions* (or *allegations*), he or she is guilty of equivocation. An equivocation is often used to intimidate a witness by presenting information as already having been accepted as true or valid when this is not established until the end of the trial.

Amphibole is the use of a faulty grammatical construction that allows more than one interpretation. For example, consider the statement by a physician, "Dr. X is the worst doctor in this city since I became a physician in this town." One linguistically correct interpretation of this sentence is that the doctor who is speaking was the worst doctor in the town before Dr. X arrived. This is obviously not what the testifier meant to imply by the statement, but it is a correct grammatical interpretation of it.

The fallacy called *composition* occurs when (1) a single or a limited number of occurrences or situations is presented and (2) then expanded inappropriately to represent more than the sum of the parts. A classic example of this seen in the courtroom is the lawyer who states, "Would you suffer for 10 cents a minute the type of pain and loss of happiness that this back-injured patient has suffered at the hands of this negligent physician?" What is not explained is the calculated *total amount of money* as represented by the expected number of minutes this person will live. The second unexplained factor in this composition is the *indefinite period of time*. This situation (10 cents a minute) calculates to $1,576,800 in 30 years.

The public misunderstanding of the use of medication represents another example of the fallacy of *composition*. For instance, it has been well emphasized by the medical community that the use of oral steroids by athletes to increase performance is dangerous. This has resulted in the public being fearful of the use of steroids for any condition.

The opposite of composition is *division*. This is a fallacy that is derived from taking a collective premise and applying it inappropriately to each of its components. The fallacy of division stems from the assumption that every group or whole is a combination of identical components or parts. This premise is often used to defend a physician in a malpractice case by the defense attorney, who emphasizes the image of doctors as persons who spend their entire lives dedicated to the pursuit of excellence and compassionate patient care. Yet any individual doctor may be an indifferent, careless physician.

Other fallacies deal not so much with errors in the use of language (mistaken use of a word or incorrect syntax of a sentence) as with misuse of the logical development of a presentation or argument. *Ad verecundiam* (appeal to authority/reverence) and *ad hominem* (appeal to bigotry) are two fallacies that focus on a person rather than on the information. Both these fallacies describe arguments based on discussing the credentials or lack of credentials of an expert rather than the relevance and accuracy of the actual information presented. *Ad verecundiam* is a false emphasis on authority or respect, and *ad hominem* refers to false attacks against the person. These two forms of the same fallacy are often used when comparing the expertise of medical witnesses, such as the false belief that a specialist always knows more than a primary physician or a university teaching physician knows more than a practicing community physician. While it might be reasonable to assume that an orthopedic surgeon would have greater expertise in issues dealing specifically with types of spinal fusion than an anesthesiologist, it would not necessarily be true that the orthopedic surgeon does a better medicolegal evaluation, particularly if the anesthesiologist specializes in musculoskeletal pain management and performs many of the newer invasive procedures, such as diskograms, facet blocks, and similar medical procedures. Our respect for higher levels of learning or greater length of experience is not unreasonable, but it can be fallaciously overemphasized as a substitute for the actual facts in medicolegal cases. If there are two medical experts of the same specialty with one being older, lawyers will present the older physician as "having more experience," whereas the younger physician will be presented as "having more up-to-date training." Ironically, neither situation, even if correct, guarantees greater knowledge.

Ad populum means "appeal to common experience" and is a somewhat more modern appeal in that it relies on the concept of the democratization of knowledge by suggesting that all people have innate natural abilities to interpret and analyze. This appeal certainly would not have worked in a society ruled by Platonic philosopher-kings. An example of this fallacy is the question, "Doctor, do you agree that X is true because X is accepted by all the doctors in the community?"

While compassion is a virtue, an argument based on *ad misericordiam* (an appeal to pity) uses pity as a mechanism for persuasion rather than a rational presentation based on fact. This appeal to pity is used subtlety when a doctor reports symptoms by stating, "The patient suffers from pain in her back," rather than simply stating, "The patient reported pain in her back." Conversely, one can create the fallacy of *false suspiciousness* by stating, "The patient claims that she has pain in her back."

The appeal to ignorance, *ad ignorantiam,* another fallacy of logic, is an attempt to win an argument based on an excessive variety of statistics and other information that the audience (usually a jury) is unable to fully analyze or check. This may be used instead of a straightforward presentation of the relevant facts.

Language and the Law

Oliver Wendell Holmes, Jr., stated, "The life of the law has not been logic; it has been experience" [6]. It is the job of the judge to ensure that evidence is reliable and fair. Thus some of the ambiguity or uncertainty intrinsic to current medical information must be modified so that a legally acceptable level of certainty about the information can be established for the final adjudication. The public has been led to believe that medicine is based on high levels of certainty.

In order to use the positive reinforcement resulting from the patient's confidence in the doctor's abilities, physicians have been disinclined to expose the limits of our actual scientific knowledge. As the ivory tower image of medicine fades, doctors are required in many ways to communicate this uncertainty as, for example, *informed consent*. However, in medicolegal settings, a doctor must be able to present medical information to a sufficient standard of legal certainty.

This chapter cannot deal with all the variations in different types of medicolegal systems, except to encourage the reader to learn more about the specific court system in which he or she may participate. Particular attention should be given to understanding the medicolegal terminology, particularly with compensation systems (Social Security, Workers' Compensation).

Language and Law: The Example of the Workers' Compensation System

Most compensation systems were developed from a governmental social policy to protect injured or ill workers by providing easy access to the benefits of treatment and financial compensation for a reduced earning capacity instead of forcing them to turn to the uncertainties of civil litigation (see Chap. 19). These systems were set up so that a disabled person would only need to get medical verification of a work-related injury as the cause in order to reach a threshold level for state or federal benefits. Unfortunately, as health care became an industry affected by economic pressures (for profit), compensation systems developed the same adversarial qualities as civil litigation situations.

Because compensation systems have more formal rules, they necessitate a greater use of certain specific words, terms, and phrases. This specific language often is interpreted mathematically to allow the calculation of monetary value for permanent disability payments and other similar benefits. While each compensation system is somewhat different, they commonly require specific terminology to be used when describing certain factors. The most frequent considerations are: (1) causation, (2) subjective factors (symptoms), (3) objective findings (results of diagnostic tests and physical examination), and (4) loss of preinjury work capacity and/or impairment and/or work restrictions. The factor of "pain and suffering" is less important and less often considered in compensation systems than in civil litigation.

The factors used to determine what qualifies as an injury or illness often differs in a compensation versus in a liability system. Most frequently, personal injuries in civil litigation result from an accident that is a single sudden, unexpected, injurious activity such as falling down in a supermarket (see Chap. 2). The concept of cumulative trauma is less frequently applied in civil litigation (except in toxic tort cases). Compensation systems often accept injuries due to repetitive microtrauma usually caused by performing the normal and expected activities of a given job. Poor ergonomic designs of workstations and the excessive duration and repetitiveness of strenuous activities may cause microtrauma. Because compensation systems deal with cumulative trauma, issues concerning hypertension, psychiatric problems, allergies, and hearing loss become subjects of medicolegal disputes.

When dealing with medicolegal systems, particularly compensation systems, it is necessary for the medical expert to learn a new vocabulary. This often includes specific, unvarying legal definitions of common words or phrases. The use of a similar but different word (such as *slight* rather than *mild*) does not carry the same legal acceptability as the specifically required term. The meanings of these specific words, or *terms of art*, are often the results of case decisions (case law). By using the identical word, you conform to established legal precedents. In the California workers' compensation system, the phrase that justifies treatment is "reasonable and necessary for the treatment or the relief of symptoms." If a defense doctor for the insurance company stated that a treating physician's medical care was "not required" instead of "not reasonable and necessary," the testimony would bear little legal weight. The term *required* in this legal setting is not the same as *reasonable and necessary.* If the applicant's treating physician tries to defend his or her care by using only the term *reasonable* but does not also use the term *necessary,* his or her documentation also would carry little legal weight. In common language, the terms *necessary* and *required* have very similar meanings, but in this legal setting, one term has legal value, whereas the other has no legal worth. The ease of access to the medicolegal vocabulary for physicians varies depending on both the system and the location. In California, there was no organized single source of legal terminology and concepts for physicians for over 50 years until the Industrial Medical Council, the state committee that deals with medical care and evaluation, wrote a physician's handbook in 1993. While not all-inclusive, this handbook resulted in a significant improvement in the quality of medicolegal reports.

Many medical terms in a compensation system are defined specifically and must be used precisely. In particular, symptoms are defined by intensity and frequency. For example, the frequency of symptoms in the California workers' compensation system is classified as occasional (25%), intermittent (50%), frequent (75%), or constant (90% to 100%). Therefore, *constant* may be used even when a symptom exists less than 100% of the time. The word *constant* is actually linguistically incorrect because *constant* refers to an unchanging quality or lack of variation. A better term for duration of a symptom at a level of 90% would be the term *semicontinuous.* If a doctor wrote the term *semicontinuous symptoms* rather than *constant symptoms,* the report would not be useful because the term *semicontinuous* is not the proper legal term. When describing the intensity of pain, the established terms are *minimal, slight, moderate,* and *severe.* If *mild* is used as the description rather than *slight,* the meaning would have no legal definition.

Language and Public Policy: The Example of Guidelines

The common source of the medicolegal language concepts used by most physicians to determine the functional loss secondary to medical conditions is the American Medical Association's (AMA) *Guides to the Evaluation of Permanent Impairment* [7]. First compiled in 1971, it is used for the evaluation of workers' compensation benefits in more than 40 states, with California being the most notable exception. The AMA guidelines are an attempt to evaluate injuries and illnesses by a permanent impairment system that can be expressed in numerical values. It is constructed as a pyramidal system in which each impairment is assigned a rating that can be combined to give a rating of whole-person impairment. While the attempt by the AMA was to develop a medical impairment rating system that was scientific, unbiased, reliable, and internally consistent, it has fallen short of its desired goal. In part due to recognition of the limits of the most recent fourth edition, the AMA in 1977 started work on a fifth edition but abandoned the effort in 1998.

Most of the problems with the AMA guidelines concern the underlying hypotheses and paradigms, which sacrificed perceived and actual loss of function and quality of life in order to maintain a rigid, mathematically consistent system. Unfortunately, many important aspects of living, including freedom from pain, were de-emphasized in order to attempt the development of a standardized, reproducible system that relies excessively on such things as range of motion. For example, a patient who is capable of spontaneous respiration but is 100% confined to a bed could be rated as having as low as a 50% whole-person impairment [7], yet such a person would have absolutely no ability to function in an open labor market. In attempting to overgeneralize, this artificial rating system has failed to meet its goal.

Conclusion

Success in modern medicine demands the sale of an image. Patients trust doctors with the sacredness of their well-being because of their demeanor and ability to communicate primarily through dialogue. Physicians are now faced with the paradox of having a better product (improved science of medicine) and yet facing a decline in social prestige (decreased art of medicine). Doctors often believe that they are effective communicators because of their high level of intelligence, their extensive academic training (necessary to be successful in college and medical school), and their practiced ability to communicate with their patients. Often physicians fail to recognize that the patient is in a dependent, nonconfrontational position. It is quite different to deal with other professional communicators, especially those in the legal profession, for whom communication has an aspect of conflict that sometimes becomes linguistic combat. By paying strict attention to how and why they are communicating medical information, physicians can become skilled participants in the medicolegal arena.

References

1. Saussure, Ferdinand de. *Course in General Linguistics,* edited by Charles Bally and Albert Sechehaye with collaboration by Albert Reidlinger; translated and annotated by Roy Harris. La Salle, IL: Open Court, 1986, c. 1983.

2. Finch, Geoffrey. *Linguistic Terms and Concepts.* New York: St. Martin's Press, 2000.

3. Grice, H. Paul. *Studies in the Way of Words.* Cambridge, MA: Harvard University Press, 1989.

4. Derrida, Jacques. *The Archeology of the Frivolous.* Pittsburgh: Duquesne University Press, 1980.

5. Kreyche, Robert J. Sources of deceit. In: *Logic for Undergraduates,* 3d ed., New York: Holt, Rinehart and Winston, 2000. P 20.

6. Holmes, Oliver Wendell, Jr. *The Common Law.* Boston: Little, Brown, 1881.

7. Doege, Theodore C. (ed), Thomas P. Houston (assoc. ed). *Guides to the Evaluation of Permanent Impairment.* Chicago: American Medical Association, 1993.

"I ask that the record show that the witness does not presume
to speak for the animal kingdom but is testifying here strictly
in his capacity as a beaver."

16

The Era of Juriscience: Evidentiary Needs in Environmental Law

LARRY A. REYNOLDS

Decision makers are asked increasingly to regulate a growing number of activities that raise complex environmental health issues [1]. These issues arise in a variety of legal contexts, including the establishment of appropriate regulatory standards, the prosecution of criminal and quasi-criminal charges for the alleged violation of environmental health protection legislation, civil actions brought by way of a growing number of toxic tort claims, and administrative hearings relating to the approval of proposed and existing activities that raise environmental health issues. In response, these decision makers are turning to the scientific and medical communities for assistance in resolving these issues. However, it is becoming apparent that science is often unable to provide the required assistance. As one author has observed:

> A recurring issue in environmental law is scientific and technological uncertainty. . . . Lawyers like to think that scientists have clear and definitive answers to certain factual questions—is this level of pollution harmful, and precisely what damage will it produce? The answer is likely to reflect a judgment, rather than a statement of fact. . . . The resolution of such mixed questions—questions of fact which carry the law with them—is one of the earmarks of environmental law. It is also one of the reasons for the problems of government agencies that seem to lag in the promulgation of standards. The impatience with agencies may be justified—but the delays in regulation and in adjudication are understandable because the field is very complex. . . . There do not seem to be any answers as yet to the many good questions lawyers and administrators ask the scientists [2].

In carrying out its environmental health decision-making responsibilities, the legal system has operated under the assumption that the scientific community is able to provide scientific information on demand and in a form compatible with the requirements of the legal system. With environmental health issues rapidly growing in number and complexity, the demands of the legal system on the scientific community are also increasing. The increasing dependence of the legal system on the scientific community with respect to matters involving environmental health decision making is pushing the scientific and legal sectors of our society into a new and closer relationship. This new and closer relationship is exposing a growing number of problems that may be indicators of fundamental incompatibilities between our society's scientific and legal systems. Moreover, these incompatibilities are creating and will continue to create problems for the legal system in carrying out its environmental health decision-making responsibilities.

This chapter will commence with an introductory discussion of the relationship between the scientific/medical and legal systems. The focus will then shift to the identification of those problems which environmental health decision makers perceive to exist with the scientific evidence presented to them—evidence on which they must base their decisions.

The Relationship of Science and Law

Historical Background

The relationship between science and law within the common-law world is a long one. As early as 1554, the English courts expressed encouragement for the use of court-appointed scientific expertise in resolving scientific issues arising within law:

> If matters arise in our laws which concern other sciences and faculties we commonly call for the aid of that science or faculty which it concerns, which is an honourable and commendable thing. For thereby it appears that we do not despise all other sciences but our own, but we approve of them and encourage them . . . [3].

In the United States, the earliest record of the use of expert witnesses at trial dates back to 1665 [4]. By 1782, the acceptance of expert scientific witnesses in England had advanced to the point where the parties called their own expert witnesses for the first time (*Folkes v. Chadd* [5]).

By the mid-1800s, however, it appears that the common-law legal system was beginning to have misgivings with respect to its relationship with the scientific community. Concerning the situation in England, one author notes

> In 1554 it might have been true that the courts adopted a generally encouraging attitude to the expert. But by the beginning of the twentieth century, a deep-seated suspicion had set in. Indeed, it was given voice in the 1870s by Sir George Jessel, Master of the Rolls, whose judicial life frequently obliged him to decide between the opinions of competing experts. According to him, the very system of the adversary trial, with its potential strength of submitting testimony to the gruelling scrutiny of cross-examination and conflicting evidence, encouraged the engagement of paid experts. Sadly, but inevitably, these mercenaries of the witness-box tended to become

locked into the forensic battalions of those who hired them. The expert might begin with integrity. But the whole pressure of the adversary system would, more often than not, force him or her to the limits of expertise. All too often, the litigant's cause would become the expert's cause, as the expert was pitched from familiar surroundings into the contest that is the hallmark of the adversary trial [6].

In the United States, concern with the use of expert scientific witnesses in trials began to appear in legal writings as early as 1897 with the appearance in the *Harvard Law Review* of an article entitled, "Expert Testimony—Prevalent Complaints and Proposed Remedies," which considered the problem of confusion among decision makers resulting from expert witnesses reaching contradictory conclusions [7].

The legal system responded to these problems by modifying legal procedures through development of a variety of rules of evidence, first at common law and later in legislation, that attempted to facilitate the admission of scientific information in legal decision-making forums while minimizing the problems created for the legal system by the inclusion of this information. For example, in most common-law jurisdictions, rules were developed that required a scientific expert to be "qualified" by a court prior to providing the court with scientific information in the form of expert evidence, that witnesses could only provide expert scientific evidence within the defined area of their expertise, and that expert scientific witnesses were prohibited from giving evidence with respect to the "ultimate issue" of a jurisprudential dispute. Most of these rules are still in effect today.

The Current Relationship between Science and Law

Today, scientific information is used most often by the legal community to assist in environmental health decision-making processes in two ways.

1. ESTABLISHMENT OF ENVIRONMENTAL HEALTH STANDARDS. The first application of scientific information within legal environmental health decision-making processes is in the establishment of environmental health standards. In setting environmental health standards, the legislator reviews the available scientific information, including any scientific uncertainties that it may contain, and integrates this information into a decision-making process that considers a variety of factors prior to making a political decision as to the appropriate "standard." Such standards most often take the form of precisely described measurable levels set out within regulations enacted under the authority of parent environmental health legislation.

2. ASSISTING ENVIRONMENTAL HEALTH DECISION MAKERS WITH FACTUAL SCIENTIFIC ISSUES ARISING WITHIN JURISPRUDENTIAL DISPUTES. The second area in which the law uses scientific information in environmental

health decision-making processes is in the use of expert scientific evidence for the purpose of providing assistance to environmental health decision makers, such as courts and administrative tribunals, with respect to factual scientific issues arising within jurisprudential disputes. In the judicial context, this purpose was summarized by the Ontario [Canada] Court of Appeal as follows:

> . . . the basic reasoning which runs through the authorities here and in England seems to be that expert opinion evidence will be admitted where it will be helpful to the jury in their deliberations and it will be excluded only where the jury can as easily draw the necessary inferences without it [8].

Thus the role of the scientific expert may be summarized as follows:

> The scientific or technical expert is an aid to factual discovery: an "expert witness" is someone who, through special training, knowledge or experience, is able to assist the legal system (a) in determining what the facts are, relevant to a particular case, and (b) by offering opinion about what the facts might mean for the reconstruction of a course of events or the outcome of a decision. It is important to note that the legal process, and not the expert, defines the factual question which it is relevant for the expert to answer [9].

Toward a New Relationship between Science and Law

Over the years, the rules of legal evidence employed by common-law jurisdictions to address the problems encountered by environmental health decision makers in the introduction of scientific information into legal environmental health decision-making processes have enjoyed a reasonable degree of success. As a result, while the relationship between our scientific and legal systems has been somewhat limited in nature, few serious difficulties have been encountered. However, there are strong indications that this situation is changing. Environmental health issues are rapidly growing in number and complexity, and with this growth, the demands of the legal system on the scientific community are also increasing.

Indicators of Evidential Problems

The demands that the legal system places on the scientific community in its attempt to address a growing number of increasingly complex scientific issues such as those created by the new generation of statutory-based civil environmental health liabilities will force our scientific and legal systems into a closer relationship. However, the success of this relationship will depend on their degree of compatibility. In this regard, we should be cautioned by the words of Dr. Richard Carpenter, who is generally credited with creation of the U.S. National Environmental Health Policy Act (NEPA) [9]. In a 1982 address to the National Science Foundation, he observed the following:

Environmental health science has not been able to deliver the facts, understanding, and predictions that were anticipated by environmental law. This mismatch of capabilities and expectations has resulted in confusion, delay, and inefficiency in governmental efforts to manage natural resources and to protect environmental health quality. The relationships between lawyers and scientists have led to familiar stereotypes: scientists are adverse to the adversary process; lawyers are unprepared academically for interdisciplinary cooperation; scientists disregard human factors; lawyers get their scientific information from popular magazines [11].

It is well accepted by the legal community that certain problems arise when an attempt is made to incorporate scientific information into legal environmental health decision-making processes. However, research in this area is limited to date and has focused primarily on process issues involving the rules of legal procedure required to accommodate scientific information. In the preface to their book, *Expert Evidence: Interpreting Science in the Law,* editors Roger Smith and Brian Wynne summarize the attitude of the legal community as follows:

> The role of scientific expertise in legal and quasi-legal decision settings is increasing steadily. What is true of the courts themselves is probably even truer of the growing number of quasi-legal settings, such as administrative tribunals. . . . Proponents of these procedures hope that the objectivity of science will provide a firm and authoritative input, giving decisions a factual basis that cannot be questioned. That the science often appears equivocal is put down to procedural problems rather than inherent properties of scientific knowledge or methods, and much debate has centered on procedural innovations which attempt to make such decisions more efficient or more authoritative. Discussion about such matters is perhaps most developed in the United States, but their relevance is everywhere apparent [12].

The failure of the legal community to recognize that problems encountered in introducing scientific information into legal environmental health decision-making processes may be symptoms that indicate the presence of more fundamental incompatibilities between the scientific and legal systems should not be surprising, given the current climate of intense pressure within which many environmental health lawyers operate [13].

Most of the information available on the issue of problems with scientific evidence introduced into legal environmental health decision-making institutions and processes is either anecdotal or based on case studies. Conclusively establishing the existence and nature of the evidential problems associated with introducing scientific information into legal environmental health decision making is a difficult task. Four reasons for this difficulty are immediately apparent. First, in the past, the limited demands by the legal system on the scientific community caused a minimal number of problems for environmental health decision makers and thereby generally failed to indicate the existence of incompatibilities between the scientific and legal systems. It is only the recent increased reliance of the legal system on the scientific community and the corresponding increase in problems experienced by the legal system in using scientific information in carrying out its environmental health decision-making responsibilities that is attracting attention to the source of these problems [14].

Second, those problems which in the past were recognized by the legal community generally were considered to be minor difficulties, attributable to shortfalls in scientific evidence. To compensate, the legal system took the position that jurisprudence would overrule juriscience and that these problems mostly could be overcome by modifications of legal procedure.

Third, the scientific and legal communities have carried out their tasks with respect to environmental health decision making in relative isolation, with little or no interaction between them. As one American jurist noted with concern, "Unless something is done to stem the seemingly pathological drive toward exclusivity of scientists and lawyers—in which each excludes the other and both exclude the people, in which we all become 'strangers in the night'—I cannot be sanguine about our children's chances for the good life" [15]. As a result of this isolation, there has been little opportunity to pursue interdisciplinary investigation of possible incompatibilities between the two systems.

Finally, an investigation of this type faces certain methodologic difficulties. For example, the identification of individual problems in environmental health decision making most often takes place on an *ad hoc* basis, wherein a problem is associated with the particular fact situation in which it arises and where an association is seldom made with other seemingly unrelated problems that may be rooted in the same fundamental science-law incompatibility that gave rise to the initial problem. From a methodologic perspective, it is difficult to cast a net wide enough to identify a sufficiently broad spectrum of environmental health decision-making problems that are traceable to common root causes of incompatibility between science and law.

Empirical Investigation

In order to overcome the difficulties in conclusively establishing the existence of evidential problems in the context of environmental health decision making, empirical research is necessary to examine the perceptions of those individuals who have had direct experience in the environmental health decision-making process. A research project entitled, "Environmental Health Decision Making: The Interfaces of Science and Law," was undertaken by the University of Alberta Department of Public Health Sciences through its Environmental Health Program. This research project explored the rapidly developing interrelationship between science and law in legal environmental health decision making by the courts and administrative tribunals in five Canadian jurisdictions (Alberta, British Columbia, Ontario, the Northwest Territories, and the Yukon Territory). This research included a series of empirical studies that examined the perceptions of four of the primary participant groups in legal environmental–environmental health decision-making processes—the judiciary, administrative tribunal members, expert scientific witnesses, and legal counsel. Respondents from each of the four groups were asked similar questions relating to their perceptions of the use of expert scientific evidence in trials and hearings.

Investigation Findings

Problems with the Quality of Scientific Information

There was considerable agreement between the decision makers and the scientific and legal communities that ". . . problems exist in environmental trials and other legal proceedings with respect to the quality of scientific information provided in the form of expert evidence by expert scientific witnesses," with 56% of judges, 60% of legal counsel, and 68% of scientists agreeing with the proposition (Table 16-1).

Problems with the Communication of Scientific Information

There also was considerable agreement between the decision makers and the scientific and legal communities that a failure to communicate exists in environmental decision-making processes. For example, 72% of judges, 85% of scientists, and 67% of legal counsel polled indicated that a problem is caused by ". . . the failure of expert scientific witnesses to effectively communicate scientific information . . . in environmental trials . . ." (Table 16-2). This leads to the conclusion that even if scientific information introduced into environmental health decision-making processes is of good quality, the communication of this evidence is creating an impediment to the availability of this information to decision makers. Even if the information is of high quality, it is of no assistance to the decision maker if it is presented in a manner that is unusable by the decision maker.

Table 16-1. Problems with the Quality of Scientific Information (Environmental Trials and Other Legal Proceedings)

"Problems exist in environmental trials and other legal proceedings with respect to the quality of scientific information provided in the form of expert evidence by expert scientific witnesses."

	Judges	Legal Counsel	Expert Scientific Witnesses	Range
Strongly agree	5.6%	11.4%	10.6%	5.6–11.4%
Agree	50.0%	47.7%	57.6%	47.7–57.6%
Undecided	27.8%	17.0%	18.8%	17.0–20.5%
Disagree	16.7%	20.5%	12.9%	12.9–20.5%
Strongly disagree	0.0%	3.4%	0.0%	0.0–3.4%

Table 16-2. Problems with Communication of Scientific Information (Environmental Trials and Other Legal Proceedings)

"Problems exist in environmental trials and other legal proceedings with respect to the communication of scientific information provided in the form of expert evidence by expert scientific witnesses."

	Judges	Legal Counsel	Expert Scientific Witnesses	Range
Strongly agree	0.0%	11.4%	27.1%	0.0–27.1%
Agree	61.1%	50.0%	54.1%	50.0–61.1%
Undecided	11.1%	11.4%	9.4%	9.4–11.4%
Disagree	27.8%	26.1%	9.4%	9.4–27.8%
Strongly disagree	0.0%	1.1%	0.0%	0.0–1.1%

Problems with the Comprehension of Scientific Information

Even if scientific information is communicated properly, it appears that those participating in environmental health decision-making processes also perceive difficulties with respect to the comprehension of this information by decision makers. With respect to the comprehension of scientific information, 55% of judges, 73% of legal counsel, and 79% of expert scientific witnesses agreed with the statement that ". . . problems exist in environmental trials and other legal proceedings with respect to the comprehension/understanding by the courts and/or legal counsel of scientific information presented in the form of expert evidence by expert scientific witnesses" (Table 16-3).

One reason given was that many legal decision makers do not understand the methods of scientific inquiry and proof. In this regard, the research project found that no less than 55% of judges, 63% of legal counsel, and 69% of scientific

Table 16-3. Problems with Comprehension of Scientific Information (Environmental Trials and Other Legal Proceedings)

"Problems exist in environmental trials and other legal proceedings with respect to the comprehension/understanding by the courts and/or legal counsel of scientific information presented in the form of expert evidence by expert scientific witnesses."

	Judges	Legal Counsel	Expert Scientific Witnesses	Range
Strongly agree	11.1%	19.3%	29.4%	11.1–29.4%
Agree	44.4%	53.4%	49.4%	44.4–53.4%
Undecided	16.7%	8.0%	11.8%	8.0–16.7%
Disagree	22.2%	19.3%	9.4%	9.4–22.2%
Strongly disagree	5.6%	0.0%	0.0%	0.0–5.6%

Table 16-4. Courts Do Not Sufficiently Understand the Methods of Scientific Inquiry and Proof (Environmental Trials and Other Legal Proceedings)

"The courts do not sufficiently understand the methods of scientific inquiry and proof."

	Judges	Legal Counsel	Expert Scientific Witnesses	Range
Major problem	16.6%	29.5%	40.0%	16.6–40.0%
Minor problem	38.8%	34.1%	29.4%	29.4–38.8%
Not a problem	11.1%	11.3%	14.1%	11.1–14.1%
Undecided/no opinion	5.5%	5.6%	7.0%	5.5–7.0%
Unfamiliar with concept	0.0%	0.0%	0.0%	0.0%

witnesses held the view that ". . . the courts do not sufficiently understand the methods of scientific inquiry and proof" (Table 16-4).

Problems with Scientific Uncertainty

The research survey results also tended to support the existence of problems with respect to uncertainty involving scientific information introduced into legal environmental decision-making institutions and processes. For example, with respect to environmental trials and other legal proceedings, 78% of judges, 60% of legal counsel, and 84% of expert scientific witnesses agreed with the statement that ". . . problems exist in environmental trials and other legal proceedings where the scientific information provided in the form of expert evidence results in uncertainty with respect to one or more scientific issues" (Table 16-5).

The relative significance of the issue of uncertainty with respect to scientific

Table 16-5. Problems Where Scientific Information Provided in the Form of Expert Evidence Results in Uncertainty with Respect to Scientific Issues (Environmental Trials and Other Legal Proceedings)

"Problems exist in environmental trials and other legal proceedings where the scientific information provided in the form of expert evidence results in uncertainty with respect to one or more scientific issues."

	Judges	Legal Counsel	Expert Scientific Witnesses	Range
Strongly agree	5.6%	11.4%	23.5%	5.6–23.5%
Agree	72.2%	48.9%	60.0%	48.9–72.2%
Undecided	5.6%	12.5%	14.1%	5.6–14.1%
Disagree	16.7%	26.1%	2.4%	2.4–26.1%
Strongly disagree	0.0%	1.1%	0.0%	0.0–1.1%

information is seen when the impacts of such uncertainty on legal environmental decision making are considered. Legal decision-making processes and institutions are founded on the requirement of resolving a jurisprudential dispute on the basis of evidence that meets a requisite standard of certainty. Decision making in the face of uncertainty with respect to scientific evidence creates a difficult task for the decision maker and goes to the heart of society's confidence in the legal decision-making framework.

Conclusion

The empirical evidence provided by the research project verifies some of the concerns in the anecdotal and case-study literature. It should provide an impetus for members of the scientific and legal communities to develop a dialogue to examine in greater detail the sources and possible solutions to these problems so that the quality of environmental health decision making ultimately will benefit.

Endnotes

1. For the purpose of this chapter, the term *environmental* refers to the natural environment and includes public health issues as they relate to the natural environment.

2. Grad, Frank P. *Treatise on Environmental Law,* Vol. I. New York: Matthew Binder, 1973 (1992 Supplement). Pp 1-25–1-26.

3. *Buckley v. Rice Thomas* (1554), 1 Pl. Comm. 118 at 124, per Saunders J.

4. *A Trial of Witches at Bury St. Edmonds* (1665), 6 Howell's State Trials 687 at 697.

5. *Folkes v. Chadd* (1782), 99 Eng. Rep. 589.

6. Freckelton, Ian R. *The Trial of the Expert: A Study of Expert Evidence and Forensic Experts.* Melbourne, Australia: Oxford University Press, 1987. Foreword, p x.

7. *Harvard Law Review* 1897;11:169.

8. *Fisher v. The Queen* (1961), 130 C.C.C. 1 (Ont. C.A.), affirmed at 130 C.C.C. 22 (S.C.C.), per Aylesworth J.A.

9. Smith, Roger, and Wynne, Brian. *Expert Evidence: Interpreting Science in the Law.* London: Routledge, 1989. P 4.

10. 42 U.S.C. 4321m, 4331–4335, 4341–4347 (1976).

11. Carpenter, Richard A. Ecology in court, and other disappointments of environmental health science and environmental health law. *Natural Resources Lawyer* 1982;15(3):573.

12. *Supra,* n. 11 at 1.

13. These pressures include heavy case loads, high expectations of clients, and the ever-present economic concerns associated with environmental health files.

14. With respect to the availability of research on the relationship between science and law generally, as recently as 1982 it was observed that ". . . there is no survey of the literature presently available. To a great extent, the literature consists only of concerns, concerns of scientists that law is out to get them and concerns of lawyers that scientists are

changing things often for the worst. The literature is surprisingly vituperative" (Gibbons, Hugh. The relationship between law and science. *Idea: The Journal of Law and Technology* 1982;22:43). Even less research is available on the relationship between science and law in the context of environmental health decision making. The available research is primarily entered in the United States, with extremely limited consideration of this issue in Canadian legal and scientific literature. Nevertheless, many of the observations found within the American literature have varying degrees of applicability to the Canadian context and hence are included.

15. Markey, Howard T. Law and science: Equal but separate. *Natural Resources Lawyer* 1982;15(3):620.

17

Evidentiary Needs in Occupational Health Law

ILISE L. FEITSHANS

The law pertaining to management of human resources, including but not limited to the Americans with Disabilities Act [1], its precursor statute, the Vocational Rehabilitation Act of 1973 [2], and the three agencies including the independent adjudicatory body created under the Occupational Safety and Health Act of 1970 [3] comprise a loosely connected legal framework within which workplace medical disputes often must be resolved. Since the birth of the Occupational Safety and Health Act in 1970, and renewed again by the Americans with Disabilities Act in 1990, Congress has spoken directly concerning law and scientific issues that have medical consequences. In the Occupational Safety and Health Act there were many ambiguities and weaknesses because of political compromise, but early case law from the U.S. Supreme Court and the courts of appeals made clear that Congress had expressed a "technology forcing" desire in several aspects of the Occupational Safety and Health Act.

Twenty years later in 1990, the U.S. Congress spoke again with the Americans with Disabilities Act [4]. This time Congress artfully drafted sweeping protections against discrimination, but only indirectly guided social change that would have an impact on medical disputes about workplace health. The Americans with Disabilities Act broadly defines terms such as *disability* and *impairment* in such a manner that new demands are made on employers to hire, place, accommodate, and promote workers who might have been disqualified previously for not being a "healthy worker." Litigation under the Americans with Disabilities Act has shown that the courts are remarkably willing to evaluate, question, and even second-guess the work of skilled medical experts regarding highly technical medical controversies.

Both statutes discussed below antedate *Daubert* and undoubtedly contributed to *Daubert*'s clear willingness to accept as admissible new types of medical evidence and expert data in courts of law compared with the previous narrow rules that governed the admission of expert testimony, especially medical evidence, at common law. It may well be that two decades of the Occupational Safety and Health Act and environmental regulatory history constituted the necessary change in the legal landscape that made the *Daubert* decision possible and that the level of comfort of admitting scientific and medical data into evidence changed as courts came to understand that many types of medical disputes will be heard and resolved by administrative agencies such as the Environmental Protection Agency (EPA), the Occupational Safety and Health Agency (OSHA), and the Occupational Safety and Health Review Commission (OSHRC)—and now the Equal Employment Opportunity Commission as it administers the Americans with Disabilities Act—in addition to the traditional uses of medical expert testimony in litigation, Social Security entitlement disputes, and pharmaceutical regulation.

The final portion of this chapter demonstrates that the U.S. Supreme Court has expanded its *Daubert*-based notions even further in the case of *Kumho Tire*, 119 S. Ct. 1167 in 1999. A decade after the passage of the Americans with Disabilities Act, the *Kumho Tire* case expanded *Daubert* to all types of expert testimony. This case puts the ball back in the experts' court, so to speak, insofar as the Supreme Court has now required that any expert must explain the basis of his or her opinion with reference to peer review and "accepted" methods of practice. This trend is completely consistent with the major thrust of the Americans with Disabilities Act, which requires employers and employees alike to present and rebut medical evidence to determine whether a person is "disabled" or "regarded as impaired" or has been properly given reasonable accommodations for employment opportunity. Taken together, the U.S. Supreme Court cases involving Occupational Safety and Health Act scientific testimony, *Daubert*, *Kumho Tire,* and the Americans with Disabilities Act all point to an unspoken reality: Our adjudication systems at nearly every level have become *de facto* science courts.

This chapter discusses the clear relationship between Occupational Safety and Health Act adjudications (whether concerning citations or at the highest standard-setting level) and Americans with Disabilities Act requirements for scientific and medical expert testimony when resolving questions of statutory interpretation. Further, this chapter takes into account these crucial scientific and medical considerations when looking to the future of legal mechanisms for medical dispute resolution and offers the following radical proposal: These illustrations make it clear that in addition to having training in the law, there should be a medical professional or epidemiologist or other scientist sitting on the U.S. Supreme Court (there is no constitutional requirement that one be a lawyer in order to serve on the U.S. Supreme Court). Moreover, scientists and medical professionals also should be required to be a part of the group of appellate judges who review the opinions of lower courts of law.

The social context in which the scientific evidence in medical disputes is currently embedded is actually one that features several separate and distinct systems fractured incongruously by design to prevent any one group or agency from overtaking the power, authority, or jurisdiction that it was delegated in the statutes that created its mission, as expressed by Congress. The reality, therefore, is twofold: First, there is no need for a proposal for science courts, as was offered in the early 1960s during the Cold War and the "space race." Our courts of law are *de facto* science courts already. Second, it is unrealistic to expect that one set of scientific rules will rule, given the underlying nature of constitutionally required limits on the delegation of authority to agencies, plenipotentiaries, bureaucrats, and elected officials. Fractured power is our nation's hallmark in governance. Thus centralized power through one set of coherent, inevitable, and powerfully admissible rules that "govern" science would be an unacceptable threat to democracy.

Instead, what is needed is not a science court nor a new set of science-evidence rules for medical evidence and related expert testimony. What is needed is scientists bringing their full participation and knowledge to existing judicial decision-making structures. In other words, medical and scientific experts should have their chance at deciding the cases once they have had adequate legal training so that we can use the existing tools to craft and employ sensible rules. Judges should be trained in science, and scientists and medical professionals should act as judges in certain types of cases.

Occupational Health Law from the Eighteenth to the Twenty-First Century

Historically in the United States, industrial accidents or massive deaths in a single occupation have been an important catalyst, if not a precursor, for legislative changes favoring increased occupational health protection. For example, in 1869, a tragic fire in Luzeren County, Pennsylvania, killed 110 coal miners. The fire started in the bottom of a shaft and flashed upward, blocking the only means of escape. The image of the dead bodies of fathers and sons, locked in each other's arms and kneeling in prayer, caused public outrage, and soon thereafter the Pennsylvania legislature passed the first Mine Safety Act. It was not until the 1880s, however, that the first company-financed medical department was instituted by the Homestead Mining Company in North Dakota. Then, in 1890, the authority to inspect mines (The Bureau of Mines) was enacted by Congress. States also began to formulate mine safety codes and statewide inspection programs. Health codes and compensation statutes already enacted in Great Britain (1890s) influenced the "experiment" of workers' compensation in New York (until that law was declared unconstitutional in 1898 because its requirement of "compulsory" adjudication was viewed as an unfair abridgment of employers' rights). The first workers' compensation law, applicable to mining, quarry, and railway workers, and providing for $10,000 in death benefits was Chapter 149 of the Maryland Acts of 1902. In that same year, Congress created the Public Health Service. In 1911, a growing body of workers' compensation laws, which allowed workers to retain the right to sue under the common law, was declared unconstitutional on the grounds that it denied the employers' rights to procedural due process. Fear that strong workers' compensation laws would be found unconstitutional caused state legislatures to subsequently write the laws narrowly.

OSHA's Role since 1970

In the United States, the Occupational Safety and Health Act of 1970 is designed for "preserving our national resources" by protecting safety and health at work. The key term is found in the title and in the purposes set forth in Section 2(b) of the Occupational Safety and Health Act of 1970, where the U.S. Congress wrote the word *health*. This 30-year-old statute is premised on the earlier international laws discussed above and clearly shares their values.

Purposes of Occupational Safety and Health Act

The field of occupational health and safety encompasses many types of work and many aspects of municipal, state, and international laws that could not be embraced by any single act of congressional legislation. Thus the federal Occupational Safety and Health Act of 1970 [5] merely represents one act among several laws governing occupational safety and health legislation nationwide. The Occupational Safety and Health Act was passed with the express purpose

> "[T]o provide safe and healthful employment and places of employment for every working man and woman in the Nation . . . by providing medical criteria which will assure insofar as practicable that no employee will suffer diminished health, functional capacity, or life expectancy as a result of his [*sic*] work experience."

Furthermore, under the Occupational Safety and Health Act, every employer has a duty to furnish to each of its employees "employment and a place of employment which is free from recognized hazards" [Sec. 5(a)(1)]. Although the U.S. Supreme Court rejected the notion that the Occupational Safety and Health Act delegated to OSHA enough authority to mandate a "risk-free workplace," the Court did endorse the notion that the Occupational Safety and Health Act is a "technology-forcing" statute in several cases. These cases ranged from standard-setting questions, such as those involving benzene and asbestos, to the day-to-day enforcement of citations adjudicated before the often underrecognized OSHRC, charged under the Occupational Safety and Health Act's statutory mission to review all enforcement proceedings. OSHRC cases consistently have upheld the agency's "technology forcing" power in the case of "recognized hazards," which are the unspecified dangers that employers are obligated to prevent, even if those hazards are not addressed in the plain meaning of the Occupational Safety and Health Act regulations. Preventing "recognized hazards" under the general duties clause [Sec. 5(a)(1)] of the Occupational

Safety and Health Act has been viewed by many as the linchpin of Occupational Safety and Health Act enforcement because it is not limited to traditional paradigms of health or safety violations; it was designed never to be outdated.

Employers must provide "employment and places of employment that are free from recognized hazards" under Occupational Safety and Health Act Section 5(a)(1). This very broad requirement includes use of the employer's existing medical data to refine working conditions by conducting internal audits, medical tests, and other industrial hygiene investigations destined to prevent harm and to ensure workplace health. Both by statutory mandate and under the Occupational Safety and Health Act's medical access standard, such information must be retrievable for employees for a period of 30 years after surveillance or exposure. One component of understanding the presence or absence of a "recognized hazard" involves risk assessment, but the precise weight to be granted to risk assessment is not settled in the current Occupational Safety and Health Act case law. The problem of what role to give risk assessment and how to steer Occupational Safety and Health Act policy in the face of scientific uncertainty has remained critical throughout the Occupational Safety and Health Act's history.

The "technology forcing" view of the employer's General Duty to prevent "recognized hazards" is consistent with the Occupational Safety and Health Act's statutory language that the three agencies created by this law should fulfill their statutory mandate by ". . . providing for research in the field of occupational safety and health, including the psychological factors involved, and by developing innovative methods, techniques and approaches for dealing with occupational safety and health problems . . ." [6].

The courts of appeal in general and the U.S. Supreme Court in particular typically have taken an expansive view of these general protections in the Occupational Safety and Health Act. From the 1975 case of *Atlas Roofing v. OSHRC* [7], the courts viewed the congressional purpose in the Occupational Safety and Health Act as painted with broad but deliberate strokes of the legislative pen. In *Atlas Roofing,* the Supreme Court noted

> After extensive investigation, Congress concluded, in 1970, that work-related deaths and injuries had become a "drastic" national problem. Finding the existing state statutory remedies as well as state common-law actions for negligence and wrongful death to be inadequate to protect the employee population from death and injury due to unsafe working conditions, Congress enacted the Occupational Safety and Health Act of 1970, 84 Stat. 1590, 29 U.S.C. Sec. 651 et seq. The Act created a new statutory duty to avoid maintaining unsafe or unhealthy working conditions, and empowers the Secretary of Labor to promulgate health and safety standards [8].

The Occupational Safety and Health Act, unlike the Americans with Disabilities Act (discussed below), does not provide for individual or private rights of action, other than the formalized complaint process that can only be pursued through an agenda at the discretion of the Secretary of Labor or in cases of criminal violations that are referred out by the Secretary of Labor and the U.S. Department of Justice.

Legislative History and Statutory Structure

Birth of the Occupational Safety and Health Act

Political action in the 1960s took many forms. Protests and riots outside legislatures as well as the writing of revolutionary new laws reframed America's way of thinking about many important social problems. Environmental issues and workplace health were among the fields that were opened up to regulation. The laws that were passed in the late 1960s and in 1970 were a landmark in applying a new understanding of science and human ecology to an old, well-established constitutional framework. At the same time, there was serious national debate about founding a purely "science" court that would require judges and practitioners to have demonstrated training in the hard sciences before litigating cases concerning pollution, adverse health effects of prescription drugs, food labeling, and the use of hazardous materials in commerce [9]. The Occupational Safety and Health Act went into effect in early 1971 and was intended to create a coherent national network from the previous patchwork of state and federal laws governing safety issues, workplace practices, and occupational health. Many commentaries on the history of occupational health suggest that the idea for it was built on the success of the Mine Safety and Health Act of the previous year. At the time, the field of industrial hygiene and the perceived scope of the Occupational Safety and Health Act's mandate embraced only a very narrow area of the regulatory rulemaking, enforcement, and administrative activities that are now considered commonplace among contemporary occupational safety and health laws. Major accidents, including one mining disaster that killed over a hundred miners, led to passage of the Mine Safety and Health Act in 1969. Many authors have astutely recognized that the Mine Safety and Health Act's passage was the result of the confluence of several political forces and that the mine disaster deaths merely brought those forces to a head. In the same heated political climate surrounding the war in Viet Nam, social protests about race relations, and the future of American society, new concern about toxins resulted in the creation of several environmental protection laws, e.g., the Toxic Substances Control Act of 1976, the Resource Conservation and Recovery Act of 1976, and the Comprehensive Environmental Response Compensation and Liability Act of 1980 (Superfund). The Occupational Safety and Health Act was written and passed in this vibrant social context, one that heralded a revolutionary acceptance of scientific and medical expert testimony in the courts and in regulatory rulemaking. This is particularly true about the Occupational Safety and Health Act, which created an agency to research occupational health issues:

the National Institute of Occupational Safety and Health (NIOSH), plus the OSHRC, an independent reviewing agency outside the traditional court system that, in theory, could be infused with special scientific expertise needed to evaluate health issues. The life given to these ideas by the birth of the Occupational Safety and Health Act and related environmental statutes may well have created a body of trans-scientific legal expertise that made the use of such testimony by the courts acceptable and thereby paved the way for the Supreme Court's *Daubert* decision.

General Purpose of Occupational Safety and Health Act

Passage of the Occupational Safety and Health Act in 1970 represented a major turning point in safety regulation in the United States. The Occupational Safety and Health Act often has been called the "Employees' Bill of Rights" because of its requirements regarding safety and health protections, information dissemination, education about workplace hazards, and potential sources of harm. The Occupational Safety and Health Act created OSHA, its so-called research arm; NIOSH; and the administrative law judiciary (OSHRC) that reviews Occupational Safety and Health Act enforcement proceedings. The major duties of these three agencies include inspection by OSHA, research by NIOSH, and adjudication by OSHRC. The general purpose of the act, "to preserve our Nation's human resources and to ensure safe and healthy working conditions for every man and woman," repeats themes that are recorded throughout the Occupational Safety and Health Act's legislative history in the congressional debates (1969–1970).

As noted by one Senator: "The real fight here is to keep from having Federal jurisdiction over industrial safety. . . . It is not new. It has been going on for so many years. . . . One of the demands of free labor has been conditions of work that allow many men and women to work within some measure of safety; in being able to do their job without fear of being maimed for life or having to be deprived of their livelihood."[10]

Occupational Safety and Health Act's Structure

Occupational Safety and Health Administration (U.S. Department of Labor): Inspection and Enforcement

An early Supreme Court case regarding the Occupational Safety and Health Act, *Atlas Roofing*, outlined in great detail the act's internal administrative law process, including the methods for determination and for appeal of decisions by the OSHRC. This process is linked under Occupational Safety and Health Act to rulemaking by the Occupational Safety and Health Administration (OSHA) and to scientific research by NIOSH. The Occupational Safety and

Health Act is responsible for promulgating and enforcing occupational safety and health standards. Occupational Safety and Health Act standards may set forth the required conditions, approaches, practices, methods, or processes reasonably necessary and appropriate to protect workers on the job. These are enforceable standards as a matter of law, but the underpinings of these laws are rooted in science. The Occupational Safety and Health Act granted the Secretary of Labor the authority to promulgate safety and health standards, inspect worksites, issue citations with monetary and other penalties, and take any measures "necessary" or "appropriate" to enforce occupational safety and health protection in the United States. The Occupational Safety and Health Act's responsibilities are formidable. Employers have a statutory duty to become familiar with the standards that apply to their enterprises and to ensure that needed engineering controls, protective gear, training in the handling of toxic and hazardous materials, and relevant medical protections are available to each employee. Section 8(e) of the Occupational Safety and Health Act describes authority to inspect working conditions and confer rights on employees or their representatives to be present during Occupational Safety and Health Act inspections.

NIOSH Research

Section 22 of the Occupational Safety and Health Act established NIOSH [10] to develop expertise in occupational health. Recognizing the inadequacy of state-of-the-art medical research regarding health effects and the impact of exposure to occupational health hazards, Senator Jacob Javits introduced the portions of the law that created NIOSH "to attract the qualified personnel necessary to engage in occupational health and safety research . . . which will more easily attract the substantial increase in funding which will be necessary to achieve the purposes of this Act."

NIOSH holds a broad range of discretionary authority to conduct research relating to occupational safety and health, including "studies in psychological factors" and exploration of "innovative methods, techniques, and approaches" for solving problems; to investigate new problems, including those created by new technology; and to study behavioral and motivational factors. NIOSH also has the statutory authority to request occupational health and safety information so that it can develop industry-wide studies of injury, illness, and disease. In addition, NIOSH has specific responsibilities in relation to Occupational Safety and Health Act standard setting, including production and annual publication of criteria to formulate standards ("criteria documents") and development and establishment of recommended safety and health standards.

OSHRC: Evidence for Medical and Technical Dispute Resolution

The legislative history of the Occupational Safety and Health Act reflects a desire to create increased confidence in the scientific expertise among administrative agencies who were delegated the authority to protect occupational safety and health by separating the enforcement and adjudication of citations and penalties, thereby avoiding a potential conflict of interest within the agency itself. Arguing for the creation of a separate adjudicatory body, Senator Javits stated: "I feel very strongly that a great element of confidence will be restored in how this very new and very wide-reaching piece of legislation will be administered if the power to adjudicate violations is in the hands of an autonomous body, more than one man, and more than in the Department of Labor itself" [11].

The OSHRC is empowered to hear all questions regarding the validity, form, or appropriateness of Occupational Safety and Health Act fines, penalties, and citations. The commission does not have the authority to hear questions regarding the validity of Occupational Safety and Health Act standards; these questions must be reviewed by a federal district court, court of appeals, or the U.S. Supreme Court. OSHRC's published opinions are available to the public. Among the hotly contested issues that have been consistent themes of OSHRC litigation since its inception are the seriousness of violations, the nature of abatement plans and related procedures, the determination of employer good faith regarding abatement plans, the implementation of in-house Occupational Safety and Health Act compliance programs, and the use of rare but often-discussed affirmative defenses for employers, such as impossibility of compliance, feasibility issues, and employee misconduct. The area of greatest litigation appears to be focused on questions of employer control of the premises and, in turn, who controls the quality of working conditions. The finding that the employer has control of working conditions triggers the General Duty section under Occupational Safety and Health Act Section 5(a)(1) even in the event that a specific hazard has not been discussed in a given Occupational Safety and Health Act standard. Also, the notion of employer control triggers liability in the event of violations or injury, even in a multi-employer worksite involving independent contractors, subcontractors, or off-site professionals.

The OSHRC's three judges review appeals of citations and have the power to affirm, dismiss, or modify penalties or alter the schedule for hazard abatement. An evidentiary hearing is held before an administrative law judge (ALJ) where the burden is on the Secretary of Labor to establish the elements of the alleged violation and the propriety of his or her proposed abatement order and proposed penalty. The ALJ is empowered to affirm, modify, or vacate any or all of these items, giving due consideration in the penalty assessment to "the size of the business of the employer . . . , the gravity of the violation, the good faith of the employer, and the history of previous violations" [12]. The ALJ's decision becomes a final and appealable order unless within 30 days a commissioner directs that it be reviewed by the OSHRC.

If review is granted, the OSHRC will hold a hearing. The OSHRC's subsequent order directing abatement and the payment of any assessed penalty becomes final unless the employer files a timely petition for judicial review in the appropriate court of appeals [13]. The Secretary of Labor similarly may seek review of OSHRC orders [14], but in either case, "[t]he findings of the Commission with respect to questions of fact, if supported by substantial evidence on the record considered as a whole, shall be conclusive" [15]. If the employer fails to pay the assessed penalty, the Secretary of Labor may commence a collection action in a federal district court in which neither the fact of the violation nor the propriety of the penalty assessed may be retried [16]. Thus the penalty may be collected without a jury passing judgment on whether the employer is guilty of a violation, and without further analysis of relevant evidence.

Americans with Disabilities Act

History and Goals of the Americans with Disabilities Act

The Americans with Disabilities Act was enacted in 1990 in response to growing public awareness and concern about discrimination against people with disabilities and the effects of such discrimination on the economic and employment opportunities available to such individuals. The Americans with Disabilities Act's statutory precursor was the Rehabilitation Act of 1973, which prohibited "any program or activity receiving Federal financial assistance" from discriminating against an individual "solely by reason of his [or her] handicap." The Americans with Disabilities Act prohibits employers from discriminating "against a qualified individual with a disability because of the disability of such individual" [42 U.S.C. Sec. 12112(a)]. *Disability* is defined as "a physical . . . impairment that substantially limits one or more of the major life activities of such individual" [Sec. 12102(2)(A)]. The EEOC regulations define *physical impairment* as "[a]ny physiological disorder, or condition . . . affecting one or more of the following body systems: neurological, musculoskeletal [etc.]" [29 C.F.R. Sec. 1630.2(h)(1)]. Note these are words of inclusion, not limitation: The clear statutory language includes a mandate that people who are actually asymptomatic or "well" can be "regarded as impaired" if they have been subjected to illegal acts of discrimination in violation of the purposes and intent of this statute.

The Americans with Disabilities Act extends its nondiscrimination mandate to private employers (Title I), state and local governments (Title II), and other private entities that provide public accommodations (Title III). In the employment context, Title I prohibits discrimination "against a qualified individual with a disability because of the disability of such individual in regard to job application procedures, the hiring, advancement, or discharge of employees, employee compensation, job training, and other terms, conditions, and privileges of employment." The discriminatory behaviors prohibited by the ADA include "limiting, segregating, or classifying" an individual adversely because of a disability, using criteria or tests that have a discriminatory effect, and failing to provide reasonable accommodations to allow an employee with a disability to participate fully in the workplace. In the post-*Daubert* era, courts have been surprisingly willing to admit, examine, and second-guess the expert opinions on highly technical medical questions concerning types of treatment, side effects of medications, the ability to "correct" a disability with treatment, or the extent to which a particular disability actually impedes a given individual's job performance.

Americans with Disabilities Act Definition of Disability

The Americans with Disabilities Act defines *disability* as (1) a physical or mental impairment that substantially limits one or more of the major life activities of such individual; (2) a record of such an impairment; or (3) being regarded as having such an impairment" [17]. This language was written in a manner that is deliberately vague in order to embrace new problems as they arise, much the way that the Vocational Rehabilitational Act of 1973 was later interpreted to deal with HIV and AIDS in the 1980s. Congress delegated the authority to interpret and implement Title I of the Americans with Disabilities Act to the EEOC, an agency that historically has considered the remedies for discrimination. To prevail on an unlawful discrimination claim under the Americans with Disabilities Act, a plaintiff must prove three things by a preponderance of the evidence: (1) he or she must show the plaintiff was disabled within the meaning of the act, (2) he or she must prove that with or without reasonable accommodation the plaintiff was a qualified individual able to perform the essential functions of the job, and (3) the plaintiff must show that he or she was discharged by the employer because of disability [18].

Correctable Disabilities

The Americans with Disabilities Act's concept of disability is becoming increasingly complex as it expands through well-honed litigation. In *Sutton v. United Air Lines* [19] and its companion cases, *Albertsons, Inc. v. Kirkingburg* and *Murphy v. United Parcel Service,* the Supreme Court examined medical evidence to determine whether or not an individual is entitled to Americans with Disabilities Act protections, even when the individual's ability to mitigate or correct his or her impairment must be considered. Each of these cases was the subject of heated medical evidence debate regarding the extent of disability, the availability of corrective devices, and their accessibility in the workplace. As a result of these cases, individuals who use medications or medical devices to correct their impairments (or who are able to compensate for their impairments without the aid of such corrective measures) may not be entitled to the law's protections—but deciding whether an individual is a part of or outside this category of people is a legal question that turns on medical evidence, to be determined on a case-by-case basis. As the next wave of post-*Sutton* Americans with Disabilities Act litigation begins to focus on what constitutes a correctable disability [20] or "imperfect" corrective measures, new plaintiffs will attempt to invoke the "disabling corrections" language in *Sutton* to argue that the side effects of their corrective measures substantially limit a major life activity. While the former group of plaintiffs is likely to present courts with relatively familiar factual disputes about the precise nature of their individual limitations, in courts that encounter disabling corrections claims, these questions indisputably will be settled by judges or administrative law officers, people with legal education making determinations under law.

We can anticipate litigation on the following issues: whether to exclude from the Americans with Disabilities Act's protections only those individuals with conditions that are truly minor and easy to correct, such as nearsightedness, and whether to include individuals with more serious conditions, such as epilepsy and diabetes, which often require disabling treatments. At least two courts have indicated a willingness to second-guess employees and their doctors by permitting employers to question the need for and appropriateness of such disabling corrections. This underscores the need to recognize that science already plays a vital role in adjudication under existing laws.

Evidentiary Requirements: The Void at the Interface between Medicine and Law

The Daubert-Kumho *Evidentiary Matrix*

As discussed in this book and in other commentaries, a quiet legal revolution occurred with the 1993 U.S. Supreme Court opinion in the *Daubert* case. As stated previously, it is likely that courts "got used to" having science around their special niches of jurisprudence after two decades of occupational health, environmental health, and disability jurisprudence that developed as the antecedent to the *Daubert* case. The social context in which there is a need for courts to competently examine scientific evidence has expanded even further in the past decade. The questions remaining for the next decade concern who is an expert and, once a court declares the testimony of an expert to be admissible, how the court is supposed to use such testimony.

Daubert terms such as "reliable," "relevant," and "methods subject to peer review and publication and generally accepted in the scientific community" have been bandied about in many different cases, with a host of different jurisprudential and scientific results. For example, cases involving birth defects from pesticide exposure *in utero* [21], chemical changes that might occur after ink has been placed on paper [22], and the absence of engineering methodology to explain opinions in an expert report have all relied on the criteria articulated in the *Daubert* decision.

In the 1999 *Kumho Tire* case [23], the Supreme Court expanded *Daubert* to embrace all types of expert testimony—a minor victory for experts whose scientifically valid testimony had not been admissible before in cases where a lower court had incorrectly given a narrow interpretation to the term *expert*. At the same time, however, *Kumho Tire* took back from the experts much more than it gave, especially for plaintiffs who sometimes can ill-afford costly expert testimony from people with sophisticated degrees. Nevertheless, even though the Court agreed that all types of experts can give admissible testimony, the Court also extended the right of judges to scrutinize the credentials and methodologies of those who proffer their expertise before the court. Thus, in a confusing outcome, the Court permitted the plaintiff's "expert" to testify but then, after reviewing the methods of his or her work, rejected this particular expert's expertise. The *Kumho Tire* case opened the door to a new breed of highly credentialed experts, who should, in theory, have testimony admitted into evidence with greater deference, and at the same time the decision reaffirmed jurisprudential primacy—asserting the right to assess another profession's expertise before accepting expert testimony (see Chap. 6).

Insofar as the Court has now required that *any* expert must explain his or her opinions by demonstrating the science and methodology on which the opinion is based, *Kumho Tire* is consistent with Occupational Safety and Health Act litigation, with NIOSH's peer-review oversight before congressional committees, and with the case law arising under the Americans with Disabilities Act in the last few years. More significantly, these cases when taken together demonstrate that trans-science jurisprudence is here to stay; courts must develop a thorough understanding of medicine and scientific principles in order to decide cases fairly.

Occupational Safety and Health Act Cases: The Law of Significant Risk

Associated Industries of New York State v. United States Department of Labor [24], one of the first decisions that demanded evidence of Occupational Safety and Health Act's administrative scheme, held invalid an early Occupational Safety and Health Administration standard that "set forth the requirement for the minimum number of lavatories in industrial establishments." In *Associated Industries*, the Court "reaffirmed" the long-standing concept that administrative determinations not supported by "substantial evidence" are not necessarily arbitrary and capricious. Nonetheless, it found that Occupational Safety and Health Act

> . . . imposes a health standard upon industrial establishments that is considerably more stringent than that which apparently has been found satisfactory by many states. . . . [The Occupational Safety and Health Administration] has an obligation to produce some evidence justifying its action.

The Occupational Safety and Health Administration attempted to justify its actions in *Associated Industries* by asserting that the standard in question was valid, pursuant to the Occupational Safety and Health Act's statutory authority, to require that workplaces be "free from recognized hazards." However, without substantial evidence relating to the need for a more stringent standard, the Occupational Safety and Health Administration arguments seemed simplistic and indeed would support virtually any discretionary action by an agency. The Court concluded that when the Occupational Safety and Health Administration seeks to institute a more stringent standard "and the proposed standard has been contested on substantial grounds, the agency has the burden of offering some explanation for adopting the standard." This case, decided decades before *Daubert* and *Kumbo Tire*, might have been tried or decided differently today because of the higher burden to scrutinize expert testimony.

In *Society of Plastic Industries, Inc. v. Occupational Safety and Health Administration* [25], the court considered whether the Occupational Safety and Health Administration had assumed a legislative role. The Court held that

> . . . [w]here explicit factual finding of safe is not possible, and the act of decision is essentially a prediction based upon pure legislative judgment, as when a Congressman decides to vote for or against a particular bill [the Court looks to the record, to determine] . . . [w]hether the agency, given an essentially legislative task to perform has carried it out in a manner calculated to negate the danger of arbitrariness and irrationality.

Nonetheless, when the Court looked with "alarm" on the "morbid" chronology of vinyl chloride exposure, unchecked by industry even after the causal relation between occupational exposure and increased morbidity was widely recognized, it was compelled to accept the agency's findings. Having demonstrated to the satisfaction of the Court the existence of a "serious health risk" based on information reported to NIOSH and independent research by others, the Court found the Occupational Safety and Health Administration's view persuasive, stating

> . . . it must be remembered that we are dealing here with human lives. . . . [I]t remains the duty of the Secretary . . . to act even in circumstances where existing methodology or research is deficient.

Therefore, the urgency of the threat to workers' health, combined with the Secretary of Labor's well-reasoned explanations, merited deference to the Occupational Safety and Health Administration's action.

This theme was repeated in *American Iron & Steel Institute (AISI) v. Occupational Safety and Health Administration,* where the Court took great care in distinguishing "determinations bottomed on factual matters" from "non-factual legislative-like policy decisions" [26]. After reviewing NIOSH testimony concerning the carcinogenicity of coke oven emissions and other data in the record, the Court employed a five-step criteria to evaluate the Occupational

Safety and Health Administration's determinations. Of the five steps in this process of judicial review, which concerned procedural requirements as well as the agency's rationale, two criteria demonstrate the significance of policy considerations. The Occupational Safety and Health Administration satisfied its burden of proof under these criteria by offering substantial evidence that "there is absolutely no safe level" for toxic coke oven emissions but that the reduced permissible exposure limit (PEL) would have demonstrable health benefits. The harm from coke oven emissions was an undisputed fact. There was evidence in the record that occupationally induced mortality could be improved by reducing occupational exposure to coke oven emissions. Moreover, acceptance of this fact among industries as well as regulatory authorities served as the basic rationale for enforcing a comparatively stringent standard. The viability of the Occupational Safety and Health Administration's methodology for achieving the standard, whose efficacy was established through the use of dose-response relationship, was the sole "scientific question" before the Court.

Litigation surrounding the validity of Occupational Safety and Health Administration standards has delayed the final implementation of many rules throughout the Occupational Safety and Health Administration's regulatory history. Both the number and complexity of these cases, however, have increased dramatically in several instances—sometimes involving some of the most improbable parties as plaintiffs or codefendants. This change in the nature of Occupational Safety and Health Administration litigation is consistent with the greater legal trend: As legal cases have become increasingly technical, legal and scientific approaches have clashed [27]. Sharp differences between legal and scientific approaches to decision-making models and growing pressure on the government to regulate areas of law that are based on scientific uncertainty have produced an awkward, if not impractical, set of precedents when juries measure scientific certainty using the rule of law. Nonetheless, this perennial struggle between scientific and legal approaches does not seem to prevent judges in particular from judging the merits of scientific studies or evaluating their findings, even though sophisticated ignorance seems to be the strongest guide. Despite a clear need for more information, courts have not been hesitant at all to leap to scientific conclusions (see Chap. 6).

The Americans with Disabilities Act's Intense Scrutiny of Impairments

Prior to the Supreme Court's decisions in *Sutton* [28] and the related "correctable disabilities" cases, there was significant disagreement among different courts whether mitigating measures should be considered when determining whether or not an individual met the Americans with Disabilities Act's definition of disability, with some cases holding that impairments should be evaluated in their uncorrected or unmitigated state when determining the applicability of the Americans with Disabilities Act and others hearing detailed medical testimony on these questions but ultimately finding against Americans with Disabilities Act coverage. New cases will require detailed examination of complex medical questions, such as whether side effects from chemotherapy prevent an individual from engaging in the major life activity of "work" or whether prosthetic limbs, antipsychotic drugs, or antiepileptic drugs (which can cause "serious negative side effects") can be regarded as Americans with Disabilities Act–covered impairments. Medical evidence is also used to determine whether a disabled individual "may be mobile and capable of functioning in society but still be disabled because of a substantial limitation on their ability to walk or run." "[T]he use or nonuse of a corrective device does not determine whether an individual is disabled; that determination depends on whether the limitations an individual with an impairment actually faces are in fact substantially limiting" and whether individuals who can correct their disabilities are still legally disabled if they can "function in society."

Examples of difficult medical judgment calls include *Wheelock v. Philip Morris,* where a federal district court in Louisiana found that an individual who experienced drowsiness caused by the drug Klonopin could not appropriately be termed an individual with a disability, and *Schwertfager v. City of Boynton Beach,* where an employer refused to accommodate an employee whose work performance suffered due to postmastectomy pain and her need for nursing assistance. The plaintiff was offered a demotion by her employer, but she refused the offer and filed suit. The court granted summary judgment to the defendant, ruling that Schwertfager was not properly classified as an individual with a disability because she did not claim to suffer any physical limitations beyond the 5-month period immediately following her surgery.

Highly complex medical testimony and medical decision making by the courts has become quite commonplace [29]. For example, in *Christian v. St. Anthony Medical Center,* the plaintiff suffered from hypercholesterolemia (excessive amount of cholesterol in her blood). The Seventh Circuit Appellate Court found that a disabling treatment could be considered a disability under the Americans with Disabilities Act, even if the underlying condition being addressed did not meet the criteria for a disability. Although her condition was not itself disabling, the plaintiff alleged that she was fired because "the defendant anticipated that she would undergo a disabling treatment—namely pheresis (or aphereisis), in which the blood is drained from the patient's body, cleansed of its cholesterol, and put back into the patient." In *Quint v. Staley* [30], a discharged employee sued her former employer under the Americans with Disabilities Act. The court of appeals held (1) that the employee's bilateral carpal tunnel syndrome, irritated ulnar nerves, and arm/shoulder syndrome constituted a "disability" within meaning of the Americans with Disabilities Act and (2) that the employee proved compensable injury under the Americans with Disabilities Act, holding that "although carpal tunnel syndrome (CTS) may not prove to be a disability within meaning of the Americans with Disabilities Act in all cases, undoubtedly it is an Americans with Disabilities Act "impairment" [31]. These cases demonstrate that courts clearly decide many contemporary evidence-based medical disputes.

Conclusion

The primacy of jurisprudence (the field of study that explains and furthers social understanding of the rule of law) is an invaluable social value that is deeply embedded in our legal structure. There is an underlying theme in all the statutes that regulate the health and safety of Americans, both at work and at leisure.

There is, however, little scientific common ground among these varying statutes other than the procedural rules that govern how they handle uncertainties. There is, for example, no specific scientific principle that can be applied to the Occupational Safety and Health Administration, OSHRC, NIOSH, EEOC, EPA, or the Food and Drug Administration (FDA) equally often or with equal reliability. This is in part the inherent limit of democracy, which requires that power be "delegated" from the power-granting authority to an agent or agency to limit the accumulation of power by any one group or entity.

This limit on power can be viewed as a weakness of the system by those who encounter the system piecemeal, without understanding the role of such limits in protecting the structure as a whole against any one group or entity overtaking the entire democracy. However, it is also the classic strong point of American democracy and therefore must be respected. It seems appropriate, therefore, to recognize that our courts of law are also in many instances medical expert courts and science courts. We should create a place for scientists who are also trained in law as an adaptation to the rapidly evolving role of scientific evidence. These scientists working for the judicial system could fill the current void in legal methods when lawyers and judges are confronted with scientific or medical issues.

The cases and statutes discussed in this chapter are just a small fraction of the science- and medicine-based litigation that is trafficked through the U.S. courts and administrative hearings each day. The volume is on an ever-increasing trajectory. These cases clearly reflect a coherent philosophy: that a rule of law that is derived from pragmatism eventually must be driven by the best science, although the rules of admissibility and standards of review necessarily differ from one statute or agency to another.

Time and again Congress has said that science and medicine have a place and should be appropriately integrated into the various parts of our legal system. The good news is that scientific evidence can be admitted more freely and subjected to a much more detailed analysis before both state and federal courts compared with the secondary status that had been accorded to similar testimony a decade or two ago. On the other hand, there is ongoing concern, however, that the courts will continue to substitute their own judgment regarding the validity, reliability, and probative value of scientific evidence. This can only be remedied by having scientists sit as judges as opposed to a "science court." The cases reviewed here make it clear that in addition to having training in the law, there should be a medical professional or epidemiologist or other scientist serving on the U.S. Supreme Court, and in turn, scientists and medical professionals who have attended law school or passed the bar also should serve as a part of the group of judges who decide appellate court cases and review the opinions of lower courts of law.

Endnotes

1. Americans with Disabilities Act of 1990, Sec. 2 et seq., 42 U.S.C.A., Sec. 12101 et seq.

2. Vocational Rehabilitation Act of 1973, Pub. L. 93-112, Sec. 504, 87 Stat. 355, 394 (1973).

3. Occupational Safety and Health Act of 1970, 29 U.S.C. 651 et seq.

4. The Americans with Disabilities Act expressly intends that "disability" determination is to be made by the fact finder on an individualized, case-by-case basis. See 42 U.S.C. Sec. 12102(2)(A) (defining *disability* as "a physical . . . impairment that substantially limits one or more of the major life activities of such individual"—terms that have been litigated heavily in the last decade.

5. 29 U.S.C. Sec. 651.

6. Occupational Safety and Health Act, Sec. 2(b), 29 U.S.C. Sec. 651.

7. *Atlas Roofing Co. v. Occupational Safety and Health Review Commission,* 518 F.2d 990 (CA5 1975), aff'd on other grounds, 430 U.S. 442 (1977).

8. *Atlas Roofing Co. v. OSHRC,* 518 F.2d 990 (CA5 1975), aff'd on other grounds, 430 U.S. 422 (1977).

9. See discussion of legislative history of Occupational Safety and Health Act in Ilise L. Feitshans, *Designing an Effective Occupational Safety and Health Act Compliance Program,* Westgroup Second (Revised) Edition, 2001.

10. See 29 U.S.C. Sec. 671(a) and (c) and S. Rep. No. 1282, 91st Congress, 2d Session at 19 (1970) and H.R. Rep. No. 1291, 91st Congress, 2d Session at 27 (1970).

11. Senate debate on Occupational Safety and Health Act of 1970 (Nov. 17, 1970), Legis. Hist. 469–470.

12. 29 U.S.C. Sec. 666(i).

13. 29 U.S.C. Sec. 660(a).

14. 29 U.S.C. Sec. 660(b).

15. 29 U.S.C. Sec. 660(a).

16. 29 U.S.C. Sec. 666(k).

17. Americans with Disabilities Act of 1990, Sec. 102(a), 42 U.S.C.A. Sec. 12112(a).

18. 172 F.3d 1, 9 A.D. Cases 242, 14 NDLR P. 231 (cite as 172 F.3d 1).

19. See Lauren J. McGarity, Disabling corrections and correctable disabilities: Why side effects might be the saving grace of *Sutton. Yale Law J* 2000;109:1161, discussing *Sutton*

v. United Air Lines, 119 S. Ct. 2139, 2145 (1999). In *Sutton,* twin sisters with severe myopia applied for employment with United Airlines as commercial airline pilots. Both Karen Sutton and her sister, Kimberly Hinton, had uncorrected vision of 20/200 or worse in both eyes and were rejected because of United's minimum vision standard, which required uncorrected visual acuity of 20/100 or better in each eye. The sisters sued United, claiming that they were rejected because of their disabilities or because United regarded them as having disabilities. In support of their contention that they were individuals with disabilities within the meaning of the Americans with Disabilities Act, Sutton and Hinton argued that their myopia significantly interfered with their ability to engage in the major life activity of working. They claimed that the court should look at their visual impairments in an uncorrected state, under EEOC guidelines. The district court dismissed their suit stating that because their vision was fully correctable, Sutton and Hinton had not demonstrated that they were individuals with disabilities or "regarded as" individuals with disabilities within the meaning of the Americans with Disabilities Act. The Court of Appeals for the Tenth Circuit affirmed; the U.S. Supreme Court upheld the Tenth Circuit's ruling. The Court found that requiring a determination of disability to be based on consideration of the individual's impairment in an uncorrected state was in conflict with the plain meaning of the statute.

20. Lauren J. McGarity, Disabling corrections and correctable disabilities: Why side effects might be the saving grace of *Sutton. Yale Law J* 2000;109:1161, discussing *Sutton v. United Air Lines,* 119 S. Ct. 2139, 2145 (1999). The EEOC has set forth three factors that should be considered in determining what constitutes a substantial limitation of a major life activity: "[t]he nature and the severity of the impairment," (2) "the duration . . . of the impairment," and (3) the "long-term impact" of the impairment. The EEOC's technical assistance manual for the Americans with Disabilities Act further states that temporary, nonchronic impairments that do not last for a long time and have little or no long-term impact usually are not disabilities. Some courts have interpreted this language to limit the classification of side effects as disabilities under the Americans with Disabilities Act, especially when those side effects may not be permanent (such as with a therapy of limited duration) or may lessen or stabilize with time (as is the case with many types of side effects).

21. *E. I. du Pont de Nemours & Co. v. Castillo,* 748 So. 2d 1108 (Fla. App.), 29/00. The primary plaintiff in this case was a child born with microphthalmia, or underdeveloped eyes. He claimed this condition was caused by Benlate, to which his mother had been exposed while he was in utero. She said she was drenched with Benlate spray while walking by a field near her home. At trial, one of the plaintiffs' causation experts testified that based on rat lavage studies and laboratory experiments on human and rat cells, he believed that fetal exposure to benomyl (the active ingredient) at a concentration of 20 parts per billion would cause microphthalmia. However, the methodology used by the plaintiffs' experts was not generally accepted in the scientific community. The court reached this holding after a thorough discussion of both the evidence, cases from other jurisdictions, and other authorities. The cases cited by the appellate court included *Daubert* (on remand to the Ninth Circuit), the *Agent Orange* case, *Allen, Brock,* and *Christophersen* from the Fifth Circuit, *Richardson v. Richardson-Merrell* (D.C. Cir.), *Lynch* (1st Cir.), *Wade-Greaux* (3d Cir.), *Cadarian v. Merrell Dow* (E.D. Mich.), *Schudel v. General Electric* (9th Cir.), and the *Havner* case from Texas. In the end the court held that we "do not conclude that epidemiological studies are a mandatory prerequisite to establish a toxic substance's teratogenicity in human beings. We do, however, conclude that where, as here, plaintiffs wish to establish a substance's teratogenicity in human beings based on animal and in vitro studies, the methodology used in the studies,

including the method of extrapolating from the achieved results, must be generally accepted in the relevant scientific community."

22. See *Learning Curve Toys, L.P. v. Playwood Toys, Inc.*, 2000 WL 343205 (N.D. Ill.), 3/31/00, denying a motion to reconsider exclusion of the defendant's expert testimony regarding the date certain writing was added to a document. The expert apparently based his conclusions on chemical changes that supposedly took place after ink has been placed on paper. Citing *Daubert,* the court declined to change its ruling. The court concluded that the expert had "failed to state the basis for his conclusion that any age difference detected by his relative age analysis reflects at least a six month gap. . . . [He] also failed to cite a specific source for his finding of statistical significance. Finally, . . . [he] failed to establish that the relative age analysis technique itself was based on methodology subjected to peer review and publication and generally accepted in the scientific community."

23. *Kumho Tire,* 119 S. Ct. 1167 (1999).

24. *Associated Industries of New York State v. United States Department of Labor,* 487 F. 2d 342 (CA2 1972).

25. *Society of Plastics Industry, Inc. v. Occupational Safety and Health Administration,* 509 F.2d 1301 (CA2 1975). See also Corn, Vinyl chloride, setting a workplace standard: An historical perspective on assessing risk, *J Public Health Policy* 1984;5:497–512, for an excellent overview of vinyl chloride's regulatory history.

26. *AISI v. Occupational Safety and Health Administration,* 577 F.2d 825 (CA3 1978).

27. See "The Courts vs. Scientific Certainty," *New York Times,* June 27, 1999.

28. *Sutton v. United Air Lines,* 119 S. Ct. 2139, 2145 (1999).

29. *Helfter v. UPS, Inc.,* 115 F.3d, 613, 617–618 (8th Cir. 1997) (plaintiff with carpal tunnel syndrome adduced no evidence concerning "various classes [of jobs] within a geographical area to which she has reasonable access," other than her own conclusory statements about her job prospects); *Crumpton v. St. Vincent's Hospital,* 963 F. Supp. 1104, 1113 (N.D. Ala. 1997) (plaintiff adduced only her conclusory deposition testimony that she was disabled from all institutional cooking jobs in her geographical area).

30. *Quint v. A.E. Staley Manufacturing Company,* 172 F.3d 1 (1999), Court of Appeals, First Circuit.

31. *Quint v. A.E. Staley Manufacturing Company,* 172 F.3d 1 (1999), citing Americans with Disabilities Act of 1990, Sec. 102(a), 42 U.S.C.A. Sec. 12112(a); 29 C.F.R. Part 1630, App., Sec. 1630.2(j).

18

Medical Disputes Involving Substance Use in the Workplace and in Athletic Competition

KENT W. PETERSON

WILLIAM J. JUDGE

DONNA R. SMITH

Few would deny that both the workplace and amateur and professional sports in the United States face a problem with drug and alcohol use. There is, however, significant debate over the solutions to this problem. Testing employees and athletes for the use of prohibited substances is controversial. This controversy is becoming more acute with the proposal to expand the established urine and breath test procedures to include alternatives such as hair, saliva, and sweat patches. Issues laid to rest years ago about the validity and reliability of test methods are again being raised. The accuracy of these alternative test methods will be challenged under the new standards of admissibility following the 1993 U.S. Supreme Court decision in *Daubert v. Merrell Dow Pharmaceuticals, Inc.* [1] and the recently revised *Federal Rules of Evidence*, Rule 702.

This chapter provides a brief history of workplace drug testing, summarizes the standard of practice that has evolved from federal guidelines in both the Department of Health and Human Services and the Department of Transportation, reviews specific criteria for expert testimony required by the *Daubert* decision and *Federal Rules of Evidence*, Rule 702, and outlines some of the issues facing the use of these newer tests following *Daubert*. It also describes the kinds of disputes arising in sports testing for prohibited substances and reviews how these disputes are adjudicated.

Workplace Drug Use: Magnitude of the Problem

Americans represent only 5% of the world's population, yet we consume nearly 60% of all illegal drugs produced [2]. According to the National Institutes of Health, alcohol and drug abuse cost this country $246 billion each year [3]. At work, employers have experienced these costs in decreased productivity, increased accidents, increased absenteeism, increased turnover, and increased medical expenses.

American businesses paid an estimated $81.6 billion in 1990 in lost productivity from alcohol and drugs due to premature death ($37 billion) and illness ($44 billion); 86% of these combined costs was attributed to alcohol [4].

As employers became more aware of the issue, it was noted that

- Seventy percent of admitted current drug or alcohol users are employed at least part time.
- More than 7% of employed Americans admitted heavy drinking (which is defined as five or more drinks on 5 or more days within the past 30 days).
- Full-time workers aged 18 to 49 years who reported current illicit drug use were more likely than those reporting no current illicit drug use to state that they had worked for three or more employers in the past year (9.3 versus 4.3%), had taken an unexcused absence from work in the past month (12.9 versus 5.0%), had involuntarily left an employer in the past year (24.8 versus 15.4%), and had been fired by an employer in the past year (2.3 versus 1.2%) [5].

According to a national survey conducted by the Hazelden Foundation, more than 60% of adults know people who have gone to work under the influence of drugs or alcohol [6]. Other available information shows the following:

- A survey of callers to the national cocaine help line revealed that 75% reported using drugs *on the job.*
- Sixty-four percent admitted that drugs adversely affected their job performance.
- Forty-four percent sold drugs to other employees.
- Eighteen percent had stolen *from coworkers* to support their drug habit [7].
- Alcoholism causes 500 million lost work days each year [8].

According to a government-sponsored survey, drug-using employees are 2.2 times more likely to request early dismissal or time off, 2.5 times more likely to have absences of 8 days or more, 3 times more likely to be late for work, 3.6 times more likely to be involved in a workplace accident, and 5 times more likely to file a workers' compensation claim [9].

Results from a U.S. Postal Service study indicate that employees who tested positive on their pre-employment drug test were 77% more likely to be discharged within the first 3 years of employment and were absent from work 66% more often than those who tested negative [10].

As one Department of Labor report states:

> Statistics such as these suggest not only that workplace substance abuse is an issue all employers need to address, but also that it is an issue that can be successfully prevented. Taking steps to raise awareness among employees about the impact of substance use on workplace performance, and offering the appropriate resources and/or assistance to employees in need, will not only improve worker safety and health, but also increase workplace productivity and market competitiveness [11].

Faced with a problem of this magnitude, employers have increasingly turned to drug and alcohol testing to help solve the problem. For more than 10 years, private employers in the transportation industry have been compelled by the federal government to perform urine and breath tests to identify and discipline workers who use drugs or alcohol [12]. These test methods have gained general acceptance by the courts [13]. Today, competitive forces and the need for faster turnaround times have led to the development of alternative test methods such as instant on-site urine tests, hair testing, fingernail test results, and sweat patches [14]. Increasingly, employees who test positive are disciplined based on test results using these and other "cutting edge" scientific methodologies. Challenges to these new tests surely will follow.

Chronology of Workplace Drug and Alcohol Testing

In response to alcohol abuse problems among World War II veterans, employers began instituting employee assistance programs (EAPs) in the 1940s. Drug testing and drug deterrence programs in America's workplaces were public policy initiatives born in the 1980s. The roots of workplace drug testing programs can be traced to the military drug programs initiated in the post-Vietnam era of the mid-1970s. When effective screening technology was developed during the Vietnam war, the U.S. military instituted mandatory random urine drug testing, using observed collection methods. The military programs were developed and implemented to deter military personnel from using illegal drugs that were readily available and a "fact of life" during duty in the Far East and to identify individuals who continued to use illegal drugs after their return to the United States. Returning vets with drug problems coincided with a sharp increase in illegal drug use by the U.S. population in general.

In the early 1980s, private employers began requiring drug and alcohol testing of certain classes of employees. There was wide variation in drugs tested for, types of specimens and methods of collection, analytical procedures used, reporting of laboratory results, criteria for interpreting laboratory results, etc. [15].

The first federal initiative in drug testing outside the military environment was signed by President Reagan in 1986 as part of his administration's "War on Drugs" [16]. The order required the federal executive agencies to implement drug testing policies and programs for safety-sensitive federal employees. The Executive Order was followed by Public Law 100-171, which established the funding and statutory authority for the comprehensive testing programs [17]. The Department of Health and Human Services (DHHS) was charged with the responsibility of establishing guidelines and procedures for the federal urine drug testing programs and for overseeing the implementation of the policy and programs; the DHHS Mandatory Guidelines for Federal Workplace Drug Testing Programs were issued in April 1988 [18].

These DHHS guidelines became the model for the Department of Transportation's (DOT) drug testing procedures (specified in 49 CFR 40), issued in December 1989 [19]. The DOT regulations initially covered 3.5 million civilian employees in safety-sensitive jobs in the interstate airlines, railroad, trucking, mass transit, and pipelines industries as well as the Coast Guard. The number of transportation workers covered subsequently has been expanded to more than 7 million. These DHHS/DOT procedures quickly emerged as the definitive standard of practice not only for federally mandated "regulated testing" but also in the "unregulated" private sector, where there was considerable variation regarding drugs tested for, collection procedures, chain-of-custody procedures, use of noncertified labs, cutoff levels, use of medical review officers and substance abuse professionals, on-site testing, and other matters.

Other federal agencies have adopted different drug testing standards, including the Department of Defense (DOD), which still uses directly witnessed specimen collection, and the Department of Energy (DOE), which has long required on-site screening tests for both illicit drugs and alcohol. The Omnibus Transportation Act of 1991 introduced a sweeping change by further requiring the DOT to test for alcohol among most transportation workers. The DOT eventually chose breath alcohol testing rather than blood or urine alcohol tests [20].

Several legal actions were filed against these rules. In some cases, implementation of the DOT rules was delayed in whole or in part. At issue in most of the litigation were Fourth Amendment concerns about employees insufficiently protected from unreasonable search and seizure. The DOT rules were upheld in all cases except one. The Federal Transit Administration (FTA) rule mandating drug testing in transit systems nationwide that were recipients of FTA funding was vacated by a federal court on the grounds that the FTA did not have regulatory authority over the transit systems. Thereafter, the drug testing rule issued by the FTA was withdrawn, and drug testing for safety-sensitive transit employees was not conducted under federal authority. This action became very significant in the years to follow, because it was the 1991 New York City subway accident that ultimately resulted in passage of the Hollings-Danforth bill (which corrected the flaw the federal court identified in the FTA rules) mandating alcohol and drug testing in the transit, aviation, commercial motor vehicle, and rail industries.

Drug Testing Basics

The 1988 DHHS Mandatory Guidelines covered three areas: specimen collection, laboratory analysis, and review of results by a physician acting as a medical review officer. The Substance Abuse and Mental Health Services Administration's (SAMHSA) National Laboratory Certification Program sets standards for certifying laboratories that perform drug tests under federally regulated testing provisions. All DHHS-regulated tests must consist of two parts: a screening test using one laboratory method (one of several types of immunoassays) and a confirmation test using a second method (gas chromatography–mass spectrometry, or GC-MS). This dual testing is intended to ensure that no falsely positive tests occur.

A medical review officer (MRO) is "a licensed physician . . . who has knowledge of substance abuse disorders and has appropriate medical training to interpret and evaluate an individual's positive test result together with his or her medical history and any other relevant biomedical information" [21]. An MRO must receive and review laboratory drug test results and, in the case of a positive result, evaluate the individual's medical explanation for the positive result. For example, positive results may accompany use of a prescription analgesic containing codeine, use of a prescription medication for Parkinson's disease (which can cause a positive result for amphetamines), or ingestion of poppy seed bagels (which can produce a positive result for morphine). An MRO must verify a positive laboratory result.

It is important to recognize that a verified positive drug test means only that a drug was present in the urine (or other specimen) at or above a designated cutoff level of measurement. A positive drug test does not mean that the individual was intoxicated, under the influence of the substance, impaired, or addicted.

There are six basic situations where tests for use of illicit drugs are performed among applicants or employees in safety-sensitive positions: employment or preplacement, postaccident, reasonable suspicion ("for cause"), random, return-to-work, and unannounced testing after rehabilitation (follow-up). Five classes of drugs are tested for under the DHHS regulations: marijuana (tetrahydrocannabinol), cocaine, phenclidine (PCP), amphetamines (amphetamine or methamphetamine), and opiates (heroin, morphine, or codeine). Other classes of drugs tested for in nonregulated settings include barbiturates and tranquilizers.

Alcohol tested under DOT regulations also requires a screening and a confirmation test. An approved oral fluid or nonevidential breath testing device may be used for screening, but an evidentiary-quality breath alcohol testing device must be used for confirmation, and the test must be performed by a trained and certified breath alcohol technician (BAT). Under rare circumstances, a blood alcohol test can be used, such as in a postmortem investigation in the railroad industry.

In recent years, substance abuse professionals (SAPs) have been designated in federal regulations as the persons responsible for evaluating workers who have verified positive drug tests to determine whether they are abusing drugs or need treatment and, after treatment, whether there has been successful rehabilitation and the ability to safely return to work. In most instances, the SAP can decide whether the worker will undergo future unannounced follow-up testing.

Litigation Background

When a test is positive for the presence of a controlled substance or alcohol, employers typically take disciplinary action. This often leads to arbitration hearings, court actions, unemployment compensation hearings, and/or workers' compensation benefits hearings [22]. Drug and alcohol test results and their methodology are at issue in a wide variety of work-related disputes, including workers' compensation claims, unemployment awards, claims for disability benefits, insurance coverage, and professional licensure status. Nonworkplace settings in which drug and alcohol use is an issue include schools, parental rights hearings, parole violations, and will contests.

When an applicant has not been hired or an employee has been terminated because of a positive drug or alcohol test result, a lawsuit may follow. The applicant or former employee usually will claim, among other things, that the test result is inaccurate. It will be asserted that the collection, laboratory analysis, or medical review of the sample were conducted negligently. It is likely that experts in the field of drug and alcohol testing will be hired both to attack and defend the test result and its methodology [23]. Motions will be filed in court to exclude both. In light of the Supreme Court decision in *Daubert v. Merrell Dow Pharmaceuticals, Inc.* [24] and the subsequent revisions to the *Federal Rules of Evidence*, Rule 702, under what conditions should these scientific test results be admitted and expert testimony heard? First, we turn to a brief description of legal framework. After all, in workplace drug testing cases, if the result is excluded, the case is over.

Expert Scientific Testimony and Federal Rules of Evidence, *Rule 702*

To be successful in either defending a drug test result or preventing that result's admission in any legal controversy, the testimony of an expert will be useful in explaining the basic science of the test, its process, and the result. The admissibility at trial of such expert scientific testimony is governed in the federal courts by *Federal Rules of Evidence,* Rule 702 [25], which provides as follows:

> If scientific, technical, or other specialized knowledge will assist the trier of fact to understand the evidence or to determine a fact in issue, a witness qualified as an expert by knowledge, skill, experience, training, or education, may testify thereto in the form of an opinion or otherwise [26].

It has been noted that "as far back as the fourteenth century, scientific evidence has posed profound challenges for the law" [27]. At bottom, many of these challenges arise from fundamental differences between the legal and scientific processes. Although the specific contours of each domain remain unclear, most commentators agree that the cultures and purposes of law and science differ in important ways. The legal system embraces the adversary process to achieve "truth," for the ultimate purpose of attaining an authoritative, final, just, and socially acceptable resolution of disputes. Thus law is a normative pursuit that seeks to define how public and private relations should function. The scientific community also engages in a quest for "truth." In contrast to the law's vision of truth, however, science embraces empirical analysis to discover truth as found in verifiable facts. Science is thus a descriptive pursuit that "does not define how the universe should be but rather describes how it actually is" [28].

These differences between law and science have posed both systemic and pragmatic dilemmas for the law and the actors within it [29]. On the one hand, scientific evidence holds out the tempting possibility of extremely accurate fact finding and a reduction in the uncertainty that often accompanies legal decision making. At the same time, however, scientific methodologies often include risks of uncertainty that the legal system is unwilling to tolerate. Moreover, in almost every instance, scientific evidence tests the abilities of judges, lawyers, and jurors, all of whom may lack the scientific expertise to comprehend the evidence and evaluate it in an informed manner [30].

In *Daubert v. Merrell Dow Pharmaceuticals, Inc.* [31], the Supreme Court set forth four parameters to help the trial court in deciding whether an expert's testimony should be admitted into evidence: (1) whether a theory or technique can be (and has been) tested, (2) whether it has been subjected to peer review and publication, (3) whether, in respect to a particular technique, there is a high known or potential rate of error and whether there are standards controlling the technique's operation, and (4) whether the theory or technique enjoys general acceptance within a relevant scientific community.

The trial court serves as the "gatekeeper" and must determine the admissibility of expert testimony using these four criteria. The Court made it clear that the *Daubert* factors are not a "definitive checklist or test" [32] and that the "gatekeeping" inquiry must be tied to the facts of each case [33].

Faced with a proffer of expert scientific testimony, the trial judge must determine at the outset, pursuant to Rule 104(a) [34], whether the expert is proposing to testify to (1) scientific knowledge that (2) will assist the trier of fact to understand or determine a fact in issue. This entails a preliminary assessment of whether the reasoning or methodology underlying the testimony is scientifically valid and of whether that reasoning or methodology properly can be applied to the facts at issue [35].

The *Daubert* Court effectively overturned the long-accepted *Frye* standard [36], in which expert testimony was considered admissible only insofar as it was based on a technique that was "generally accepted" in the scientific community. However, *general acceptance* is "not a necessary precondition to the admissibility of scientific evidence" [37]. Indeed, the Court specifically declined to require *general acceptance* when it rejected the *Frye* rule. General acceptance is but one factor that is considered along with all other factors relevant to the Rule 702 inquiry. Since the *Daubert* decision, other courts have expanded on the *Daubert* factors [38]. For example, the Third Circuit Court of Appeals delineated the relevant factors as follows:

1. whether a method consists of a testable hypothesis;
2. whether the method has been subject to peer review;
3. the known or potential rate of error;
4. the existence and maintenance of standards controlling the technique's operation;
5. whether the method is generally accepted;
6. the relationship of the technique to methods which have been established to be reliable;
7. the qualifications of the expert witness testifying based on the methodology; and
8. the non-judicial uses to which the method has been put [39].

The Court concluded by emphasizing that the "inquiry envisioned by Rule 702 is . . . a flexible one" and reminded the trial courts that the "focus . . . must be solely on principles and methodology, not on the conclusions they generate." The Court also noted that the trial courts should be mindful of other applicable rules in assessing a proffer of expert scientific testimony under Rule 702. Specifically, this refers to Rule 703, which provides that expert opinions based on otherwise inadmissible hearsay are to be admitted only if the facts or data relied on are of a type reasonably relied on by experts in the particular field in forming opinions; Rule 706, which allows the court in its discretion to procure the assistance of an expert of its own choosing; and Rule 403, which permits the exclusion of relevant evidence if its probative value is substantially outweighed by the danger of unfair prejudice, confusion of the issues, or misleading the jury.

Daubert *Applied to Workplace Drug Testing*

Millions of workplace drug tests are conducted in this country each year. Approximately 5% of those tests are positive. As a result, many workers involved are subject to discipline. Typically, these tests are conducted under federal urine testing guidelines that have been in place for more than 10 years or breath alcohol testing guidelines that have been in place for 5 years [40]. The urine drug testing process consists of a collection of a urine sample, shipment to one of 67 government-certified drug testing laboratories [41], and review by a licensed MRO. When challenged, each step could require "an expert" to explain the process. Most critical are the laboratory analysis and medical review of the sample.

Established Test Process

Drug tests required under federal programs and those in states where federal guidelines are required or applied test for drugs in urine and alcohol in breath. The DOT-regulated drug tests must be submitted to a laboratory facility certified by SAMHSA. These laboratory facilities are closely regulated, including a rigorous quality control program. Strict chain-of-custody procedures must be maintained for each sample that crosses the laboratory threshold. Each sample is subject to analysis as follows:

Initial test. The initial test shall use an immunoassay that meets the requirements of the Food and Drug Administration (FDA) for commercial distribution. Specified initial cutoff levels shall be used when screening specimens to determine whether they are negative for the five drugs or classes of drugs [40 CFR part 40.29(e)].

Confirmatory test. All specimens identified as positive on the initial test shall be confirmed using gas chromatography–mass spectrometry (GC-MS) techniques at specified cutoff levels for each drug. All confirmations shall be by quantitative analysis. Concentrations that exceed the linear region of the standard curve shall be documented in the laboratory record as "greater than highest standard curve value" [40 CFR part 40.29(f)].

The most widely used analytical methods that meet these specifications are the enzyme-multiplied immunoassay technique (EMIT or CEDIA) and the kinetic interaction of microparticles in solution (KIMS) test. These are popular because they are inexpensive, require little formal training for operators, have a short analysis time, and can detect a wide range of drugs [42]. Experts, however, regard these as suitable only for preliminary screening, due to their propensity for error. They have been criticized because of the tendency to yield false-positive test results based on cross-reactivity with legitimate drugs and certain foods. The manufacturers have recommended, and federal rules require, that a positive test result be confirmed with another analytical method, thereby essentially conceding that they are neither valid nor reliable as a single testing method.

The analytical method that experts consider to be the most accurate and reliable means of confirming positive screening results is GC-MS. A 1996 survey of 25 technical experts revealed that GC-MS is the only confirmation test that, when used in conjunction with the preceding screening tests, is rated "fully defensible against legal challenge" for a wide range of drugs [43]. The federal government requires that all federal employers use GC-MS to confirm positive test results from initial screening methods. The only disadvantages of GC-MS are its high cost and complexity. Over the past 12 years, courts have consistently determined that a combination of EMIT confirmed by GC-MS is valid and reliable [44].

A drug testing program includes more than the analytical methods used to detect illicit drugs in urine samples; it also includes the quality assurance procedures of the drug testing laboratories. Employers can maximize the accuracy and reliability of the analytical approaches of their drug testing programs by selecting laboratories that follow strict quality assurance procedures. The laboratory should use qualified personnel who adhere to chain-of-custody procedures in handling samples. External quality control procedures also contribute to the accuracy and reliability of drug testing programs. Thus an employer should compare the performance of its laboratory with that of other laboratories. The danger of using poor quality control procedures is illustrated by a challenge to the accuracy of drug tests administered by the military in 1981. Because the military used an inaccurate confirmatory technique and selected laboratories with poor quality assurance procedures, military tribunals ordered the reinstatement of thousands of servicemen. Thus, even if an employer uses the most reliable and accurate analytical techniques available, a drug testing program is only as defensible as the quality assurance procedures of the testing laboratory.

The Alternative Testing Procedures and Daubert/Rule 702

Employers and their advisors must assess the advantages and disadvantages of moving away from test procedures and methods now readily accepted by the courts to an arena of unknowns. Urine testing for controlled substances and breath or saliva testing for alcohol are considered established test methods. Testing for controlled substances using hair, saliva, and sweat patches have not yet reached this status. It is appropriate to assess each proposed test matrix and examine its prospects under *Daubert*. Additionally, it is appropriate to examine the issues facing specimen validity testing, on-site (instant) test kits, and testing urine for alcohol under *Daubert* [45]. For the purposes of this discussion, we will focus on hair testing in light of *Daubert*. However, the same analysis would apply to each of the above-mentioned alternate matrices or tests.

Hair Testing

Examining hair for the presence of illicit substances is not new [46]. However, its application to the workplace is relatively recent [47]. Of the thousands of court decisions dealing with workplace drug testing, fewer than 50 address this issue [48]. At least one state supreme court has addressed the admissibility of hair test results and expert testimony in light of *Daubert*. In *Nevada Employment Security Department et al. v. Holmes*, the Nevada Supreme Court cited *Daubert* and concluded that radioimmunoassay (RIA, hair) testing, especially when coupled with a confirmatory GC-MS test, is now an accepted and reliable scientific methodology for detecting illicit drug use [49]. In so concluding, the court agreed that the positive test result demonstrated work-related misconduct warranting a denial of unemployment benefits. It is instructive to note that the Nevada Supreme Court concluded that the test result in this case was, *when coupled with a confirmatory GC/MS test,* an accepted and reliable scientific methodology for detecting illicit drug use [50].

It is important to keep in mind that the admissibility of scientific expert testimony must pass a two-step test: (1) whether the expert would testify to valid scientific knowledge and (2) whether that testimony would assist the trier of fact *with a fact at issue* [51].

The facts at issue must be decided in view of the adversarial setting and a myriad of issues such as the burden of proof required, the legislative intent (if any), and the public-policy concerns of that particular forum. For example, in the *Holmes* case discussed earlier, a fair reading of the court's decision reveals an overriding emphasis on the need to stem the tide of illicit drug use at work. In workers' compensation cases, there is an ever-present legislative intent to liberally interpret the law in favor of the claimant.

A handful of trial courts have addressed the use of hair test results in criminal cases [53], parole hearings [54], child custody matters [55], and military court martial proceedings [56]. Only a handful of state appellate courts have addressed the use of hair testing in employment termination matters. In *Bass v. Florida Department of Law Enforcement* [57], a Dade County corrections employee was terminated after her urine tested positive for the presence of cocaine. When Bass learned of the results of the urine test, she voluntarily underwent further drug testing. The results of these subsequent tests, which included a hair analysis test, showed no evidence of cocaine use. Included in the results was a report by an expert witness that suggested a scientific basis for a false-positive reading on the initial urinalysis test.

At a formal hearing, Bass sought to introduce evidence of the hair analysis test and the letter from the expert explaining how a false-positive reading could have been obtained on the urinalysis. The hearing officer refused to admit this evidence [58]. Upon appeal, the court ruled that the hair analysis testimony had been erroneously excluded, reversed the final order, and remanded the case for further proceedings [59]. After a hearing on remand, the hearing officer again recommended revocation of criminal justice certification. The Criminal Justice Standards and Training Commission entered a revocation order, which Bass appealed. The Florida Appellate Court again reversed the decision and again ordered the commission to consider the hair test report submitted by Bass's expert. On remand, the commission considered the expert's report and dismissed the case against Bass, thereby reinstating her license [60].

Despite the limited number of court decisions on the subject of hair testing, there is significant pressure to consider this method for use in federal testing programs [61]. If legally challenged, could hair testing survive a *Daubert* hearing? We consider below each of the elements of the *Daubert* standard.

WHETHER A THEORY OR TECHNIQUE CAN BE (AND HAS BEEN) TESTED. Given the paucity of court cases in which hair test results have been admitted, the claims of accuracy and reliability voiced by some hair test advocates have yet to be verified. In fact, independent studies raise serious questions about the use of hair testing in the workplace [62]. In 1994, a conference on hair testing was held, sponsored by the federal Division of Workplace Programs (DHHS) Center for Substance Abuse Prevention. "It was clear from the conference presentations that the science of testing hair for drugs of abuse continues to have analytical inconsistencies that undermine confidence in the accuracy, reliability, and fairness of such test results" [63].

Casserly noted that

> The scientific community does not question whether hair analysis can detect the presence of drugs in hair. More than eighty studies worldwide attest to this fact. But some scientists do question how to interpret the outcome of these positive results. Tom Mieczkowski, a criminologist, stated that scientists question the "interpretation of hair analysis outcomes and how these outcomes may or may not be appropriately employed." H. Westley Clark, an addiction-medicine specialist, stated that "there are no standards on which people agree, and there are no agreed-upon cutoffs below which a test will be called negative, as there are in urinalysis" [64].

The continuing controversies surround issues such as environmental contamination, absorption, and racial, gender, and age bias. The exact mechanism by which drugs are absorbed into the hair is unknown. Commentator Casserly provides the following succinct discussion of the issues [65]:

> Martha R. Harkey described two theories of how drugs are absorbed into one's hair. One theory suggests that: [drugs] enter the growing hair follicle by passive diffusion from the capillaries at the base of the hair follicle. According to this model, drugs are trapped in the hair cells during early development, are bound in the hair shaft during keratogenesis, and can be detected in the hair shaft as it emerges from the scalp. . . . In this model, drug concentration in hair should be proportional to the drug concentration in blood at the time of hair synthesis. The time of drug

ingestion also can be calculated from the location of the drug along the hair shaft (assuming a constant hair growth rate of one centimeter per month) [66].

Casserly continues:

Another theory suggests that . . . [drugs] may be absorbed into hair from capillaries, sebaceous glands, sweat glands, as well as from the external environment. Using this model, drugs could be incorporated into hair from multiple pools during various times of the hair life cycle (i.e., from blood during growth and differentiation, from sweat and sebum after formation, and from the external environment after formation) [67].

A study conducted by the University of California, Davis, Medical School found that clean hair samples tested positive for cocaine after being handled by individuals who had ingested cocaine. This study indicates that it is difficult to determine if a positive result occurs because of drug ingestion or external exposure.

Another study conducted by the University of Alabama, Birmingham, analyzed hair samples from 35 children who lived in homes in which crack cocaine was smoked routinely. The study found that two-thirds of the children (many of whom were 8 years old or younger) tested positive for cocaine. The study abstract stated that "if one assumes that young children are not intentional cocaine users, these results show that their hair can become cocaine positive through passive exposure" [68].

In response to these criticisms, hair test advocates claim that proper washing methods eliminate all environmental contaminants. However, scientific critics argue that the advocate's special washing method cannot be scientifically confirmed because they have never voluntarily handed over their data to independent researchers. In fact, various studies done of similar washing methods show conflicting results, but independent scientific studies "concluded that similar washing of artificially contaminated hair left enough cocaine behind to cause false-positive results" [69]. A study by D. Blank and D. Kidwell "reported failure to successfully wash cocaine from hair soaked in strong aqueous concentrations of cocaine" [70].

There are unresolved issues concerning the absorption rate of drugs in hair, relating to individual differences in hair texture and type. Some scientists argue that two individuals may ingest the same amount of drugs but have different results on their hair tests due to absorbency rates. This may occur because "hair morphology and physiology differ with race, gender, and age. . . ." The exact way in which these differences affect hair analysis outcomes is not known [71].

Others have pointed to studies that demonstrate the possibility of "built-in racial bias" in hair testing [72]. Additionally, another study conducted by the Center for Human Toxicology at the University of Utah "raises the possibility that women's hair might hold more drug residue than men's" [73].

WHETHER IT HAS BEEN SUBJECTED TO PEER REVIEW AND PUBLICATION. As the preceding discussion indicates, papers on hair testing have been published frequently [74], but they have not necessarily received peer review. In fact, the unwillingness of hair test advocates involved in the commercial promotion of hair testing to submit their procedures to peer review has been criticized greatly [75] and is the subject of some frustration in the field.

WHETHER, IN RESPECT TO A PARTICULAR TECHNIQUE, THERE IS A HIGH KNOWN OR POTENTIAL RATE OF ERROR AND WHETHER THERE ARE STANDARDS CONTROLLING THE TECHNIQUE'S OPERATION. The possibility of error has been noted [76]. At a minimum, the potential for error cannot be ruled out with any degree of scientific certainty [77].

WHETHER THE THEORY OR TECHNIQUE ENJOYS GENERAL ACCEPTANCE WITHIN A RELEVANT SCIENTIFIC COMMUNITY. The relevant scientific community (forensic toxicologists) continues to question the use of hair testing in the workplace [78]. Relatively few court decisions have addressed the admissibility of hair test results. To attempt a glimpse at the future, it is instructive to look at the cases that have involved hair test results to see what, if any, extenuating factors may have affected the outcome (see Appendix 18A). It is likely that attempts to discipline a current full-time worker based on a hair test will face a tough challenge under *Daubert*.

Athletics and Sports Drug Testing

Testing for drug use by athletes has become an increasingly common component of organized sports—at the academic, amateur, and professional levels. Recent U.S. court cases have dealt with drug testing of public school student athletes, college players, Olympic competitors, and professional athletes. The International Olympic Committee (IOC) has had "doping control" or athlete drug testing at the center of its medical commission functions for over two decades. In 2000, the United States created a national sports drug testing agency, the U.S. Anti-Doping Agency (USADA), and established a White House Task Force on Drugs in Sports.

Sports drug testing historically has been focused on deterring and detecting "cheating" by athletes who use performance-enhancing substances to achieve an unfair competitive advantage. In the United States, and more recently in international Olympic sports communities, there has been a move toward including testing for illegal drug use by athletes, regardless of whether the use is intended for athletic performance enhancement. The IOC's list of banned or prohibited substances for Olympic competition now includes cocaine, marijuana, and morphine [79].

The *de facto* standard of practice in sports testing are the IOC Anti-Doping

Rules. In 1999, the International Standards Organization (ISO) issued specifications for sports antidoping programs and procedures [80]. Both the IOC Anti-Doping Rules and the ISO standards for doping control programs contain criteria for prohibited drugs, specimen collection, specimen analysis, results management, and athlete sanctions. Many drug testing programs in U.S. collegiate and professional sports use a combination of workplace and sports antidoping procedures. The IOC and ISO standards are based on forensic principles for collecting, transferring, and analyzing specimens and include provisions for test results management. They also include "due process" guarantees for the athlete during adjudication and sanctions procedures.

The basic framework for sports testing is in many ways similar to workplace testing. The sports or athletic organization is analogous to the employer, and sanctions for positive tests are imposed by the sports organization. Some sports organizations conduct their testing programs using internal staff and resources; others contract the functions to sports testing companies or agencies. The National Collegiate Athletic Association (NCAA), for example, contracts its collegiate sports testing to a private-sector company. The U.S. Olympic Committee contracts with USADA to perform sports testing of U.S. Olympic athletes. Many professional sports organizations contract with companies that also conduct workplace testing for employers.

In general, athletic testing programs are much more comprehensive than workplace testing programs. Because the focus is primarily on drug use for enhancing athletic performance, the major class of drugs targeted is anabolic steroids. Sports testing panels often include anabolic steroids, diuretics (used to mask anabolic steroid use), stimulants, and narcotics. In some sports, particularly endurance and strength events, testing for drugs used to manipulate blood properties, such as erythropoietin (EPO) is common. The IOC list of prohibited substances contains over 150 drugs or drug metabolites.

Many sports testing programs are structured to include in-competition and out-of-competition testing. In-competition testing is conducted immediately before or just after the athlete participates in the sports event. Out-of-competition testing may occur at any time, by random selection of athletes or by testing at training camps or practice sessions. Some sports testing programs have a follow-up testing component to monitor athletes who have been suspended or placed on a probationary status for a prior violation.

Urinalysis is the most commonly used methodology in sports testing today. However, blood samples are used for some forms of sports testing, especially for EPO, human growth hormone, and other substances used to alter blood chemistry. Urinalysis is conducted in specialty laboratories, using GC-MS or MS-MS technology. The IOC establishes cutoff levels for the drugs, but most levels are set at the lowest limits of detection because the IOC program is aimed at detecting trace amounts of the prohibited drugs. Some substances, such as caffeine, have administrative cutoff levels where "excessive" use of the specific drug is prohibited in a competition setting. The IOC has an international laboratory accreditation program, similar to the DHHS National Laboratory Certification Program. There are currently 23 IOC-accredited drug testing laboratories; with two located in the United States. The ISO has published laboratory standards for sports testing, and several laboratories in the United States have achieved ISO certification under the ISO standard.

Urine specimen collection procedures for sports testing are based on forensic standards. In most IOC and professional sports testing, a split sample is required. Minimum urine volume is usually 70 to 80 ml due to the expanded testing panel. Generally, athletic testing includes use of some type of a custody and control form to document the collection process. In IOC testing, all collections are directly observed by a witness. In academic and professional sports testing, collection procedures similar to those used by DHHS or DOT are followed. Collection kits for IOC and professional sports testing may include glass bottles with intricate self-sealing caps for storing and shipping the urine samples.

Sports testing programs vary in how the MRO is employed. Many programs use a "medical exemption" process to address issues of athletes using prohibited drugs for bona fide medical reasons. The medical exemption process involves a physician or board of physicians designated by the sports organization whose responsibility is to review medical documentation submitted by the athlete and his or her physician. When an athlete and his or her physician feel that use of a prohibited substance is medically indicated, the athlete is required to request a medical exemption prior to administration of the prohibited drug. If the request for medical exemption is approved, a positive result for that drug(s) on a subsequent test is then "disqualified" (declared negative). Some sports testing programs use an MRO to review all test results and to contact the athlete on positive tests to determine if the athlete has a medical explanation for use of the prohibited drug. In these circumstances, the physician must determine if use of the drug was medically appropriate and not for purposes of enhancing performance. In some sports testing programs, the test results are reported directly to the sports organization, and the athlete must initiate any medical review of a positive finding through the sports organization's appeal process. However, in most sports testing programs, testing of the split specimen of a positive test is "automatic" and usually is conducted at the same laboratory that did the original analysis.

Testing of adolescents is fairly common in sports testing programs in the United States because many school athletes, Olympic athletes, and some professional sports athletes are under 18 or 21 years of age. In public school athletic testing programs, parental consent to drug testing generally is required. The athlete will not be allowed to participate without the parent's consent to drug testing. Usually, the parent is not present during the drug testing. Test results are often reported to the school's testing coordinator and, after review, are released to the student and the parents. In collegiate testing programs, parental consent, even for students under 18 or 21, is not required. In Olympic and professional sports testing, parents, guardians, or agents must sign consent forms allowing the underage athlete to participate in sanctioned competition, and these consents include participation in the sports drug testing program. In IOC and professional sport testing programs, results are not released to the parent or guardian.

Disputes or appeals concerning sanctions imposed as a result of a positive drug test in athletic testing programs vary. The IOC and ISO standards for sports testing prescribe a progression of hearings and appeals for the athlete. The IOC requires that the sports organization afford the athlete a hearing at which he or she can appear, with legal representation, if desired, or at which written submissions on behalf of the athlete are considered. The hearing panel or committee makes a determination of the sanctions to be imposed and a finding of a drug program violation. Members of the hearing panel are often appointed by the sports organization and must be "independent" of the organization. A typical hearing panel is composed of a physician, laboratory scientist, and attorney. All the panel experts usually have a recognized background in sports medicine, drug testing science, and sports dispute adjudication. Following the decision of the hearing panel, the athlete or the sports organization can appeal the panel's findings to a "court of last resort." In programs using the IOC or ISO models, the International Court of Arbitration for Sport (ICAS) is the appellate organization. In NCAA sports testing, some U.S. professional sports testing programs, and the U.S. Olympic Committee's programs, the Athletic Arbitration Association (AAA) is the appellate arbitrator [81].

As with most drug testing programs, disputes surrounding sports drug testing involve the specimen collection procedures, the accuracy and validity of laboratory findings, and issues surrounding "alternative explanations" for why the athlete's specimen contained a prohibited drug. Many recent sports testing disputes have centered on issues about possible sources of prohibited drugs or their metabolites. For example, many over-the-counter dietary supplements, widely available in the United States, are alleged to contain precursor or analogue substances that may yield metabolites of anabolic steroids when taken by athletes who engage in strenuous physical training or competition.

The arena of sports testing, particularly at the professional and Olympics levels, often involves some form of dispute resolution for most positive test findings. Because a positive test carries sanctions that can range from monetary fines to suspensions from competition to permanent bar from competition, the stakes for an athlete are very high. In addition, many professional athletes' endorsement contracts also contain restrictive language concerning drug test violations. Potential loss of earnings is substantial for a professional athlete found guilty of a doping offense. Another factor that has an impact on the dispute-resolution process is the public nature of sports drug testing programs.

Unlike in workplace testing, where public disclosure of test results generally is prohibited, IOC and other athletic drug testing programs require a public announcement of an athlete's violation of the organization's antidoping rules.

A factor in dispute resolution in athletic drug testing is the establishment of "intent"—or did the athlete use the prohibited drug with the intent of enhancing his or her athletic performance. While some athletic drug testing programs test only for "illicit" or Drug Enforcement Agency (DEA) Class I and II substances, most programs in professional and Olympic sports are focused on "performance enhancing" drugs or "doping methods." The primary objectives are to detect and deter the use of drugs that can give an athlete an unfair advantage in competition. Thus most sports testing programs include a strict liability provision that holds the athlete responsible for any prohibited substance found in his or her system. If the athlete needs to use a prohibited drug for medical treatment purposes, a physician or panel of physicians appointed by the sports organization must approve the athlete's request for a medical exemption, documented by the treating physician, for use of the banned substance. In the absence of a medical exemption, the athlete must prove that "exceptional circumstances" existed that caused the athlete to have the prohibited drug(s) in his or her system. *Exceptional circumstances* may exist if an athlete has unknowingly been given a prohibited substance by a coach, trainer, or physician or when use of an over-the-counter preparation containing a prohibited substance (e.g., ephedrine, caffeine, etc.) is determined to have been insignificant in enhancing the athlete's performance. In general, exceptional circumstances, if accepted in the dispute-resolution or adjudication process, may have an impact on the severity of the sanctions imposed, but it will not negate the finding of a drug rule violation.

The role of the physician in dispute resolution in athletic testing programs is a significant one. Because the issues of the effects of drugs on athletic performance, the role of drugs in injury treatment and recovery, and the judgment of whether a prohibited drug is used for appropriate medical reasons or for unfair competitive advantage are central to determining violations of sports drug rules, the physician's professional opinion is critical. This is underscored by the evolution of athletic drug testing programs over the past decade in which medical review boards and appeals panels (that include a physician) have become a mandatory part of the process.

As the allegations of improved athletic performance through chemical manipulation increase, sports testing programs will be even more visible in professional and amateur athletics. And because huge sums of money are involved in organized sport at all levels, disputes over the accuracy and quality of drug testing results will continue to be of great concern to athletes and their athletic organizations.

Endnotes

1. 509 U.S. 579, 113 S. Ct. 2786 125 L. Ed. 2d 469, (1993).

2. *www.dol.gov/asp/public/programs/drugs/workingpartners/educate.htm.*

3. *www.dol.gov/asp/public/programs/drugs/facts.htm*, citing *The Economic Costs of Alcohol and Drug Abuse in the United States.* Rockville, MD: National Institute on Drug Abuse, National Institute on Alcoholism and Alcohol Abuse, 1992.

4. *Substance Abuse and Mental Health Statistics Sourcebook.* Rockville, MD: Substance Abuse and Mental Health Services Administration, U.S. Department of Health and Human Services, May 1995. P 3.

5. *An Analysis of Worker Drug Use and Workplace Policies and Programs.* Rockville, MD: Substance Abuse and Mental Health Services Administration, DHHS, August 1999 (*http://www.samhsa.gov/OAS/wkplace/httoc.htm*).

6. *Addiction in the Workplace Survey.* Center City, MN: Hazelden Foundation, October 22, 1996 (*www.dol.gov/asp/public/programs/drugs/facts.htm*).

7. *www.dol.gov/asp/public/programs/drugs/facts.htm.*

8. *Treatment is the Answer: A White Paper on the Cost-Effectiveness of Alcoholism and Drug Dependency Treatment.* Laguna Hills, CA: National Association of Treatment Providers, March 1991.

9. Backer, T. E. *Strategic Planning for Workplace Drug Abuse Programs.* Rockville, MD: National Institute on Drug Abuse, 1987. P 4.

10. Normand J, Salyards S, Maloney J. An evaluation of preemployment drug testing. *J Appl Psychol* 1990;75(6):629–639.

11. *http://www.elaws.dol.gov/asp/drugfree/benefits.htm.*

12. *Mandatory Guidelines for Federal Workplace Drug Testing Programs,* initially published April 11, 1988 (53 *Fed Reg* 11979). One commentator has noted that 97% of this country's drug tests are conducted through urinalysis. See Casserly, Evidentiary and constitutional implications of employee drug testing through hair analysis. *Cleveland–St. Louis Rev* 1997;45:469.

13. *Skinner v. Railway Labor Executives Association,* 489 U.S. 602, 109 S. Ct. 1402, at 1411; 103 L. Ed. 639 (1989). See *Boston Police Department v. Campbell et al.,* 1997 Mass. Super, LEXIS 285 (1997), where the court noted that urine drug testing by means of EMIT, confirmed by GC-MS, "approaches 100% accuracy."

14. Draft proposal of test guidelines, DHHS, March 10, 1998; available at *http://www.ol2 .net/guidance/samhsahair.htm.*

15. Peterson KW. Employee drug screening: an overview of implementation issues. *Clin Chem* 1987;33:54B–60B.

16. Autry J. The Drug-Free Workplace Program: Guidelines for drug abuse policy, education, testing and rehabilitation. In: Peterson KW (ed). *Drug and Alcohol Testing and Medical Review Officer Information Handbook.* Arlington Heights, IL: American College of Occupational and Environmental Medicine, 1998. Table 1.

17. *Id.*

18. Substance Abuse and Mental Health Services Administration. Mandatory guidelines for federal workplace drug testing program. *Fed Reg* 1994;59(110):29908–29931. In: Peterson KW. *Drug and Alcohol Testing and Medical Review Officer Resource Manual.*

Arlington Heights, IL: American College of Occupational and Environmental Medicine, 1999. Pp 1.1–1.24.

19. Department of Transportation. Title 49 CFR Part 40: Procedures for transportation workplace drug and alcohol testing programs. In: Peterson KW. *Drug and Alcohol Testing and Medical Review Officer Resource Manual*. Arlington Heights, IL: American College of Occupational and Environmental Medicine, 1999. Pp 1.27–1.86.

20. Department of Transportation. Limitation on alcohol use by transportation workers. *Fed Reg* 1994;59(31):7302–7338.

21. DHHS mandatory guidelines. *Id.*

22. "There are few activities in our society more personal or private than the passing of urine." *Skinner v. Railway Labor Executives' Association*, 489 U.S. 602, 617, 109 S. Ct. 1402, 103 L. Ed. 2d 639, (1989), quoting *National Treasury Employees Union v. Von Raab*, 816 F.2d 170, 175 (5th Cir. 1987), aff'd in part and vacated in part, 489 U.S. 656, 109 S. Ct. 1384, 103 L. Ed. 2d 685 (1989).

23. "In response to the question: 'Is that your conclusion that this man is a malingerer?' Dr. Unsworth responded: 'I wouldn't be testifying if I didn't think so, unless I was on the other side, then it would be a posttraumatic condition.' " *Ladner v. Higgins*, 71 So. 2d 242, 244 (La. Ct. App. 1954), quoted in Confronting the new challenges of scientific evidence. *Harvard Law Rev* 1995;108:1481.

24. 509 U.S. 579, 125 L. Ed. 2d 469, 113 S. Ct. 2786 (1993).

25. But note Conley. *Essay: The Science of Gatekeeping: The Federal Judicial Center's New Reference Manual on Scientific Evidence*, 74 N.C. L. Rev. 1183 (April 1996), where the authors point out that "*Daubert* leaves unanswered a number of questions, including the relationship between Federal Rule of Evidence 702, which focuses on the reliability of the expert's methods, and Rule 703, which deals with the acceptability of the expert's sources. There is also a legitimate question whether Federal Rule of Evidence 403, which invites courts to balance the probative value of any evidence against the potential for prejudice, gives trial judges what is effectively a blank check in the scientific evidence context."

26. Most states have adopted similar if not identical language. See, e.g., *Wilt v. Buracker*, 191 W. Va. 39; 443 S.E.2d 196, and *Maritime Overseas Corporation v. Ellis*, 971 S.W.2d 402 (1998).

27. Confronting the new challenges of scientific evidence. *Harvard Law Rev* 1995; 108:1481.

28. *Id.*

29. *Id.*

30. *Id.* See also Conley. *Essay: The Science of Gatekeeping: The Federal Judicial Center's New Reference Manual on Scientific Evidence*, 74 N.C. L. Rev. 1183 (April 1996); Edmond, Trashing "Junk Science" *1998 Stanford Technical Law Rev* 1998;3, in which the authors introduce their discussion by stating: "One very significant fact to be considered is whether the experts are proposing to testify about matters growing naturally out of research they have conducted independent of litigation or whether they have developed their opinions expressly for purposes of testifying. . . . [I]n determining whether proposed expert testimony amounts to good science, we may not ignore the fact that a scientist's normal workplace is the lab or the field, not the courtroom or the lawyer's office."

31. 509 U.S. 579, 125 L. Ed. 2d 469, 113 S. Ct. 2786 (1993). *Daubert* concerned the

admissibility of scientific evidence proffered by plaintiffs who alleged that the prescription antinausea drug Bendectin, marketed by defendant and ingested by pregnant women, caused birth defects.

32. *Daubert,* at 593; see also *Kumho Tire Company, Ltd. v. Patrick Carmichael, etc., et al.,* 526 U.S. 137 (1999).

33. *Id.*

34. *Federal Rules of Evidence,* Rule 104(a), provides "Preliminary questions concerning the qualification of a person to be a witness, the existence of a privilege, or the admissibility of evidence shall be determined by the court, subject to the provisions of subsection (b) [pertaining to conditional admissions].

35. *Daubert,* at 592–593. The Court held that these matters should be established "by a preponderance of proof" (*Daubert,* at 593 n.10) and identified some "general observations," relevant to the proponent's burden, while acknowledging that the factors it identified were not all-inclusive ("many factors will bear on the inquiry").

36. *Frye v. United States,* 54 App. D.C. 46; 293 F. 1013 (1923).

37. *Daubert,* at 597.

38. See *In re: TMI Litigation,* 193 F.3d 613 (Third Circuit 1999).

39. *In re: TMI Litigation,* citing *United States v. Downing,* 753 F.2d 1224 (3d Cir. 1985), and *In re: Paoli Railroad Yard PCB Litigation,* 35 F.3d 717 (3d Cir. 1994), *cert. denied,* 115 S. Ct. 1253 (1995).

40. 49 CFR part 40. While it is true that these rules only apply to employers regulated by a federal agency such as the DOT, many states have enacted laws that require private, nonregulated employers to follow these federal rules (e.g., *Iowa Code Annual,* Sec. 730.5). It is not unusual for employers to follow federal guidelines to take advantage of workers' compensation or unemployment benefits (e.g., Ala. Code Sec. 25-5-330 to 24-5-340) or as a requirement of collective-bargaining agreements.

41. *www.SAMHSA.gov.*

42. Fogel. Survey of the law on employee drug testing. 42 *University of Miami Law Rev* 1996;42:553.

43. *Id.*

44. See *National Treasury Employees Union et al. v. Von Raab,* 489 U.S. 656, 672, 109 S. Ct. 1384, 1394 (1989), finding that the combination of EMIT and GC-MS tests "is highly accurate, assuming proper storage, handling, and measurement techniques." The Court also noted that the union in that case did not dispute the evidence that the follow-up test, GC-MS, is almost always accurate, assuming proper storage, handling, and measurement techniques (*Von Raab,* at 1394, n.2).

45. *Specimen validity testing* means checking samples for adulterants or attempts at substitution.

46. Casserly. Evidentiary and constitutional implications of employee drug testing through hair analysis. 45 *Cleveland–St. Louis Law Rev* 1997;45:469, noting that hair testing for drugs was used as far back as 1954.

47. *Id.,* at n.85 and accompanying text, citing a 1990 report prepared by a committee of the Society of Forensic Toxicology (SOFT) in which it was determined that "the use of hair analysis for employee and pre-employment screening is premature and cannot be sustained by current information on hair analysis for drugs of abuse."

48. One commentator suggests that the limited number of hair test cases is due to the

"concern over the accuracy of hair testing." Wefing. Employer drug testing: Disparate judicial and legislative responses. *Alberta Law Rev* 2000;63:1.

49. *Nevada Employment Security Department et al. v. Holmes,* 112 Nev. 275, 914 P.2d 611 (1996).

50. *Id.* (emphasis added).

51. *Walker v. Soo Line Railroad Company,* 208 F.3d 581 (7th Cir. 2000).

52. *Bryant v. Tidy Building Services,* 678 So. 2d 48 (La. App. 1996).

53. See *United States v. Foote,* 898 F.2d 659 (8th Cir. 1990), where the court denied a motion to compel the arresting officer to submit to a hair test for cocaine.

54. See *United States v. Madina,* 749 F. Supp. 59 (E.D.N.Y. 1990), where the court admitted hair test results in a probation revocation proceeding.

55. *Burgel v. Burgel,* 533 N.Y.S.2d 735 (App. Div. 1988).

56. *United States v. Bush,* 44 M.J. 646 (C.M.A. 1996).

57. 712 So. 2d 1171 (Fla. Ct. App. 1998).

58. *Bass v. Florida Department of Law Enforcement, Criminal Justice Standards and Training Commission,* 627 So. 2d 1321, 1321–1322 (Fla. 3d D.C.A. 1993) (Ferguson, J., concurring).

59. *Id.,* at 1321.

60. Statement of J. White, Assistant General Counsel, Florida Department of Law Enforcement, Criminal Justice Standards and Training Commission, telephone interview, October 13, 2000. Mr. White also indicated that no "*Daubert*-type" hearing was held. Ms. Bass represented herself at the initial proceeding and introduced the expert's report. As the case proceeded, the commission did not have an opportunity nor the need to introduce rebuttal expert testimony.

61. Draft proposal of test guidelines, DHHS, March 10, 1998; available at *http://www.ol2 .net/guidance/samhsahair.htm.*

62. Casserly. Evidentiary and constitutional implications of employee drug testing through hair analysis. *Cleveland–St. Louis Law Rev* 1997;45:469.

63. Draft proposal of test guidelines, DHHS, March 10, 1998: available at *http://www.ol2 .net/guidance/samhsahair.htm.*

64. Casserly. Evidentiary and constitutional implications of employee drug testing through hair analysis. *Cleveland–St. Louis Law Rev* 1997;45:469.

65. *Id.*

66. *Id.*

67. *Id.*

68. *Id.*

69. *Id.,* at n.58 and accompanying text.

70. *Id.,* at n.59 and accompanying text.

71. *Id.,* at nn.65 through 67 and accompanying text.

72. Wefing, at n.260 and accompanying text. Casserly notes that some hair test advocates point to a University of Southern Florida study that "attributed African-American subjects higher positive-test rates through hair testing to higher use of cocaine, not to any racial bias in the test" (Casserly, at n.71).

73. Casserly, at n.70 and accompanying text. Casserly points out that some hair test

advocates have argued that a double standard is used for hair analysis as opposed to alcohol testing because a standardized alcohol test is used for both sexes, although women metabolize alcohol more slowly than men.

74. *Bass v. Florida Department of Law Enforcement, Criminal Justice Standards and Training Commission,* 627 So. 2d 1321, 1321–1322 (Fla. 3d D.C.A. 1993) (Ferguson, J., concurring), where the court noted the numerous articles published by the plaintiff's expert.

75. Casserly, at n.54 and accompanying text.

76. *Id.*

77. Cone et al. Analysis of hair for cocaine. In: *International Research on Standards and Technology.* 1995. Pp 91–120.

78. Draft proposal of test guidelines, DHHS, March 10, 1998; available at *http://www.ol2 .net/guidance/samhsahair.htm.*

79. International Olympic Committee memorandum, April 1, 2000, *Prohibited Classes of Substances and Prohibited Methods.* Lausanne, Switzerland, signed by Dr. Patrick Schmasch, Medical Director.

80. International Organization for Standardization (ISO). *Publicly Available Specification (PAS) 18873, International Protocol for Doping Control.* Geneva, Switzerland, 1999.

81. National Collegiate Athletic Association (NCAA), National Center for Drug-Free Sport, NCAA Drug-Testing Program, *www.ncaa.org/sport_sciences/drug testing.*

Appendix 18A. *Hair Testing Case Outcomes and Extenuating Factors*

Case	Outcome	Factors Affecting Outcome
1. *Burgel v. Burgel* (1988)	Hair test admitted	Court expressed no opinion re: the admissibility of the results; issue was whether the wife must submit to the test; based on broad scope of discovery and her past admission of cocaine use, court said she must take the test.
2. *Garvin v. Garvin* (1990)	Hair test not admitted	Hair test reliability was not an issue; court refused to require test since there was no suspicion that the wife used drugs.
3. *Koch v. Harrah's Club* (1990)	Hair test admitted	Nevada trial court; only allowed if Harrah's agrees to allow employees to choose urinalysis to confirm; hair test alone not sufficient to terminate.
4. *U.S. v. Medina* (1990)	Hair test admitted	Parole revocation hearing (standard of proof limited)
5. *U.S. v. Foote* (1990)	Hair test denied	Criminal defendant requested arresting officer to take test; Court said no.
6. *U.S. v. Riley* (1990)	Not an issue	Dissenting Judge merely referenced hair test by analogy.
7. *In re: Adoption of Baby Boy L* (1993)	Hair test admitted	In best interest of child custody cases, courts allow liberal discovery.
8. *U.S. v. Nimmer* (1995)	Hair test admitted	Military court agreed to allow negative hair test in to refute urine test.
9. *Nevada Emp. Sec. Dept. v. Holmes*	Hair test admitted	Unemployment case, public policy to maintain safety at work; GC-MS confirmation required
10. *U.S. v. Bush* (1996)	Hair test admitted	Issue was to determine "sustained" drug use after an attempt at substituting previous sample.
11. *Hicks v. City of N.Y.* (1997)	Hair test not admitted	Court found test not reliable.
12. *Brown v. City of N.Y.* (1998)	Hair test admitted	Probationary employee; full-time workers subject to urinalysis.
13. *Bass v. Fla. Dept. Law Enf.* (1998)	Hair test admitted	No *Daubert*-type hearing held.
14. *Broadus v. Unemp. Comp Bd. of Review* (1998)	Hair test not admitted	Inability of test to pinpoint time of ingestion.
15. *In re: Nixon v. City of N.Y.* (1999)	Hair test admitted	No rebuttal expert witness offered.
16. *Ryan v. Carroll* (N.Y. 1999)	No decision	Case remanded from federal to state court; court said negative hair test result raises questions about the accuracy of the urine positive result.
17. *Wallace v. Outokumpu American Brass, Inc.* (N.Y. 2000)	No decision	Remanded from federal to state court; claim of racial bias in test.

19

Evidentiary Issues in Workers' Compensation

MICHAEL G. HOLTHOUSER

The principle behind workers' compensation is that workers are protected against financial loss due to injury on the job and employers are protected against lawsuits and unpredictable costs. Further, workers do not have to prove negligence or malfeasance on the part of employers to collect benefits. Workers' compensation in the United States has developed into a complex system of no-fault health and disability insurance that is mandated by state or federal law and is administered at the state level. Insurance services are provided by competing private carriers or by public carriers, depending on the state and the system. Coverage of workers by workers' compensation differs from system to system, typically excluding employees in banks and agriculture, the self-employed, and employees in work-places with few workers.

Workers' compensation exists to mitigate the effect on workers of wage loss, lost earnings opportunities due to disability, and medical care associated with work-related injuries and illness. Various states, the District of Columbia, Puerto Rico, and the federal government have approached this problem in slightly different ways, creating 53 systems plus certain special-purpose compensation systems. In Canada, the system developed differently and more in keeping with the European roots of workers' compensation. The Canadian pattern is more uniform, with closer similarities among the 10 provincial systems, 3 territories, and the system for federal employees. The two countries provide a natural comparison by which to explore the organizational behavior and characteristics of workers' compensation systems.

The workers' compensation system in almost every state has been in a situation of perceived crisis. In the early 1990s, a perception of fraud in the system led to widespread crackdowns, investigations, and often intrusive monitoring of injured workers. Today, the crisis in workers' compensation is largely economic. In recent years, the incidence and cost of work injuries in the United States

Portions of this chapter have been published previously in the OEM Report, March 2001, with permission of the publisher.

have reached new heights. However, this trend has stabilized recently, and injury claims are stable or decreasing, as are benefits paid. However, the costs remain much higher than in past years.

Key Concepts in Workers' Compensation

Principles

The basic principles of workers' compensation are common to almost all systems in the United States and Canada and derive from the origins of the program in nineteenth-century Germany [1].

- *No-fault* compensation is provided, except for the exclusions listed below. There is no punitive or distributive compensation based on causation or responsibility for the injury, as long as it occurred "out of and in the course of employment." The workers' compensation system itself does not determine liability, and benefits do not change whether the employer, the employee, or a third party was immediately responsible for the injury.
- *Exclusions* are specified in the legislation. Certain types of injuries are routinely excluded in the United States (in Canada, exclusions are more limited). Claims for injuries arising from malicious or self-destructive acts, horseplay, impairment by alcohol or drugs, criminal acts, or acts in violation of company policy may be denied. Injuries arising while en route to and from work are not considered work-related. Injuries that occur away from the usual workplace and outside usual working hours may or may not be covered depending on whether the worker was traveling on the job and engaged in work at the time.
- *Regulation* is separated from compensation services. Workers' compensation is separated from enforcement of occupational health and safety regulations. It is assumed that the employer will provide a reasonably safe workplace, and many carriers encourage or require employers they cover to meet safety standards. Even in British Columbia, where the workers' compensation board is responsible for occupational health and safety regulation, the functions are separated in the organization.
- *Fair compensation* in a reasonable period of time is the ultimate goal. Compensation to the injured worker is intended to be fair and timely. Although often disputed, this principle is generally maintained for simple injuries. More complicated claims often take much longer, are more likely to be denied, and are not necessarily compensated to the satisfaction of the claimant.
- *Collective liability* is the doctrine that all employers in a certain industry or classification are liable as a group for the cost of injuries arising

among workers in that classification. The workers' compensation system determines which employer the worker worked for when the injury occurred, but the purpose is not to assess liability to the individual company. The workers' compensation system is interested in which company was the employer in order to identify which carrier should provide indemnification, to provide the employer with an opportunity to dispute or support the claim, to compile a statistical database by which to set premiums for an industry (and to set the relevant categories), to compile data on which to set experience ratings for an individual employer, and to document the circumstances in the assessment of causation. However, compensation for the individual claim comes out of a pot into which all employers have paid, proportionate to the historical cost of claims in their particular classification.

- *Mandatory coverage* for workers covered under legislation is the rule, except in Texas, which allows employers to opt out of workers' compensation coverage but still holds them responsible for work-related injury benefits. Workers' compensation may not be required, depending on the jurisdiction, for small businesses (usually less than five employees), farm workers, independent contractors, domestic employees who live in private homes, maritime workers (who are covered under the Jones Act), railroad workers (covered under their own federal act), students engaged in learning activities, and unpaid volunteers. Approximately 85% of all workers in the United States are now covered; 64 to 100% of workers are covered in Canada, depending on the province.
- *Protection from litigation* is the major factor inducing employers to accept workers' compensation. Despite the fact that the government holds employers responsible for providing a safe and healthy workplace, under workers' compensation law, the employer is protected from lawsuits by the employee as part of the defining principle of workers' compensation. This largely restricts the grounds of litigation to due process within the workers' compensation system or allegations of withholding or falsifying evidence. In theory, workers' compensation is an "exclusive remedy" (defined below) and cannot be appealed to courts. In practice, litigation is a common occurrence in the United States.
- *The right of appeal* is an integral part of workers' compensation systems and built into the legislation in every jurisdiction. Claims may be appealed to the insurance carrier if they are denied. Tribunals, commissions, and administrative courts or boards, following the relevant state and federal legislation, review the decisions of workers' compensation carriers.
- *Regulation of the industry* is required in most of the United States because of the way the industry is organized. The carriers are commercial insurance companies subject to state regulatory agencies.

Definitions

Precision of language is always important in consideration of statutory matters and is particularly helpful in understanding the complexities of workers' compensation. The following are some important terms commonly used in workers' compensation and the Americans with Disabilities Act Title I (which is discussed in Chap. 20):

> *Exclusive remedy* stands for the concept that in workers' compensation the worker's sole recourse for monetary compensation or other benefits is the employer. The employer, and in Canada, both the employer and employee, cannot be sued outside the workers' compensation system, except in special instances in which there may be allegations of fraud or intentional actions by the employer that caused damages or defective or unsafe equipment or material from an external supplier.
>
> *Impairment* is a medical term and is defined by the American Medical Association (AMA) as "the loss of, loss of use of, or derangement of any body part, function, or system." Physicians generally determine degree of impairment using an AMA-designed system [2] (see Chap. 12).
>
> *Disability* is a legal and administrative term when used in workers' compensation. The AMA defines *disability* ". . . [as] an alteration of an individual's capacity to meet personal, social, or occupational demands or statutory or regulatory requirements." Disability represents the gap between what activities an individual can perform and what a specific job or labor market requires. As a legal term, its determination is unique to a particular jurisdiction and usually is defined in the workers' compensation act. Physicians generally have no special expertise for determination of disability, but they may for the determination of impairment (see Chap. 12). Under the Americans with Disabilities Act (see Chap. 20), a disability is a physical or mental impairment that limits a major life function, such as the "essential job functions." Recently, the Supreme Court of the United States has clarified the term to include only those disabilities which cannot be overcome by medical measures, e.g., controlling diabetes through the use of medication and diet. Under the Americans with Disabilities Act, a *disability* is more like a handicap. Under the act, a person has a disability if he or she considers himself or herself to have a covered disability under the act, if he or she has a record of a covered disability, or he or she is regarded by his or her employer as having a covered disability.
>
> *Handicap* is defined as an impairment that can be overcome by some type of "reasonable accommodation" of the impairment. The enforced use of reading glasses is an example. The Americans with Disabilities Act

and its earlier Canadian equivalent, the Human Rights Act, mandate greater employer attention to "reasonable accommodation" needs of those with permanent disabilities, as defined by the acts, whether or not they were "disabled" as a result of a work-related injury. The origin of this word is of interest: Destitute and maimed veterans of the Boer War were reduced to begging by the reluctance of the British government to pay pensions. They stood on the street holding their caps in their hands to receive handouts, hence *handicap*. Handicap is used in other contexts to mean the degree of accommodation or compensatory credit required to overcome an impairment, rather than the impairment itself.

Employability represents another administrative process affected by both disability and handicap; any decrease in employability as a consequence of an injury may result in economic loss to the worker, leading to a monetary award.

Temporary total disability (TTD) means that the injured worker is for some time-limited period unable to work at any type of substantial and gainful employment. The worker is entitled to a full or partial weekly wage while classified as "temporary total." These conditions are not yet permanent and are thus not covered by the provisions of the Americans with Disabilities Act.

Temporary partial disability (not used in all jurisdictions) is used when the injured worker returns to work part time or is on light or "restricted duty" and may be earning less than at the time of the injury or accident. The compensation payment makes up the difference. A return-to-work/ restricted-duty assignment may classify a worker as "temporary partial" and may trigger a cessation of "temporary total" payments (with or without a "benefits review"). This classification may have nothing to do with an employer accepting a worker back to "restricted duty." Depending on the jurisdiction, the compensation payments may stop after either a light- or full-duty release to work whether the employer does or does not accept the worker back on the job. It obviously can place the worker in a position of economic jeopardy and the physician in a difficult ethical position with his or her patient.

Work disability or *permanent partial disability* (PPD; the definition may vary from state to state) means the extent, as expressed as a percentage, to which the ability of the worker to perform work in the open labor market and to earn comparable wages has been reduced, taking into consideration the worker's education, age, training, general health, experience, and transferable skills, but he or she is capable of modified or alternative duties. PPD is determined when an injured worker has reached maximum medical improvement (MMI). There are applicable scheduled and nonscheduled benefits.

Permanent total disability (PTD; the definition will vary from state to state) occurs when the worker has been rendered completely and permanently incapable of engaging in any type of substantial gainful employment. The loss of vision, loss of limbs, or loss of neurologic functions in any combinations may constitute PTD.

Scheduled benefits are associated with impairments of certain readily identifiable body parts, such as the hand. They are predetermined, and corresponding disability tables exist. The benefits are determined as a percentage of impairment multiplied by the maximum scheduled loss from the body part. There is a maximum cap on scheduled benefits.

Nonscheduled benefits provide benefit compensation at a proportional rate to the "whole person." The *whole person* is considered 100% disability. Nonscheduled benefits are calculated at MMI and are paid as a lump-sum payment, equivalent to the average weekly rate (the average wage paid in the state), to a maximum, for the number of weeks allowed for the "whole person" reduced by the "whole person" impairment for the injury. Such settlement is intended to close out wage loss or indemnity payments. Medical payments may continue indefinitely and are not influenced by the settlement.

Causation involves the determination of whether a job activity or work injury actually caused impairment. This issue precipitates major disputes within the administrative sectors of the workers' compensation system, so its determination is of prime importance. While this task is simple when a fracture of a tibia occurs following a fall at work, it is much more difficult when, for example, a customary work activity results in nonspecific low-back pain. Often the determination depends entirely on the history derived from the worker and is a question of fact decided legally rather than a medical determination. Despite this, most systems require physicians to determine causation after an occupational injury is reported.

Exacerbation usually implies a temporary appearance or manifestation of previous injury, whereas *reinjury* or *aggravation* usually implies a fresh incident producing additional impairment to the previously injured anatomic region.

Apportionment concerns the the degree to which an occupational disorder is the result of either occupational or nonoccupational conditions (see Chap. 11). Thus it divides responsibility for any given permanent impairment among employers/insurers or between one employer/insurer and the private resources of the worker. Only impairment, not causation, is apportioned in standard workers' compensation procedures. Many states do not recognize apportionment. Apportionment is often an issue when successive injuries result in additional degrees of disability or multiple insurers become involved in a claim. Various factors, such as job description, mechanism of injury, clinical course, and stability of the medical condition, are useful in arriving at apportionment conclusions.

Second-injury funds are special funds, in some states, set aside to cover additional disability arising from a second, unrelated injury to a disabled person. They reflect the trend that second injuries often incur significantly greater cost than first injuries. In addition, injured workers with existing permanent impairment have less functional reserve, and the second injury adds to the existing level of impairment. This typically pushes the impairment rating into a much higher level of disability and therefore cost. On occasion, injury to one body part reduces the worker's capacity to accommodate or adapt to another injury. (For example, injury to an arm on the same side as a preexisting leg injury makes it difficult to use crutches.) Employers may assume that the previously injured worker also may be at greater risk for serious injury because of factors related to the first injury, such as deconditioning, residual functional impairment, and a tendency to overreact, although the evidence for this is weak. Some employers still believe in the theory that certain workers are "accident prone." Second-injury funds remove liability from an industrial classification in order to reduce the exposure of employers to an adverse experience rating. Second-injury funds were developed after World War II to encourage employers to hire disabled veterans without concern for the effect on their insurance premiums or experience rating. Now they are used to encourage the employment of workers with PPDs. These special insurance pools are sometimes funded by special assessments or by setting aside general revenues, without regard to industry classification. Second-injury funds are often underfunded and in deficit. For example, the Kentucky second-injury fund has a $2 billion dollar deficit. The Americans with Disabilities Act has eliminated much of the rationale for second-injury funds by prohibiting employer discrimination against disabled workers.

Maximum medical improvement (MMI) may not be full recovery but is the point in medical treatment when, for practical purposes and with reasonable medical care, no significant further improvement is expected. An alternative term for MMI is *permanent and stationary* (P&S) and *medical stability*. This is usually the time when the injured party's impairment is rated for the purposes of determining the amount of a settlement.

Independent medical evaluation (IME) refers to a one-time medical evaluation of an injured worker for purposes of impairment rating or evaluating treatment being rendered by the treating physician or the determination of whether or not the injured worker has reached MMI. The term also may refer to the medical examiner, who typically is the physician assigned by the administrative agency to carry out such an evaluation (see related discussions in Chaps. 9, 12, and 13).

Treating physician is the physician responsible for medical treatment as opposed to consultants or physicians who conduct IMEs. The treating physician may refer the injured worker to a specialist or to another physician for consultation or treatment. The physician to whom the worker is referred is called a *referral physician*. The referral physician may assume full care responsibilities for the injured worker, in which case he or she becomes the treating physician. The treating physician is sometimes called the "gatekeeper" of the system because he or she opens the door into workers' compensation by filing a "physician's first report" establishing the claim and directs access to care. In managed-care operations, insurance carriers may have their own gatekeepers to specialized care. In various systems, the treating physician or system gatekeeper's approval must be obtained for a worker to seek special medical consultation or testing.

The Economics of Workers' Compensation

Workers' compensation cannot be understood without knowledge of the economic stakes and incentives. From the point of view of health care providers, it is usually considered a special class of payment and treated as just another form of insurance. However, workers' compensation is best understood as a massive, parallel system of health care that has its own rules and characteristics but which shares providers with the general health care system.

Workers' compensation benefits are widely viewed as transfer payments, such as welfare, but this is incorrect. They are insurance benefits paid from a risk pool, which is structured by actuarial principles and projected costs. Workers' compensation coverage distributes risk, like any insurance, and confers protection from potentially greater loss to any one employer. Premiums are a tax only in the sense that they are mandatory, for coverage of designated qualifying employees, like Social Security. Like unemployment insurance for employees, they insure against future loss.

Occupational Disorders

In the United States, approximately 11 million work injuries occur each year [3] and account for 19% of the 57 million injuries due to all causes in the United States [4]. The direct cost of workplace injuries is estimated to be as high as $111 billion, equivalent to 3% of the U.S. gross national product [5]. Indirect costs (i.e., loss of production, vocational rehabilitation, hiring and retraining costs, etc.) account for at least an equivalent amount. Workers' compensation does not cover all these costs, of course. It is limited to medical care, indemnification for lost wages due to disability and time off work, and death benefits to survivors.

Benefits

Benefits in the United States are typically 100% reimbursement for approved medical care and rehabilitation on a fee schedule set by the state. This fee schedule is usually more generous than in the past when compared with care reimbursement through other benefits systems and compares favorably with Medicare reimbursement. Compensation for lost income varies but typically is based on two-thirds of current wages or salary, tax-free (or 90% in Canada). Wage-loss benefits begin immediately in some states or after a waiting period, usually 3 days but as long as a week, in others.

In 1998, according to data compiled by the National Academy of Social Insurance [6], workers' compensation benefit payments rose slightly to $41.7 billion, after a 7-year decline that ended in 1997, from a peak of $45.7 billion in 1992. In 1998, workers' compensation cost employers $52 billion, or $431 per covered worker, continuing a downward trend from a peak of $60.8 billion in 1993. Not surprisingly, the largest workers' compensation benefit payments were in the larger states, but some states were exceptionally high (percentages refer to the difference between 1997 and 1998): California $7.4 billion (+ 4.3%), Florida $2.2 billion (− 4.7%), and Pennsylvania $2.4 billion (− 0.9%). Others rose exceptionally between 1997 and 1998 but began from a relatively small base: Utah $0.2 billion (+ 38.5%, following a marked decline between 1996 and 1997), Tennessee $0.5 billion (+ 19.7%), and Alabama $0.6 billion (+ 16.0%). Of interest as benchmarks and because they are used as comparisons elsewhere in this chapter are New York $2.4 billion, Texas $1.5 billion, Massachusetts $0.6 billion, and Kentucky $0.5 billion.

Insurance

In the United States, workers' compensation carriers at the state level are mostly for-profit insurance companies that are subsidiaries or branches of larger insurance companies, such as Liberty Mutual, CNA, Fireman's Fund, Travelers, and The Hartford. They are regulated by insurance commissions or workers' compensation boards to ensure fair pricing, adequate service, and compliance with the state workers' compensation law. Six states (Nevada, Ohio, North Dakota, Washington, West Virginia, and Wyoming) and all Canadian provinces have single public carriers that function as regulated monopolies.

Twenty-four states also have state insurance pools for high-risk employers that have poor safety records or high rates of claims. This so-called residual market is not attractive to commercial insurance companies but needs insurance to operate. The state provides insurance services for these high-risk employers at high rates. Employers also may self-insure in 47 states if they are large enough to have the assets to set aside a fund large enough to cover anticipated claims. Most self-insured companies hire specialty firms to manage their claims but pay the claims themselves.

Workers' compensation insurance is funded by employers—employees are not expected to make a contribution. The premiums for the insurance are calculated on the basis of a rate common to the industry classification that is applied to the payroll size and the occupational classification of employees and adjusted usually by an experience rating. The experience rating takes into account the employer's individual history of costs and injury rates. Because risks are pooled for an industrial classification, improving the experience rating represents the major opportunity for a company to reduce its own premium and the only strong incentive in the system for an individual employer to improve injury rates.

Costs

The cost of workers' compensation is of increasing concern to most employers. Until relatively recently, it was simply considered one of the costs of doing business. At 1 to 3 percent of payroll, or approximately 10% of group benefit costs, the numbers often were not big enough to attract much attention. Reductions in workers' compensation costs usually were aimed at premium or program administration expenses. In reality, only about 20% of the workers' compensation costs are fixed. The remaining 80% relate to loss itself [7]. This relaxed view of workers' compensation's nonadministrative costs began to change when administrators began noticing that in the United States, medical costs for treatment of workers' compensation injuries were increasing much more rapidly than the rate of group health insurance for treatment of similar conditions [8]. There are many reasons for this, including lack of oversight of treating physicians in the past, and there has been a tendency to ascribe injuries to the worksite, because workers' compensation will pay 100% of the medical bills and provide wage replacement. As group health benefits continue to be reduced through job changes, higher deductibles, and increasing copays, the incentive to shift care to the workers' compensation system is greater than ever [9]. Plant closings, buy-outs, and downsizings also contribute to "cost shifting" as the costs of injuries are shuffled among successor companies and onto society when unfunded liabilities outlive companies that close. These adverse changes have been blunted somewhat recently by workers' compensation reforms, including case management and utilization review.

These costs are reflected in rising premium rates for non-self-insured employers and increased expenses for the self-insured. For example, from 1988 to 1991, workers' compensation premium rates grew 25% per year in Massachusetts. This rapid premium escalation plagues other states as well and has led to efforts to reform the system, such as introduction of other cost-containment strategies (e.g., managed care). The cost of workers' compensation has caused many states to use their reforms of workers' compensation law to attract new businesses.

This form of employer-oriented reform and cost cutting has been labeled "corporate welfare" and a "race to the bottom" by some because it is characterized by critics as a subsidy to industry and a means of reducing real costs that industry responsibly should shoulder. It is also criticized on the grounds that employers likely to be attracted by low workers' compensation costs may not be safety-conscious or good corporate citizens. Advocates counter that less expensive workers' compensation costs are a valid consideration for employers, even in low-risk industries, especially when companies plan relocations or new facilities.

It is a common belief that medical costs are largely responsible for the continued growth in the cost of the workers' compensation system. This perception is reinforced by the fact that the cost of medical treatment is rising more rapidly in workers' compensation than in health care in general. However, indemnification costs for lost wages generally are greater than the cost of medical care. Historically, medical costs have accounted for about one-third of direct costs and indemnity (wage loss replacement) payments for the remaining two-thirds [10]. The trend in many jurisdictions is for the two to become more even as the cost of medical care rises faster than the cost of wage replacement.

Medical care costs are incurred at the time of service and are rarely open-ended in workers' compensation, although they may be for serious permanent disability requiring long-term treatment. Wage replacement costs are high, proportionate to the amount of time the worker is off work, and may be ongoing for permanent disability claims until a settlement is reached. Thus most workers' compensation carriers are strongly motivated to get the worker back to work as soon as possible. However, if there is no realistic prospect of return to work, the foremost interest of the carrier is to keep medical care costs to a minimum.

This explains some of the curious aspects of medical care provided under workers' compensation. Workers' compensation carriers are now trying to manage (or ration) the care they pay for, sometimes in a manner more like health management organizations than traditional indemnifying insurance companies. However, they often allow chiropractic services and sometimes other forms of unproven or alternative health care, such as acupuncture, which would be denied by most other insurers. The reason is that many occupational injuries, most notoriously chronic back pain, are difficult to manage, and a troublesome subset of cases results in difficult management problems, especially unexplained disability, chronic pain, and prolonged time off work. Conventional medical treatment for these problems is expensive and often not very effective. Alternative treatment generally is less expensive, whether or not it is effective.

Rehabilitation services have a special place in workers' compensation services. Intensive rehabilitation may speed early and safe return to work. However, it also provides a means of monitoring the progress of injured workers and assessing their fitness to work. This usually can be done by a rehabilitation therapist much more efficiently and at much lower cost than by return visits to a physician, who usually is not trained to perform such assessments anyway.

Temporary disability implies that there is a prospect for the worker to return to his or her usual work. Early and safe return to work, so that the worker is quickly reintegrated into the workplace and does not lose skills, strength, or conditioning and does not face an increased risk of reinjury or present a risk to others, is the ideal in managing cases in workers' compensation. This often means that workers' compensation carriers will accept premium costs for corrective or curative medical care, intensive rehabilitation, and frequent return visits to monitor residual impairment when the worker is expected to return to work. Setting the expectation for early return to work at the start of treatment in appropriate cases is best done by the treating physician. It should be considered an integral step in treating workers with compensable injuries or illnesses.

Most injured employees with work injuries return to work within the same period of time as those with non-work-related injuries of the same type. It is a minority of injured workers who drive up the disproportionate medical and indemnity costs found in the workers' compensation system. For example, an analysis of cost per case of compensable low-back pain for 98,999 Liberty Mutual workers' compensation cases indicated an average cost per patient of $6807 (averages are influenced significantly by extreme values at either end of the range of values) compared with a median cost per patient of $392 (median values are the center-most figure in the range and are not influenced by extreme values). These patients often can be identified early, when aggressive case management is likely to be most effective.

History and Evolution

Workers' compensation is the oldest variety of government-mandated social insurance still in existence. Because it is so old, it has accumulated numerous complications and anomalies. When it was first introduced, however, it was a major reform that greatly simplified and rationalized the handling of occupational injuries.

The modern form of workers' compensation has its roots in personal injury compensation. Personal injury claims for work-related injuries always represented a large and important class of legal claims but originally were treated as any other personal injury except in the calculation of compensation, which very early took into account lost earnings.

Injuries and diseases were known to occur in ancient times among workers. Hazardous jobs often were performed by slaves or prisoners. Prisoners and slaves taken in war were considered expendable, but the labor of slaves had value, and compensation was owed to the slave owner if the slave was injured or killed.

The Code of Hammurabi, the remarkable legal system devised by a Babylonian king in about 1800 B.C., included monetary payments for work-related injuries, in addition to the traditional eye-for-an-eye and tooth-for-a-tooth formula for personal injury. Similar systems are described in the Old Testament (Exodus 21:18–19). In Roman times, employers and slave owners had a duty to care for injured workers.

In the Middle Ages, beginning about A.D. 1000, merchant and craft guilds were formed to protect the interests of their members. Even pirates of the 1700s had a complex compensation system. For example, 600 pieces of eight (the equivalent of a Spanish dollar) were paid for the loss of a right arm. This amount was more than 1 year's pay and was equivalent in total benefits to about $120,000 in 1990 dollars [11]. It is presumed that this represented the equivalent of total disability, because it would have been difficult for the armless pirate to have pursued his or her (there were female pirates) regular occupation without being able to wield a cutlass.

When industry was based on limited technology, crafts, and traditional sources of power, the potential for disabling injury on a large scale was limited. The Industrial Revolution brought the exploitation of much more powerful sources of energy and technology fraught with new hazards. With the introduction of the steam engine came the dawn of the Industrial Revolution but with it far more dangerous machinery. Process speeds, material volume, and variety increased through more powerful transportation, manufacturing, and processing equipment. The kinetic energy involved in manufacturing increased, as did the use of energy, chemical contamination, and the accompanying potential for injury and disease. The pace of technology introduction into commerce far outstripped ability of society to deal with the results.

In many countries, especially England and Scotland, increasing agricultural productivity led to rural unemployment at about the same time. People left their rural environments and family support systems and ventured into cities and mill towns where gainful employment was available. However, the transition from traditional village economics to a wage economy was brutal. Traditional rural transactions were based on personal relationships, seasonal employment, competitive local markets, and often barter or informal credit. In the new industrial economy, employment was deemed to be entering voluntarily into the service of an employer, regular hours had to be kept (sometimes 6 days a week), goods and services often were available only at company stores, and cash was the only acceptable means of payment. Because of the exploding demand for labor, men, women, and children all worked, and as the labor shortage eased, the lower wages for women and children were used to undercut the wages of men, who were usually the principal breadwinners. If the breadwinners became ill or injured in their employment and were not able to work, they quickly became unable to provide for themselves and their families, thus becoming a burden on society.

By the latter half of the nineteenth century, the situation had created a social crisis. Disabled industrial workers, including some children, were a prominent segment of the impoverished underclass in American, English, and European cities. Widows and orphans from households in which the breadwinner had died on the job were often turned out on the street, especially if the employer owned their housing, and were forced to beg or turn to crime. Prostitution was a common fate for girls who could not keep a job due to injury, illness, or incapacity and who were without the support of their families. One need only view many of the silent motion pictures created around the turn of the twentieth century to observe how unbelievably bad working conditions truly were.

In the United States and Canada, many of the people performing the heavy, dirty, or dangerous work were immigrants. Many understood English poorly, further complicating the process of communicating safety instructions. Upton Sinclair, in his famous book, *The Jungle,* chronicles the horrors of the meatpacking industry in the early 1900s, as seen through the eyes of Lithuanian immigrants.

Workers were not the only segment of society to endure inhumane conditions at this time. There was general disdain for the injured and disabled, particularly due to the legacy of the doctrine of "social Darwinism" that gained ground in the mid-nineteenth century, thereby relieving the conscience of the monied classes. As mentioned earlier, disabled soldiers returning to Great Britain from the Boer War were forced to beg for relief by extending their upside-down military caps to passersby in public places, and this was the origin of the term *handicap.* Disabled workers and their families similarly had to beg for community support. As the numbers of these people increased in the public view, the obvious need for a support system developed.

With the industrial system in crisis, there developed the idea that a social support system might confer political benefits. By providing social security, the government could win the allegiance of the people. This idea was attractive after the profound unrest in all industrial societies and the many revolutions in Europe in the nineteenth century. In 1854, Prussia required employers in certain industries to contribute to accident funds, which were administered by representatives of employers under government supervision. The "Iron Chancellor," Prince Otto Eduard Leopold von Bismarck, creator and first chancellor of the German Empire, was concerned that the dignity of German workers was diminished by the squalid conditions in which they were placed when disabled through work. He reasoned that employers should fund a system of wage-loss compensation for workers injured on the job because it was the employers who controlled the worksites and derived the benefit of the workers' labor (a concept that would not be alien to his German contemporary, Karl Marx). Bismarck proposed a compulsory mutual liability concept of "one for all and all for one" and this legislation was enacted in 1884, making this the first workers' compensation statute.

In the English-speaking world, England had led the way into the Industrial Revolution and had passed the first Public Health Act in 1848. However, England was anything but revolutionary in dealing with labor issues. Its approach to addressing its growing problem of injured and disabled workers and the misfortune that befell their families was, weakly, to encourage voluntary programs based on *noblesse oblige*. As the crisis worsened, the British (including Scottish) approach was far more employer-oriented. England passed the Employer's Liability Act in 1880, which permitted an injured worker to recover up to 3 years' wages from his or her employer under very restrictive circumstances. The effect of this legislation often was nullified because workers could waive their rights to benefits on hire, a procedure actively encouraged by their employers. By 1897, the Employers' Liability Act had run its course. England subsequently passed workers' compensation acts in 1897 and 1906, which, unlike the German mutual liability system, adopted an individual liability concept [12]. Employers were required to have insurance coverage for their injured workers or to be self-insurers. If employers failed to have one of the two forms of coverage, they were individually open to suit. If the employer was solvent, there was a chance of recovery, but if not, the suit would be fruitless for the injured worker and his or her attorney. British schemes for compensating workers diverged further after the National Health Service (NHS) was formed and became a form of industrial injury insurance supplementing medical care coverage by the NHS.

The third model came from a relative laggard in the Industrial Revolution, Russia. An elaborate schedule was developed in 1907 relating injuries and physical impairment to percentage of total disability. Disability was rated in terms of lost earning capacity and modified depending on specific job requirements. This same concept served as the basis for the California Industrial Accident Act of 1914 [11].

Today, the United States, Canada, and Australia are the only nations with workers' compensation systems that are based on state or provincial legislation and administration. All other countries that have workers' compensation or "social insurance" have national programs.

United States

There had been several decades of experience with these various models before the United States began to respond. Before the widespread introduction of a workers' compensation system, when a worker became sick or injured in the course of his or her employment, the sole remedy was to sue the employer for damages. By the turn of the century in the United States, injured or ill workers could sue their employers for injuries that occurred on the job. This was more theoretical than practical, however.

Common law in the United States held that a "master" or employer was responsible for injury or death of employees "resulting from a negligent act by him [or her]." This required the injured party to prove that his or her injury was the result of negligence by the employer. This was not easy. An attorney had to be hired and paid, witnesses had to be arranged, and the process required time. There also was the potential for personal threats to the injured worker and his or her family by unscrupulous employers. Most workers did not have the resources to obtain justice under this system. Moreover, employers had potent common-law defenses, referred to as the "unholy trinity," that could be used to fend off such lawsuits. These defenses included contributory negligence, the fellow servant rule, and the assumption of risk. *Contributory negligence* meant if a worker did anything that contributed to the injury at issue, then the employer was not responsible for what happened to the employee and was thus not negligent. The *fellow servant* rule held that if a coworker or fellow employee did something to cause the injury, then the injured party had to recover damages from the coworker because the employer had not been negligent. Under the *assumption of the risk* doctrine, an employee who entered into employment in an industry known to be associated with hazards, e.g., mining, assumed those risks, thus absolving the employer from negligence if the worker was injured.

In addition to the "unholy trinity" of defenses, other legal defenses were available under common law to employers in the United States including acts of God, acts of a third party, inevitable accident, duty of care, no proximate cause, justification, self-defense, statutes of limitations, difficulty in determining and accessing defendants, and lack of evidence. Furthermore at that time, under common law, employers had no liability for injured workers' dependents, and any cause of action terminated on the worker's death [13]. The rising tide of injured and nonproductive employees placed an ever-larger burden on relatives, churches, and charitable institutions. This situation ultimately was seen as unfair because although the employer reaped the benefits of the employee's work, with the legal advantages on their side, employers bore little risk. The time was ripe for social change.

Early reforms in the United States typically took the form of so-called employer liability acts that covered only the most hazardous industries and removed only some of the employer's legal defenses. Employer support for some form of "automatic" compensation grew as the costs of litigation and employer-sponsored "welfare plans" increased. The labor movement, which initially opposed automatic compensation, changed its position when it found that employer liability acts did not resolve the compensation problems arising from workplace accidents. With the combined support of both employers and labor, "no fault" compensation plans soon followed [14].

In 1911, Wisconsin enacted the first constitutionally valid statute to become effective and thus also the oldest social insurance program in the United States. Also in 1911, Washington State implemented a system in which the state became the monopoly provider of workers' compensation insurance. The private insurance industry organized a successful lobby to dissuade most other states from implementing similar monopoly state funds. Today, seven states have a monopoly provider workers' compensation insurance provider scheme. Thus workers' compensation became the only social program to involve the use of private insurance carriers. In the same year, the New York Court of Appeals ruled that the state's workers' compensation legislation was unconstitutional on the grounds of "deprivation of property without due process of law." Other states anxious to avoid similar judicial review on the grounds of constitutionality, and subject to pressure by industry lobby groups, incorporated various limiting provisions in their legislation, including exclusions to the categories of industries covered, mandatory waiting periods, statutory maximums to indemnity benefits, and cash benefits determined as a proportion of earnings [15].

Despite the constitutional challenges to an automatic and mutual system of employer liability for work-related injuries and illness, the scope of workers' compensation in North America gradually increased over the next three decades as the economies rapidly expanded. Both the complexity and cost of the system increased dramatically as both industries and labor forces grew, as related workplace risks increased, and as specialized expertise in disability and risk management was developed and applied to workers' compensation. By 1920, most states had passed workers' compensation legislation, and by 1949, all states in the United States had workers' compensation programs.

Occupational disease laws were not passed until 1917, starting in Massachusetts and California; all state laws did not cover occupational diseases until 1976. Part of the reason for the slow adoption of occupational disease compensation laws was fear of liability because of the long latencies and the lack of a definite onset of many occupational diseases. In addition, the sudden trauma of an occupational injury, which generally was used to determine causation and to define compensability, was missing, so any expansion of coverage required an expansion of thinking [16].

Comparison of Canadian and American Systems

Development of workers' compensation in Canada, on the other hand, was unfettered. There was no written constitution to raise concern. In contrast to the market-driven approach to workers' compensation supported by Americans, Canadians favored strong government participation and universally adopted a monopoly public-sector model like that in Washington State. However, starting in Ontario in 1915 and spreading to most other provinces, Canadian provincial legislation came to incorporate a pattern of jurisdiction-specific coverage exclusions and benefits similar to those found in the United States.

Many of the problems Canada faced were shared with the United States in a rapidly developing, resource-based economy dependent on immigrants for labor and distant owners, often British or American, for capital. The labor market was tight at times but became saturated after World War I, leading eventually to desperate conditions that culminated in the shocking events of the Winnipeg General Strike of 1919, perhaps North America's closest brush with a socialist revolution. With the only safety nets provided by charitable organizations, injured workers who could not afford legal counsel had no recourse and no prospects in such a strained economic system.

National and state or provincial leaders came to realize that an entirely new set of principles outside existing common-law and employer liability legislation were needed to protect workers, industry, and the public welfare purse from the consequences of job-related accidents and deaths. They were helped in this realization by the growing importance of urban voters at the turn of the century. Politicians in both the United States and Canada became more responsive to needs and aspirations of these new voters. Commissions, in both the United States and Canada, in the early 1900s examined the various workers' compensation models used in Great Britain, Germany, and elsewhere. Most jurisdictions concluded that the German comprehensive compulsory mutual insurance system administered by representatives of employers and workers under state supervision was the most appropriate starting point for the development of their own systems [14].

Workers' compensation in Canada took a different path to development, rejecting the British system and opting instead for a system closer to the original German system than the insurance scheme that was later adopted in the United States. Sir William Meredith reported to the Ontario legislature in 1913 that it was his opinion that a collective system of liability with employers divided into groups, similar to the German system, rather than individual liability, like the British system, would be better suited to the conditions and circumstances of Ontario. The basis of Sir Meredith's successful proposal was "an historic compromise" between the interests of employers and workers for the mutual benefit of each as well as a benefit to the public welfare. The employers would submit to the levy of taxes on their industries and receive protection from expensive litigation, whereas workers would give up their precarious right to sue and receive in return a stipulated amount based on their economic position in the community. "Both . . . as well as the State as a whole, benefit from the elimination of the friction and loss which necessarily attends Litigation." The 1915 Ontario Workers' Compensation Act became the foundation of the modern Canadian system. For strong industries, particularly the public utilities, the Ontario system permitted self-insurance; for all others, it required a compulsory system based on mutual insurance principles.

There are fundamental differences between the Canadian and U.S. systems:

- *Private-sector involvement* is significantly different between the two North American neighbors. In Canada, workers' compensation insurance is provided through provincially mandated not-for-profit service monopolies. There is no competition and thus no consumer choice for covered industries. In contrast, workers' compensation in the United States is provided through public-private or private-private competition except for seven states where a public monopoly provider operates. Except for these few state monopolies and where state agencies operate in competitive markets, most workers' compensation insurers in the United States are for-profit companies.

- *Separation of service delivery and regulatory functions* is also a major area of difference. Authority to enact and to change workers' compensation legislation rests with the provincial and state governments in Canada and the United States. In effect, Canadian boards act as custodians or stewards of the "historic compromise" between the interests of employers and workers. They both determine and enforce their own policies and standards. They are not only an insurer but also a tribunal with public-law duty to adjudicate each claim fairly, impartially, and according to law. In contrast, in the competitive workers' compensation system in the United States, the regulatory and service-delivery functions are divided between one or more government agencies that regulate the system and various public and private organizations that deliver services subject to those regulations.

- *Regulation* required to manage the two systems differs. The adoption of a competitive profit-making structure in almost all the U.S. workers' compensation systems brought with it the need for government to develop and maintain a complex and costly regulatory and monitoring framework intended to both set out the conditions of competition for the industry and protect the interests of workers, employers, and the public. In Canada, the adoption of a not-for-profit exclusive public-provider approach avoided profit-making conflict-of-interest problems and allowed governments to vest workers' compensation agencies with both service-providing responsibilities and regulatory authority. This approach, when coupled with appropriate vehicles to safeguard public interest (legislative change authority, board of directors appointments, public inquiry authority), permitted the Canadian systems to avoid many of the overhead costs inherent in third-party regulation of the industry.

- *Litigation* varies significantly. "Exclusive remedy" legislation in the United States may be viewed as being roughly comparable with the Canadian "historic compromise" in that American workers trade the possibility of civil lawsuit for an assurance of certain benefits. However, unlike the Canadian systems, those in the United States involve state courts extensively in the appeals process and allow for civil lawsuits against employers, insurers, and third parties in a variety of circumstances. Workers and employers have the right of appeal in both the Canadian and U.S. systems, and multilevel appeals processes are employed. However, in Canada, this right of appeal is exercised through a nonlitigious discovery process not involving any burden of proof and operating outside the regular court system. Furthermore, in the Canadian system when evidence is judged to be evenly balanced, the matter is typically decided in favor of the claimant, because claimants are given the benefit of the doubt. In contrast, in the United States, an adversarial appeals process operates in which lawyers play a prominent role and unresolved appeals ultimately come before state courts. Significant additional costs are borne by the workers' compensation system in the form of attorneys' fees, medical witness fees, administrative overhead for the formal hearings and records, and prolonged absences of appellants from work due to disputed claims [17].

- *Cost* is substantially less in Canadian systems. Much of this difference is the result of decreased administrative costs.
- *Liability* is more sharply restricted in Canadian systems. An important distinction between the Canadian and U.S. systems is that in Canada, all employers and employees are immune from civil actions arising from work-related accidents. In the United States, only the employer is generally immune from suit. Much of the Canadian system's success is due to this distinction. The result of the universal immunity from suit provision is that all costs of compensation are passed on to the general public in the price of goods and services. The Canadian system is therefore more efficient, cost-effective, and nonlitigious compared to the United States, where operating costs are substantially higher and workers gain fewer benefits due to the costs of litigation and the need to make a profit by the private insurance carriers [18].
- *Benefits* are structured differently in Canadian systems. Benefits have increased dramatically over the years, growing from 50% of gross wage loss to as high as 90% of lost net wages in some Canadian jurisdictions. Workers in most U.S. states receive two-thirds of their gross earnings tax-free. Periodic cost-of-living adjustments to pensions are made in recognition of inflation, and the system has expanded benefits to include psychological and physical rehabilitation, dental care, prescription drugs, nursing attendants, home care allowances, and vocational rehabilitation, including business assistance grants, training on the job, and a host of other benefits [18]. As of 1995, six Canadian jurisdictions also provide a noneconomic loss award based on clinical impairment determined by objective medical assessment. These noneconomic awards cover nonwage replacement for general damages such as pain and suffering, loss of enjoyment of life, and loss of future opportunities. Normally, these payments are capped at a fixed amount subject to annual cost-of-living adjustments and, because of the no-fault system, are significantly less than a litigant would receive in a successful tort action [19].

Claims Management

As a form of social insurance, workers' compensation was designed to be an accessible remedy for damages and to prevent devastating loss. It was never designed to be an entitlement, exercised as a matter of right on demand. Numerous tests are required—of employment, of causation, of fitness-for-duty, and of earnings. The system also was designed for straightforward injuries, not occupational diseases or cumulative injury. Chronic disorders, those with latency periods, multifactorial disorders, and episodic disorders (such as asthma) present claims-management difficulties for the system and are the subject of many disputes. On the other hand, the system works efficiently and acceptably well for the great majority of claims.

Access to benefits can be challenging if all parties involved are not in agreement and the system is full of ambiguities. For those involved in the care of ill or injured workers, mastering or at least coping with the various systems of workers' compensation delivery can be challenging. For those who represent employers or employees, understanding the system is key to deriving the maximum benefits available to those who need them. For insurers and case managers, it is the fiduciary matrix in which they operate as they attempt to appropriately control access to benefits.

Eligibility and Jurisdiction

Not all employees are protected by workers' compensation insurance. About 85 to 87% of American workers and 64 to 100% of Canadian workers are covered [15,16]. Furthermore, not all workers are considered employees. For example, domestic servants in a private home, professional athletes, many contract and subcontract workers, some seasonal agricultural workers, independent truckers, clergy, volunteers, workers in nonprofit organizations, and workers in banks and financial institutions are excluded from coverage by workers' compensation in one or more workers' compensation systems [15]. Questions about the applicability of workers' compensation to employees working at home who become injured will require further clarification. Generally, the principal site of employment determines the workers' compensation jurisdiction. However, with interprovincial, international, and interstate work, there may well be confusion regarding the appropriate jurisdiction. Because there are significant differences in the benefits extended to workers across various jurisdictions, there is naturally an incentive to seek benefits in the most generous one.

There are specified claim filing requirements in most jurisdictions. An employer usually must be notified within 30 days of the injury or illness. A claim must be filed within 1 year for a disability claim and within 2 years by dependents for a death claim. These claim filing requirements can make getting compensation for an occupational disease problematic because there are often long latencies in occupational diseases, far beyond 1 or 2 years, and there can be confounding by multiple etiologies for the disease and lack of specificity of the pathology observed by the physician.

An injured worker may forfeit his or her right to medical treatment cost coverage and indemnity if he or she is intoxicated or in violation of known drug-free workplace policies. If a worker is not using required safety gear and/ or is not following established safety procedures when he or she is injured, his or her benefits may be reduced by 25% in some jurisdictions, echoing the former contributory negligence common-law defense used by employers. Benefits may be lost if a claimant is incarcerated because of criminal activities. Workers' compensation benefits are at risk if a worker refuses to return to work after being cleared, even at a modified capacity, if work is available. Injured workers cannot collect (tax free) workers' compensation benefits together with additional salary or other forms of compensation that are, in combination, in excess of the worker's preinjury pay from the injury employer.

Claims Handling

Once an injury occurs, the clock starts for several important time limits. As mentioned previously, an injury or illness must be reported to the employer within 30 days. A claim must be filed within 1 year for a nondisabling injury or within 2 years for a disabling injury or death. In some jurisdictions, these statutes of limitations apply to the discovery or diagnosis of an occupational disease rather than the injury itself.

In the United States, there is great variation in who selects the treating physician. In 24 of the 53 jurisdictions, the employer decides whom the worker should see first. In 27, the employee may decide. In 2, there are state panels that designate preferred providers, i.e., physicians allowed to treat workers' compensation cases. Limitations also are imposed on some services. For example, Florida restricts the use of chiropractors to 18 treatments. Workers are free to get additional care or to seek care outside such restrictions, but their expenses will not be reimbursed.

Claims may be filed by the worker, by the employer, or most commonly, by the physician. The *physician's first report* is an essential document that provides the circumstances of the injury, the diagnosis and the basis for it, and the treatment rendered at the time. Along with the emergency room report, if care was sought in an emergency department, these documents set the tone as well as the foundation in fact for all subsequent documentation in the case. This is why they must be as accurate as possible. Unfortunately, both these reports usually are filled out by physicians without training in workers' compensation or occupational medicine. The history is often lacking pertinent details. The forms almost always are designed for acute injuries and require specific dates for the injury, treatment, and expected return to work. Reports for chronic conditions and occupational diseases are particularly problematic with such forms.

Claims are managed by the workers' compensation carrier, usually by a case manager who makes an initial determination. This may require further investigation, the advice of a medical advisor, or the services of an independent medical examiner. Claims that are denied may be appealed, usually first to the carrier itself and then to some public tribunal or administrative court.

There are many grounds to deny a claim. The most fundamental is whether the injury actually arose out of work, even if it happened on the employer's property. For example, recreational injuries on company property generally are not considered to be work-related. An injury in the company parking lot once one has arrived at the workplace may be. (Evidentiary issues are discussed below.)

There are many other grounds for denying a claim besides lack of a demonstrable relationship to work. Fraud is suspected commonly but probably makes up only a small fraction of claims. Cases of suspected fraud are often investigated with intrusive methods. Surveillance by video and interviews with neighbors and coworkers often are used to identify malingerers or workers exaggerating their symptoms.

Disability and Return to Work

The workers' compensation system originally began as a wage-loss system designed to pay compensation for the duration of the disability or, if permanent disability resulted, the difference between what a worker earned at the time of the accident and what he or she was able to earn after the accident. Over time, some jurisdictions adopted a prescribed- or defined-benefit system based on specified time periods and/or predetermined financial benefits; others, for ease of administration, opted for an average disability award system based primarily on physical impairment. This latter system is referred to by some as the "meat chart," a reminder of the picture of the steer displayed above the butcher's meat refrigerator delineating the various cuts of meat. The "meat chart" concept often results in a disparity of benefits. For example, many workers with permanent clinical impairment are able to return to their jobs without wage loss or loss of opportunity but still receive lifetime pensions for their work-related accident; however, the same clinical impairment to other workers may prevent these individuals from returning to the same type of employment or the same wage level, and the scheduled permanent partial disability award granted for their injury may not adequately recognize their true functional disability. While a "meat chart" system may fairly recognize clinical impairment, it has no relationship to functional disability, and many jurisdictions are returning to basics by recognizing that functional disability, tied to impairment of earnings capacity, is the appropriate basis for determining workers' compensation awards [18].

Questions of whether or not an injured worker is ready to return to work can lead to litigation if there is disagreement between the injured worker and the treating physicians. This is especially likely to occur if the physician is not familiar with the functional requirements of the worker's job and the employee's true functional capacity or there is a mismatch between the worker's functional capacity and the requirements of the job. Also, when the worker has been away from the job for an extended period of time, performs heavy work for a low wage and under adverse environmental conditions, and there is animosity present between the worker and his or her supervisor or when there is chronic or operant pain and the worker is getting conflicting advice from medical practitioners other than the treating physician, representatives, and/or attorneys, it is not surprising that he or she would not be thrilled with the prospect of returning to the job [20]. Job requirements may remain static in certain occupations, i.e., felling trees, but the body naturally ages over time. There are few 50-year-old lumberjacks. Employers are sometimes unreasonable in their expectations of older employees, especially if they have been performing heavy work for the majority of their working lifetime. Employers significantly contribute to prolonging the disability period and the indemnity payments they make by not offering light, limited, or restricted duty. The physician should be knowledgeable about both the requirements of the job and the functional capacity of the injured employee to perform the requirements of the job.

Litigation

As a general rule in Canada and the United States, any issue or matter arising out of legislation is disputable unless the clear and unambiguous wording of the relevant statute precludes it. There are ambiguous phrases in workers' compensation laws. The causation of some injuries and illnesses is debatable. Decisions must be made about return to work and how long indemnity and other benefits should continue. These ambiguous areas create a breech in the workers' compensation "exclusive remedy" approach and add significantly to the burden on administrators and the health care delivery system.

Workers' compensation is founded on an inquiry model, not an adversarial model, one with the objective of providing wage-loss replacement and medical treatment for the injured worker and distributing the cost to the consuming public in the prices of goods and services. If there is a genesis to compensation law, it arises more out of contract than tort law. It is, in effect, a statutory condition that forms part of the worker's contract of employment and is a benefit to all workers covered by the legislation in no less a manner than other statutory conditions of work, such as minimum-wage and hours-of-work legislation. The purpose of workers' compensation laws is to set aside one body of rules arising out of the common law and establish another in its place.

From a legal perspective, workers' compensation legislation generally applies in lieu of all rights or causes of action a worker or his or her dependents are or might become entitled to against his or her accident employer and against any employers or workers of those employers in Canada who are subject to the legislation. In a civil action, after all legal costs are paid, and after the employer, insurer, or workers' compensation authority is reimbursed the costs of the claim, the worker is entitled to any excess funds.

As mentioned previously, in the United States, only the accident employer is immune from lawsuits by its workers, and even then, in several states, the employer may be sued if it is found that he or she committed an intentional tort. This distinction from the monopolistic collective protection and exclusive jurisdiction concept developed in Canada is a significant reason why litigation is much less in Canada than in the United States. Further, a combination of the Canadian universal health care system, the dearth of litigation, and the Canadian nonprofit system largely contributes to lower insurance rates than the private accident insurance rates found in the United States [21].

Given the impossibility of providing an absolutely satisfactory definition of the phrase *arising out of and in the course of employment,* this pivotal question is often the subject of appeal, but it is not, however, the most frequent issue of dispute. That distinction falls to disputes over cash payments that are based on the duration of entitlement, the degree of disability, or both. Other issues such as medical and vocational benefits are also disputed frequently. This applies as a general rule in both Canada and the United States [22]. Where involvement by professional litigators or advocates was a rarity 10 to 15 years ago in Canada, it is now common.

Evidentiary Issues

The initial point of entry in any jurisdiction is determined by establishing whether the injury arose "out of and in the course of employment." Causation between the injury and the job must be established. The connection between an event and the result is not always clear. Nontraumatic heart conditions, nonspecific low-back pain, and congenital and other pre-existing conditions can all confound the determination of causation. Because many, but not all, workers' compensation cases are "OSHA recordable," and because the performance of managers, supervisors, and safety professionals is frequently tied to OSHA-recordable rates, there is often a double incentive in the United States to deny the work-relatedness of injuries.

When a definitive cause and effect is not obvious, it may place entitlement to workers' compensation in doubt. The workers' compensation claims adjudicator, administrator, or case manager must decide one way or the other in such circumstances.

Much of the rest of this book is devoted to issues of evidence that apply to workers' compensation and similar adjudication systems. These issues will not be repeated here. The particular evidentiary issues for workers' compensation are the following:

- Relationship to work.
- Identification of the employer at the time of the injury.
- Causation:
     Arising out of work.
     Competing theories or alternative explanations.
     Distinguishing from natural aging in degenerative conditions (e.g., osteoarthritis of cervical spine).
- Appropriateness of treatment.
- Reasons for disqualification.
- Impairment:
     Determining and rating impairment level.
     Determining when maximum medical improvement occurs.
- Fitness to work.
- Return to work.
- Modified work, if available.
- Accommodation required, if any.

Standards of Certainty

Evidence in workers' compensation is usually, but not always, medical evidence and invariably is required so that a determination can be made regarding cause, degree, or duration of disability. Where ambiguity exists and causation connections are not apparent, substantial reliance is placed on medical opinion. These cases make up the bulk of appeals.

Like any other expert opinion, expert medical opinion frequently will present the adjudicator, or "finder of facts," with conflicting findings often couched in conditional language, i.e., *might, could,* or *maybe*. Similarly, it is not uncommon for expert medical opinion to mix the concepts of probability and possibility [23]. The burden of proof is on the claimant to show that the claim is valid. This is made easier to achieve in most adjudication hearings because the policies of most systems require that the claimant be given the benefit of the doubt. One need only be 50% sure to make a judgment in the claimant's favor but must be 51% sure to deny the claim. In principle, one is only required to demonstrate a "balance of probabilities," not "more likely than not," at each step of the process. This is very different from the usual standard of certainty required in the health sciences, which at a minimum typically requires 95% certainty (the familiar $p < 0.05$) [24]. Generally, certainty less than 50% is considered *possibility* and certainty above 50% is considered *probability* for causation or work-relatedness determination.

It is doubtful that any clinician truthfully can say that he or she is 51%, 62%, or 78% sure of his or her decision. Nevertheless, the important distinction is to be convinced that it is "more likely than not" when giving an opinion about work-relatedness. If a reporting physician opines that an injury is "possibly related" to the work performed, the claim can be denied. Therefore, it is very important that physicians making the determination of *causation* be precise in the terminology used to avoid iatrogenic cost and delay in receipt of benefits by injured workers.

Novel and Occupational Disease Claims

New or newly identified medical conditions pose great problems for the management of claims in workers' compensation. Conditions such as chronic fatigue syndrome, chronic pain, myofascial pain, carpal tunnel syndrome, and environmental illness are difficult to define (either in causation, clinical causation, or both). There are experts on both sides with conflicting strong opinions about whether or not these ambiguous conditions exist at all in the individual. It is not unusual to have experts reviewing the same information and arriving at completely different conclusions. This can place the decision maker in the position of appearing arbitrary in his or her decision. An adjudicator usually will deny compensation benefits when a subjective symptom (usually pain) is unsupported by objective findings (observations or test results that are not under the control of the claimant, i.e., degrees of motion, a fracture, or loss of deep tendon reflexes). Subjective findings are reports of pain or a positive straight-leg-raising test.

Another area of contention is that of the personal physician's opinion versus that of an expert. The personal physician may be a generalist, whereas the expert has specialty credentials in the area in question. The generalist has seen the injured or ill party on many occasions and is convinced regarding the condition's work-relatedness, whereas the expert who has vast experience with the medical condition at issue and who has extensive knowledge about the epidemiology of the problem may rule this out on the basis of one IME with the worker. Expert opinion usually is considered *prima facie* weight of evidence, especially in situations where the expert is a member of an impartial review panel, as is required in many states.

Presumption

Presumptive clauses are yet another way that causation can be determined. Presumption concludes that a single factor, (i.e., occupational exposure, such as coal mining), is "more likely than not" the cause of a given outcome (Black Lung or coal workers' pneumoconiosis) in a group. Many systems of law permit the presumption that the identified factor is the cause of a specific health problem for every member of a group unless there is compelling evidence to the contrary. Presumption is reflected in the development of lists for compensation of occupational diseases. Rebuttable presumptions can be challenged. This can lead to protracted legal disputes with politicians, employer groups, medical and other scientific experts, and regulatory authorities. Physicians involved in treating or advising patients with conditions involving presumptions must be thoroughly familiar with the medical literature on the topic and with the political and legal environment surrounding the issues under consideration when giving their opinions. (See Chap. 14.)

Reforming Workers' Compensation: A Tale of Two States

Attempts are under way on both sides of the U.S.-Canadian border to make reforms in the workers' compensation system to keep it a just, efficient, and viable social benefit system while at the same time eliminating the waste, fraud, and abuse that exists. For illustration purposes, reform measures undertaken in two states, Massachusetts and Kentucky, will be reviewed.

Massachusetts

Following an unsuccessful attempt at reform in 1985, Massachusetts found itself in the position of having no standard of care for ill or injured workers, a situation shared by many workers' compensation jurisdictions. There were low return-to-work results derived from the system. Highly skilled physicians were unwilling to treat ill or injured workers because of the heavy administrative burden placed on them by the system, a low fee schedule, and long delays in receiving the insurer's payment. Unchecked fraud existed. There appeared to be no oversight of an out-of-control, inadequate system. There were high medical and indemnity costs with no employer control. Businesses were threatening to leave the state if significant changes to the workers' compensation system were not forthcoming. The program's administrative body, the Department of Industrial Accidents (DIA), had one of the worst reputations of all state agencies. Frustrated, the Massachusetts legislature demanded reform within 180 days.

Following much work, numerous reforms demanded were implemented and are working well.

- The appointment of a medical consultant consortium (MCC) to advise the DIA on health care provided to ill or injured workers.
- The appointment of a 13-member health care services board (HCSB) to develop
  Eligibility criteria for an impartial physician roster and quality assurance mechanisms to maintain it.

Guidelines for review of complaints regarding practitioners by ill or injured workers.

Utilization review (UR) draft regulations and complaint process.

- The creation of workers' compensation preferred provider (PPA) arrangement draft regulations.
- The establishment of a quality control system within the DIA to review and monitor the total range of utilization of health care services provided to ill or injured workers [25].

By 1998, all components were finally in place and working smoothly. Costs have plummeted. There were double-digit decreases in premiums in the 4-year period from 1994 to 1998. Complaints about the UR process decreased steadily, and only a small proportion of complaints were found to be legitimate. Currently, there is nearly 100% compliance with the UR regulations. The *prima facie* weight of evidence of impartial physicians' opinions and findings binding all parties has greatly reduced the number of disputed cases awaiting legal hearings [26].

Kentucky

The state of Kentucky took a more evolutionary approach to reform than did Massachusetts. During the 1970s and 1980s, business development in the state was minimal due, in part, to workers' compensation rates that were substantially higher than those in neighboring states. Recognizing the need to deal with these costs, the state general assembly began reforming the system by first addressing spiraling workers' compensation medical costs.

In 1989, Kentucky implemented its first Official Medical Fee Schedule for Workers' Compensation, defining by statute the upper limits of "reasonable." Four years later, in 1993, the state embraced the philosophy of managed care for workers' compensation cases. House Bill (HB) 928 allowed employers, for the first time, to limit the employee's choice of treating physicians. Prior to this, injured employees could choose whomever they wished as their treating physician, and employers had no voice in the selection process. Under HB 928, an employer who joined a certified managed-care program (managed-care organization, or MCO) could require injured workers to choose from a panel of physicians designated by the MCO. MCOs are required to meet rigorous standards insofar as number and specialty of physicians available within given geographic areas. Unauthorized, nonemergency treatment outside the MCO panel for a work-related injury was not the financial responsibility of the employer or its insurance carrier. Other provisions of HB 928 provided for case management, pharmaceutical management, and other important cost-containment measures. MCOs producing the best results have been those which blended lean panels of physicians with excellent clinical skills together with sensitive and effective communications between physicians, employees, case managers, claims adjusters, and employers, i.e., those who are stakeholders or who have an appropriate role in the case.

Not all insurance carriers were quick to take advantage of managed care in workers' compensation. Regulations that were considered onerous and "parochial" caused many nationwide carriers to resist adopting the very programs for which they had lobbied for years.

In order to induce carriers to participate in certified MCOs, the state Department of Workers Claims, by administrative regulation, required all insurers and the self-insured that were not otherwise part of a certified MCO to perform mandatory UR on all cases that either exceeded $3000 in medical expenses, resulted in more than 30 days' lost time, or involved hospitalization or outpatient surgery. Such UR plans must be approved by the state, with annual reporting to the department and fines of up to $3000 for failure to comply.

In 1996, Kentucky strongly addressed the indemnity portion of workers' compensation through HB 1. HB 1 essentially eliminated the plaintiff attorneys from involvement in workers' compensation cases by reducing their maximal allowable fees to an unrealistic amount. To fill the advocacy void created by this provision, the state created the staff position of "benefits advisor." The benefits advisor assists the worker in filing a workers' compensation claim and moving the claim through the newly reformed judicial structure. This structure relied heavily on "arbitrators" who attempt to efficiently settle cases through an arbitration process, somewhat similar to the Canadian system. Only if and when the arbitration process failed would a case proceed to an administrative law judge and a more formal hearing. After assessing the results of the new system and receiving unrelenting criticism from the trial bar, the general assembly eliminated the arbitrator position in 2000 and raised the cap on attorney's fees to an amount that once again encourages all plaintiff attorneys to participate in the system. Significant reductions in indemnity benefits also were enacted in 1996 and have had a major impact on decreasing rates in the state. Many people feel that the reform effort went too far in favor of business (although Kentucky benefits are still significantly above those of most neighboring states, and the general assembly is expected to restore a portion of the benefit that was taken away in 1996).

HB 1 also dealt with the politically charged behemoth of Kentucky workers' compensation, the conundrum of coal workers' pneumoconiosis or Black Lung. Historically, benefits for impairments due to Black Lung have served as the financial underpinning for many poor communities in eastern Kentucky. Judicial interpretations of state statutes resulted in rulings of PTD, and hence lifetime benefits, for workers who could do many kinds of labor except the mining of underground coal. Disability was granted based on changes in a worker's chest radiographs, even if the worker also was a heavy tobacco smoker (which can cause similar radiographic "profusion" changes) and even though the coal worker had no significant reduction in breathing capacity. Determining who was, in fact, permanently and totally disabled was a clear example of "dueling doctors," in which the same plaintiff-oriented physicians offered opinions routinely opposed by the same group of defense-oriented physicians. To remove bias from the system and the "dueling doctors," the state created two "centers of excellence" at the state's two medical colleges, where a select group of expert physicians examine the worker and available medical information and then issue a finding to the court as to the worker's impairment. Mere changes in a worker's chest x-ray are no longer sufficient to qualify for benefits, and any decrease in breathing capacity less than 25% of predicted is no longer compensable. Legislative changes in 2001 are expected to restore minimal benefits in minimal cases [27].

Other Special Workers' Compensation Systems in the United States

There are various forms of workers' compensation and special acts in the United States that apply to injured workers depending on the business sector in which the employer operates. These regulations differ significantly and those who work with injured workers must be familiar with their provisions.

In the United States, railroad workers are covered under the Federal Employee Liability Act (FELA). Railroad workers must litigate disputed claims, but the standard for winning is set lower than in most tort litigation. This legislation came long before state workers' compensation systems and represented a response to four major problems: the unresponsiveness of courts in conventional litigation; the problem of jurisdiction (because railroads were interstate commerce), labor unrest in the industry; and the increasing injury rate in an industry central to the industrial economy of the day.

Civilian workers of the U.S. government are covered under the Federal Employees' Compensation Act (FECA). FECA is often considered a model workers' compensation system for workers' compensation reform because of its administrative simplicity and national coverage. The Longshoremen and Harbor Workers' Compensation Act covers maritime workers on navigable waters of the United States, whereas the Jones Act covers U.S. seamen. The Federal Black Lung Act (Title IV of the Federal Coal Mine Safety and Health Act of 1969 as amended in 1972, 1978, and 1981) provides benefits for total disability or death caused by coal workers' pneumoconiosis. The federal Social Security Disability Insurance program covers disabilities, which generally exclude occupational injuries [16]. Disability resulting from occupational exposures that are not recognized as work-related often are covered by Social Security. The Veterans Health Administration provides care and compensation for "service-connected disabilities." The Department of Energy has two programs that apply to nuclear workers, one primarily for radiation exposures and one for chemical hazards.

Summary

Although workers' compensation systems are very expensive, they represent social evolution at its best, and form an essential part of the social safety net enjoyed by people who live and work in North America. As these systems approach their centennial, it is clear that reforms are needed and that vigilance is required to prevent erosion of previously enacted reforms. The workers' compensation system truly is "an historic compromise" between all interested parties and one deserving of society's support and protection.

References

1. Plumb JM, Cowell JWF. Workers' compensation systems: An overview of workers' compensation. *Occup Med* 1998;13(2):244.

2. Cocchiarella L, Andersson GBJ. *Guides to the Evaluation of Permanent Impairment,* 5th ed. Chicago: American Medical Association, 2001. Preface, p iii.

3. Roseman S, Miller T, Douglas J. *The Costs of Occupational Traumatic and Cumulative Injuries.* Washington: The Urban Institute, 1991. P 32.

4. Antonakes J. Claims cost of back pain. *Best's Review* 1981:36.

5. Miller T, Roseman J. *Saving Money by Saving Lives.* Washington: The Urban Institute, 1990. P 36.

6. Mont D, Burton JF Jr, Rena V. *Workers' Compensation: Benefits, Coverage, and Costs, 1997–1998—New Estimates.* Washington: National Academy of Social Insurance, 2000.

7. Douglas JR. *Managing Workers' Compensation: A Human Resources Guide to Controlling Costs.* New York: Wiley, 1994. P 3.

8. Douglas JR. *Managing Workers' Compensation: A Human Resources Guide to Controlling Costs.* New York: Wiley, 1994. P 9.

9. Harris JS. *Workers' compensation.* In: McCunney RJ (ed), *A Practical Approach to Occupational and Environmental Medicine,* 2d ed. Boston: Little, Brown, 1994. P 572.

10. Rice D, Mackenzie E, et al. *Cost of Injury in the United States: A Report to Congress.* Institute for Health and Aging, University of California, and the Injury Prevention Center, Johns Hopkins University, 1989. P 2.

11. American Academy of Orthopaedic Surgeons. *A Physician's Primer on Workers' Compensation.* Committee on Occupational Health, 1992.

12. Carr JD. Workers' compensation systems: Purpose and mandate. *Occup Med* 1998;13(2):417–418.

13. Carr JD. Workers' compensation systems: Purpose and mandate. *Occup Med* 1998;13(2):419.

14. Plumb JM, Cowell JWF. Workers' compensation systems: An overview of workers' compensation. *Occup Med* 1998;13(2):242.

15. Plumb JM, Cowell JWF. Workers' compensation systems: An overview of workers' compensation. *Occup Med* 1998;13(2):243.

16. Harris JS. *Workers' compensation.* In: McCunney RJ (ed). *A Practical Approach to Occupational and Environmental Medicine,* 2d ed. Boston: Little, Brown, 1994. P 568.

17. Plumb JM, Cowell JWF. Workers' compensation systems: An overview of workers' compensation. *Occup Med* 1998;13(2):246–247.

18. Carr JD. Workers' compensation systems: Purpose and mandate. *Occup Med* 1998;13(2):420.

19. Carr JD. Workers' compensation systems: Purpose and mandate. *Occup Med* 1998;13(2):420–421.

20. Bigos SJ, et al. The prospective study of work perceptions and psychosocial factors affecting the report of back injury. *Spine* 1991;16:1.

21. Carr JD. Workers' compensation systems: Purpose and mandate. *Occup Med* 1998;13(2):421.

22. Harte D, Smith DA. Workers' compensation systems: Purpose and mandate. *Occup Med* 1998;13(2):424–425.

23. Harte D, Smith DA. Workers' compensation systems: Purpose and mandate. *Occup Med* 1998;13(2):425.

24. Guidotti TL. Workers' compensation systems: Purpose and mandate. *Occup Med* 1998;13(2):292–293.

25. Feedman JL, Campbell JJ, Hashimoto D, Ward D. Workers' compensation systems: Purpose and mandate. *Occup Med* 1998;13(2):382.

26. Feedman JL, Campbell JJ, Hashimoto D, Ward D. Workers' compensation systems: Purpose and mandate. *Occup Med* 1998;13(2):387.

27. Faris WV. Personal communication, President of Occupational Managed Care Alliance, Inc., a Kentucky-based managed care organization, 2000.

20

Evidentiary Requirements under the Americans with Disabilities Act

CHRISTINA GUEROLA SARCHIO

Overview of the Americans with Disabilities Act

In 1990, Congress found that approximately 43 million Americans had one or more physical or mental disabilities and that this number was increasing as the population grew older [1]. Congress felt that this "discrete and insular minority" had faced restrictions and limitations, experienced a history of purposeful unequal treatment, and had been "relegated to a position of political powerlessness in our society" [2]. Moreover, Congress stated that "the continuing existence of unfair and unnecessary discrimination and prejudice denies people with disabilities the opportunity to compete on an equal basis and to pursue those opportunities for which our free society is justifiably famous and costs the United States billions of dollars in unnecessary expenses resulting from dependency and nonproductivity" [3].

Accordingly, Congress enacted the Americans with Disabilities Act of 1990 to address the major areas of discrimination faced daily by individuals with disabilities [4]. The Americans with Disabilities Act provides civil rights protection in specific contexts such as employment, public accommodations, public services, and transportation [5]. The language of the Americans with Disabilities Act, however, does not always answer the question of whether an individual qualifies as disabled under the statute [6]. Thus courts must decide on a case-by-case basis whether an individual has a disability before looking to whether the Americans with Disabilities Act was violated. Many litigating parties employ expert witnesses to assist the court in this endeavor.

This chapter will examine the role that experts play in helping to determine whether an individual is disabled under the Americans with Disabilities Act, including (1) the various ways attorneys use experts in Americans with Disabilities Act litigation, (2) how attorneys select and prepare expert witnesses, and (3) courts' requirements for qualifying an expert witness and allowing the expert to testify at trial.

Expert Testimony in Americans with Disabilities Act Litigation

Experts have become critical in helping courts and juries decide whether an individual is disabled within the meaning of the Americans with Disabilities Act. Experts can help a complainant satisfy his or her burden of proof or can help the defense disprove his or her disability. In fact, some courts have found that the absence of a medical expert can be a factor in determining that a complainant has presented only speculation in support of his or her claim [7]. There is no general rule, however, "that medical testimony is always necessary to establish disability" [8]. Nevertheless, attorneys employ experts for two main purposes: (1) to evaluate an individual's disability and (2) to discredit the opposing expert's opinion testimony.

Determining Disability

In order to prevail on an Americans with Disabilities Act claim, an individual must prove that he or she is disabled. In defining *disability* under the Americans with Disabilities Act, Congress adopted the definition of *handicapped* employed in the Rehabilitation Act of 1973 [9]. Congress intended the analysis of the older term to apply to the new term [10]. In addition, Congress wanted the relevant case law developed under the Rehabilitation Act to apply to the Americans with Disabilities Act [11]. Thus courts can look to prior judicial interpretations under each statute to determine whether an individual meets the legal definition of disabled.

The Americans with Disabilities Act defines *disability* as "a physical or mental impairment that substantially limits one or more of the major life activities" [12]. In order to evaluate whether an individual is disabled, this chapter will describe how the expert witness can determine if the individual (1) has a physical or mental impairment that (2) limits one or more major life activities and (3) is substantial [13]. In addition, this chapter also will discuss recent Supreme Court rulings stating that the consideration of whether a person is substantially limited in a major life activity must take into account any "mitigating measures," such as medication, used to minimize the disability [14].

PHYSICAL OR MENTAL IMPAIRMENT. The Americans with Disabilities Act itself neither defines physical or mental impairment nor provides a list of conditions it deems impairments. Congress purposely omitted such a list because it wanted the act to be "elastic enough to incorporate new disorders that develop in the future" [15]. Nevertheless, because courts have relied in part on the act's legislative history and agency interpretations in deciding what impairments are covered under the Americans with Disabilities Act [16], expert witnesses and attorneys can look therein for guidance as to what impairments the act covers.

Congress stated that it considered the following conditions, diseases, and infections as protected: orthopedic, visual, speech, and hearing impairments; cerebral palsy; epilepsy; muscular dystrophy; multiple sclerosis; asymptomatic and symptomatic human immunodeficiency virus (HIV) infection; cancer; heart disease; tuberculosis; alcoholism; diabetes; and past drug addiction [17]. With regard to mental impairments, covered conditions include any mental or psychological disorder, such as mental retardation, organic brain syndrome, emotional or mental illness, and learning disabilities [18]. More specifically, Congress intended to cover mental disorders diagnosed from the *Diagnostic and Statistical Manual of Mental Disorders* [19].

To further assist courts in interpreting and applying the Americans with Disabilities Act, Congress delegated to the Equal Employment Opportunity Commission (EEOC) the authority to issue regulations [20]. EEOC regulations define physical impairment to mean any physiological disorder or condition, cosmetic disfigurement, or anatomical loss affecting one or more of the following body systems: neurological, neuromuscular, special sense organs, cardiovascular, reproductive, digestive, genitourinary, hemic and lymphatic, skin, and endocrine [21].

Although the EEOC adopted Congress's description of mental impairments listed above, the EEOC's several exceptions to this definition include transvestism, transsexualism, pedophilia, exhibitionism, voyeurism, gender identity disorders not resulting from physical impairments, or other sexual behavior disorders; compulsive gambling, kleptomania, or pyromania; or psychoactive substance use disorders resulting from current illegal use of drugs [22]. EEOC regulations do not consider homosexuality and bisexuality impairments, and therefore, they are not disabilities [23]. Once an individual has established that he or she suffers from a physical or mental impairment, the individual must then demonstrate that the impairment limits a major life activity.

MAJOR LIFE ACTIVITY. The EEOC defined *major life activities* as those basic activities which the average person in the general population can perform with little or no difficulty [24]. These activities include everyday functions such as "caring for oneself, performing manual tasks, walking, seeing, hearing, speaking, breathing, learning, and working" [25].

Given that most Americans with Disabilities Act lawsuits involve discrimination in the workplace, it is important for the expert witness and the attorney to understand what it means to be limited in the major life activity of working. The EEOC has stated that because an individual cannot perform a "particular job for one employer or because he or she is unable to perform a specialized job or profession requiring extraordinary skill, prowess or talent" does not make that individual substantially limited in the major life activity of working [26]. Rather, an individual is substantially limited in working if the individual is significantly restricted in the ability to perform a class of jobs or a broad range of jobs in various classes when compared with the ability of the average person with similar qualifications to perform those same jobs [27]. Factors specific to the major life activity of working include the geographic area to which the person has reasonable access, the job from which the individual had been disqualified because of an impairment, and other dissimilar jobs in the geographic area that the individual is disqualified from due to the impairment [28].

The EEOC's aforementioned list regarding life activities is not exhaustive. Other major life activities include, but are not limited to, sitting, standing, lifting, and reaching [29]. Once the court has determined that the activity is major, the court must then consider whether the impairment substantially limits that life activity.

SUBSTANTIAL LIMITATION. According to EEOC regulations, one is substantially limited if one cannot perform an activity others can perform without the impairment or if the individual is significantly restricted in the performance of such an activity [30]. In considering whether an impairment substantially limits a major life activity of the individual, the expert witness needs to assess (1) the nature and severity of the impairment, (2) the duration or expected duration of the impairment, and (3) the expected or actual permanent or long-term impact of the impairment [31]. Therefore, when an impairment significantly restricts the duration, manner, or condition under which an individual can perform a particular major life activity, as compared with an average person in the general population, his or her impairment is deemed substantially limiting.

MITIGATING MEASURES. Expert witnesses must now also consider whether an individual's disability is correctable. "[T]he determination of whether an individual is disabled should be made with reference to measures that mitigate the individual's impairment . . ." [32]. For instance, in *Sutton,* the complainants had uncorrected vision over 20/200 [33]. The complainants applied for airline pilot positions, but United Air Lines rejected them because it required a minimum uncorrected vision of 20/100 [34]. The Supreme Court found that the complainants were not disabled under the Americans with Disabilities Act because they could fully correct their visual impairments with eyeglasses [35].

The Court stated that one has a disability if, notwithstanding the use of a corrective device, that individual is substantially limited in a major life activity [36]. For example, individuals who use prosthetic limbs or wheelchairs may be mobile and capable of functioning in society but are still disabled because of a substantial limitation on their ability to walk or run [37]. The same may be true of individuals who take medicine to lessen the symptoms of an impairment so that they can function but nevertheless remain substantially limited [38].

The use or nonuse of a corrective device does not by itself determine whether an individual is disabled; that determination "depends on whether the limitations an individual with an impairment actually faces are in fact substantially limiting" [39]. Thus, when evaluating the effects of the mitigating measures, the expert witness ought to look at the symptoms and limitations the individual experienced *before* using the mitigating measure and compare them with an individual's abilities *after* using the mitigating measure.

COURTS' INTERPRETATIONS OF THE AMERICANS WITH DISABILITIES ACT. When making the disability determination under the Americans with Disabilities Act, courts must evaluate each impairment on a case-by-case basis [40]. This is so because what may impair one individual may not be as limiting to another. Thus it is extremely difficult for an attorney to offer the expert witness specific guidance on whether a court will conclude that a specific impairment constitutes a disability.

Generally, however, courts have found that the Americans with Disabilities Act does *not* cover the following physical impairments: arthritis, asthma, carpal tunnel syndrome, chemical sensitivity, chronic fatigue syndrome, hypertension, and obesity [41]. Courts also have excluded the following mental impairments: fear of heights, paranoid schizophrenia controlled with medication, stress management requiring medication, bipolar model disorder, sexual behavior disorders, and violent temper [42].

On the other hand, courts have found that the Americans with Disabilities Act protects the following mental impairments: panic disorders, nervous conditions, anxiety disorders, apraxia, emotional conditions, personality disorders, mental illness, paranoia and paranoid schizophrenia, anxiety neurosis, manic depression or bipolar disorder, extreme stress reaction, claustrophobia, dysthymia, agoraphobia, and phobic reaction to carbon monoxide [43].

Thus attorneys should alert their expert witnesses to past court decisions relevant to the impairment in dispute. Additionally, court decisions may provide insight as to the type of expert evidence courts generally have found unreliable. This may prove invaluable to the expert witness both as a way to guard against potential problems and as a tool to criticize the opposing expert's methods.

Discrediting the Opposing Expert

An expert witness can ascertain the strengths and weaknesses of the opposing side's medical evidence [44]. Notably, the retained expert can evaluate the opposing expert's credentials and qualifications, review the opposing expert's relevant publications and previous case participation, and identify any inconsistencies with his or her proposed testimony.

There are various avenues for discrediting the opposing expert. For instance, the expert can be questioned about conflicting scientific literature: Are there any studies or publications that contradict the expert's position? Depending on whether the opposing expert testifies for the complainant or the defendant, other criticisms may include failure to obtain an adequate history of the patient, failure to use the accepted diagnostic system, failure to consider other, non-proximately caused stressors, failure to rule out the transient side effects of any of the complainant's medications, failure to communicate with other treating specialists, bias in reporting due to economic considerations (how much a party is paying the expert or a desire to continue the doctor-patient relationship), failure to conduct an adequate differential diagnosis and rule out other mental or physical conditions that could cause the plaintiff's symptoms, and failure to rule out malingering [45].

Thus, in order to successfully litigate an Americans with Disabilities Act case, employing an expert witness can be extremely helpful, if not essential. Once the decision to retain an expert has been made, it is crucial for the attorney to properly select and prepare the expert witness.

Selecting and Preparing the Expert Witness

As the use of expert witnesses in Americans with Disabilities Act litigation has become more prevalent, experts have opined on an ever-expanding range of issues. Attorneys should decide whether to hire a generalist or a specialist and determine whether the expert will testify in court or simply serve as a consultant on the case. After an attorney hires the expert, he or she must ensure that the expert is properly prepared to assist with the case.

Selecting the Expert

Two types of experts can be used in Americans with Disabilities Act litigation: (1) those expected to testify at trial and (2) those employed to assist, usually before trial, with case preparation [46]. The distinction is important because the expert who will *not* be called to take the stand need not have the same qualifications as one who will testify.

When selecting an expert witness, the attorney should look for particular credentials and characteristics. The expert witness must be knowledgeable about and familiar with the particular disability at issue. An expert with clinical experience with the disability is invaluable, as is an expert who has authored publications and studies on the subject. The attorney should evaluate the expert's demeanor, as well as assess the likelihood that the expert witness may get rattled on cross-examination. The attorney also needs to probe for any incidents that may reflect unfavorably on the witness's character, such as sanctions from licensing agencies, termination from employment, lawsuits, or arrests.

Furthermore, the attorney must find out whether the expert has testified previously predominantly for plaintiffs or for defense. In order to maximize credibility, the expert should have worked previously on behalf of both sides. Of course, the attorney needs to determine whether there is a positional conflict in an expert's past reports or testimony and whether the conflict is potentially fatal to the case.

There are numerous sources from which an attorney can obtain leads on retaining potential expert witnesses. Generally, the complainant or plaintiff in the litigation will present his or her treating physician to explain to the court the history of his or her disability. Treating physicians, however, typically testify about the facts and their clinical observations and may be reluctant to address causation or other broader issues [47]. Consequently, the complainant may need to employ other experts to better guide the court.

The treating physician is a good source for a recommendation of an expert witness. For additional reliable sources of potential experts dealing with Americans with Disabilities Act cases, the attorney can consult with other lawyers and experts, look to authors of literature discussing the particular disability involved, contact associations representing the disabled, or contact colleges and universities. Various companies will match an expert witness to a case for either a finder's fee or a retainer. These companies frequently advertise in litigation periodicals, such as *Trial Magazine,* published by the Association of Trial Lawyers of America, or *ABA Journal,* published by the American Bar Association, or on the Internet [48]. Regardless of where the attorney ultimately finds the expert witness, it is essential that the attorney prepare the expert witness to deal with the onset of litigation.

Preparing the Expert

The attorney should guide the witness according to whether the expert will be testifying or simply consulting on the case. A consulting expert will need less guidance than a testifying expert. Typically, the consulting expert will evaluate the claims and report his or her findings to the attorney. If the expert is going to testify in the case, then he or she must prepare an expert report. The testifying expert likely will begin testifying by giving evidence at a deposition. If the case survives pretrial motions, specifically a *Daubert* [49] motion, which challenges the admissibility of the expert's report and proposed testimony, then the expert also should expect to testify at trial.

THE EXPERT REPORT. The attorney and the expert witness initially must discuss the scope and structure of the report. First, they must agree on the general points the report should cover. Also, they should discuss whether drafts of the report will be circulated and whether they will keep those drafts. Opinions of consulting experts are not subject to legal "discovery," whereas the opposing side can, and will, request an expert's communications, correspondence, and documents related to the litigation [50]. Thus the parties should establish beforehand whether they can and should destroy drafts once the report is complete. Additionally, the parties must set a timetable for the report's preparation and production because if a party does not serve the report on the opposing side in a timely manner, the court may preclude the introduction of evidence from the expert [51].

Before compiling the report, the expert witness should carefully review pertinent documents, including the complainant's medical records, the complainant's deposition testimony, other experts' deposition testimony, and their reports. The expert witness also should keep up to date on the current literature and studies regarding the disability at issue.

It is also highly recommended that the expert witness personally conduct a physical or mental examination of the complainant [52]. This prevents the opposition from criticizing the expert for relying on alleged incomplete, one-sided, or second-hand information. In reviewing the medical records and conducting an examination of the complainant, the expert need not worry about doctor-patient confidentiality because the complainant waives that right when bringing an Americans with Disabilities Act lawsuit [53].

The report must contain the following information: (1) a complete statement of all opinions to be expressed and the basis and reasons for them, (2) the data or other information considered by the expert in forming the opinions, (3) any exhibits used as a summary of or support for the opinions, and (4) the expert's qualifications [54]. Under the rubric of expert qualifications, the expert report also must include (1) a list of all publications authored by the expert witness within the preceding 10 years, (2) the compensation to be paid for the time and testimony, and (3) a listing of any other cases in which the witness has testified as an expert at trial or by deposition within the preceding 4 years [55].

DEPOSITION AND TRIAL. The prospective expert witness needs thorough preparation for his or her deposition and trial testimony. Ideally, an attorney should conduct mock proceedings with simulated cross-examination. It may even be useful for the expert to view the courtroom before testifying.

At deposition, the examining attorney will seek to uncover areas to bolster a *Daubert* challenge and for impeachment at trial. Therefore, it is essential that before the deposition, and preferably before the finalization of the expert report, the expert witness review the complainant's medical records, deposition testimony of key witnesses, and important studies or treatises in support of the expert's findings. The examining attorney will certainly ask the expert witness about his or her qualifications and credentials, including the witness's publications, as well as litigation experience.

Additionally, the examining attorney will review the report thoroughly with the expert witness, ask questions about the factual predicate for the expert's opinion and how the expert reached particular conclusions, and inquire about the substance of any articles or studies relied on. The attorney also may ask the expert to identify leading authorities in the field, including other experts and medical literature. The expert witness should tread cautiously when asked whether particular authors or texts are authoritative [56]. The opposition potentially could employ those authors as experts and, if they have not already, scrutinize the cited texts for information contradicting the expert witness's findings.

The expert witness also may receive and be asked to comment on discovery materials and deposition transcripts that the expert previously may not have seen. The examining attorney does this to test whether the expert witness will change his or her theory of the case if given new or varied facts. Again, the expert witness needs to be careful not to fall into hypothetical or rhetorical traps.

The examining attorney also may attempt to goad the expert into a debate in order to portray the expert as cantankerous, arrogant, or condescending. The expert should conduct himself or herself respectfully yet firmly in answering opposing counsel's questions. In his or her testimony, whether at deposition or at trial, the expert must understand the questions and respond to them directly, fairly, and without volunteering additional or extraneous information. Most important, the expert must be able to reduce scientific and technical theories to clear, concise terminology that can be readily understood by the court and the jury. Cases very often are decided on the credibility and likability of the expert witness.

Expert Witness Qualification

The trial court must ensure that all expert testimony meets a threshold standard of reliability and relevance before admitting it [57]. The court also must determine whether the expert testimony in question meets two essential requirements: (1) that the testimony relies on scientific, technical, or other specialized knowledge and (2) that it assists the trier of fact in understanding the evidence or determining a fact at issue [58].

The first requirement focuses on whether the expert's opinion is reliable, i.e., whether the "reasoning or methodology underlying the opinion is scientifically valid and trustworthy" [59]. Exclusion of expert testimony is justified when the flaws in method or procedure demonstrate a lack of "good grounds" for the opinion [60]. The Supreme Court announced a general checklist that should be employed in making this determination: (1) whether the scientific theory had been tested, (2) whether the theory or technique has been subjected to peer review and publication, (3) the known potential rate of error, and (4) the general acceptance of the theory or technique [61].

The Supreme Court recently held in the *Kumho Tire* case that the *Daubert* requirements apply to all experts in all cases, thus extending *Daubert* to experts testifying in Americans with Disabilities Act cases. *Kumho Tire* also emphasized that the inquiry into whether an expert is reliable is "a flexible one," and the factors articulated in *Daubert* "do not constitute a 'definitive checklist or test'"

[62]. Rather, the inquiry "must be 'tied to the facts' of a particular 'case'" [63]. In other words, "the factors identified in *Daubert* may or may not be pertinent in assessing reliability, depending on the nature of the issue, the expert's particular expertise, and the subject of his [or her] testimony" [64]. In fact, the Supreme Court went on to recognize that not all the *Daubert* factors necessarily apply, even in a case where the reliability of scientific testimony is challenged [65]. The point is to ensure that an expert, "whether basing testimony upon professional studies or personal experience, employs in the courtroom the same level of intellectual rigor that characterizes the practice of an expert in the relevant field" [66].

Conclusion

The passage of the Americans with Disabilities Act to eradicate disability discrimination has led to new issues for courts to address, and as a result, expert witnesses play a crucial role in this type of litigation. Expert testimony in Americans with Disabilities Act cases, therefore, requires the same attention and preparation as other cases. Experts can help prove or disprove disability claims, but it is imperative for the parties to carefully select and prepare their experts for the rigors of the courtroom. In particular, the experts must be prepared to face the court's gatekeeping check under *Daubert* that only allows the admission of reliable and relevant expert testimony.

Endnotes

1. 42 U.S.C.S. Sec. 12101(a)(1) (2000).

2. 42 U.S.C.S. Sec. 12101(a)(7) (2000).

3. 42 U.S.C.S. Sec. 12101(a)(9) (2000).

4. 42 U.S.C.S. Sec. 12101(b)(4) (2000).

5. 42 U.S.C.S. Sec. 12101(a)(3) (2000).

6. Kamholz, Sheryl Rebecca. Note: The Americans with Disabilities Act: Advocating judicial deference to the EEOC's mitigating measures guidelines. *Boston University Public Interest Law J* 1998;8:100.

7. See *Welsh v. City of Tulsa,* 977 F.2d 1415, 1419 (10th Cir. 1992) (plaintiff not handicapped where he failed to present evidence that diminished sensory perception in two fingers substantially limited his ability to perform physical tasks).

8. See *Katz v. City Metal Co.,* 87 F.3d 26, 32 (1st Cir. 1996) (a reasonable jury could find that an individual who had a heart attack and was limited in his ability to breathe and walk was disabled under the Americans with Disabilities Act without expert medical testimony).

9. The Rehabilitation Act of 1973, 29 U.S.C.S. Secs. 791–794, was enacted to prohibit discrimination against handicapped individuals among federal agencies, government contracts, and other recipients of federal funds [29 U.S.C.S. Sec. 793 (2000)]. Because of the Rehabilitation Act's limited scope of application, however, it proved somewhat

ineffectual in combating discrimination. See Gould, Keri K. Symposium, and equal protection for all. . . . The Americans with Disabilities Act in the courtroom. *Journal at Law & Health* 1993–1994;8:127–129; see also 29 C.F.R. Sec. 1630.2(g) (2000).

10. See McDevitt, William J. Defining the term "disability" under the Americans with Disabilities Act. *St. Thomas Law Rev* 1988;10:284.

11. *Id.*, at 284, n.22 [citing H.R. Rep. No. 101-485, pt. 3, at 27 (1990), reprinted in 1990 U.S.C.C.A.N. 445, 450].

12. 42 U.S.C.S. Sec. 12102(2) (2000).

13. See McDevitt, *supra*, n.10, at pp 284–285.

14. See *Sutton v. United Air Lines, Inc.*, 527 U.S. 471 (1999); *Murphy v. United Parcel Service*, 527 U.S. 516, 521 (1999).

15. H.R. Rep. No. 101-485, pt. 3, at 27 (1990), reprinted in 1990 U.S.C.C.A.N. 445, 450.

16. In recent Supreme Court decisions, however, the Court sidestepped some agency regulations while agreeing with others. See Barhorst, Stacie E. Note: What does disability mean: The Americans with Disabilities Act of 1990 in the aftermath of *Sutton, Murphy,* and *Albertsons. Drake Law Rev* 1999;48:153, 170.

17. Gould, *supra*, n.9, at p 130 nn.60–61 [citing 28 C.F.R. Sec. 35.104 (1993), and S. Rep. No. 101-116, at 22 (1989)].

18. *Id.*

19. *Id.*, at p 130, n.63 [citing 135 Cong. Rec. S10772 (daily ed Sept. 7, 1989) (statement of Sen. Armstrong)].

20. Barhorst, *supra*, n.16, at p 140.

21. 29 C.F.R. Sec. 1630.2(h)(i) (2000).

22. 29 C.F.R. Sec. 1630.3(d)(1)–(3) (2000).

23. 29 C.F.R. Sec. 1630.3(e) (2000).

24. 29 C.F.R. Sec. 1630.2(j)(i) (2000).

25. 29 C.F.R. Sec. 1630.2(i) (2000).

26. Barhorst, *supra* note 16, at pp 143–144, n.38 (citing 29 C.F.R. pt. 1630, App. at 348).

27. *Id.*, at 144, n.46 (citing 29 C.F.R. pt. 1630, App. at 349).

28. *Id.*, at 144.

29. 29 C.F.R. Sec. 1630.2(i).

30. 29 C.F.R. Sec. 1630.2(j)(1) (2000). The Supreme Court stated that the EEOC's "substantially limits" standard, while requiring a significant restriction in an individual's manner of performing a major life activity, should not be equated with a mere difference in the performance of the activity between an impaired and nonimpaired individual. See Rydel, Peter K. Comment: Redefining the right to reproduce: Asserting infertility as a disability under the Americans with Disabilities Act. *Albany Law Rev* 1999;63:604–605, n.30 [citing *Albertsons, Inc. v. Kirkingburg*, 527 U.S. 555 (1999)].

31. 29 C.F.R. Sec. 1630.2(j)(2) (2000).

32. *Sutton*, 527 U.S. at 475.

33. *Id.*

34. *Id.*, at 488–489.

35. *Id.*, at 482.

36. *Id.*, at 488.

37. *Id.*

38. *Id.*

39. *Id.*

40. 28 C.F.R. Sec. 35.104 (2000).

41. *Murphy,* 527 U.S. at 516 (an employee with high blood pressure that was controlled by medication is not a person with a disability under the Americans with Disabilities Act); *Broussard v. University of California,* 192 F.3d 1252, 1258 (9th Cir. 1999) (carpal tunnel syndrome did not limit any major life activity); *Gutridge v. Clure,* 153 F.3d 898, 901 (8th Cir. 1998) (an employee's five surgeries for carpal tunnel syndrome did not create a record of impairment under the Americans with Disabilities Act because he did not show that he was substantially limited in a major life activity), *cert. denied,* 526 U.S. 1113 (1999); *Francis v. City of Meriden,* 129 F.3d 281, 286 (2d Cir. 1997) (obesity, except where it relates to physiologic disorder, is not an impairment); *Hamm v. Runyon,* 51 F.3d 721, 725 (7th Cir. 1995) (a probationary postal employee who was discharged for tardiness failed to show that his arthritis was a disability in that he never contended it substantially limited a major life activity); *Maulding v. Sullivan,* 961 F.2d 694, 698 (8th Cir. 1992) (alleged sensitivity to chemicals that prevented plaintiff from performing only lab work but did not substantially limit employment as a whole held not to be a handicap), *cert. denied,* 507 U.S. 910 (1993); *Tangires v. Johns Hopkins Hospital,* 79 F. Supp. 2d 587, 593 (since plaintiff had not availed herself of proper medical treatment for her asthma, she was not a qualified individual with a disability who was protected by the provisions of the Americans with Disabilities Act), aff'd, 200 U.S. App. LEXIS 23555 (4th Cir. Md. Sept. 20, 2000).

42. Lars, Noah. Pigeonholing illness: Medical diagnosis as a legal construct. *Hastings Law J* 1999;50:241, 177, n.135.

43. *Id.*

44. Blend, Julie E. Using expert witnesses in employment litigation. *Rev Litigation* 1998;17:39.

45. Fitzpatrick, Robert B. Working with mental experts on workplace claims: Some practical advice. *ALI-ABA Course No. SC08,* July 1997.

46. Harrell, P. Arley. A new lawyer's guide to expert use. *Practical Lawyer* 1993;39(2):55.

47. If the complainant does not include his or her treating physician among the list of witnesses, opposing counsel should investigate the circumstances surrounding that decision. The attorney may come to learn that the treating physician has information helpful to defeat the complainant's claims.

48. The search term *expert witness* resulted in hundreds of hits, including *www.expertlaw .com, www.expertpages.com, www.lawinfo.com,* and *www.witness.net.* Individual expert Web sites also can be found.

49. See *Daubert v. Merrell Dow Pharm., Inc.,* 509 U.S. 579 (1993).

50. See *Federal Rules of Civil Procedure* 26(b)(4)(B).

51. See *Federal Rules of Civil Procedure* 26(a)(2)(C).

52. The federal rules allow an examination of a party when the mental or physical condition of that party is in controversy (*Federal Rules of Civil Procedure,* Rule 35).

53. Jacobs, Roger B. Defense of claim brought under the Americans with Disabilities Act. *American Jursiprudence Trials* 1994;49, Sec. 30, para. 171.

54. See *Federal Rules of Civil Procedure* 26(a)(2)(B).

55. *Id.*

56. When asked about specific medical textbooks or literature, expert witnesses are often reluctant to admit that they have either not read such literature or are not especially familiar with it. Thus the witness may concede that it is authoritative without knowing the particulars of the text. One way to address this predicament is for the expert witness to state that textbooks generally are not authoritative because they are updated frequently or that some parts are authoritative whereas others are not. See Deposing the adverse party's expert witness. *Ohio Personal Injury Practice* Sec. 5.17 (2000 ed). Prior to the deposition, the attorney and the expert witness should decide how to manage this likely scenario.

57. *Daubert,* 509 U.S. at 589.

58. *Trevino v. City of Rock Island Police Department,* 91 F. Supp. 2d 1204, 1205 (C.D. Ill. 2000) (plaintiff's expert testimony was barred because his personal experience as a monocular police officer did not give him genuine expertise on the subject and expert failed to substantiate his opinion) [relying on *Kumho Tire Co. v. Carmichael,* 526 U.S. 137 (1999)].

59. Koral, Alan M. Discussion points on the use of expert witnesses. *Practising Law Institute* 1998;586:351 (relying on *Daubert,* 509 U.S. at 590–591).

60. *Id.*

61. *Id.*

62. *Trevino,* 91 F. Supp. 2d at 1206.

63. *Id.*

64. *Id.*

65. *Id.*

66. *Id.*

21

Parity for Mental Health Issues

SUSAN SILVERMAN

Mental health, as it affects the workforce, is the subject of increasing legislation and is now receiving greater national attention because its effects have an impact on a significant percentage. However, society continues to think of mental illness as a distinct class of disease and to treat it differently from physical illness. At best, the result is a discrepancy in treatment; at worst, these patients suffer from outright discrimination.

Workers' compensation boards usually have highly restrictive policies for mental illness claims. These are much more difficult to document and to win on appeal than physical injury claims. In the courtroom, injuries to the mind are much more difficult to prove than injuries to the body, and damages for mental disturbance are viewed more skeptically by jurors. Indeed, damages for "pain and suffering" are often the butt of jokes about the legal system, clearly implying that the awards are not deserved.

Mental illness is just as much the result of interplay between biological and external causal factors as physical illness. Yet we avoid accepting mental illness as a compensable condition or as an outcome of causal factors in the environment (in this case, mostly social) or the workplace. There are many reasons for this aversion to accepting parity between mental illness and physical illness; they include

- The diagnosis of mental illness relies on subjective findings and involves considerable interpretation. The finer points of diagnosis often are not distinguishable by laypersons.
- Stereotypes abound about the mentally ill. Senator Thomas Eagleton would have achieved the Democratic endorsement for the position of Vice President of the United States if his medical records indicated treatment for a broken leg instead of treatment for depression. In 1972, past treatment for a psychiatric problem made his nomination politically unacceptable.
- Many people believe that the mentally ill are people who cannot handle

stress or who are weak and unfit. This folk theory makes it difficult to demonstrate that work-related stress may have contributed to mental disability.

- Stress arises in daily life as well as in the workplace or as a response to the broader social environment. There is no way to measure, let alone apportion, the effect of stress from different sources.

- Mental disability is difficult to measure. It cannot be quantified easily on an impairment scale, and an individual's ability to cope varies day by day.

- Mental illness is presumed to be chronic and long-lasting. The costs are assumed to be unpredictable in the individual case and very high in the aggregate. The damages in such cases may appear well out of proportion to the liability in common situations of workplace-related stress.

- Negative stereotypes about psychiatrists abound (e.g., abhorrence re-garding treatment methods of the past, such as excessive electroconvul-sive therapy, and innumerable popular jokes about Freud), which undermines confidence in their testimony.

- Lingering social discrimination against the mentally ill results in negative attitudes and often victim blaming among juries, particularly when substance abuse is involved.

- Mentally ill persons, especially when they are not acutely psychotic, may behave in ways that annoy or seem willful to jurors, who are then inclined to consider the behavior to be voluntary and abusive.

These attitudes are rarely articulated out loud. Rather, they form the cultural backdrop of a general reluctance in our society to deal with the issue of mental illness. Proponents who argue for the end of the distinction between mental and physical health are not directly opposed by those in favor of maintaining the disparity. Those opposed to equality in care and treatment between mental and physical disabilities ("parity") have voiced their opposition in economic terms. They argue that we cannot expend the dollars necessary to achieve this objective, laudable though it may be, at this time. Those who oppose parity proclaim that America cannot afford to add to its cost of production the "bil-lions" needed to achieve mental health parity when our global competitors are not faced with such a cost. Those in favor of parity respond that the cost to the nation of lost worker hours and wasted human resources is a constant drag on our ability to compete in the global marketplace.

These arguments were neatly summarized by Cook:

Insurers articulate many reasons for limiting mental health care benefits, stressing cost containment and the relative subjectivity of mental treatment. Where cost-reduction is the goal, mental health services seem to be an easy target: the services are relatively confined to a single area of medicine, are socially stigmatized, and the efficacy of mental therapy is believed to be less obvious or documented. Furthermore, "mental disorders are not as easy to define as other illnesses," and "mental health problems are subjective." As a result, insurers assert that the duration of psychiatric treatment is often indefinite. Insurers fear a version of adverse selection attributed to mental health care: insurers, believing that people have advance notice of a current or incipient need for psychiatric services or counseling, fear that people will shop around for the best mental health coverage [1].

The economic argument also features a fear of the "thin wedge." If workers' compensation systems were more liberal in accepting claims for major, totally disabling mental illness as an outcome of work, there would be many more claims for lesser degrees of disability. If there were more claims for lesser ratings, the partial disability awards would be based on highly subjective evidence because there is no standard or commonly accepted method applicable to mental illness either for assessing impairment or translating impairment into disability. Mental illness is easier than physical illness to fake. Malingering would be an even more serious problem than it is today. Patients would go "doctor shopping" for the highest impairment rating and least favorable prognosis. It would be impossible to draw the line between grades of mental illness, and the floodgates would open for claims reflecting the stress of daily life. The fear is that the compensation system would soon collapse or premiums would become intolerable, just from this category of claim alone.

This chapter examines the issue of parity as it has been addressed by recent legislation and looks at how that legislation has been interpreted by the judicial system.

The Federal Legislative Framework for Parity in Mental Illness

Alcohol, Drug Abuse, Mental Health Reorganization Act

By 1992, the significant problems and social costs of mental illness to the United States had finally generated serious national concern. As a result of this increased national awareness and in an attempt to streamline the cost of prevention and treatment, the U.S. Congress passed the Alcohol, Drug Abuse, Mental Health Reorganization Act [2]. This act significantly altered the federal government's involvement in and increased the national commitment to mental health care. The experts who testified before Congress clearly presented the social ills affecting significant portions of the American population. In its passage of the act, Congress recognized a problem and acted with the hope that recognition of the problem someday would lead to its solution. Few advocates for the addicted and mentally ill would deny that much more could have been done.

The Alcohol, Drug Abuse, Mental Health Reorganization Act combined, in part, essential portions of legislation already on the books to ensure that treatment and prevention of mental illness were streamlined and coordinated.

While there were several new segments of legislation within the act, three prior statutes were essential to the core formation of the new legislation. These are

- The Alcohol, Drug Abuse, and Mental Health Amendments of 1984.
- The State Comprehensive Mental Health Services Act of 1986.
- The Protection and Advocacy Act for Mentally Ill Individuals.

Alcohol, Drug Abuse, and Mental Health Amendments of 1984 [3]

This legislation established block grants for alcohol, drug abuse, and mental health programs. Under these amendments, states may use their allocation for

(1) Planning, establishing, maintaining, coordinating and evaluation projections for the development of more effective prevention, treatment and rehabilitation programs and activities to deal with alcohol and drug abuse; and
(2) Grants to community mental health centers for the following services and for planning, administration and educational activities related to these services: Services for chronically mentally ill individuals, which include identification of chronically mentally ill individuals and assistance to such individuals in gaining access to essential services through the assignment of case managers . . . [4].

State Comprehensive Mental Health Services Act of 1986 [5]

This act focused on providing block grants to states to provide community mental health services. In addition,

The state plan shall provide for the establishment of and implementation of an organized community-based system for chronically ill individuals. . . . The state plan shall describe services to provide to chronically mentally ill individuals to enable such individuals to gain access to mental health services, including access to treatment, prevention, and rehabilitation services [6].

Protection and Advocacy Act for Mentally Ill Individuals [7]

The Protection and Advocacy Act for Mentally Ill Individuals was enacted in 1986 in response to a study conducted by the Senate Labor and Human Resources Committee. This act sought to address allegations of widespread abuse and neglect of individuals in psychiatric institutions. In addition, the Alcohol, Drug Abuse, Mental Health Reorganization Act mandated that the Health Care Financing Administration should study the barriers to insurance coverage for the treatment of mental illness and substance abuse [8].

Mental Health Parity Act of 1996 [9]

The debate as to whether or not there should be parity between benefits for mental illness and physical illness for those in the workforce is one that needs to be resolved in the legislative arena, not left to the courts, which can only interpret, to the best of their ability, congressional intent. Stronger and more concise language in statutes dealing with employee benefits is required. The conflict between the social desire to ensure parity and unease over the economic costs to America's employers remains unresolved. For example, The Health Insurance Portability and Accountability Act of 1996 [10,11] was passed by Congress without any provisions for parity.

In 1996, Congress examined the complex problem of treating mental and physical health on an equal basis. The Mental Health Parity Act of 1996 became the first legislation aimed at parity of treatments and related costs. While the law ensures that lifetime limits for mental and physical illness are the same [12], it does nothing to help eradicate the disparity between reimbursement schemes for hospital lengths of stay and services provided [13]. Furthermore, the law is not applicable to employer groups with fewer than 50 employees [14]. In addition, if an employer experiences a 1 percent increase in the cost of its health benefit plan, it becomes exempt from the requirements of the act [15].

Beginning in 1998, when both types of benefits were offered, employer groups had to set the annual and lifetime dollar limits on mental health benefits equal to those for physical health benefits. The Mental Health Parity Act only affects health plans that choose to offer mental health benefits and does not apply to services for substance abuse or for chemical dependency treatments [16]. It allows different cost-sharing arrangements, limits on inpatient days, and medical necessity provisions [17]. It applies to self-insured Employee Retirement Income Security Act of 1974 (ERISA) plans [18], insured plans, and the Federal Employee Health Benefits Program [19], but it does not apply to individual health insurance policies, Medicare, or Medicaid standard and risk programs [20].

The passage of the Mental Health Parity Act has created much controversy in the business and insurance communities. Most articles appearing in business and insurance journals question the legislation on economic grounds. The act provides the business community with an opportunity to re-evaluate its programs and to implement programs that are cost-effective. The National Association of Health Underwriters, which opposed the act, predicted that the law would drive up premiums and encourage employers to curtail coverage [21]. A report issued by the actuarial firm of Milliman & Robertson "estimated an overall health insurance increase of 2.5 percent on typical preferred provider organization (PPO) plans if full parity existed" [22], whereas a Congressional Budget Office (CBO) study predicted a 4 percent increase [23].

There is no clear consensus on what impact the Mental Health Parity Act will have on employer-sponsored benefits. For example, Xerox Corporation stated that parity between mental and physical illnesses "will cost corporations and insurance companies and . . . [health maintenance organizations] a lot of money" [24]. Xerox anticipated that the legislation "will cost us [Xerox] money" and was "going to make it more difficult to manage mental health care" [25].

> If mental health parity results in increased health insurance premiums, we [the business community] can expect continued erosion in employment-based health insurance coverage. The Congressional Budget Office (CBO) has estimated that as many as 800,000 workers and their dependents can lose health insurance coverage, while WWW [Watson Wyatt Worldwide] estimated that between 1.1 million and 3.2 million individuals would lose coverage, and PW [Peat Marwick] estimated that 1.7 million individuals would lose coverage [26].

The financial impact of the Mental Health Parity Act will not be known until employer groups analyze their benefit costs after enactment of the law. At that point, the true financial significance of the act will be known, but until then, organizations can only have best-guess estimates of their benefit program cost increases. Passage of the Mental Health Parity Act affords employer groups an opportunity to look at their mental health benefit programs and find ways to maintain, or even possibly reduce, costs.

The field of behavioral health care has progressed to a level where proper care can be rendered effectively with plan designs that do not increase employer costs. Relatively few patients currently exceed the preceding benefit design, so increasing maximums or imposing other requirements should not lead to uncontrollable costs [27].

The Employee Benefit Research Institute (EBRI), in analyzing mental health care benefits and the cost of mental health parity, drew a comparison between their workers and/or their families whose employers fully financed health insurance. The researchers documented a drop of approximately 10 percent from 1988 to 1995 for employers defraying costs of all health care. EBRI found that health plans took a two-tiered approach, the higher tier available to physical conditions and the lower tier available for mental conditions [28].

> Because of the social stigma attached to mental health care and the subjectivity inherent in the patient's assessment of the need for this care, the demand for it is much more price sensitive than that for other forms of health care. This price sensitivity is apparent not only in the overall demand for care but also in the demand for specific providers and sites of care [29].

EBRI, assuming full parity between the mental and physical coverage under health plans, cited several other independent studies of major actuarial firms, all of them concluding that the increased cost for full parity would run from a low of 2.5 percent to a high of 11.4 percent of premium [30]. The CBO's study, also cited in the EBRI report, estimated from 4 to 5.3 percent of premium [31]. The EBRI report immediately was labeled by the National Mental Health

Association "as an attempt to impede parity efforts in state legislatures," and the association accused the report of being highly biased and produced by the insurance industry [32].

The CBO has estimated the cost of full parity to be $65 billion. It is anticipated that this cost will be paid through increased insurance and health care premiums, but possibly employees consequently will receive either smaller increases in salary or reduced medical benefits [33]. While this figure may be high, it should be compared with the potential savings to American business in productivity, estimated to be as high as $130 billion [34]. One commentator summed up the anticipated effects of parity in this manner: "Confusion looms in mental health coverage as a new federal law aimed at expanding mental health benefits may allow—or even encourage—companies to provide less coverage" [35].

Thus the parity debate has been framed in economic terms. Will a dollar spent on mental health care produce more than a dollar of increased productivity from the American workforce? Parity has not yet been made a social issue, i.e., whether America feels that the treatment of mental conditions is a desirable objective in itself. There is little doubt that the Mental Health Parity Act in its present form has so many escape mechanisms that it borders on being an exercise in futility.

Judicial Interpretation of Parity Issues in the Americans with Disabilities Act

The Americans with Disabilities Act, enacted in 1990, has been perceived by some advocates as an appropriate vehicle for the accomplishment of parity by a judicial interpretation of its provisions. However, the majority of courts who have considered the issue have employed judicial restraint and relied on strict construction of the language of the act. The Sixth Circuit, for example, reviewed the disparity between benefits available for physical conditions as compared with mental conditions in *Parker v. Metropolitan Life Insurance Company* [36].

Quida Sue Parker's severe depression was covered under the terms and conditions of the policy issued by Metropolitan Life, which provided disability benefits. Ms. Parker participated in the disability plan that was offered by her employer. Because her disability was deemed to be "nervous and/or mental," her insurance ceased to pay benefits after 24 months. Had her disability been defined as physical, her benefits would have continued until she reached age 65. One of the issues presented on appeal to the Sixth Circuit was whether Parker's employer, in providing inferior health care benefits to those who suffer mental illness as compared with those who suffer from physical illness, violated Title III of the Americans with Disabilities Act. Title III of the act specifically prohibits the provision of unequal or separate benefits by a place of public accommodation [37].

A three-judge panel of the Sixth Circuit (the *Parker* court) held that such discrimination violated the terms and provisions of Title III of the Americans with Disabilities Act. The court found that insurance products fell within the language of Title III; by offering Quida Sue Parker goods and services that were different from those which are provided to other individuals, Met Life violated the statutory mandate [38]. The *Parker* court reviewed the legislative history of the Americans with Disabilities Act and relied on a portion of the report of the House of Representatives that stated: "In sum, [the Americans with Disabilities Act] requires that underwriting and classification of risks be based on sound actuarial principles or be related to actual or reasonably anticipated experience" [39]. The court decided that the disparity contained in the insurance policy, treating mental and physical disability differently, violated Title III of the Americans with Disabilities Act.

However, defendants sought a rehearing en banc on the panel's disposition of Parker's Title III claim [40]. In an 8 to 5 decision, the Sixth Circuit reversed the prior panel decision, holding that Met Life's insurance policies were not an item or a good offered by a place of public accommodation. The court opined that long-term disability plans offered as an employee benefit are not a public accommodation; therefore, the terms and conditions of Title III of the Americans with Disabilities Act, which is restricted to places of public accommodation, did not apply.

In arriving at this judgment, the Sixth Circuit applied the doctrine of *noscitur a sociis* [41]. This legal doctrine instructs that "a . . . term is interpreted within the context of the accompanying words 'to avoid the giving of unintended breadth to the Acts of Congress'" [42]. Because the insurance policy was not within the intended coverage of Title III of the Americans with Disabilities Act, the issue of parity between benefits available for physical versus mental conditions was moot.

Prior to *Parker*, the First Circuit decided the *Carparts Distribution Center* case [43]. However, other circuits have interpreted this section of the Americans with Disabilities Act differently, as did the dissenting judges in the *Parker* case. The executors of the estate of an employee who suffered from AIDS brought suit alleging that his health benefit plan had a discriminatory lifetime cap of health benefits to AIDS patients. The First Circuit addressed the issue of whether a defendant who provides medical plans could be considered a public accommodation under Title III. The First Circuit held:

> Whether establishments of "public accommodation" are limited to actual physical structures is a question of first impression in the Circuit. For the following reasons we find they are not so limited and remand to the district court . . . [44].

As did the Sixth Circuit in *Parker*, the First Circuit in *Carparts* examined the legislative history of the Americans with Disabilities Act. Based on that legislative history, the First Circuit found that the disparity in benefits to those with specific disabilities would no longer be permitted. The purpose of Title III of the Americans with Disabilities Act is

> . . . to bring individuals with disabilities into the economic and social mainstream of American life . . . in a clear, balanced, and reasonable manner. In drafting Title III, Congress intended that people with disabilities have equal access to the array of goods and services offered by private establishments and made available to those who do not have disabilities [45].

Unlike the Sixth Circuit, the First Circuit decided that neither Title III nor the regulations made any reference to physical boundaries or physical entry, and therefore, the AIDS cap was discriminatory [46]. The Sixth Circuit disagreed with this interpretation and pointed out that the Americans with Disabilities Act does not mandate equality between individuals with different disabilities. The act simply prohibits discrimination between the disabled and the nondisabled [44]. Given the conflicting judicial decisions, the issue remains whether, in the employment arena, Congress establishes parity through the Americans with Disabilities Act. The issue ultimately may have to be resolved by the Supreme Court or be addressed by further legislation.

Ambiguity, Economic Realities, and Insurance

Assume that a 38-year-old woman complains of the following continuing physical symptoms: headaches, lack of appetite, rapid pulse, stomach aches, and insomnia. Past history shows that the patient has a very mild case of hypertension that has been under control with diet and exercise and that her gallbladder was removed 6 months ago. A complete physical examination is conducted, but a physical cause for her continued symptoms cannot be determined conclusively. The patient denies any serious external stresses that may be contributing to these symptoms.

The symptoms presented could be due to depression or a yet undiagnosed physical ailment. What are the physician's next steps? Should all organic possibilities be ruled out by extensive and sophisticated testing, or should the physician consider prescribing an antidepressant and recommend that the patient consult a mental health professional? The decision may be made, in part, by what type of insurance the patient has and how that insurance reimburses for physical and mental disorders [47]. Studies demonstrate that individuals who may have a potential mental health risk, unlike individuals who consider their physical health below average, do consider their mental health status when selecting insurance coverage [48]. "The choice between traditional and full coverage and HMO coverage for policyholders who have a family member suffering from a mental health problem may be colored by the extent of coverage for mental health services . . ." [49].

Consider the same facts, but the woman is over 65 years of age and has primary insurance offered through Medicare. While mental health benefits are covered under Medicare Parts A and B, disparity between mental and physical illnesses still exists:

> . . . many experts believe that Medicare-covered mental health services remain inaccessible and underused by the elderly. Among reasons cited for the underuse are Medicare's complex coverage rules and a reimbursement methodology that continues to reflect restrictions and payment differentials that do not apply to the reimbursement of non-mental health services [50].
>
> If a patient is hospitalized, the benefits with respect to deductible and coinsurance are the same for a physical illness or mental illness [51], but, as with private insurance, Medicare has different reimbursement schemes, ranging from a fixed case rate to reasonable and customary costs, depending on where the psychiatric services are provided [52]. If outpatient services are provided, Medicare, like private insurance organizations, has a different schedule of benefits and reimbursement methodology [53]. Medicare even has gone as far as setting higher coinsurance and dollar amount allowances for outpatient mental health services.

> The rationale for setting the outpatient mental health services at a higher coinsurance rate was to protect the federal government from payment for services thought to be induced by a lower rate for those services, rather than by need for the services by the patient. In other words, it was feared that the patient, who did not actually need such services, would use them if they were subject to only a 20% coinsurance rate, thus causing inappropriate overuse of the services. This phenomenon, known as "moral hazard," was considered to be particularly worrisome for outpatient psychotherapy [54].

Legislative and judicial attempts have so far fallen short of defining whether a disease is physical or mental in origin, thereby adding to the confusion surrounding the issue of parity. If parity is not to be achieved, it is then essential that the economic forces that control insurance benefits provide clear, concise, and medically agreed on definitions of physical diseases versus mental conditions. If parity is achieved, such distinctions will have no meaning in economic terms.

In *Philips v. Lincoln National Insurance Company,* this ambiguity and lack of definition allowed the court to hold that medical conditions that are organic in nature fall outside the scope of the mental illness provision and that the limitations on mental illness do not apply [55]. The expert witnesses could not agree on whether the diagnosis of "congenital encephalopathy," which is organic in nature but can give rise to a "cluster of behavioral disorders" [56], is a physical illness or a mental illness. There was consensus among the experts only on the fact that "certain mental illnesses can be organically based" [57].

Cause or origin classifies illness, and if the origins are physical in nature but the patient exhibits mental symptoms, the controversy and ambiguity are heightened [58]. Psychiatrists have testified that psychiatric disorders are organic in nature and therefore should be classified as a physical disorder.

[Bipolar affective disorder] . . . was an illness of the brain and body rather that of the mind and stemmed from a chemical imbalance which responds to medication. This illness, like many others, . . . manifests some behavioral or emotional disturbances, but the causes of those manifestations are physical and biological in nature as distinguished from mental [59].

[The] . . . physiological disease processes cause the most serious psychiatric disorders. Among them were manic-depressive illness and schizophrenia. The only psychiatric disorders that . . . did not have a physiological but rather a functional cause are ". . . diseases that we would classify as problems in living such as marital disorders, alcoholism, substance abuse . . ." [60].

Despite these decisions, employer groups and insurance groups have not sought to tighten the policy language regarding what constitutes mental illness and thus prevent a judicial finding of ambiguity in the schedule of benefits. For example, Northwestern Memorial Hospital [61], the City of Chicago [62], and Blue Cross and Blue Shield of Illinois HMO [63] define *mental illness* to "mean those illnesses classified as disorders in the *Diagnostic and Statistical Manual of Mental Disorders* published by the American Psychiatric Association. . . ." Notwithstanding the American Psychiatric Association's classification system, psychiatrists, medical practitioners, and the judicial system still have difficulty in labeling a medical condition physical or mental.

Nevertheless, in 1997, Texas took a major step forward when it passed a bill ending insurance discrimination against people with serious brain disorders. . . . "As new wonder drugs continue to improve the quality of life of the mentally ill, it's time for the country to turn its back on essentially medieval approaches. A continued push for mental health parity and responsible managed care could easily spell the end for many of the gratuitous tragedies that too often accompany mental illness" [64].

Conclusion

Until recently, Congress, state legislatures, and the judicial system have not evidenced serious concern regarding the discrimination practiced by employers, insurance companies, and medical providers against those suffering from mental health disabilities. There is no question that disparity between physical and mental illness still exists. Today's health care debate is structured in terms of the economics of the health care delivery system. The advocates of parity, whether accomplished legislatively, judicially, or administratively, must first concentrate on the American worker. The ultimate goal is to eliminate any distinction in insurance coverage that prevents a person from being a productive member of the workforce. If meaningful legislation cannot be passed that is supported by the economic community as well as by those lobbying for equal treatment for mental illness, on a case-by-case basis, this will only serve to perpetuate the problem instead of resolving it.

Endnotes

1. Cook, Youndy C. Messing with our minds: The mental illness limitation in health insurance. *University of Miami Law Rev* 1996;50:345, 346.

2. Alcohol, Drug Abuse, Mental Health Reorganization Act of 1992, Pub. L. 102-321 (S. 1306), 106 Stat. 323 (codified as amended in scattered sections of 42 U.S.C., enacted July 19, 1992).

3. Alcohol Abuse, Drug Abuse and Mental Health Amendments of 1984, Pub. L. 98-509, 98 Stat. 2353 (codified as amended in scattered sections of 42 U.S.C.A.).

4. *Id.*

5. State Comprehensive Mental Health Services Plan Act of 1986, Pub. L. 99-660, 100 Stat. 3795 (codified as amended in scattered sections of 42 U.S.C.A.).

6. *Id.*

7. Protection and Advocacy Act for Mentally Ill Individuals of 1986, Pub. L. 99-319, 100 Stat. 478 (codified as amended in scattered sections of 42 U.S.C.A.).

8. See n.15. 42 U.S.C. 285p, Alcohol, Drug Abuse, Mental Health Reorganization Act, Sec. 703.

9. The Mental Health Parity Act of 1996, Pub. L. 104-204 (H.R. 3666), 110 Stat. 1936 (codified as amended in scattered sections of 29 and 42 U.S.C., enacted September 24, 1996).

10. Health Insurance Portability and Accountability Act of 1996, Pub. L. 104-91 (H.R. 3103), 110 Stat. 1936 (codified as amended in scattered sections of 29 and 42 U.S.C., enacted August 21, 1996).

11. "Under the Health Portability and Accountability Act of 1996 (HIPPA), group health plans, including HMO plans, are subject to certain requirements regarding portability of insurance coverage through limitations on the pre-existing condition exclusions, prohibitions on excluding individuals from coverage based on health status, and guaranteed renewability of health insurance coverage for plan years beginning after June 30, 1997." Rutkowski, Arthur D., and Rutkowski, Barbara Lang. Health Insurance Portability and Accountability Act of 1996: Are you in compliance with the law? *Employment Law Update, West* 1997;1.

12. See n.31 at Sec. 712(a)(1).

13. *Id.,* at Sec. 712(b)(1)(2).

14. *Id.,* at Sec. 712(c)(1)(B).

15. *Id.,* at Sec. 712(c)(2)(C).

16. *Id.,* at Sec. 712(e)(4).

17. *Id.,* at Sec. 2705(b)(2).

18. *Id.,* at Sec. 702.

19. *Id.,* at Sec. 703.

20. The Domenici-Wellstone Mental Illness Parity Provision: What the New Law Will Do and Not Do, American Psychiatric Association Fact Sheet. Washington, D.C.: American Psychiatric Association, 1997.

21. Hann, Leslie Werstein. Unintended consequences. *Best's Review: Life-Health Insurance Addition* 1997;97:56.

22. West, Diane. Mental parity report irks proponents. *National Underwriter Life & Health Financial* 1997;99:1.

23. *Id.*

24. Katz, David M. Firms afraid mental "parity" will increase benefit costs. *National Underwriter Life & Health Financial* 1996; 41:42.

25. *Id.*

26. *Issues in Mental Health Care Benefits: The Costs of Mental Health Parity.* Washington, D.C.: Employee Benefit Research Institute, Brief Number 182, February 1997. Pp 1, 11.

27. Bradman, Leo H. One view of mental health parity. *National Underwriter* 1997;101:S7.

28. *Issues in Mental Health Care Benefits: The Costs of Mental Health Parity.* Washington, D.C.: Employee Benefit Research Institute, Brief Number 182, February 1997. Pp 1, 9–11.

29. *Id.*, at 13.

30. *Id.*, at 9.

31. *Id.*

32. West, Diane. Mental parity report irks proponents. *National Underwriter Life & Health Financial* 1997;11:1.

33. Fischer, Mary Jane. CBO: Mental health amendment will cost $65B. *National Underwriter Property & Casualty* 1996;1.

34. See n.14.

35. See n.43 at 56.

36. *Parker v. Metropolitan Life Insurance*, 99 F.3d 181 (6th Cir. 1996), *rev'd en banc* 121 F.3d 1006 (6th Cir. 1997).

37. *Parker v. Metropolitan Life Insurance Co.*, 121 F.3d 1006, 1010 (6th Cir. *en banc*, 1997).

38. *Parker v. Metropolitan Life Insurance Co.*, 99 F.3d 181, 188 (6th Cir. 1996).

39. *Id.*, at 190.

40. *Parker v. Metropolitan Life*, 121 F.3d 1006, 1010 (6th Cir. *en banc*, 1997).

41. "It is known from its associates." The meaning of a word is or may be known for the accompanying words. Under the doctrine of *noscitur a sociis*, the meaning of questionable or doubtful words or phrases in a statute may be ascertained by reference to the meaning of other words or phrases associated with it [*id.*, at 1014, quoting *Black's Law Dictionary*, 1060 (6th ed, 1990)].

42. *Id.*, at 1014.

43. *Carparts Distribution Center, Inc. v. Automotive Wholesaler's Assoc. of New England*, 37 F.3d 12 (1st Cir. 1994).

44. *Id.*, at 18.

45. *Id.*, at 19 (internal citations omitted).

46. *Id.*, at 9.

47. Freedman, Alfred M., et al. *Issues in Psychiatric Classification: Science, Practice and Social Policy.* New York: Human Science Press, 1986. P 163. "The financial arrangements with which the physician deals, however tangentially, have an effect which cannot be

denied or underestimated in coloring one's medical thinking. The provision of health care and the financing of health-related benefits do not exist, separate from each other, on two separate tracks."

48. Deb, Partha, et al. Choice of health insurance by families of the mentally ill. *Health Economics* 1996;5:74.

49. *Id.*, at 65.

50. Sherman, Jeremie J. Medicare's mental health benefits: Coverage, use, and expenditures. *Journal of Aging and Health* 1996;8:55.

51. *Id.*, at 57.

52. *Id.*, at 62.

53. *Id.*, at 58–59.

54. *Id.*, at 59.

55. *Id.*, at 310–311.

56. *Id.*, at 304.

57. *Id.*, at 305.

58. *Arkansas Blue Cross and Blue Shield, Inc. v. John Doe*, 733 S.W. 2d 429, 431 (Ark. App. 6th 1987).

59. *Id.*, at 431.

60. *Equitable Life Assurance Society of the United States v. Berry*, 212 Cal. App. 3d 832, 840 (Cal. App. 3d 1989).

61. Northwestern University Group Major Medical Hospitalization Insurance, ASOA, p 15.

62. City of Chicago. *Employee Benefits Handbook.* Printed December 1994. P M-30.

63. *HMO Illinois, a Blue Cross HMO: Your Certificate of Health Care Benefits.* GB-16 HCSC, January 1995. P 47.

64. Estrada, Richard. A push for mental health parity. *Chicago Tribune,* October 21, 1997, at Sec 1, p 17.

22

Medical Evidence and the Professional Standard of Care

SARA ROSENBAUM

This chapter begins with a brief overview of the history of the professional standard of care and the evidentiary rules that historically have applied to standard-of-care litigation in a health care quality context. The chapter then examines the evolution of the role that the professional standard of care has come to play in prospective treatment-related coverage decision making, as well as the growing use of standardized practice guidelines to set the standard of care in managed-care contractual arrangements. The chapter concludes with a discussion regarding the evidentiary implications of the growing use of standardized practice guidelines to guide coverage decision making by managed-care corporations.

In the past, health insurers were passive payers, and the only medical care disputes that raised professional standard-of-care questions were those which involved the quality of medical care itself. However, in the modern health system, managed-care decision making, with its emphasis on prospective coverage, and cost containment have become the norm. For all but the wealthiest Americans, coverage decisions effectively determine the quality and accessibility of medical treatment [1]. The rise of medical judgment as an integral part of insurance coverage has led to a significant debate at the highest policy levels over the evidentiary standards and methods used by insurers to determine the proper standard of care for individual patients and thus the treatment for which they should be covered. The essence of this debate is whether standardized treatment approaches and modalities (i.e., generalized practice guidelines) should ever be conclusive evidence regarding the proper standard of care in an individual pa-tient's case. I argue that even if standardized guidelines were shown to be both reliable and relevant to a specific patient, the quality of medical care depends on the resolution of treatment decisions resting on particularized, individual clinical judgment.

Origins and Evolution of the Professional Standard of Care

Evidence regarding the quality of medical care has been a matter of judicial focus for more than two centuries [2]. From the beginning of the modern era in medical care quality litigation, the resolution of medical quality disputes turned on whether a plaintiff could show that a defendant had breached the "professional standard of care." Under eighteenth-century common law, courts ruled that in order to recover damages against a physician, a plaintiff would have to demonstrate that the defendant violated the customs and standards of his or her own profession, as testified to by other professionals. Thus, in an early action against a surgeon for substandard practice, the English courts ruled that the plaintiff had to prove that the defendant had violated "the usage and law of surgeons . . . the rule of the profession . . ." as demonstrated through the testimony of other surgeons [3]. From these early decisions, evidence regarding the standard of care came to depend for both its reliability and its relevance on the *custom of the profession itself as defined by members of the profession* and without regard to other possible evidence about the reasonableness of such custom or practice. The practical import of such a standard was to chill medical liability litigation, because an injured person would have to find an expert who would present testimony against another health professional regarding the defendant's possible violation of professional custom [4].

Furthermore, until the middle of the twentieth century, courts severely limited the geographic scope of relevant evidence regarding the standard of care to the locality in which the defendant actually practiced, thereby further inhibiting individuals' ability to bring quality-of-care claims. By the late nineteenth century, a number of courts had held that a physician practicing in a small town or rural area was

> . . . bound to possess that skill only which physicians and surgeons of ordinary ability and skill, practicing in similar localities, with opportunities for no larger experience, ordinarily possess; and he was not bound to possess that high degree of art and skill possessed by eminent surgeons practicing in larger cities and making a specialty of the practice of surgery [5].

Other courts required injured persons to prove not merely a breach of the standard of care in "similar localities" but actually to show that the defendant's conduct violated the custom of the precise locality in which the defendant practiced [6].

The "same or similar locality" standard itself led to extensive litigation regarding whether a particular standard was in fact the standard for a same or similar locality [7]. Application of the locality rule had several effects. The first was its consequences for an injured person's ability to bring *any* action, because the rule effectively restricted a plaintiff to the use of expert testimony from geographic colleagues of the defendant. The second effect of the locality rule was to render irrelevant evidence regarding developments in the standard of practice, thereby insulating small-town practitioners (most physicians at the time) from any legal obligation to modernize their practice techniques in the face of advances in medical care.

Ultimately, this very narrow and provincial vision of the professional standard of care gave way to more modern thinking. First, the locality rule gave way to a national standard of care. Second, custom, as the exclusive matter of relevance, gave way to a broader concept of reasonableness, particularly in the case of informed consent [8].

By the middle of the twentieth century, the evolution of medicine and a growing concept of "social egalitarianism" throughout all dimensions of the U.S. legal system had revolutionized the judicial approach to evidence of the standard of care in medical liability cases [9]. Courts no longer limited plaintiffs to the presentation of evidence regarding the standard of care from the same or similar locality in which a defendant practiced but permitted a far broader scope of evidence. Consistent with advances in social policy thinking, and in the face of evidence regarding the increasing standardization of medical training and education and the use of national accreditation standards, courts began to hold physicians to

> . . . that degree of care and skill which is expected of a reasonably competent practitioner in the same class to which he [or she] belongs, acting in the same or similar circumstances. Under this standard, advances in the profession, availability of facilities, specialization or general practice, proximity of specialists and special facilities, together with all relevant considerations, are to be taken into account [10].

Under this "national standard of care," evidence related to medical practice on a national scale became relevant, as did the testimony of outside experts regarding the standard of care in areas other than the one in which the defendant practiced. To be sure, as this excerpt from the *Shilkret* case underscores, a defendant could show that the actual circumstances of practice constrained his or her ability to adhere to a higher standard of care and that despite the defendant's diligence on a patient's behalf, such care could not be achieved. At the same time, as the local habits and customs of physicians gave way to more global expectations of health quality, the approach of courts to evidence also changed [11].

In addition, deference to evidence of professional custom gave way to the admissibility of evidence regarding the reasonableness of professional custom and practice itself in light of advances in medical knowledge and medical management technique. This willingness to allow evidence that challenged the reasonableness of claims of professional custom had its roots in liability cases outside the medical context [12], but by the second half of the twentieth century courts were ready to challenge the conclusiveness of medical claims of custom, particularly in circumstances where available and relatively inexpensive technologies should have caused custom to evolve [13].

Thus, while evidence of professional custom remains relevant in modern legal practice, a determination of whether the professional standard has been met turns on whether, in light of all relevant circumstances in the context of a particular case, a practitioner's conduct and judgment can be considered professionally reasonable. Thus the central question for judicial resolution becomes whether a defendant acted in a reasonably professional manner given the totality of circumstances surrounding the case [14]. The relevant evidence in such a case is the testimony of professionals and experts [15], as well as other evidence of professional reasonableness, including evidence of advances in medical technology, evidence regarding the availability of knowledge regarding appropriate approaches to the treatment and management of complex conditions, and the results of relevant and reliable scientific studies that meet the types of standards articulated by expert bodies [16].

Nor has evolution in the professional standard of care been limited to physicians and other health professionals. Since the mid-1960s, courts have accepted the proposition that health care corporations, including hospitals and, more recently, health maintenance organizations (HMOs) and other managed-care organizations could be held liable for the substandard performance of their corporate duty of care [17].

Medical Judgment Decision Making by Public and Private Insurers in a Coverage Context and the Emergence of Standardized Practice Guidelines: Implications for Liability

As recently as a generation ago, the professional standard of care had little to do with health care coverage. In 1980, the vast majority of Americans with employer-sponsored health insurance obtained their coverage through "conventional" insurance arrangements, under which insurers left most questions of medical judgment up to treating physicians and denied coverage for treatment, if at all, only on a retrospective (post-treatment) basis [18]. Employer-sponsored plans were not alone in the degree of discretion they accorded physicians; managed care was virtually nonexistent in public insurance programs such as Medicare and Medicaid.

To be sure, under conventional insurance, disputes arose over coverage as insurers increasingly turned to retrospective review to contain costs. By definition, however, these disputes arose after treatment had been furnished. While they raised matters of great economic significance for insured persons, the disputes did not affect access to care itself. Furthermore, these disputes tended to turn on legal questions of contractual interpretation rather than medical evidence [19]. Consequently, evidence related to the standard of medical care tended to be an issue only in the context of medical liability litigation, where the quality of medical care was at issue.

The advent of the managed-care era effectively has extended the debate over application of the professional standard of care to medical care coverage itself, not only the quality of care. The reason for this lies in the essential objectives and features of the modern managed-care arrangement. As used in this chapter, the term *managed care* denotes any contractual arrangement in which an entity sells to a purchaser and its sponsored members a product that insures individuals for medical care services furnished by the entity through its network of health care professionals who are selected by the entity and whose medical treatment decisions are reviewed by the entity in advance of or concurrent with the provision of care [20]. A managed-care network can be tightly or loosely organized, and review over professional treatment decisions can be rigorous or limited [21]. However, under this working definition, the critical element that distinguishes managed care from conventional coverage is control by the managed-care entity of medical judgment through various enforcement tools that include utilization review, selective contracting, and use of practice guidelines coupled with physician incentives [22].

Harold Luft, a leading expert in managed care, has observed that physician conduct is what is managed in managed care [23]. As a result, the advent of managed care has directly refocused the basic issue of medical judgment away from the treating physician and toward the corporation. Regardless of whether the matter is framed as one of health care *quality* or health care *coverage*, the matter to be resolved in a medical dispute is whether the medical judgment that was exercised met the professional standard of care.

The power of managed-care companies to effectively determine the standard of care through coverage decisions has been illustrated by a series of cases involving persons who have been injured by managed-care coverage decisions [24], the most compelling of which may be *Corcoran v. United HealthCare, Inc.* [25]. The *Corcoran* case is a landmark decision that concerns the application of the federal Employee Retirement Income Security Act (ERISA) to damages claims for negligent coverage decision making by health insurers under employer-sponsored plans. In *Corcoran,* the plaintiff, a woman with a documented history of preterm labor, sought round-the-clock hospitalization coverage during the final portion of her second pregnancy in order to avert infant death. Her physician repeatedly argued for advanced hospitalization care for his patient in light of her medical history; the defendant, which performed utilization management services for a self-insured employer-sponsored health plan, denied the request and instead prescribed part-time home nursing. The plaintiff, who had been placed in a hospital pending defendant's decision, went home after being informed that she would be covered only for part-time home care. Within days of her return, she lost her baby one evening after the part-time home health nurse had left for the day.

The *Corcoran* decision triggered national news coverage as well as congressional hearings over the ruling, which shielded the insurer from liability for damages under the principles of ERISA preemption [26]. The hearings brought to light the health insurer's application of its pregnancy management practice guidelines as well as its rejection of individualized evidence presented by the patient's physician and its substitution of a care plan for that recommended by the physician. Because the company was shielded from liability under the rules of preemption, the question of whether its exercise of judgment was substandard in the plaintiff's case was never answered.

The intersection between medical judgment and the professional standard of care on the one hand and medical care coverage on the other has been reinforced over the years by experts such as David Eddy, who has written extensively about the link between health care financing and health quality:

> Coverage criteria [in insurance plans] constitute a contract between health plans and their members on how the members' money will be spent. . . . [They function] to ensure that plans do not waste the members' money on non-medical, ineffective, or harmful practices. . . . A second purpose that evolved over the last two decades is to improve quality. . . . [G]aps in knowledge [about the effectiveness of medical practices] exist because practices that provide some hope of benefit are disseminated before the . . . actual benefit can be confirmed through clinical research. . . . The best way to correct this problem is to insist on good evidence of effectiveness before allowing a practice to be disseminated. Because coverage criteria sit astride the flow of money, they are in an excellent position to do this. . . . [C]overage criteria help plans achieve the seemingly contradictory objectives of controlling costs while simultaneously increasing quality [27].

As Dr. Eddy's writings suggest, purchasers of health insurance and group health plan sponsors have come to expect insurers and health plan administrators to exercise medical judgment regarding the appropriateness of care in the context of performing their coverage-related tasks. Furthermore, the role of payers in treatment decisions shows up in actual coverage language. And finally, there is at least limited evidence that a revolution is under way in the manner in which the coverage provisions in insurance contracts are structured: Insurers may be in the process of moving away from contracts that vest discretion in insurers to exercise medical judgment regarding the application of broad coverage rules to individual treatment cases and toward agreements that incorporate fixed and standardized treatment guidelines directly into the terms of an insurance con-tract.

This movement away from broad coverage limits coupled with retention of medical judgment discretion and toward fixed contractual coverage rules is the result of concern on the part of insurers of their potential liability for judicial reversal of their decisions to deny or limit treatments. The actual number of legal challenges to coverage denials is undoubtedly few in relation to the number of denials (particularly because, in the case of ERISA-covered plans, administra-tors and insurers are shielded for damages flowing from substandard coverage decision making). At the same time, cases such as *Corcoran* suggest that rather than making the careful and rigorous judgments about the proven benefits of care that Dr. Eddy advocates, companies may engage in arbitrary decision making that has no evidentiary basis and that rests on what, in a few particularly notorious instances, can only be termed an outrageous abrogation of a company's fiduciary obligations.

For example, in *Bedrick v. Travelers Insurance* [28], the insurer's utilization manager denied physical therapy for a child with cerebral palsy on the rationale that children with cerebral palsy have a chronic condition from which they will not recover; therefore, physical therapy could never be beneficial. When cross-examined at trial regarding her conclusions, the manager offered a reference to a single article in the *New England Journal of Medicine* of questionable relevance. Similarly, in *Wickline v. State of California* [29], the medical review branch of the California Medicaid agency prematurely discharged a woman (who ultimately lost her leg) from a hospital without reviewing her medical records, consulting with her treating physician, or making the type of rigorous individual factual determination as to her continued need for care that patient-oriented medical judgment considerations would require [30].

This exposure to liability in individual cases under agreements that reserve to the insurer the power to make individual medical necessity decisions has caused companies to turn to legal approaches, long advocated by certain leading law experts, to build express coverage terms directly into the face of the agreement [31]. The use of treatment guidelines as express contractual provisions has two important yet seemingly contradictory, consequences. First, in the context of a challenge to an insurer coverage decision, testimony regarding the professional standard of care in a particular case becomes irrelevant because the standardized practice guidelines conclusively determine coverage. In other words, guidelines are becoming a matter of basic contract design rather than a method for applying broad contractual terms to an individual case. Thus, in *Jones v. Kodak,* a woman who needed extended treatment for alcohol addiction was completely precluded from appealing her ERISA employer plan's denial of coverage because the court determined that the treatment she could receive was limited to the treatment guidelines that had been incorporated directly into the terms of the agreement between her employer and the mental health care plan it offered [32]. In the court's opinion, it was irrelevant that the guidelines as applied to this individual case were inappropriate (a fact admitted to by the insurer's own utilization reviewer); coverage had been limited to potentially substandard care as a matter of contractual agreement.

Second, and paradoxically, if standardized guidelines are either inappropriate or else are inappropriately applied by a managed-care organization to an individual case, substandard practice rules may subject a managed-care organization to medical liability for injuries sustained as a result of medical care practice carried out under the guidelines. Thus, in *Bauman v. United HealthCare, Inc.* [33], an HMO was found potentially liable for the death of a newborn infant following what turned out to be the baby's premature discharge under the company's 24-hour length-of-stay rule [34]. The guidelines in the case were viewed not as a standard of coverage but as the standard of care that the HMO built into its corporate practice. As a result, the HMO was potentially corporately liable, as would be any health care corporation for poor quality of care management and oversight. At a subsequent trial, evidence of the professional reasonableness of the company's practice guidelines would be directly relevant, as would evidence regarding how such guidelines are to be used and applied in individual patient cases [35]. Furthermore, under the concept of the professional standard of practice, which focuses on the quality of care for an individual patient, it is doubtful that any practice that entails the unquestioning application of a practice protocol to a patient without considering the individual facts of the case would be considered reasonable.

Thus, while the incorporation of standardized guidelines into an agreement may shield an insurer from coverage liability and a challenge based on the professional standard of care to its decisions, substandard guidelines ultimately can subject a company to a classic lawsuit based on theories of medical care negligence and liability. Despite this seeming contradiction, this result is consistent with what the Supreme Court in *Pegram v. Herdrich* termed the "hybrid nature" of managed-care corporations [36], which both make coverage decisions and furnish treatment. Unlike the *Corcoran* case, which challenged the company's conduct in its capacity as a coverage decision maker, a legal action against an employer-sponsored health plan that is predicated on theories of medical quality can be brought without running afoul of ERISA preemption [37]. Where standardized guidelines are challenged in a quality-of-care context, testimony regarding the extent to which practice based on such guidelines satisfied a professional standard of care would be directly relevant. Furthermore, in cases in which a defendant cannot demonstrate through expert testimony that its guidelines, as designed and applied, meet professionally reasonable standards, adherence to such guidelines would be deemed to be irrelevant to the issue of quality [38].

Congressional Oversight of Managed-Care Treatment Decisions

During the 1999–2000 legislative session, the 106th Congress actively debated managed-care quality reform. The debate was far-ranging and reached no resolution. However, one of the most high-profile matters that arose, and one that has received enormous state legislative attention as well [39], is the issue of external review of coverage-related treatment decisions by managed-care companies and the scope and quality of evidence that must be considered in individual cases. To the extent that coverage is limited by the incorporation of practice guidelines directly into the terms of a coverage agreement as in the *Kodak* case, any individual external review of coverage would be precluded because the issue becomes contract design rather than its application. However, incorporation of guidelines into contracts is only an emerging trend; most coverage agreements continue to be drafted broadly. As a result, agreements continue to delegate medical judgment discretionary powers to insurers and health plan administrators, and external reviews of individual determinations will continue to play a central role in any managed-care regulatory debate.

While many aspects of managed care reform aroused great controversy with no agreement between Republicans and Democrats, relative unanimity was reached regarding key elements of the external review process. The House-Senate conference negotiators agreed on the need for a more active process of external review of health plan coverage decisions because of the effects of such decisions on health care access and quality. In particular, negotiators reached a tentative agreement on three matters related to medical care disputes and evidence. These areas of agreement were embodied in a Republican-sponsored version of managed-care quality legislation introduced late in the 106th Congress [40].

The first matter addresses access to external review. The legislation would provide for external review in any case involving a "medically reviewable decision." Such decisions are defined to include any case "that requires an evaluation of the medical facts by a health care professional [41]." Second, the bill provides for what amounts to a *de novo* standard of review during the review process by clarifying that the external review is a "new, independent determination" as to whether the original plan decision should be upheld, reversed, or modified [42]. By this standard, the bill permits the introduction of evidence that had not been considered previously by a health plan and also permits external review experts to take a fresh look at the evidence that plan administrators and insurers relied on to reach their decisions.

Finally, negotiators articulated an evidentiary rule for the external review process [43]. The evidence that an independent medical review panel "shall" consider includes (1) "appropriate and available evidence and information," including the plan or insurer's own determination and the "evidence, guidelines, or rationale used by the issuer in reaching such determination," (2) the recommendation of the treating health care professional and "the evidence, guidelines, and rationale" used by the professional, (3) any "additional relevant evidence or information" obtained by the independent medical review panel or submitted by the plan, issuer, participant, beneficiary, or treating health professional, and (4) the plan coverage document.

This language casts a spotlight on the issue of relevant evidence and information and underscores the need for evidentiary standards regarding the measurement of information and the minimum threshold that such information should have to satisfy before it can be considered by a review panel. The language of the measure also can be thought of as a public policy acknowledgment of the impact of managed-care coverage decision making not only on access to coverage but also on the quality of care itself. In other words, the legislation recognizes the consequences of coverage decisions and establishes a *de novo* review process

[44] that provides plan members with an independent evaluation of a health care corporation's medical judgment to determine if that judgment is in accord with relevant evidence and the facts of the individual's case.

Conclusion: The Evidentiary Implications of an Evolving Approach to Medical Care Decision Making in the Modern Health Care System

We have examined the evolution of the professional standard of care as a paradigm for measuring health care quality and, second, as the standard by which the reasonableness of coverage decision making is to be measured. The cases and legislation discussed illustrate a willingness on the part of the judicial and legislative branches to subject medical decisions and conduct to scrutiny for reasonableness, as well as a refusal to give conclusive deference to claims of custom or discretionary authority.

At the same time, the *Kodak* decision brings to light a trend that could significantly shield coverage decisions made by health plans and their networks from any external scrutiny under a professional standard of practice. However, the *Bauman* decision suggests that if substandard practice guidelines result in death or injury, a managed-care company, like other corporate health providers, could face direct liability under quality-of-care theories that apply a professional standard of care.

Nevertheless, the ability of injured persons to sue to recover damages for substandard managed care is of little comfort, however, in the context of systemic quality concerns. Studies of medical liability claims suggest that these actions are so rare—and, when they do occur, potentially so unrelated to the actual incidence of medically induced injury—that medical liability litigation cannot provide the type of overall health care quality accountability mechanism that any health system needs [45].

Evidently, in the market-based environment that surrounds the U.S. health system, the means for ensuring better health care quality is through the act of purchasing itself. While the courts need educating to recognize the proper use and application of standardized practice guidelines, group health care purchasers need similar training. Reading actual guidelines used in managed care gives a clear indication of why scrutiny is so important. Typically, these guidelines are shielded from view because they are considered proprietary. However, consider the following guidelines, from the Milliman and Robertson actuarial firm, that are meant to serve as a guide for managed-care corporations regarding the standard of primary care practice:

A. The number of visits per member should be no more than 4 visits per year.
B. Seventy percent to 80 percent of members will be seen by a physician during a given year.

C. The visits per members should be no more than 5 visits per member seen per year.

D. Primary care physicians should comprise 70 percent to 80 percent of the total visits. This percentage will be higher for pediatric patients and lower for adults under the care of family practitioners or internists.

E. Referrals to specialists should be no greater than 0.5 per member per year.

F. Ambulatory visits by specialists should average no more than 2.5 visits per referred patient per year. This average will include mental health services with as many as 6 visits per member seen per year.

G. Ancillary services should average less than one ancillary service per visit when there has been a large number of visits.

H. The services per encounter should be no more than 2.0 services per encounter.

I. The total number of office visits including primary care visits, specialist consultations, outpatient mental health care, and periodic health appraisals, as well as new patient visits, should exceed the number of ancillary services, including laboratory testing, radiology testing, other miscellaneous medicine services, immunizations, injections and physical therapy visits.

When one or more of these guidelines are exceeded, our chart reviews have revealed an unacceptably high number of unnecessary services [46].

Whether this guideline should be used to guide network selection, credentialing, compensation of network providers, or decisions regarding the appropriateness of care depends on whether it is a good guideline. The Institute of Medicine (IOM) not only has emphasized the limited use that should be made of even good guidelines but also has identified the essential features of good guidelines. According to the IOM, in order to be of acceptable quality, guidelines must exhibit certain attributes. First, they must be valid, by which the IOM means that the guidelines must lead to the health and cost outcomes projected, when followed. The IOM notes that prospective assessments of guideline validity would consider projected outcomes and costs of alternative courses of action, the relationship between the evidence and the recommendations, the substance and quality of the clinical and scientific evidence cited, and the means used to evaluate the evidence [47]. Guidelines that simply rest on actuarial estimates of the frequency with which certain diagnostic or treatment procedures are done or that appear to rest on no evidence whatsoever would fall far from this test.

A second measure of good guidelines according to the IOM is their reliability and reproducibility. By this the IOM means, first, that a second group of experts could produce the same results if given the same evidence and methods for guidelines development and, second, that if given the same circumstances the guidelines are interpreted and applied consistently [48]. Third, the IOM identifies clinical applicability. By this the IOM standards require that "the guidelines should be as inclusive of appropriately defined patient populations as scientific and clinical evidence and expert judgment permit and that they should explicitly state the population" to which they apply [49]. Fourth, the IOM identifies guideline clarity as essential, meaning that they should use unambiguous and precise language, define terms clearly, and use "logical and easy to follow modes of presentation" [50]. Fifth, the IOM recommends the use of a multidisciplinary process to develop the guidelines that includes not only experts but representatives of affected populations [51]. Sixth, the IOM recommends scheduled reviews to determine if revisions are warranted [52]. And finally, the IOM emphasizes the need for meticulous documentation of the process by which guidelines are developed [53].

In sum, if the trend toward the contractual incorporation of practice guidelines is to continue (and the industry's desire to reduce its own treatment discretion and "incentivize" physician practice and performance suggests that it will), then group health care purchasers will need to learn how to conduct evidentiary evaluations of what constitutes a good guideline so that they can make informed decisions regarding which guidelines (if any) should be contractually specified and what types of contractual limits should be placed on their use.

Purchasers need training in the evaluation of practice guidelines, particularly when they become part of the contractual process. Two issues need to be addressed. The first is the minimum elements of acceptable guidelines. Here, the IOM report is quite useful in guiding purchasers through the series of evidentiary matters that they must address. Second is the question of the legal implications of agreeing to a contract that incorporates standardized coverage as an irrebuttable standard of coverage. While in the short run the use of guidelines in this manner can lessen the incidence of coverage challenge, in the long run, and given the movement by courts to recognize theories of medical liability against managed-care plans, the use of fixed guidelines actually could spur additional quality-of-care–related litigation.

The IOM study and a voluminous body of quality-of-care and coverage decisions case law are a testament to the inability to excise individual judgment from medical treatment decision making. Putting aside the technical problems with guidelines and the limited number of good guidelines that exist, as the Supreme Court reminded the nation in *Pegram v. Herdrich,* in the end, the quality of care comes down to medical judgment, which can only happen on an individualized basis. As has been noted on numerous occasions, medical practice, whether by individual physicians or through health care corporations, has a "core ethical dimension" that requires health professionals to use their "knowledge of the particular patient in deciding the course of treatment along with the patient" [54]. Even where there are good general data, it is ethically wrong to blindly apply them to individual patients without patient-based considerations. For this reason, and in the end, the professional standard of practice remains the only viable standard to ensure accountability in health care, and the evidentiary needs that flow from this standard will continue to be highly central to the training of law and policy professionals. Furthermore, as the modern health care era ushers in the expanded use of treatment guidelines, a new effort is needed to train purchasers, public policy makers, the bar, and judges alike in the evidentiary predicates of acceptable guidelines and their proper use.

Endnotes

1. Rosenbaum S, Frankford D, Moore B, and Borzi P. Who should determine when health care is medically necessary? *New Engl J Med* 1999;340:229–233.

2. Rosenblatt R, Law S, and Rosenbaum S. *Law and the American Health Care System.* New York: Foundation Press 1997; 2000–01 Supplement, Ch. 3A.

3. *Slater v.* Baker and Stapleton, 95 Eng. Rep. 860, 862 (King's Bench, 1767). See Rosenblatt et al., *supra,* n.1, at 843.

4. Law S. and Polan S. *Pain and Profit: The Politics of Malpractice.* New York: Basic Books, 1978. Pp 7–8.

5. *Small v. Howard,* 128 Mass. 131, 132, 35 Am. Rep. 363, 365 (1880). See Rosenblatt et al., n.2 *supra,* at 843–844.

6. Rosenblatt et al., n.2 *supra,* at 844.

7. Waltz T. The rise and gradual fall of the locality rule in medical malpractice litigation. *DePaul Law Review* 1968;18:408–412.

8. In *Canterbury v. Spence,* 464 F.2d 772 (D.C. Cir., 1972) the court held that other than in very narrow circumstances, the professional standard played no role in measuring the negligence of physicians in an informed consent context, because medical judgment, which gave rise to the professional standard itself, did not come into play in the context of the duty to disclose risks and benefits or a patient's right to self determination.

9. Rosenblatt et al., n.2, *supra,* Ch. 3C.

10. *Shilkret v. Annapolis Emergency Hospital,* 349 A.2d 245, 249–250 (Md. 1975).

11. *Hall v. Hilbun,* 466 So. 2d 856 (Miss. 1985) (overturning the locality rule and permitting testimony by a national expert in a post-surgery medical management liability case).

12. *The T. J. Hooper,* 60 F.2d 737 (2d Cir., 1932).

13. See, e.g., *Helling v. Carey,* 519 P.2d 981 (Wash. 1974) (ophthalmologist could be found liable for plaintiff's blindness which resulted from the failure to administer a glaucoma test that was not recommended under professional practice standards on an individual as young as the plaintiff); *Washington v. Washington Hospital Center;* 579 A.2d. 177 (D.C. App. T., 1977) (hospital liable for the asphyxiation of a patient whose lack of oxygen during a botched anesthesia procedure could have been detected with the use of a simple carbon dioxide monitor in the operating room).

14. *The T. J. Hooper,* n.12, *supra; Helling v. Carey,* n.13, *supra. Washington v. Washington Hospital Center,* n.13, *supra.*

15. Finder JM. The future of practice guidelines: Should they constitute conclusive evidence of the standard of care? *Health Matrix: Journal of Law and Medicine* 2000;10:67–117.

16. See, e.g., IOM, *Clinical Practice Guidelines: Directions for a New Program.* Washington, DC: National Academy Press, 1990.

17. *Shilkret v. Annapolis Emergency Hospital,* n.8, *supra; Darling v. Charleston Memorial Community Hospital,* 211 N.E.2d 253 (Ill., 1965) (a hospital may be found liable for

direct negligence where it failed to adequately exercise a reasonable standard of care in the management of patients; *Bauman v. United HealthCare*, 193 F.3d 151 (3d Cir., 1999); *cert. denied*, 120 S. Ct. 2143 (2000).

18. Rosenblatt R, Law S, and Rosenbaum S. *Law and the American Health Care System.* New York: Foundation Press, 1997; 2000–01 Supplement, Ch. 2(J).

19. *Id.*, Ch. 2B. For a case that illustrates traditional medical care dispute resolution relating to coverage see *Van Vector v. Blue Cross Association*, 365 N.E.2d 638 (Ill. App. Ct., 1977) (insurer breached the terms of its contract with the insured by exercising retrospective treatment decision-making powers that overrode the judgment of the treating clinician).

20. Rosenblatt et al., n.2, *supra*, Ch. 2(J).

21. *Id.*

22. *Id.* The legality under federal employee benefit law of managed care arrangements that use physician incentives was upheld by the United States Supreme Court in a case challenging the use of such arrangements as a breach of fiduciary duty under the Employee Retirement Income Security Act in *Pegram v. Herdrich*, 120 S. Ct. 2143 (2000).

23. Miller RH and Luft HS. Managed care plan performance since 1980: A literature analysis. *JAMA* 1994;271:1512.

24. See cases noted in Rosenblatt et al., n.2, *supra*, Ch. 3(I).

25. 965 F.2d 1321 (5th Cir., 1992); *cert. denied*, 506 U.S. 1033 (1993).

26. One of the most legally remarkable aspects of U.S. law in the area of insurer liability for negligent coverage decision-making concerns ERISA preemption of state law remedies for injuries caused by negligence related to coverage determinations. One of the most complex areas of federal civil law, ERISA and its sweeping preemption provisions prohibit the recovery of damages by persons who are injured by the negligent coverage decisions made by their employer-sponsored health plans. Modeled on trust law concepts, ERISA (whose principal purpose was protection of the nation's employer-sponsored pension system) itself provides no basis for the recovery of damages. Much has been written on the preemptive effects of ERISA in the area of personal injury law and the 106th Congress extensively debated (without resolution) the question of whether such preemption should be modified or rolled back entirely. Borzi P and Rosenbaum S. *An Analysis of the Senate and House Passed Managed Care Patient Protection Legislation.* Washington, DC: Kaiser Family Foundation, May 2000. *www.kff.org.* See generally Rosenblatt et al., n.2, *supra*, Ch. 2(C) and 3(I).

27. Eddy DM. Benefit language: Criteria that will improve quality while reducing costs. *JAMA* 1996;275:650–651.

28. 98 F.3d 149 (4th Cir., 1996).

29. 239 Cal. Rptr. 810 (Cal. App. 1986); petition for review dismissed, 741 P.2d 613 (Cal., 1987).

30. In *Wickline* the agency ultimately was found not liable for her injuries because the physician's acquiescence to the decision of the agency without protest was determined to be the cause of her injury.

31. Havighurst CC. Altering the applicable standard of care. *Law and Contemporary Problems* 1986;49:257–292. Havighurst CC. Prospective self denial: Can consumers contract today to accept health care rationing tomorrow? *U. Penn. Law Review* 1992;140:1755–1804. See Rosenblatt et al., n.2, *supra*, at 1000–1001.

32. *Jones v. Kodak.* 169 F.3d 1287 (10th Cir., 1999).

33. See n.17, *supra.*

34. See also *Moscovitch v. Danbury Hospital,* 25 F. Supp. 2d 74 (1998) (managed care organization potentially liable for the death of an individual who was allegedly prematurely discharged from an inpatient mental health facility under company practice guidelines).

35. In its study of practice guidelines, the Institute of Medicine has cautioned that guidelines are appropriate to guide treatment decisions, not to dictate them. IOM, *Clinical Practice Guidelines: Directions for a New Program.* Washington, DC: National Academy Press, 1990. P 2.

36. Pegram, n.22, *supra,* at 2165.

37. The exemption of health care quality cases from ERISA preemption was established in the landmark case of *Dukes v. U.S. HealthCare, Inc.,* 57 F.3d 350 (3d Cir., 1995); *cert. denied,* 116 S. Ct. 564 (1995). The liability of ERISA sponsored plans for injuries flowing from the exercise of medical judgment, whether in a context of coverage or quality, may have been further broadened by the Supreme Court's decision in *Pegram,* n.20, *supra.*

38. Finder, n.15, *supra.*

39. Dallek G and Pollitz K. *External review of health plan decisions: an update.* Washington, DC: Institute for Health Care Research and Policy, Georgetown University, May 2000.

40. H.R. 5628 (106th Cong., 2d Sess.).

41. ERISA §503 as added by H.R. 5628, Subtitle C.

42. *Id.*

43. *Id.*

44. Under current federal law related to employer-sponsored health plans, there is no external review system. Persons denied care must appeal directly from the health plan's determination to courts which in turn severely limit their scope of review to an "abuse of discretion" standard unless there is no evidence of an intent to delegate coverage decision-making discretion to the plan administrator or insurer. Courts may also use a less limited standard of review where there is evidence of conflict. *Firestone Tire and Rubber v. Bruch,* 489 U.S. 101 (1989); *Bedrick v. Travelers Insurance Co.,* n.28, *supra.*

45. Harvard University. *Patients, Doctors and Lawyers: Medical Injury, Malpractice Litigation, and Patient Compensation in New York.* Cambridge, MA: Harvard University Press, 1990.

46. Milliman and Robertson, Health Care Management Guidelines, Vol. 3: Ambulatory Care Guidelines, 1.1 (1995).

47. IOM, *supra,* at 10.

48. *Id.*

49. *Id.*

50. *Id.*

51. *Id.*

52. *Id.*

53. *Id.*

54. Rosenbaum et al., *supra,* n.1 at 230.

*Appendices*_____

Introduction

TEE L. GUIDOTTI

The three appendices that follow are case studies to illustrate the application of the evidence-based approach to scientific testimony. They are drawn from real life and are adapted from reports to workers' compensation agencies adjudicating difficult cases. Each addresses a problem in evaluating individual cases from group experience, and each rests on scientific rather than legal issues.

The three case studies are very different. Case Study 1, on chromium, is a relatively easy problem despite the technical content. The degree of technical detail in the report was required to address concerns raised by the claimants' representatives, but the issue on which the cases hinged was much simpler and more direct—Was there any significant exposure at all? It is very common in occupational disease claims to find that exposure assessment is the key to understanding the issues.

Case Study 2, on transformer fluids, is slightly more difficult. This case study involves an evaluation of the consistency and reliability of the literature on health risks associated with polychlorinated biphenyl compounds (PCBs). In reading this case study, it is useful to remember that whatever the gaps and uncertainties in the literature, there is a much greater body of scientific knowledge on PCBs than on most other potentially toxic exposures. In terms of the completeness of the scientific literature, this is almost as good as it gets. It is also useful to remember that this case study has no implications for the evaluation of the hazard presented by PCBs and the basis for remedial action to reduce human exposure. (PCBs are no longer manufactured. Control efforts are directed at destroying or preventing the release of stocks that have already been produced.) This case study only applies to the experience of a particular group of workers and the state of the art regarding PCB-associated risks that apply to their experience on a "more likely than not" basis.

Case Study 3 is a report intended to provide a scientific basis for the development of a compensation policy for asbestos-related cases. It is much more difficult than the first two case studies. Fortunately, the literature on asbestos is more complete than the literature on almost any other toxic exposure. To a greater degree than the literature on PCBs, this is truly as good as it gets. The technical issues and uncertainties, such as whether an elevation of lung cancer risk among asbestos-exposed workers is only associated with the presence of fibrosis, are unavoidable. Decisions must be made in real time; claims cannot be suspended awaiting further scientific evidence. For a public agency or insurance carrier working under the direction of public regulations and/or specific legislation, these decisions must be seen to be reasonable. A policy that is based on a minority scientific interpretation, an interpretation that appears arbitrary, or one that is likely to be invalidated by new information not only is indefensible but also is a threat to the credibility of the organization. As much as possible, reasonable policy decisions must be based on scientific consensus.

Case Study 1: Cancer Risk Associated with Chromium Exposure from Drinking Water

HAROLD E. HOFFMAN

This case study involves a superficially plausible association, inconsistencies in the literature, and a highly technical problem. In the end, the interpretation was very simple. The case dealt with the same issue as the popular movie *Erin Brockovitch* released in 2000. As in the movie, there was considerable confusion over the toxic substance in question, which is a form of chromium.

Problem

Several Canadian asbestos mine workers were diagnosed with cancer, including non-Hodgkin's lymphoma, prostate carcinoma, gastric adenocarcinoma, renal cell carcinoma, and carcinoma of the gastrointestinal tract.

The mine, located in Atlantic Canada, began production in 1963 and was decommissioned from 1981 to 1982 [1]. The principal concern was contamination by chromium in drinking water on the asbestos mine site because chromium was found in a concentration that exceeded the *Guidelines for Canadian Drinking Water Quality* [2]. Chromium is known to be a human carcinogen, and its association with lung cancer is well established.

Excessive chromium levels were found in drinking water at the site. From 1995 to 1997, chromium levels increased from 0.003 to 0.084 mg/liter (3–84 μg/liter), exceeding the recommended value of 0.05 mg/liter (50 μg/liter) for drinking water provided in the Canadian drinking water guidelines [2]. Chromium concentrations decreased with depth from a range of between 380 and 650 mg/kg at 2.5 cm to 160 mg/kg at 100 cm [1]. These concentrations are likely a reflection of the loading from industrial activity.

The concentration of chromium in the pond sediment was 398 mg/kg in

1981, which is within the range of chromium concentrations detected in the upper layers of the sediment in 1997, suggesting that there has been little sediment accumulation since the closing of the mine in 1981–1982 [1]. In addition, the pond water is also likely to contain higher concentrations of dissolved metals today than it did 40 years ago [1]. Drinking water was obtained from the pond on the site.

Issues

The following key issues were identified:

1. Does the scientific literature support an association between the diagnosis of carcinoma and ingestion of chromium at the level noted in the 1998 water sampling?
2. What are the other likely sources of chromium?
3. Is it possible that chromium could be ingested from other sources?
4. How much chromium must be ingested and what is the time frame before an association with carcinoma can be established?
5. What is the expected latency period before the onset of carcinoma?
6. What types of cancer, supported by scientific literature, are associated with the ingestion of chromium?
7. If there is a tenuous association with carcinoma, would the risk of cancer be increased if there were other causative factors involved, i.e., if a worker also was exposed to asbestos dust?
8. To what degree would the risk be increased?
9. Are there any tests to determine the levels of chromium ions in the bodies of living claimants?

Regulatory Guidelines for Chromium in Drinking Water

The Health Canada maximum acceptable concentration for chromium in drinking water is 50 μg/liter, or 0.05 mg/liter [2]. This is consistent with both international and American standards. The U.S. Food and Nutrition Board has recommended 50 to 200 μg/day of chromium as safe and adequate [3].

The U.S. Environmental Protection Agency (EPA) drinking water standard is 100 μg/liter (100 ppb), but in many states the standard is 50 μg/liter (50 ppb) [4]. Most other countries have set drinking water standards less than 50 μg/liter (50 ppb) [4].

The U.S. EPA has set drinking water standards as follows [5–7]:

Maximum contaminant level goals (MCLG): 0.1 mg/liter. MCLG is the maximum level of a contaminant in drinking water at which no known or anticipated adverse effect on the health effect of persons would occur and which allows for adequate margins of safety. MCLGs are nonenforceable public health goals [8].

Maximum contaminant level (MCL): 0.1 mg/liter. MCL is the maximum permissible level of a contaminant in water that is delivered to any user of a public water system. MCLs are enforceable standards. The margins of safety in MCLGs ensure that exceeding the MCL slightly does not pose significant risk to public health.

Health advisory level (HAL) (child): 1 to 10 days: 1 mg/liter; longer term: 0.2 mg/liter. Most countries have set drinking water standards that are usually less than 50 μg/liter (50 ppb) [4].

The World Health Organization (WHO) suggests a permissible level of chromium(VI) in drinking water of 40 μg/kg [9].

Chromium Compounds

Chromium generally is present in low concentrations in Canadian surface waters [2]. In the Great Lakes, chromium concentrations range from 0.0002 to 0.019 mg/liter, and chromium concentrations in Canadian rivers range from 0.002 to 0.023 mg/liter [2]. Canadian drinking water supplies have chromium concentrations from 0.014 to 0.009 mg/liter, with a median concentration of chromium of 0.002 mg/liter [2].

The carcinogenicity of chromium in solution is critically affected by the speciation by ion type, or redox state, which is also known as the *valence*. We have no record of the valence of chromium at the mine. It has not been standard practice to speciate metal ions, which means to determine their redox potential or valence, in occupational hygiene or environmental monitoring studies in the past, although this practice is now becoming widespread. However, this is so because the predominant species of various metals in water under various conditions is generally known. The valence state of chromium of greatest hazard to human health is hexavalent [also written as Cr(VI), or Cr^{6+}]. Chromium(VI) is almost solely a product of human activity; it rarely exists in nature. Trivalent chromium [Cr(III), or Cr^{3+}] is an essential nutrient of no known toxicity. Metallic chromium (Cr, or Cr^0) does not exist in solution; it is all ionized.

Chromium(III) is more likely to predominate in fresh water unless large amounts of chromium(VI) have been added [10]. Chromium exists in oxidation states from −2 to +6 valence. The most important stable states are 0 (elemental metal), +3 (trivalent), and +6 (hexavalent). Chromium(II) is an essential dietary mineral in low doses. Metallic chromium(0), divalent chromium(II), and trivalent chromium(III) are relatively nontoxic [11]. Chromium(VI) is classified by the U.S. EPA as an inhalation carcinogen [12].

Water-soluble chromium(III) compounds are nontoxic because they are not well absorbed into the body, and even if absorbed, they enter the cell poorly

[4]. However, water-soluble chromium(VI) compounds are extremely toxic because they resemble phosphate and are actively transported into all cells of the body in place of anions, such as phosphates [4]. Once inside the cell, chromium(VI) is reduced to reactive intermediates [chromium(V) and chromium(IV)] and stable chromium(III). Chromium(III) binds tightly to cellular ligands and is an important mediator of chromium(VI) toxicity and carcinogenesis, because all the chromium(VI) is eventually converted to chromium(III) in the cell [4]. In central Canada, surface water concentrations range from 0.2 to 44 µg/liter [13]. A survey of Canadian drinking water supplies gave an overall median level of chromium of 2 µg/liter, with a maximum of 14 µg/liter (raw water) and 9 µg/liter (treated water) [13].

In nature, chromium exists primarily in the trivalent state [14]. In a location where chromite ore was processed for 60 years, 2.6% of the soil chromium was chromium(VI) [14].

Chromium is found in nature only in the combined state and not as the element [15]. During chlorination of drinking water, chromium(III) may be oxidized to chromium(VI) [16].

Dietary Exposure to Chromium

Food is a major source of chromium intake [13]. Chromium(III) is an essential nutrient [4,17]. Chromium concentrations in foods include milk (0.06 mg/kg), meat (0.07 mg/kg), cereal (0.17 mg/kg), potatoes (0.05 mg/kg), fruits (0.06 mg/kg), and sugars (0.34 mg/kg). Commercial seafood contains 0.13 to 0.85 mg/kg. Wines available in Canada contain between 0.02 and 0.06 mg/liter chromium. Approximately 63% of chromium in foods is present in the hexavalent form. The total daily intake of chromium from water is about 10% of the total dietary intake [2].

People who drink high-chromium water (50 µg/liter) receive about half their chromium intake from food and half from drinking water [18]. People who drink water with average levels of chromium (5 µg/liter) receive about 91% of their chromium from food and 9% from water [18].

Toxicokinetics of Chromium Compounds

Toxicokinetics is the study of how compounds foreign to the body behave as they enter, pass through, and are transformed in the body's systems. The toxicokinetics of chromium compounds have been the subject of extensive investigation. Chromium(VI) accumulates in liver, kidney, and bone if the concentration of chromium(VI) in drinking water is in the range of 0.45 to 25 ppm [4]. Chromium(III) in drinking water results in substantially less chromium in liver, kidney, and bone. Thus the body burden of chromium(VI) is much more closely associated with cumulative intake than chromium(III).

Absorption

Chromium(III) compounds are poorly absorbed into the body regardless of the site of exposure [4]. Oral absorption of chromium(III) ranges from 1 to 3% [4].

Costa reported that chromium(VI) compounds are readily absorbed by inhalation and ingestion [4]. Water-soluble chromium(VI) compounds are better absorbed from the gastrointestinal tract than chromium(III) compounds [4]. As much as 10% of oral chromium(VI) is absorbed [4].

Several investigators have stated that human ingestion of soluble chromium(VI) in drinking water at levels of 1 to 10 ppm is safe because of the high capacity of the gastrointestinal tract to reduce chromium(VI) to chromium(III) [4]. However, a substantial amount of chromium(VI) was bioavailable following ingestion of drinking water [4]. Costa stated "the claim that chromium(VI) ingestion will not result in human absorption due to an efficient reduction to chromium(II) by stomach acid is not supported" [4]. Oral administration of chromium(III) will yield substantial levels of chromium(III) in tissues such as the lungs, spleen, and heart [4]. Rates of chromium uptake from the gastrointestinal tract are relatively low, with chromium(VI) being more readily absorbed than chromium(III) [16]. Less than 1% of inorganic chromium(III) and about 10% of inorganic chromium(VI) is absorbed from the gastrointestinal tract [16].

The recommended dietary intake of chromium(III) is 50 to 200 µg/day [17]. Estimates of dietary chromium(III) absorption range from 0.5 to 2.0% [18] to 0.1 to 3% [2]. About 2 to 10% of the hexavalent chromium ingested is absorbed [2]. Chromium(VI) compounds are reduced to chromium(III) compounds in the stomach, accounting for the relatively poor gastrointestinal absorption of orally administered chromium(VI) compounds. Gastric juice inhibits absorption of both trivalent and hexavalent inorganic chromium and partially reduces the hexavalent form to the trivalent form [2]. Under physiologic conditions, chromium(VI) is rapidly reduced to chromium(III) [19].

Human gastric juice is quite efficient in reducing chromium(VI) and in decreasing its mutagenicity [20]. The reducing capacity of the stomach is an important protective barrier against ingested chromium [20].

The Canadian Centre for Occupational Health and Safety considers metallic chromium practically nontoxic by ingestion and not absorbed into the body. Even if it is oxidized to chromium(III) by stomach acids, the process would be slow, and chromium(III) is poorly absorbed and not toxic.

Chromium(VI) compounds are reduced to chromium(III) before reaching the circulation [9]. Further reduction occurs in the blood [21]. Only 1 to 25% of a dose of chromium(III) is absorbed following ingestion [11]. Hexavalent salts are converted by gastric juices to the trivalent form prior to absorption [11]. The average uptake of chromium(VI) in a human study was 10.6% [22]. After absorption, chromium(III) does not readily cross cell membranes but binds to plasma proteins. Chromium(VI) after absorption is rapidly taken up by erythrocytes and reduced to chromium(III) inside the cell.

Finley et al. [12] found that humans who ingest chromium(VI) at concentrations of up to 10.0 mg chromium(VI) per liter absorb chromium(III) [rather than chromium(VI)] because of gastric reduction of the ingested chromium(VI). Therefore, they concluded that the drinking water standard of 0.1 mg chromium(VI) per liter is safe [12].

Kerger et al. [23] found that the upper gastrointestinal tract and the blood provide sufficient reducing potential to prevent any substantial systemic uptake of chromium(VI) following drinking water exposures at 5 to 10 mg chromium(VI) per liter. The gastrointestinal tract and blood are effective in reducing chromium(VI) to chromium(III) [23].

Kuykendall et al. [24] showed that oral chromium(VI) was reduced in the stomach and small intestine, followed by systemic uptake, distribution, and excretion as chromium(III). The lack of substantial chromium(VI) uptake into the bloodstream after ingestion of oral bolus doses at 10,000 μg chromium(VI) suggests that oral exposures in humans are not hazardous [24].

In drinking water, chromium(VI) in concentrations of 10 mg/liter or less is completely reduced to chromium(III) prior to systemic distribution [25].

Metabolism

Chromium(VI) compounds are subject to early metabolism prior to distribution in the circulation. Chromium(VI) is reduced intracellularly to chromium(III). Chromium(VI) readily passes through cellular membranes, but chromium(III) does not cross cellular membranes [22]. Therefore, when chromium(VI) enters cells, it is reduced to chromium(III) and does not readily diffuse out of the cell [22].

Distribution

Absorbed chromium (oxidation state unknown) is widely distributed throughout the body [22]. Chromium(VI) compounds easily cross cell membranes and exert a genotoxic effect [26,27]. The major sites of chromium accumulation, transported bound to the iron plasma protein transferrin, are the spleen, liver, and kidney [22,27]. Chromium(VI) is widely distributed [4]. Chromium(III) and chromium(VI) are mainly deposited in blood, liver, spleen, body soft tissues, and bone [27].

Excretion

Of the total dose of labeled chromium administered, 89.4% was excreted in the feces, and 2% was excreted in the urine [22].

Health Effects

Alexeeff et al. [22] could not establish a causal relationship between chromium exposures and nonrespiratory cancers in humans. Bednar and Kies [28] reported that drinking water in 453 Nebraska communities showed a mean chromium level of 0.002 mg/liter, with a range of less than 0.001 to 0.01 mg/liter. The maximum allowable level was 0.05 mg/liter. Chromium in drinking water did not appear to be associated with cancer deaths in Nebraska residents [28].

Bick et al. [29] studied a community where chromium(VI) from cooling water towers was dumped on the desert floor, flowing to an underground aquifer that served as the sole source of water for residents. Drinking water contained hexavalent chromium ranging from 0.5 to 25 mg/liter [29]. Two patients with Hodgkin's disease were presented. For patient 1, the exposure period was at least 16 years, and the time interval between initial exposure and diagnosis was 29 years. For patient 2, the exposure period was 23 years, and the time interval between initial exposure and diagnosis was 21 years. The authors reported the observed incidence to be 65 to 92 times the expected incidence [29]. "This may be a chance occurrence; however, clinicians should be aware of the potential association between chromium exposure and Hodgkin's lymphoma" [29]. Nevertheless, the limited number of cases weakens the study.

Furthermore, there were striking inconsistencies in the authors' report of conclusions drawn from medical literature and the actual source study itself. This is a lesson in caution in relying on conclusions based on one group's interpretation of another study.

The Canadian Centre for Occupational Health and Safety states that no adequate human or animal information is available regarding carcinogenicity [15]. The International Agency for Research on Cancer (IARC) considered the evidence for designating chromium(VI) as a cause of cancer at sites other than the lungs to be insufficient [13]. IARC's evaluation of carcinogenic risk is Group 3 (not classifiable) [15].

Cohen and Costa [30] reported that the levels of metals in water are several orders of magnitude lower than those encountered in occupational situations. No significant increases in carcinogenic health hazards were observed from exposure to chromium in water [30].

Costa concluded that chromium(VI) can be readily absorbed by ingestion and is a potential carcinogen [4]. "Exposure of humans to any amount of chromium(VI) (water soluble and insoluble) by inhalation, ingestion, and on the skin should always be avoided" [4].

De Flora et al. [20] hypothesized that the efficiency of chromium(VI) reduction in the stomach explains the very low toxicity and lack of oral carcinogenicity of chromium(VI) by ingestion. Later, these authors stated that reduction of chromium(VI) by saliva and gastric juice may explain a lack of oral carcinogenicity [26]. Further reduction of absorbed chromium(VI) occurs in the blood of the portal vein and the liver. Therefore, oral chromium(VI) is very unlikely to induce tumors [26].

Health Canada reported that "in humans, exposure to hexavalent chromium salts for periods of 2 to 26 years has been implicated as a cause of cancer of the digestive tract. . . . However, a recent report by the U.S. Environmental Protection Agency states [that] there are inadequate data to conclude that chromium is carcinogenic via ingestion" [2].

Jaworski [10] found no reports of cancer caused by ingested chromium(VI), probably because chromium(VI) is rapidly reduced to chromium(III) in acidic gastric juice [10]. Chromium(III) compounds appear not to be carcinogenic [10].

Kapil and Keogh, in an ATSDR report [16], concluded that no cancers, other than lung cancer, are associated with occupational chromium exposure. They stated that there was insufficient evidence to consider the nonrespiratory cancers to be of a causal nature.

The U.S. Department of Health and Human Services found no evidence of carcinogenicity in animal studies [17]. In a 1997 study by Zhang and Li, the department concluded that exposure to chromium(VI) was not responsible for cancers in the regions of study. The lack of dose-response relationship and the relatively short latency period did not support a relationship between cancer and chromium(VI) [31].

The U.S. EPA found insufficient data to perform a quantitative risk analysis for cancer following oral exposure to chromium [18]. The risk of cancer following ingestion of chromium in drinking water at 100 μg/liter appears to be negligible [18]. Furthermore, the EPA in *Current Drinking Water Standards* described potential health effects from ingestion of water with chromium to be allergic dermatitis but did not mention cancer [8].

Conclusion

Oral chromium(III) is nontoxic and noncarcinogenic to humans. The scientific consensus is that ingested chromium(VI) is poorly absorbed from the gastrointestinal tract. Although Costa considered chromium(VI) to be readily absorbed by ingestion, other researchers did not support this finding. No evidence of human cancer from oral exposure to chromium was found in the scientific literature.

The specific answers to questions in the inquiry were as follows:

1. Does the literature support a relationship between the diagnosis of carcinoma and ingestion of chromium at the level noted for 1998 water sampling?
   The scientific literature does not support a relationship between carcinoma and ingestion of chromium at any level. The levels reported in the most recent water sampling are not of concern. The existing water quality in the pond on the site from which drinking water was obtained is considered a worst-case scenario for historical water quality. The maximum recently measured drinking water total chromium (III and VI) concentration was 85 μg/liter (0.084 mg/liter). In fresh water, chromium(III) usually predominates over chromium(VI). Therefore, the chromium(VI) component would be substantially less than 85 μg/liter, so the chromium(VI) levels likely would not be above the recommended levels.

2. What are the other likely sources of chromium?
   Food is a major source of chromium intake. At least half the chromium intake is from food, as described earlier.

3. Is it possible that chromium could be ingested from other sources?
   The major sources of ingested chromium are food and drinking water.

4. How much chromium must be ingested and over what time frame before an association with carcinoma can be established?
   There is no evidence that any amount of ingested chromium can cause cancer.

5. What is the expected latency period before the onset of carcinoma?
   Because there is no evidence that oral (ingested) chromium causes cancer, the question of latency does not apply.

6. What types of cancer, supported by scientific literature, are associated with the ingestion of chromium?
   No cancers are related to the ingestion of chromium.

7. If there is a tenuous association with carcinoma, would the risk of cancer be increased if there were other causative factors involved, i.e., if a worker also was exposed to asbestos?
   The ingestion of chromium does not make humans more susceptible to cancers caused by other agents. The exposure to carcinogens (not oral chromium) does not make humans more susceptible to develop cancer from chromium.

8. To what degree would the risk be increased?
   The risk of cancer is not increased from ingestion of chromium.

9. Are there any tests to determine the levels of chromium in the bodies of living claimants?

Because chromium cannot be considered the cause of these cancers, there is no reason to test for chromium. Chromium(VI) is rapidly converted into chromium(III) in the stomach as well as in the blood. Therefore, any body fluid measurements would describe chromium(III) levels. This chromium(III) level would be irrelevant because chromium(III) is not carcinogenic.

References

1. Fracflow Consultants. Geochemical investigation into historic water quality of the pond on site from which drinking water was obtained at Advocate mine. Report to Worker's Compensation Commission of Newfoundland and Labrador, June 1998.

2. Health Canada. *Guidelines for Canadian Drinking Water Quality.* January 1979, updated September 1986.

3. Canadian Centre for Occupational Health and Safety. Chromium. *Cheminfo* 1998; 98-3 (Cheminfo Record Number 910).

4. Costa M. Toxicity and carcinogenicity of Cr(VI) in animal models and humans. *Crit Rev Toxicol* 1997;27(5):431–442.

5. U.S. Environmental Protection Agency. *Drinking Water and Health Contaminant Specific Fact Sheets for Consumers.* Washington, DC: EPA Office of Ground Water and Drinking Water, 1998.

6. U.S. Environmental Protection Agency. *Drinking Water Regulations and Health Advisories.* Washington, DC: Office of Water, EPA-822-B-96-002, October 1996.

7. U.S. Environmental Protection Agency. *Technical Drinking Water and Health Contaminant Specific Fact Sheets.* Washington, DC: EPA Office of Ground Water and Drinking Water, 1998.

8. U.S. Environmental Protection Agency. *Current Drinking Water Standards.* Washington, DC: EPA Office of Ground Water and Drinking Water, 1999.

9. Leonard A, Lauwerys RR. Carcinogenicity and mutagenicity of chromium. *Mutat Res* 1980;76:227–239.

10. Jaworski JF. *Environmental and Nutritional Effects of Chromium: Chromium Update 1984.* National Research Council of Canada, Subcommittee on Heavy Metals and Certain Other Elements, 1984.

11. Geller RJ. Chromium. In: Sullivan JB, Krieger GR (eds). *Hazardous Materials Toxicology: Clinical Principles of Environmental Health.* Baltimore: Williams & Wilkins, 1992. Pp 891–895.

12. Finley BL, Kerger BD, Katona MW, et al. Human ingestion of chromium(VI) in drinking water: Pharmacokinetics following repeated exposure. *Toxicol Appl Pharmacol* 1997;142:151–159.

13. World Health Organization. *Guidelines for Drinking Water Quality,* Vol. 2: *Health Criteria and Other Supporting Information.* Geneva: WHO, 1993. P 11.

14. Von Burg R, Liu D. Chromium and hexavalent chromium: Toxicology update. *J Appl Toxicol* 1993;13(3):225–230.

15. Canadian Centre for Occupational Health and Safety. Chromium. *Cheminfo* 1998; 98-4 (Cheminfo Record Number 547).

16. Kapil V, Keogh J. Chromium toxicity. In: *ATSDR Case Studies in Environmental Medicine.* Washington: U.S. Department of Health & Human Services, June 1990.

17. U.S. Department of Health & Human Services. *Draft Toxicological Profile for Chromium (Update).* Washington, DC: DHHS, August 1998.

18. U.S. Environmental Protection Agency. *The Drinking Water Criteria Document on Chromium.* Document TR-1242-64A. Washington, DC: U.S. EPA, December 20, 1990.

19. Herold DA, Fitzgerald RL. Chromium. In: Seiler HG, Sigel A, Sigel H (eds). *Handbook on Metals in Clinical and Analytical Chemistry.* New York: Marcel Dekker, 1994. Pp 321–329.

20. De Flora S, Badolati GS, Serra D, et al. Circadian reduction of chromium in the gastric environment. *Mutat Res* 1987;192:169–174.

21. Lukanova A, Toniolo P, Zhitkovich A, et al. Occupational exposure to Cr(VI): comparison between chromium levels in lymphocytes, erythrocytes, and urine. *Int Arch Occup Environ Health* 1996;69:39–44.

22. Alexeeff GV, Pinter SP, Zeise L. Chromium carcinogenicity: California strategies. *Science of the Total Environment* 1989;86:159–168.

23. Kerger DB, Finley BL, Corbett GE, et al. Ingestion of chromium(VI) in drinking water by human volunteers: Absorption, distribution, and excretion of single and repeated doses. *J Toxicol Environ Health* 1997;50:67–95.

24. Kuykendall JR, Kerger BD, Jarvi EJ, et al. Measurement of DNA-protein crosslinks in human leukocytes following acute ingestion of chromium in drinking water. *Carcinogenesis* 1996;17(9):1971–1997.

25. Paustenbach DJ, Hays SM, Brien BA, et al. Observation of steady state in blood and urine following human ingestion of hexavalent chromium in drinking water. *J Toxicol Environ Health* 1996;49:453–461.

26. De Flora S, Serra D, Camoirano A, Zanacchi P. Metabolic reduction of chromium, as related to its carcinogenic properties. *Biol Trace Element Res* 1989;21:179–187.

27. Nieboer E, Yassi A, Haines AT, Jusys AA. *Effects of Chromium Compounds on Human Health.* Ontario: Ministry of Labour, December 1, 1984.

28. Bednar CM, Kies C. Inorganic contaminants in drinking water correlated with disease occurrence in Nebraska. *Water Resources Bulletin* 1991;27(4):631–635.

29. Bick RL, Girardi TV, Lack WJ, et al. Hodgkin's disease in association with hexavalent chromium exposure. *Int J Hematol* 1996;64:257–262.

30. Cohen MD, Costa M. Chromium compounds. In: Rom WM (ed). *Environmental and Occupational Medicine,* 3d ed. Philadelphia: Lippincott-Raven, 1998.

31. Zhang JD, Li SK. Cancer mortality in a Chinese population exposed to hexavalent chromium in water. *J Occup Environ Med* 1997;39(4):315–319.

Case Study 2:
Risk Associated with Exposure to Transformer Fluids

HAROLD E. HOFFMAN

This case study assesses a group of claims with a common exposure history. Because the principal constituents of transformer fluids are suspected carcinogens, there was a superficial plausibility in the association. Evaluation of the epidemiologic and toxicologic evidence leads to a clear result.

Essential Issues

A workers' compensation commission requested an evaluation of the scientific literature for evidence of a causal relationship between occupational exposures to electrical transformer fluids and development of cancer. Electrical workers, among others, had suffered carcinomas of the pancreas, esophagus, stomach, colon, bladder, prostrate, lung, and bronchi, as well as acute myelogenous leukemia and non-Hodgkin's lymphoma.

Potential for Exposure

Occupational exposures to transformer fluids may occur due to leaks, maintenance, recycling, removal of fluids, fire, sampling, testing of fluids, and adding fluids. Electrical workers, power line repairers, and hazardous waste workers may be exposed. Compliance with protective equipment was not optimal in the power industry in the past, although it has improved greatly in recent years [1].

Transformer Fluids

The constituents of electrical transformer fluids that are suspected of causing cancer are polychlorinated biphenyls (PCBs), a large and diverse family of 209 chemicals, of which approximately 20 are present in various mixtures in any one formulation of electrical transformer fluids. Most transformer fluids that contained PCBs were formulated with relatively low chlorination percentages (as expressed by Arachlor numbers), and the compounds tend to be less carcinogenic than PCBs with higher chlorination levels [2]. (For example Arachlor 1242 is a mixture of PCBs containing 42% chlorine by weight. It is less toxic and is presumed to be less carcinogenic than Arachlor 1254, which is 54% chlorine. Both are common transformer fluids.) Other constituents of transformer fluids have not been implicated as carcinogens.

Electrical transformers and capacitors require askarels, which are electrical insulating (dielectric) fluids. Askarels are blends of PCBs and solvents and contain 40 to 70% PCBs in solvents such as trichlorobenzene and tetrachlorobenzene. Some fluids contained only 10% PCBs. PCBs were used in askarels because of their electrical insulation (high dielectric constant), thermal insulation, thermal stability, flame resistance, noncorrosiveness, and ease of manufacture. Askarels do not produce explosive gases in electric arcing.

PCBs were used in electrical equipment where fire would be disastrous. By 1976, PCBs were in 5% of transformers and 95% of capacitors produced in the United States [3,4]. Now, fewer than 5% of transformers have PCBs. Although all electrical transformers and capacitors are closed systems, fluctuations in temperature stress them and cause leaks.

PCBs were produced in the United States from 1929 to 1977 [3,4]. Although PCB production was banned in 1979 due to potential health risks, many older electrical devices continue to contain PCBs. In other devices, there may be residues of PCB-contaminated mineral oil that was used as replacement fluid.

PCBs were substituted with mineral oil in the following manner: (1) replacement of a complete transformer or capacitor, (2) leaving the PCB-filled equipment in service until replacement was required, and (3) draining the PCB and replacing with non-PCB fluid. PCB-filled transformers were refilled with mineral oil and either dibutylphenol or dibutylparaeresol.

Contaminants in the electrical device fluids include degradation products from heated PCBs [1]. At high temperatures, PCBs degrade to polychlorinated dibenzofurans (PCDFs), polychlorinated dibenzodioxins (PCCDs), and polychlorinated quarterphenyls (PCQ) [1,4]. These compounds are recognized to have carcinogenic activity, and the potential carcinogenicity of PCBs as a class is complicated by the presence of these hazardous contaminants. Their effects cannot be easily isolated from those of the parent PCBs. However, populations at risk would have been exposed to the mixtures as a whole, so there is little need to attempt to assess the risks independently.

Overview of PCBs

PCBs are chlorinated biphenyl compounds. There are 209 different PCB compounds (congeners) with from 1 to 10 chlorine atoms attached to a biphenyl

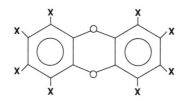

polychlorinated biphenyl

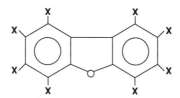

**polychlorinated
dibenzodioxins (dioxins)**

**polychlorinated
dibenzodifurans (furans)**

Figure A2-1   X = potential attachment site of a chlorine atom.

molecule. PCBs are mixtures of many isomers and compounds. Mixtures contain an average of three atoms of chlorine per molecule (42% chlorine) to five atoms of chlorine per molecule (54% chlorine). PCBs of 42 and 54% chlorine (Arachlor 1242 and 1254) were found commonly in insulating liquids in electrical capacitors and transformers (Fig. A2-1).

PCBs are readily absorbed through the respiratory tract, gastrointestinal tract, and skin and are stable, fat-soluble, and poorly excreted [5]. Occupational exposure is primarily through the skin and by inhalation.

PCBs are metabolized in the liver. Highly chlorinated isomers are more resistant to metabolism, enabling them to persist longer [5]. Stearic effects around the central carbon–carbon bond affect activity as a xenoestrogen or estrogen receptor inhibitor.

PCBs distribute to fatty tissue because of their lipophilic nature, and more than 90% of the general population have detectable levels of PCBs in adipose tissue [2]. Fat levels of PCBs are 300 to 400 times higher than serum levels

[2]. Transplacental distribution also occurs, and metabolites of PCBs are excreted into bile, feces, and breast milk. Urinary excretion is low [5].

Review of Epidemiologic Studies

The first group of studies showed evidence for various associations, some of which were of concern in this group of workers. Bertazzi et al. [6], in an historical cohort mortality study, found a total of 14 neoplasms in their group of PCB-exposed workers, including stomach, pancreas, liver, biliary tract, hematologic system, and lung. A causal association was not established because of the small number of cases (Table A2-1). The cases reported by Bertazzi et al. [6] often have implausibly short lengths of exposures (lung cancer after 0.1 and 0.5 years of exposure, liver cancer after 0.3 years of exposure, stomach cancer after 0.5 years of exposure, Hodgkin's disease after 0.2 years of exposure).

Brown and Jones [7], in an historical cohort mortality study, observed a small number of deaths with inconclusive results. In a 1987 update, evidence suggested that occupational exposure to PCBs might be associated with an excess risk of mortality from cancer of the liver, gallbladder, and biliary tract [8]. The study was limited by (1) possible misclassification, (2) cancer types different from those found in animals exposed to PCB, and (3) the pattern of risk by latency and duration of employment not consistent with that of an occupational carcinogen.

Gustavsson et al. [9] conducted a historical cohort mortality study and found that the total deaths, total cancer deaths, and incident cancer cases were not significantly elevated. In 1997, Gustavsson and Hogstedt [10] conducted a follow-up study; deaths and cancers corresponded closely to those expected. The study was small but well designed.

Loomis [11] conducted an historical cohort mortality study with 138,905

Table A2-1. Bertazzi et al. 1987 Study

Cancer Type	National References		Local	
	SMR	CI	SMR	CI
Malignant tumors				
Male	253	144–415	274	104–300
Female	156	—	226	123–385
GI tract				
Male	346	141–721	274	112–572
Lung				
Male	250	—	187	—
Hematologic				
Male	375	—	263	—
Female	266	—	377	115–877

men. The companies in the study did not have historical records of PCB exposures that were documented; therefore, an expert panel estimated exposures. Mortality from malignant melanoma of the skin was increased among men with the longest employment in jobs potentially exposed to PCB insulating fluids and increased with cumulative exposure to PCB insulating fluids. Limitations of the study included limited exposure assessments, worker use of personal protective equipment, inability to separate effects of pure PCBs from other constituents of dielectric fluids, lack of information on concentration or chemistry of exposures, and sunlight exposure.

Sinks et al. [12] conducted an historical cohort study. A significant increase was seen in malignant melanomas (SMR 4.1; CI 1.8–8.0). The National Institute for Occupational Health and Safety (NIOSH) concluded that workers at this plant were at excess risk of malignant melanoma [13]. Exposures to ultraviolet radiation and photosensitizing agents were likely confounding factors.

The next studies were more problematic.

Emmett et al. (part I) [14], in a cross-sectional study, found no cancer except for two exposed workers with melanoma. The temporal relationship between the exposure and the melanoma was not specified. Goldsmith and Guidotti [15], in a geographic mortality analysis, concluded that some excess risk may occur in electrical workers exposed to soldering fumes, nonionic radiation, and PCBs in transformers.

Greenland et al. [16] conducted a case-control study with poor employment records and poor exposure assessments. Study power was limited, and several biases may have affected the results. The only positive association was between resins and lung cancer, which may have been due to confounding by asbestos.

Hay and Tarrel [17] conducted an historical cohort study of workers exposed to phenoxy herbicides and PCBs in sprayed waste transformer oil. There were too few deaths from malignancy to permit analysis. Hunter et al. [18], in a case-control study, measured PCBs in cancer patients and controls. The study had 240 cases of breast cancer from a population of 32,826 women. The authors did not observe an increased risk of breast cancer with relatively high levels of plasma 1,1-dichloro-2,2-bis(p-chlorophenyl)ethylene and PCBs.

Rothman [19] conducted a nested case-control study. Serum concentrations of PCB were strongly associated with risk of non-Hodgkin's lymphoma. The findings are considered hypotheses-generating. Hsieh et al. [20] did a cohort study of ingestion of rice oil with polychlorinated derivatives including PCBs. The standardized mortality ratio (SMR) for Hodgkin's disease was elevated. The dose of ingested PCBs is much higher than likely to be accounted for by workplace exposure.

Yassi et al. [21] conducted an historical cohort mortality study on transformer workers in Winnepeg (study has been critiqued by Wong [22]). Standardized mortality ratios for digestive and pancreatic cancers were higher in the factory departments where transformers were assembled than in factory departments where the exposures were thought to be lower [3].

Hoffmann [23], in a literature review, considered organochlorines including PCBs to be a risk factor for non-Hodgkin's lymphoma. Exposure assessments were very limited. All organochlorine exposures were reviewed rather than focusing on PCB or transformer fluid exposures.

One study [24] yielded a relative risk for bladder cancer in electricians at electrical power stations that was elevated but did not achieve statistical significance (RR 1.3, 95% CI 1.0–1.8).

Summary of Literature Reviews

The first group of studies reviewed represent a high level of evidence, with authoritative review or reasonably definitive studies of demonstrably high quality. The International Agency for Research on Cancer (IARC) has determined that PCBs are probably carcinogenic to humans (Group 2A) [25,26]. This assessment is based on limited evidence of cancer in humans (mostly liver, but some evidence for other sites as well) and sufficient evidence of carcinogenicity to experimental animals. Because the numbers were small, dose-response relationships could not be evaluated, and the role of compounds other than PCBs could not be excluded, therefore the evidence was considered to be limited. Based on cancer bioassays in animals, the U.S. Department of Health and Human Services has determined that PCBs reasonably may be anticipated to be human carcinogens [3]. Moreover, the Environmental Protection Agency (EPA) also determined that PCBs are probable human carcinogens [3].

Studies of PCB-exposed workers conducted prior to 1995 provided inconclusive or no evidence regarding carcinogenicity in humans following inhalation, oral, or dermal exposures regarding carcinogenicity in humans following exposure to PCB [3,27]. Kimbrough [28] did not find consistent data regarding the increase in overall mortality or in specific cancer mortality of workers exposed to PCBs.

Most of the studies reviewed by Silberhorn et al. [29] were inconclusive because they lacked statistical power. However, studies of Yusho victims suggest that exposure to PCBs may result in an increased risk of hepatocellular carcinoma. Based on these studies and studies of carcinogenicity in animals, Silberhorn et al. concluded that PCBs are likely to be human carcinogens.

Wong [22] found a lack of consistency between previous studies and the absence of an exposure-response relationship. These results argue against a causal association between PCB exposure and liver and gallbladder cancer. A review by James et al. [30] found no cancer risk associated with exposure to PCBs.

Applying the method of meta-analysis to four historical cohort studies, the Industrial Disease Standards Panel of the Ontario (Canada) Ministry of Labour [31] found a probable connection between occupational exposure to PCBs and cancers of the liver, biliary tract, and gallbladder. Evidence from animal studies was included in the evaluation. Of the original studies, only one study reported a significant increase in liver and gallbladder cancer. Wong [22] and the authors of this study argued against an association. Steineck et al. [32] reviewed a single study on PCB and cancer.

Interpretation

Although animal studies show potential carcinogenic risk from chronic PCB exposure, human studies are inconclusive [1]. PCBs are, however, usually considered probable human carcinogens [5]. Workers exposed to PCBs demonstrate a suggestion of increased risk of pancreatic cancer, cancer of the brain, and malignant melanoma. Other studies have found no evidence of excess cancer risk associated with PCB exposure [5].

Some evidence exists for an association between brain cancers and melanoma and exposure to PCBs [33]. A cluster suggested the possibility of a relationship between PCB exposures and kidney cancer in utility workers [33]. No increased risk of breast or endometrial cancer has been observed in humans [5]. There is no suggestion in the literature of a cancer risk arising from exposure to non-PCB-containing transformer fluids.

Consistency and Specificity of the Association

The traditional Hill criteria (see Chap. 5) for establishment of a causal relationship are not conclusive regarding PCB exposure and cancer [34]. Consistency of findings is not present. Specificity of types of disease with specific exposures is not present. The only Hill criterion satisfied by the existing data is temporality.

Conclusion

There was no convincing pattern of mortality associated with exposure to PCBs (and by extension to electrical transformer fluids) for any of the cancers of concern [i.e., pancreas, esophagus, stomach, colon, bladder, prostrate, lung, acute myelogenous leukemia (AML) or non-Hodgkin's lymphoma (NHL)]. The evidence is insufficient to conclude that there is an association between exposure to PCBs (and by extension to transformer fluids) and these specific cancers. Only melanoma, an improbable association most likely confounded by ultraviolet radiation exposure during outdoor work on capacitors, is consistently elevated. This cancer may be work-related in outdoor workers quite apart from PCB exposure.

Although data from Bertazzi [6] are strongest, the findings are not strongly suggestive when aggregated categories, such as gastrointestinal cancers, are broken down. The authors state that "no clear-cut and definite conclusion regarding the association between cancer of the gastrointestinal (GI) tract and exposure to PCBs can be drawn from the results of the study. There is no consistent trend visible to us that would lead to a conclusion of association" [6].

Several of the studies, including that of Bertazzi, have had sufficient power to address the issue of consistency. Even the Industrial Disease Standards Panel, which conducted a meta-analysis for selected cancers (e.g., hepatic, biliary tree, and gallbladder), did not conclude that there was an association for the nine cancers of concern.

In conclusion, there is no compelling evidence for an association between PCB exposure or other constituents of transformer fluids and cancers of the pancreas, esophagus, stomach, colon, bladder, prostate, lung, AML, or NHL. The various data that now exist do not suggest an association that is consistent, specific, or strong enough in any of these site-specific cancers to warrant a presumption of relationship to work. Therefore, at present, there is no corroborated evidence in the literature that would support the conclusion that exposure to electrical transformer fluids is associated with an elevated risk of these cancers.

Table A2-2 beginning on p. 391 lists additional references on PCBs besides the ones cited in this appendix.

References

1. Calise A, Shih RD. Electricians. In: Greenberg MI (ed). *Occupational, Industrial, and Environmental Toxicology.* St. Louis: Mosby, 1997. Chap. 11, pp 83–97.

2. Rom WN. *Environmental and Occupational Medicine,* 2d ed. Boston: Little, Brown, 1992.

3. Agency for Toxic Substances and Disease Registry. *Toxicological Profile for Polychlorinated Biphenyls.* Washington, DC: U.S. Department of Health and Human Services, Public Health Service, September 1997.

4. Safe S, Hutzinger O. PCDDs and PCDFs: Sources and environmental impact. In: Safe S, Hutzinger O (eds). *Environmental Toxin Series 3.* Berlin: Springer-Verlag, 1990. Pp 1–20.

5. La Dou J. *Occupational and Environmental Medicine,* 2d ed. Stanford, CT: Appleton & Lange, 1997. Pp 464–466.

6. Bertazzi PA. Cancer mortality of capacitor manufacturing workers. *Am J Indust Med* 1987;11:165–176.

7. Brown DP, Jones M. Mortality and industrial hygiene study of workers exposed to polychlorinated biphenyls. *Arch Environ Health* 1981;36(3):120–129.

8. Brown DP. Mortality of workers exposed to polychlorinated biphenyls: An update. *Arch Environ Health* 1987;42(6):334–339.

9. Gustavsson P, Hogstedt C, Rappe C. Short-term mortality and cancer incidence in

capacitor manufacturing workers exposed to polychlorinated biphenyls (PCBs). *Am J Indust Med* 1986;10:341–344.

10. Gustavsson P, Hogstedt C. A cohort study of Swedish capacitor manufacturing workers exposed to polychlorinated biphenyls (PCBs). *Am J Indust Med* 1997;32: 24–239.

11. Loomis D. Cancer mortality among electric utility workers exposed to polychlorinated biphenyls. *Occup Environ Med* 1997;54:720–728.

12. Sinks T, et al. Mortality among workers exposed to polychlorinated biphenyls. *Am J Epidemiol* 1992;136(4):389–398.

13. Sinks T, et al. *Health Hazard Evaluation Report.* Bloomington, IN: Westinghouse Electric Corporation, Indiana State Board of Health, NIOSH, HETA 89-116-2094, January 1991. Pp 1–27.

14. Emmett EA, et al. Studies of transformer repair workers exposed to PCBs: I. Study design, PCB concentrations, questionnaire, and clinical examination results. *Am J Indust Med* 1988;13:415–427.

15. Goldsmith JR, Guidotti TL. Environmental factors in the epidemiology of lymphosarcoma. *Pathol Ann* 1977;2(pt 2):411–425.

16. Greenland S, et al. A case-control study of cancer mortality at a transformer-assembly facility. *Int Arch Occup Environ Health* 1994;66:49–54.

17. Hay A, Tarrel J. Mortality of power workers exposed to phenoxy herbicides and polychlorinated biphenyls in waste transformer oil. *Ann NY Acad Sci* 1997;837:138–156.

18. Hunter DJ, et al. Plasma organochlorine levels and the risk of breast cancer. *New Engl J Med* 1997;337(18):1253–1258.

19. Rothman N. A nested case-control study of a non-Hodgkin's lymphoma and serum organochlorine residues. *Lancet* 1997;350:240–244.

20. Hsieh SF, et al. A cohort study on mortality and exposure to polychlorinated biphenyls. *Arch Environ Health* 1996;51(6):417–424.

21. Yassi A. Cancer mortality in workers employed at a transformer manufacturing plant. *Am J Indust Med* 1994;25:425–437.

22. Wong O. Pancreatic cancer in workers at a transformer manufacturing plant. *Am J Indust Med* 1995;27:905–910.

23. Hoffmann W. Organochlorine compounds: Risk of non-Hodgkin's lymphoma and breast cancer? *Arch Environ Health* 1996;51(3):189–192.

24. Steineck G. Industry related urothelial carcinogens: Application of a job exposure matrix to census data. *Am J Indust Med* 1989;16:209–224.

25. Agency for Toxic Substances and Disease Registry. *Public Health Statement on PCBs.* Washington, DC: U.S. Department of Health and Human Services, Public Health Service, June 1989.

26. IARC. *IARC Monographs on the Evaluation of the Carcinogenic Risks to Humans: An Updating of IARC Monographs,* Vols. 1 to 42. Lyon, France: Supplement International Agency for Research on Cancer, 1987.

27. Agency for Toxic Substances and Disease Registry. *Tox FAQs Polychlorinated Biphenyls (PCBs).* Washington, DC: U.S. Department of Health and Human Services, Public Health Service, September 1997.

28. Kimbrough RD. Polychlorinated biphenyls (PCBs) and human health: An update. *Crit Rev Toxicol* 1995;25(2):133–163.

29. Silberhorn EM, Glauert HP, Robertson LW. Carcinogenicity of polyhalogenated biphenyls: PCBs and PABs. *Crit Rev Toxicol* 1992;20(6):440–496.

30. James RC, Busch H, Tanburro CH, et al. Polychlorinated biphenyl exposure and human disease. *J Occup Med* 1993;35(2):136–148.

31. Industrial Disease Standards Panel (Government of Ontario). *Report to the Workers' Compensation Board on Occupational Exposure to PCBs and Various Cancers*. Toronto, Ontario: IDSP, December 1987.

32. Steineck G, Plato N, Alfredsson L, Norell SE. Urothelial cancer and some industry-related chemicals: An evaluation of the epidemiologic literature. *Am J Indust Med* 1990;17:371–391.

33. Rosenstock L, Cullen MR. *Textbook of Clinical Occupational and Environmental Medicine*. Philadelphia: WB Saunders, 1994.

34. Hill AB. The environment and disease: Association or causation? *Proc R Soc Med* 1965;58:295–300. As reported in Greenland S (ed). *Evolution of Epidemiologic Ideas: Annotated Readings on Concepts and Methods*. Chestnut Hill, MA: Epidemiology Resources, Inc., 1987.

Bibliography

Boffetta P, Kogevinas M, Simonato L, et al. Current perspectives on occupational cancer risks. *Int J Occup Environ Health* 1995;1(4):1–11.

Case RA. Some environmental carcinogens. *Proc R Soc Med* 1969;62:1061–1066.

Cogliano VJ. Assessing the cancer risk from environmental PCBs. *Environ Health Perspect* 1998;106(6):317–323.

Committee on the Assessment of Polychlorinated Biphenyls in the Environment. *Polychlorinated Biphenyls, Chemical and Toxicity Data as Required by FIFRA and TSCA Guidelines* (Appendix D). Washington, DC: National Academy of Science, 1974. Pp 143–169.

Emmett EA, Maroni M, Jefferys J, et al. Studies of transformer repair workers exposed to PCBs: II. Results of clinical laboratory investigations. *Am J Indust Med* 1988;14:47–62.

Eschenroeder AQ, Doyle C, Faever EJ. Health risks of PSC spills from electrical equipment. *Risk Analysis* 1986;6(2):213–221.

Hansen LG. Stepping backward to improve assessment of PCB congener toxicities. *Environ Health Perspect* 1998;106(suppl 1):171–189.

Monsanto Material Safety Data Sheet on Polychlorinated Biphenyls. Monsanto Company, St. Louis, 1988.

Rosenman KD. Dioxin, polychlorinated biphenyls and dibenzofurans. In WN Rom (ed). *Environmental and Occupational Medicine*, (2d ed). Boston: Little, Brown, 1992. Pp 927–933.

U.S. Environmental Protection Agency. PCBs: *Cancer Dose-Response Assessment and Application to Environmental Mixtures*. Washington, DC: National Center for Environmental Assessment, EPA/600/p-96/001F, September 1996.

Table A2-2. Additional References on PCBs (October 1, 1998)

Author	Article	Journal	Paper Type	Comments	Conclusion
ATSDR	Toxicological Profile for PCBs	U.S. DHHS 1997	Review	Studies of PCB-exposed workers have not provided consistent information regarding an increase in overall mortality or in specific cancer mortality attributable to PCBs.	Inconclusive
ATSDR	PCBs: Public Health Statement	June 1989	ATSDR statement	PCBs reasonably may be anticipated to be carcinogens. "Other studies of people with occupational exposure suggest that PCBs might cause liver cancer." "While the role of PCBs in producing cancer . . . in humans cannot be clearly delineated, the suggestive evidence proves an additional basis for public health concern about humans who may be exposed to PCBs."	Inconclusive
ATSDR	ToxFAQs: Polychlorinated Biphenyls	September 1997	ATSDR fact sheet	The Department of Health and Human Services (DHHS) has determined that PCBs reasonably may be anticipated to be carcinogens.	Inconclusive
Bertazzi PA	Cancer Mortality	*Am J Indust Med* 1987; 11:165–176	Cohort	Suggestion of an increase in cancer of GI and lymphoid tissues but was *not* statistically significant.	No increase in cancer
Boffeta P	Current Perspectives	*Int J Occup Environ Health* 1995;1(4)	Review	Group 2A: Probably carcinogenic to humans. Liver, bile ducts, leukemia, lymphoma.	Probably carcinogenic
Brown DP	Mortality of Workers Exposed to PCBs	*Arch Environ Health* 1987;42(6)	Cohort	This study provides limited information indicating that occupational exposure to PCBs may be associated with an excess risk of mortality from cancer of the liver, gallbladder, and biliary tract.	Inconclusive
Brown DP	Mortality and Industrial Hygiene Study of Workers Exposed to PCBs	*Arch Environ Health* 1981;36(32)	Cohort	Small number of deaths. Among the cancer causes, there was increased cancer of the liver and rectum. However, the findings for liver cancer do not reflect a relationship with latency.	Inconclusive

(continued)

Table A2-2. Continued

Author	Article	Journal	Paper Type	Comments	Conclusion
Calise A	Occupational Industrial and Environmental Toxicology	Greenberg MI. *Occupational Industrial and Environmental Toxicology,* 1997	Textbook	Animal studies show potential carcinogenic risk from chronic PCB exposure, but human studies are inconclusive. PCBs are considered probable human carcinogens.	Inconclusive; probable human carcinogens
Emmett EA	Studies of Transformer Repair Workers exposed to PCBs, Part I	*Am J Indust Med* 1988;13:415–427	Cross-sectional	For transformer use, the Aroclors were usually combined with trichlorobenzene in 60:40 to 70:30 mixtures called *Askarels*. PCBs typically were used in transformers inside buildings, where protection against fire was paramount.	No increase in cancer
Emmett EA	Studies of Transformer Repair Workers Exposed to PCBs, Part II	*Am J Indust Med* 1988;14:47–62	Cross-sectional	Cancer was not studied.	—
Goldsmith JR	Environmental Factors in the Epidemiology of Lymphosarcoma	*Pathology Annual, Part 2,* 1997;12	Geographic mortality analysis	Occupational data indicate that electrical workers have some excess risk of lymphosarcoma.	Inconclusive
Greenland S	A Case-Control Study of Cancer	*Int Arch Occup Environ Health* 1994;66(1):49–54	Case-control	Weak study.	Inconclusive
Gustavsson P	Short-Term Mortality and Cancer Incidence in Capacitor Manufacturing	*Am J Indust Med* 1986;10:341–344	Cohort	No increased cancer.	No increase in cancer
Gustavsson P	A Cohort Study of Swedish Capacitor Manufacturing workers exposed to PCBs	*Am J Indust Med* 1997;32:234–239	Cohort	The study is too small to infer association between PCBs and cancer, but the findings are consistent with previous studies.	Inconclusive
Hay A	Mortality of Power Workers	*Ann NY Acad Sci* 1997;837:138–156	Cohort	Too few deaths from malignancy.	Inconclusive

Author	Title	Citation	Type	Findings	Conclusion
Hoffmann W	Organochlorine Compounds: Risk of Non-Hodgkin's Lymphoma and Breast Cancer	*Arch Environ Health* 1996;51(3):189–192	Review	"Currently, OCs are considered to be an established risk factor for NHL." "Results for breast cancer are less conclusive."	NHL: PCBs are a suggested risk factor for NHL. Breast cancer: inconclusive
Hsieh S	Cohort Study on Mortality and Exposure to PCBs	*Arch Environ Health* 1996;51(6):417–424	Cohort	Increased SMR 61.17, CI 1.55–340 for Hodgkin's disease.	Inconclusive
Hunter DJ	Plasma Organo-chlorine Levels and the Risk of Breast Cancer	*New Engl J Med* 1997;337(18):1253–1258	Case-control	No evidence of an increased risk of breast cancer.	No increase in breast cancer
IARC	Evaluation of Carcinogenic Risks to Humans	An updating of *IARC Monographs*, Vols. 1 to 42, Suppl 7, 1987	Review	The available studies suggest an association between cancer and exposure to PCBs. The increased risk from hepatobiliary cancer emerged consistently in different studies. PCB is classified as Group 2A. Evidence was considered limited.	Limited evidence for cancer; probably carcinogenic to humans
Industrial Disease Standards Panel Ontario Ministry of Labour	Report on Occupational Exposure to PCBs and Various Cancers	1987	Review	1. Probable connection between liver, biliary tract, and gallbladder cancers. "When the cohorts are combined in a meta-analysis, compelling epidemiological evidence of excess cancers appears for the liver, biliary tract, and gallbladder." 2. No probable connection between any other site-specific cancer. 3. Recommendation for workers' compensation responsibility for claims arising from liver, biliary tract, and gallbladder cancers among workers with occupational PCB exposure of at least 3 months and with a latency period of 5 years.	Probable connection between liver, biliary tract, and gallbladder cancers
Industrial Disease Standards Panel Ontario Ministry of Labour	Response to Supplementary Questions Arising from IDSP Report No. 2	IDSP Report No. 2A, January 1990	Review	Liver, biliary tract, and gallbladder cancers discussed.	Probable connection between liver, biliary tract, and gallbladder cancers

(continued)

Table A2-2. Continued

Author	Article	Journal	Paper Type	Comments	Conclusion
James RC	PCB Expsore and Human Disease	*J Occup Med* 1993;35(2):136–148	Review	No cancer increase.	No increase in cancer
Kimbrough RD	Mortality Study in PCB Capacitor Workers	*Clin Toxicol* 1997:35	Retrospective mortality study of capacitor workers	Previously reported cancer increases among PCB-exposed workers were not confirmed.	No increase in cancer
Kimbrough RD	Polychlorinated Biphenyls and Human Health	*Crit Rev Toxicol* 1995;25(2):133–163	Review		Inconclusive
La Dou J		*Occupational Environmental Medicine*, 2d ed. Stanford, CT: Appleton & Lange, 1997. Pp 464–466.	Textbook	There has been no increased risk of breast or endometrial cancer in humans. Workers exposed to PCBs have a suggestion of increased risk of pancreatic cancer, brain cancer, and malignant melanoma. Other studies have found no evidence of excess cancer risk associated with PCB exposure.	No clear evidence of increased risk of cancer
Loomis D	Cancer Mortality among Electric Utility Workers Exposed to PCBs	*Occp Environ Med* 1997;54:720–728	Retrospective cohort	Large sample size. Detailed exposure data. Attempts to measure several confounders. "PCBs are carcinogenic to humans, with malignant melanoma being of greatest concern."	Malignant melanoma
Monsanto	MSDS on PCBs Polychlorinated Biphenyls (PCBs) Case No. 1336-36-3		MSDS	Not a scientific document	—
National Toxicology Program		Eighth Report on Carcinogens	Review	Inadequate evidence for carcinogenicity in humans. A slight increase of incidence of cancer, particularly melanoma of the skin has been reported.	Inadequate evidence for carcinogenicity in humans
Rosenman KD	Dioxin, Polychlorinated Biphenyls, and Dibenzofurans	Rom NR. *Environmental and Occupational Medicine*, 2d ed. Boston: Little, Brown, 1992. P 927	Textbook	Combining results from cohorts showed a significant increase in cancers of the liver, biliary tract, and gallbladder. Further studies were suggested. One study reported an increase in melanoma.	Inconclusive

Author	Citation	Type	Findings	Conclusion
Rosenstock	Pp 821–823	Textbook	In occupational cohorts, some evidence for brain cancers and melanoma have been presented but not confirmed. A cluster suggested the possibility of a relationship between PCB exposures and kidney cancer in utility workers.	No clear evidence of increased risk of cancer
Rothman N	A Nested Case-Control Study of Non-Hodgkin's Lymphoma	*Lancet* 1997;350:240–244	Case-control	Small size (case 74, controls 147). The study cannot support a causal relationship between PCB and non-Hodgkin's lymphoma but should be regarded as hypothesis-generating.	No significant relationship
Silberhorn EM	Carcinogenicity of Polyhalogenated Biphenyls: PCBs and PBBs	*Crit Rev Toxicol* 1990;20(6):440–496	Review	Although there is certainly no justification for a causal relationship, several of the epidemiologic studies do point to an association between some forms of cancer and exposure to PCBs. Most of these studies are inconclusive because they lack statistical power.	Inconclusive
Sinks T	Health Hazard Evaluation Report	Westinghouse Electric Corp., Bloomington, Indiana (Indiana State Board of Health), NIOSH, Jan 1991, HETA 89-116-2004, pp 1–27.			
Sinks T	Mortality among Workers Exposed to PCBs	*Am J Epidemiol* 1992;136(4):389–398	Cohort	The small number of observed deaths resulted in risk estimates with broad confidence intervals. Some evidence of an association between PCB exposure in an occupational environmental and mortality from malignant melanoma.	Inconclusive
Steineck G	Urethelial Cancer and Some Industry-Related Chemicals	*Am J Indust Med* 1990;17:371–391	Review	Paucity of data.	Inconclusive

(continued)

Table A2-2. Continued

Author	Article	Journal	Paper Type	Comments	Conclusion
Steineck G	Industry-Related Urethelial Carcinogens	*Am J Indust Med* 1989;16:209–224	Cohort	For electricians in electric power stations exposed to PCBs, the relative risk for bladder cancer was 1.3 (1.0–1.8). Although the report stated, "The present study gives some support for a causal relation between exposure to . . . PCB, and development of urothelial cancer," this is not strong evidence as the CI included 1.0.	Inconclusive
U.S. Department of Health & Human Services	Toxicological Profile for Polychlorinated Biphenyls (Update)	U.S. Department of Health and Human Services, Public Health Service, September 1997	Review	Page 7: "Studies of workers do not provide enough information to determine if PCBs cause cancer in humans. Based on the cancer in animals, PCBs can reasonably be anticipated to be carcinogens. IARC has determined that PCBs are probably carcinogenic to humans. The EPA has determined that PCBs are probably human carcinogens." Pages 32–36: "Several studies with inhalational exposure to PCBs were reviewed, and all results were considered to be inconclusive. No studies were located regarding cancer in animals after inhalation exposure to PCBs." Page 94: "No studies were located regarding carcinogenicity in humans following oral exposure to Aroclor PCB formulations." Page 106: "No studies were located regarding cancer in humans after dermal exposure to PCBs."	Inconclusive
U.S. EPA	PCBs: Cancer Dose-Response	National Centre for Environmental Assessment	Review	Limited to inadequate evidence of carcinogenicity.	Inclusive
Wong O	*Am J Indust Med*	1995;27:905–910	Critique	Reviews study by Yassi et al.	—
Yassi A	*Am J Indust Med*	1994;25:425–437	Historical cohort mortality study	See critique by Otto Wong in *Am J Indust Med* 1995;27:905–910.	Increased pancreatic cancer

Case Study 3: Apportionment of Asbestos-Related Disease

TEE L. GUIDOTTI

Few toxic exposures have received more attention in the past century than asbestos. Asbestos may cause a variety of life-threatening health outcomes. Some of them, such as lung cancer, are characteristic outcomes associated with but not specific to asbestos. Some, such as mesothelioma and asbestosis, are highly specific but uncommon [1–3]. In North America and Europe, particularly in Great Britain and France, there is an epidemic of asbestos-related lung cancer and mesothelioma as workers who were exposed during the 1960s and 1970s pass through the expected latency period and have achieved an age of peak risk. Asbestos is both a huge ongoing problem in occupational health and a model on which principles of evidence-based medical dispute resolution can be tested.

Here, I will explore the use of apportionment by cause in asbestos-related diseases where other putative risk factors, such as cigarette smoking, may be present. This discussion also serves as an example of the analysis of a complicated and sometimes contradictory scientific literature. The form of analysis is an application of the evidence-based approach advocated in this book.

Much is known about asbestos-related conditions. A great deal of work has been done in the laboratory on the mechanisms by which asbestos causes cancer, although much remains uncertain. What we know about the effects of asbestos on human beings is derived from population studies. The body of literature in epidemiology on asbestos-exposed workers is enormous. However, epidemiologic studies of populations at risk can only yield generalities. An epidemiologic study is a guide to what may be happening in a given case, and individual evaluation is essential to the fair adjudication of such cases. Bringing evaluation down to the individual case is often an ambiguous and uncertain undertaking. As noted in Chapter 11, assignment of attributable risk is an epidemiologic concept but apportionment applies to the individual. Apportionment is most defensible when the evidence is based on a group or population. For the individual, however, apportionment is a best estimate only.

Asbestos-related disease appears to be greatly under-recognized. Nevitt et al. [4] examined workers' compensation claims in Washington state during the period 1982 to 1986 for a high-risk population in which occupational disease already had been diagnosed at a university-affiliated clinic. Only half the claims in the state system were in fact accepted [4]. Criteria for acceptance were inconsistent among systems and within the state system; there was no or an unexpectedly low correlation between claim acceptance and chest film (by the ILO Classification, described below), presence of restrictive changes, smoking status, or concurrent obstructive lung disease. This unsatisfactory state of affairs is by no means uncommon.

Other studies of asbestos-related injury claims have shown similar results [4–6]. Together, these studies have demonstrated a lower rate of claim submission, lower rates of claims acceptance, and a higher mortality from potentially asbestos-related disease, including such characteristic disorders as asbestosis, among workers potentially eligible for compensation. After decades of research and discussion, many of the most basic issues related to asbestos are still in dispute. While some of these issues are slowly reaching consensus, controversies are still unresolved. For example, two of the more vigorous disputes are over the following issues:

- The risk associated with exposure to chrysotile in real terms. Scientists generally agree that the level of risk for most outcomes is lower compared with amphiboles.
- Whether there is a very large interaction between asbestos exposure and smoking that elevates the risk of lung cancer disproportionately. Early studies demonstrated alarmingly large interactions. Subsequent studies, particularly of chrysotile, have shown fewer or no interactions.

Interestingly, the most fundamental issue of all, whether our conventional statistical framework developed for population studies can be applied retrospectively to individual risk, is almost never mentioned (see Chapter 9).

In the presence of such controversy, it makes sense to avoid setting a policy for evaluating individual cases based on one interpretation or a single school of thought. For the purposes of a workable policy, I propose that the assumptions and findings admissible for apportionment should satisfy certain basic criteria:

- *They should be robust.* The underpinnings of a defensible policy for apportionment should not be highly sensitive to data from individual, unreplicated studies or other sources of substantial uncertainty.
- *They should be evidence-based.* Not every issue germane to a responsible policy is addressed in the scientific literature, and few are thoroughly explored by a large number of studies of very high quality. The best

evidence should prevail, as reflected in peer-reviewed studies whenever possible.

- *They should be based on the totality of evidence and on evaluated knowledge.* Although individual findings may be in dispute, the general outline of asbestos-related disease is known and should be reflected in a defensible policy.
- *When the data are not clear, they should be based on the most likely and the worst cases, giving the benefit of the doubt to the worker.* This concept for adjudication as a whole is specified in most workers' compensation legislation.
- *They should acknowledge controversy.* When a critical issue is not settled, the policy should make allowances for reasonable recognition of both sides of the argument.

Characteristics of Asbestos as a Hazard

This discussion assumes that the reader has a general familiarity with asbestos and asbestos-related disease. Suffice to say that this mineral has been widely and heavily used since the late nineteenth century because of its fireproofing, insulation, and chemical resistance properties. The use of asbestos increased greatly around the time of World War II. Asbestosis (the specific disease caused by asbestos) is a type of pneumoconiosis, a family of diseases caused by the deposition of dust in the lungs and the lung's response to its presence. Asbestosis has been known since the 1920s; lung cancer associated with asbestos exposure was recognized in the 1940s. Despite this knowledge, asbestos was poorly controlled. When the health hazards associated with asbestos became undeniable in the 1970s, asbestos-containing materials were mostly withdrawn from the market. An outright ban was imposed by the European Community in 1999. Health problems continue today as a consequence of past exposure; new exposure may occur when asbestos is removed from structures where it was placed decades ago.

There are two major types of asbestos: *chrysotile,* or "white asbestos," which consists of sheets rolled into long, hollow fibers, and *amphiboles,* which are solid fibers. There are many types of amphibole asbestos, of which crocidolite, or "blue asbestos," is the most potent in producing adverse health effects such as lung cancer and asbestosis. Chrysotile is the predominant form mined in North America and was used previously in insulation and most other products. Chrysotile fibers tend to dissolve in the body over time, so fewer fibers are retained in the lungs. All asbestos, but particularly the amphiboles, fragments into even smaller fibrils over time and/or when they are disturbed. The smaller fibrils are now suspected to be the most carcinogenic.

Chrysotile is often described as presenting less risk of adverse outcomes than amphibole asbestos, and this is correct [7]. However, the magnitude of risk associated with exposure to chrysotile is not clear, in part because of differences in the populations and occupational settings in which these risks have been studied.

Studies of Quebec asbestos miners [8,9] and local residents of mining communities [10] have demonstrated lower estimates of risk for mesothelioma and lung cancer than are observed among miners of the amphibole minerals. However, studies of miners and others with "upstream" exposure in the asbestos manufacturing process do not necessary replicate the risk associated with exposure of end users of chrysotile products [11]. McDonald and McDonald (quoted in Bignon and Brochard [7]) perceptively observed that a "major problem remains to explain why the risk in relation to exposure has been so much higher in the textile industry than in mining and milling—at least of chrysotile . . . ." Recently mined and milled chrysotile may vary considerably in distribution of fiber size, fragmentation, and number, including fibers in the submicroscopic range that are not easily counted from worked and fractured chrysotile [11,12]. McDonald et al. [13] suggested that this was an explanation for the markedly elevated incidence of lung cancer in one textile plant in the United States; this plant showed a 50-fold steeper exposure-response relationship compared with Canadian mining and milling operations. Thus it is not prudent to accept the risk estimates for chrysotile asbestos miners as definitive estimates of risk of end users, such as insulators.

The landmark early studies of asbestos workers in North America, especially insulation workers, were conducted on populations exposed primarily to chrysotile, and their risk estimates are much greater than those observed among miners [14]. Quebec chrysotile miners historically have demonstrated unremarkable trends in total mortality and all cancers, although demonstrating mortality from pneumoconioses, mesothelioma, and the mortality experience does not appear to be closely correlated with dust exposure [8,15]. The lower risk associated with mining and, to a lesser extent, milling is apparent when risk estimates are sorted by industry and fiber type [16]. These studies also demonstrated a relationship to cigarette smoking that constitutes one of the major examples in toxicology of interaction. This interaction is not consistent across industries and appears to be weak or even nonexistent for chrysotile miners in Quebec [15] but has been demonstrated for insulation workers. The knowledge available from the totality of the literature therefore provides a set of principles used in the following sections to create a robust, practical approach to apportionment in asbestos-related disease.

For the foregoing reasons, it makes sense to develop an approach that does not depend on whether chrysotile or amphibole asbestos exposure is at issue and to use estimates that reflect the experience of workers in end-use occupations rather than mining.

Asbestosis

Asbestosis is the characteristic pneumoconiosis associated with inhalation of asbestos fibers. The term should never be used generically to refer to asbestos-related disorders because this leads to unnecessary confusion [17].

Like all pneumoconioses, asbestosis consists of the direct effect of the dust and also of the effect on the lung of the reaction to its presence. In asbestosis, the pulmonary response is exuberant fibrosis, occurring in parenchyma (alveolar region) of the lung, initially adjacent to the airways in response to an alveolitis, or inflammation of the airspaces. Early asbestosis resembles the disease known as *usual interstitial pneumonia* (UIP), a synonym for *fibrosing alveolitis* and *idiopathic pulmonary fibrosis*.

Characteristic of both early asbestosis and UIP is the presence of an inflammatory reaction that can be measured by bronchoalveolar lavage (BAL), in which cells and secretions from the deep lung are obtained by bronchoscopy. With advancing disease, the fibrosis becomes more extensive and is more likely to be associated with other asbestos-related changes in the thorax. The diagnosis of asbestosis is usually made on the chest film, but computed tomography (CT) and high-resolution computed tomography (HRCT) are used increasingly to establish the diagnosis [18]. Both are more sensitive than conventional chest radiography in identifying interstitial fibrosis [19].

The final common pathway for both asbestosis and UIP, and for a variety of other pneumoconioses, is a coarse pattern of parenchymal fibrosis called *honeycombing*. Asbestosis is characterized by the presence of asbestos fibers and asbestos bodies, which distinguishes the condition from UIP and other fibrogenic pneumoconioses. Asbestos bodies are much easier to see but are much less common than asbestos fibers. Recently, new cases of asbestosis have not been as severe as in the past, when honeycombing and fibrous bands were common in advanced asbestosis cases. Fibers from tissue recovered at autopsy or biopsy sometimes were difficult to visualize because of the mass of scarred tissue, but total fiber counts from ashed tissue were very high in such cases [20].

The process of fibrosis in asbestosis is relatively localized to the interstitium (the structural connective tissue in the lung that lies between alveoli), which over time becomes thicker and more diffuse. Initially, the fibrosis begins as isolated patches that coalesce into rough or spiky-shaped masses that appear as irregular opacities on a chest film. These opacities are most frequent, and therefore most dense, on the chest film in the lower lung fields. Over time, they appear to coalesce into larger masses or opacities and sometimes may present as nodules, in which case cancer must be ruled out, or as bands of fibrosis. Ultimately, the scarring may become gross and interfere with the mechanical function of the lung.

In asbestosis, the airways are also affected, but not as much as the paren-chyma. Pulmonary function studies may show a mild obstruction to airflow, particularly early in the course of the disease [18,21]. In more advanced or rapidly progressing cases of asbestosis, this obstructive component is usually soon overwhelmed by a progressive restrictive disease, at least in part due to air trapping [22] that limits the capacity of the lungs and that ultimately may cause respiratory insufficiency. In less advanced or progressive disease, there is an accelerated loss of ventilatory capacity, sometimes appearing before radiographi-cally evident asbestosis. In such cases, however, the progression of the chronic airflow obstruction is greater with greater profusion of irregular opacities on the chest film [23]. Combined restrictive and obstructive deficits in asbestos-exposed workers seem to be associated with greater functional impairment [24].

Because it is difficult to appreciate obstructive disease against a background of severe restrictive disease, the airways component of asbestosis has not received much attention until recently. Pleural fibrosis is particularly associated with these restrictive changes and probably represents the contribution of mechanical changes in the chest wall, but this is a relatively minor effect [25–27]. Pulmonary function studies also show a reduced diffusing capacity because of both delayed diffusion across the thickened interstitium and mismatching of blood and air in the alveolar region resulting from the disruption of the fibrosis. This mismatching is also a reason for the progressive desaturation of oxygen in the blood that eventually results in hypoxemia and clinical respiratory insufficiency in severe cases. Mild cases of asbestosis may not necessarily show this interference with gas exchange, and blood gases may be normal in such cases.

All varieties of asbestos, chrysotile and amphiboles, may cause asbestosis at sufficiently high exposure levels. Commercially available asbestos often was a mixture of these fiber types anyway, so making fine distinctions is not usually warranted in practice. Unlike other outcomes associated with asbestos, there is no evidence that cigarette smoking plays any role in contributing to the onset of asbestosis or that the effects of asbestos exposure and cigarette smoking are positively interactive in causing enhanced asbestosis [28]. There is some evidence that once established, asbestosis may be enhanced by cigarette smoking, with an increased frequency of opacities detectable by HRCT for the same degree of asbestos exposure [29]. Because the frequency of opacities does not correlate closely with changes in pulmonary function and therefore impairment, it is not clear that this finding can be used as the basis for an apportionment formula.

The implications of these data simplify apportionment in most cases. Because asbestosis is a disease that is only caused by exposure to asbestos, and because other risk factors play only a very minor role in modifying the outcome associated with the fibrosis (as opposed to complications such as cancer), there is no basis for apportionment by cause. If the diagnosis is asbestosis and causation can be established, the apportionment by cause is 100% attributable to asbestos, and all respiratory impairment resulting from the fibrotic component of the disease is asbestos-related.

The general rule is that in the presence of asbestosis, all respiratory impairment should be apportioned to asbestos. This should be a rebuttable presumption. The exception may be a very mild case of asbestosis with minimal or no functional impairment associated with marked obstructive changes in a heavy smoker, a characteristic smoking-related respiratory impairment. In such a case, the restrictive component of the disease would be considered asbestos-related, and the obstructive component [taken as $FEV_1/FVC(\%)$ rather than FEV_1 compared with predicted] more than likely would reflect the influence of cigarette smoking. The treatment in such a case would then parallel that given below for chronic obstructive airways disease.

Chronic Obstructive Airways Disease

It has been known for many years that exposure to asbestos is associated with obstruction to airflow as well as restrictive changes. However, chronic obstructive airways disease (COAD) has not been emphasized as an asbestos-related outcome and has not been accepted by compensation agencies as a presumption or scheduled occupational disease. There are several reasons for this reluctance to recognize asbestos-related COAD. The most influential probably has been that the effect of cigarette smoking is not easily separated from asbestos exposure and has confounded the association, influencing agencies and adjudicators to attribute all the cause to the smoking [30]. Another factor is that the predominant effect in advanced asbestosis is restrictive disease, and the obstructive changes associated with lesser degrees of asbestosis largely have been overlooked [21,23]. Yet another factor is that mandated surveillance for asbestos-exposed workers, such as the OSHA asbestos standard in the United States, has emphasized early identification of restrictive changes and changes in the forced vital capacity (FVC) rather than the forced expiratory volume in 1 second (FEV_1).

Adults lose a fraction of their lung capacity and airflow velocity, as measured by routine spirometry, with age; this loss is predictable and for FEV_1 averages 30 ml/year. In theory, any person who lived long enough would develop obstructive disease once the natural loss progressed far enough. Pulmonary injury may accelerate this loss, and in cigarette smokers, this rate of loss may easily double or triple so that, during their lifetime, they dip well below the normal range and develop incapacity or the condition known as chronic obstructive pulmonary disease (COPD).

COPD and the less common term COAD are usually synonymous, but here COAD will be used to refer to the class of obstructive lung disorders and COPD to the specific disease. COPD refers to chronic lung diseases in which the outflow of air is obstructed: emphysema or chronic bronchitis or both, often with some element of asthma. Almost all COPD, except for certain rare diseases

Figure A3-1. Bronchogenic carcinoma in an asbestos cement pipe worker against a background of asbestosis.

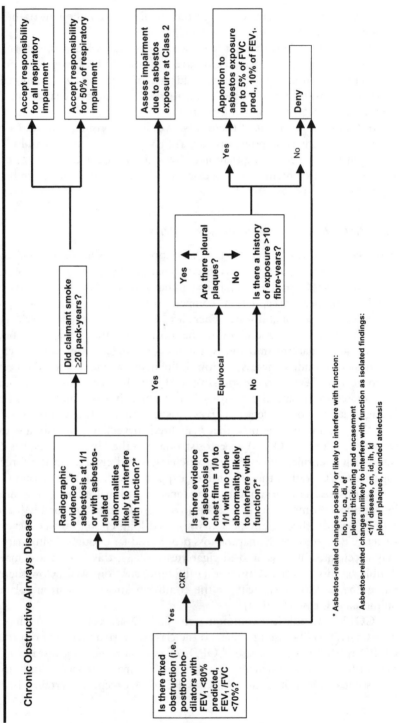

and rare occupational conditions, is caused by cigarette smoking. COAD is used here, purposefully, as the more general term in order to ensure that airways changes in general, including those associated with asbestos exposure, are not confused with the complex illness associated with cigarette smoking that most clinicians have in mind when they refer to COPD.

It is now well established that asbestos-exposed workers show accelerated loss of airflow and are at risk for obstructive airways disease [31–36]. Those with signs of early parenchymal fibrosis appear to be at higher risk for more rapid decline [37]. Functional changes are also correlated with respiratory symptoms such as cough, wheeze, and shortness of breath [38]. Asbestos-exposed workers who develop persistent respiratory symptoms are at risk for even more rapid loss of pulmonary function [38]. In addition, there is experimental evidence for a positive interaction (synergy) in airflow obstruction between asbestos exposure and cigarette smoking because of changes in compliance in the walls of small airways [39].

Studies of nonsmoking asbestos-exposed workers confirm that asbestos exposure alone can accelerate loss of pulmonary function [18,31,33,40–43]. The two studies that permit inference of the rate of loss of FEV_1 [33,41] suggest that the accelerated rate of decline, over the usual 30 ml/year, is on the order of 30 to 60 ml/year, or a doubling or tripling of the normal rate. The decline in FEV_1 was greater with higher exposure levels. This is in the same range as the effect of cigarette smoking.

The pathology and physiology of this effect are reasonably clear. The alveolitis induced by asbestos begins at the respiratory bronchiole, which is anatomically adjacent to the terminal and other small bronchioles. As well, there may be direct inflammation of the bronchiolar wall in response to deposited asbestos fibers [39,44]. The adjacent alveolitis changes the compliance of the walls of the small airways (which are membranous, unprotected by cartilage) and, together with loss of the elastic recoil of the surrounding lung parenchyma, causes a progressively larger fraction of the population of small airways in the lung to close earlier on expiration, trapping air and introducing resistance to airflow. Asbestos therefore causes a small airways disease that appears first as reduced flow rates in the midexpiratory part of the spirogram, which reflects airflow in the small-diameter but high cross-section peripheral airways, where normally there should be very little resistance to flow. This may occur with or without early signs of asbestosis [18]. Sarič and Perič (1996, unpublished) have proposed that this process follows an initial phase of several years in which small airways airflow actually increases due to stabilization of the bronchiolar wall by fibrosis.

Cigarette smoking induces a focal bronchiolitis and minimal adjacent alveolitis in much the same way. Over time, a loss of elastic recoil, early collapse of the bronchiole, and small airways disease ensue. An important component of this process, also presumably critical in asbestos-related bronchiolitis, is the release of inflammatory mediators and protease enzymes that degrade structural protein, resulting in local tissue destruction. This progresses to overt emphysema. To date, there is no evidence for an interaction between cigarette smoking and asbestos as a cause of small airways disease or loss of FEV_1 [31,33,40,41,43]. One may assume, therefore, that the two exposures contribute more or less independently to risk.

Given this apparently independent contribution to risk, apportionment by cause can be applied as a tradeoff between the contribution of asbestos exposure and the contribution of cigarette smoking to the degree of impairment because COAD is manifested by and defined by increased resistance to airflow. A reasonable method is needed for apportioning the relative contribution of cigarette smoking and asbestos in an asbestos-exposed worker who is impaired, with a reduced FEV_1. This might be done in three ways: (1) Assessing the rate of loss of pulmonary function specific to the worker (smoking or nonsmoking) prior to exposure to asbestos, (2) extrapolating the rate of loss, and (3) determining the difference between the predicted rate of loss and that observed, which is assumed to be due to asbestos exposure. The relative contribution of each to the last relevant set of pulmonary function studies would be the apportionment attributed to each cause.

This approach is most rigorous but depends on having at least two FEV_1 determinations prior to beginning work involving exposure to asbestos. This is not realistic in most cases. Variability in spirometric measurements is enough to obscure or exaggerate such changes when the tests are performed in different laboratories. Workers who have had routine spirometry are also likely to have had the test as surveillance for dust exposure in an earlier job or because they had a lung disease; in either case the predictive value of the baseline rate of change of FEV_1 is reduced, but it would be even more important to obtain individualized results. Removal from exposure to asbestos would not normally present a problem in interpretation because the accelerated decline in FEV_1 continues for at least 10 years [33].

When a baseline FEV_1 is available, assume that the rate of loss of pulmonary function due to aging is the average of 30 ml/year, extrapolate the expected rate of loss to current pulmonary function, and determine the difference between the predicted rate of loss and that observed. This difference is assumed to be due to asbestos exposure in a nonsmoker and apportioned between the two in a smoker exposed to asbestos. The relative contribution of each to the last relevant set of pulmonary function studies would be apportioned based on the Ohlson data [21] described below, with the functional loss due to asbestos taken from Ohlson et al. and the balance attributed to smoking.

This method can be used in cases where pre-exposure pulmonary function levels are not known, which is the majority of cases. This is not individual-specific but is based on group norms for rate of change of FEV_1. Spirometric variability remains a problem. This method would probably underestimate the apportioned contribution of asbestos because the Ohlson data reflect functional loss in healthy workers.

• Assess current pulmonary function and compare it with predicted values; then apply a crude rule of thumb to the difference: 50% apportionment to asbestos and 50% to cigarette smoking.

This method has the advantage of simplicity but cannot take into account degrees of exposure or smoking history. It is probably an overestimate (thereby "giving the benefit of doubt to the worker," appropriate to workers' compensation) because it is unlikely that asbestos exposure would be responsible for as much as 50% of isolated obstructive impairment. The following are proposed as essential criteria for a definition of substantial contribution:

• The contribution to the outcome (regardless of the subsequent impairment) should be demonstrable in some way or inferred from population data; a history of nominal exposure or the presence of a marker that does not correlate with risk is not enough.
• The contribution should be on the same order of and significant relative to natural individual variation and loss of function in progression of the disease. For example, if the normal adult change in FEV_1 is -30 ± 7 ml/year and -60 ± 10 ml/year is associated with COPD by age 60, an additional incremental loss of 10 ml/year due to an occupational exposure would clearly be significant (representing one-third of the contribution leading to pathology), but 5 ml/year would not be so significant because it falls within the range of measurement error and normal variation. In practice, the "noise" in measurement and lack of baseline measurements may make this approach difficult to apply.
• In cases where impairment results from loss of function due to the disease outcome, the proportion of impairment contributed by the cause in question should be enough to change the prognosis or clinical course, in other words, enough to make a difference in a borderline case.
• Whatever the contribution to the outcome, it should plausibly relate to the permanent impairment. In other words, if the presence of a pleural plaque does not predict airflow obstruction, demonstration of a pleural plaque cannot be used to suggest a substantial contribution of asbestos in causing airflow obstruction, notwithstanding their association with a restrictive component of reduced ventilatory capacity [45].

Applying these criteria, one may derive a reasonable test for substantial contribution in asbestos exposure, as demonstrated below. As a practical matter, individual awards at such low levels of impairment in the absence of a test would be small, but there could be many of them. A small error on the side of inclusiveness is not very expensive, but the total absence of a test would place a huge demand on the system.

Defining Substantial Contribution *in Asbestos Exposure: COAD*

One approach to defining *substantial contribution* is to identify a level of exposure commonly associated with definite functional changes that may be of significance in the progression of disease. In the real world, detailed exposure information over the lifetime of a worker is simply not available. In practice, this may mean resorting to general or approximate categories.

When there is a possibility of error, the policy in workers' compensation is to give the benefit of the doubt to the worker. Estimates of substantial contribution therefore should be set at a level that will include all or almost all claimants who are likely to be affected by their exposure and to exclude as many claimants as possible who are not likely to have been affected, but erring on the side of inclusion.

If half the impairment is due to an occupational cause, then the disorder is presumptively occupational and qualifies as an occupational disease. If less than half, then the contribution may be significant but is not the major determinant of disease. If the impairment is not sufficient to push an otherwise fit person into a level of impairment recognized by workers' compensation, it would be inconsistent to call it a substantial contribution for purposes of compensation. Therefore, an exposure that causes a lesion so trivial that it cannot be discerned in the contribution to total impairment cannot be considered a substantial contribution. As a practical matter, therefore, one is concerned about contributions to the apportionment of predominantly nonoccupational disease from 5 to 50 percent.

Ohlson et al. [21] presented data that relate lung function as a percentage predicted from regression equations by exposure category for asbestos workers. These data are cross-sectional in a stable, aging workforce without evidence of asbestos-related disease or evidence of significant outmigration. Although a longitudinal study would be preferable, these data do reflect the realities of clinical presentation. Notwithstanding that the regression never dipped below the range of normal, Ohlson's data show a relationship between very mild impairment and exposure and are particularly useful in defining the relationship between exposure and response for changes so subtle that they could not be appreciated by any other means (Table A3-1).

There are two ways of reading such a regression. It may be read as a prediction for the entire population and therefore a best estimate for the individual or as an average for the population with variability among individual subjects so that a small subset of subjects might have a markedly greater loss than the average. The authors comment that "the group exposed to dust with compara-

Table A3-1. Lung Function as a Percentage Predicted from Regression Equations by Exposure Category for Asbestos Workers (Data from Ohlson et al., 1984)

Fiber-Years	0–14 ($n = 41$)	15–22 ($n = 42$)	23+ ($n = 41$)
FVC	96.1	95.4	94.6
FEV$_1$	92.8	91.8	90.5

tively low asbestos fiber concentration had a minor impairment of lung function, . . . " both smokers and nonsmokers, and variance was low in this population. They do not identify a subset with disproportionately poor pulmonary function, although such a subset would be of greatest concern.

The Ohlson data show a linear relationship with a very slight slope and are clearly reflective of a mild effect in a population with generally preserved pulmonary function. It is therefore a useful data set for the purpose of defining substantial contribution.

The standard convention in pulmonary function testing is to consider both FVC and FEV$_1$ as abnormal only when they fall below 80% of predicted as adopted by the *AMA Guides to the Evaluation of Permanent Impairment*. Functional impairment for most people, other than athletes, is generally not demonstrable until at least this much function has been lost. FVC is less obviously linked to symptomatic impairment than FEV$_1$ and seems to be less impaired in asbestos-related disease than FEV$_1$, at least in the earliest stages. Therefore, FEV$_1$ should be used as the most sensitive indicator of effect. If one assumes that 20% of FEV$_1$ must be lost before impairment is obvious, what fraction of that 20% must result from a given cause before it can be considered *substantial?*

For a disorder to result in a loss of FEV$_1$ sufficient to push a normal person who smoked across the line into clinical impairment, perhaps half this residual may be required; this is a clinical impression not easily validated by data. Thus a level of exposure sufficient to result in loss of 5% of function is a reasonable threshold for what is substantial. This is also reasonable considering that it exceeds the measurement error of careful spirometry by the American Thoracic Society (ATS) criteria.

Referring to Table A3-1 [21], a loss of only 5% of FEV$_1$ would correspond to approximately 10 fiber-years of asbestos exposure. This number can now be compared with other derivations as an estimate of a reasonable exposure level constituting substantial contribution.

If the effect of an exposure to asbestos, for example, were only to produce a pleural plaque, it might qualify as a tissue injury in pathologic terms but not as a cause of an outcome leading to impairment. The tissue injury did not interfere with function. In some compensation systems, the worker is still entitled to compensation for an asbestos-related condition, i.e., medical costs for annual surveillance, but not for permanent impairment. However, if one demonstrates that the same exposure to asbestos resulted in a decrement in pulmonary function that falls outside the range of normal variability and could mean the difference between impairment and freedom from impairment in a worker developing COAD, this would constitute a substantial contribution. Unfortunately, there is no relationship demonstrable between the loading of fibers required to produce a plaque and that required to contribute to airflow obstruction, so plaques cannot be used as a marker of substantial contribution, and the absence of plaques cannot be used to rule out a substantial contribution [45].

Lung Cancer

Lung cancer is a much more difficult apportionment problem than either of the two asbestos-related outcomes discussed earlier [46]. There are many causes of lung cancer, many of them occupational and one major lifestyle cause, cigarette smoking. Apportioning between occupational and nonoccupational causes of lung cancer in a worker exposed to asbestos, therefore, is almost always an issue of ruling out the significance of other occupational exposures and then estimating the most likely contribution of asbestos against that of cigarette smoking.

Relationships Between Smoking and Asbestos Exposure

Complicating matters is the fact that there is controversy over the positive interaction between asbestos exposure and smoking in conferring risk of lung cancer. In this section the issue will be addressed from a somewhat different point of view. The essential issue for purposes of apportionment and assessing causation is not whether an interaction exists but whether the evidence supports the assumption of a presumption among smokers. In other words, do smokers exposed to asbestos experience at least a doubling of their risk compared with unexposed smokers? The evidence suggests that whether an interaction exists or not, such a presumption is justified.

In the classic studies conducted on insulation workers and other groups in the 1970s, it was observed that asbestos exposure alone conferred a risk of lung cancer approximately 5 times the baseline risk of a nonsmoking person not exposed to asbestos. Cigarette smoking alone conferred a risk approximately 10 to 15 times that of the baseline. However, the combination of work-related asbestos exposure and cigarette smoking was associated with a risk of 50 to 100 times the baseline, far greater than if both risks were simply added and roughly what one might expect if they were multiplied, and provides a classic example of multiplicative (synergistic) interaction.

This interaction reflects an underlying biological mechanism. This mechanism clearly acts to amplify the effects of the exposure to asbestos to greatly enhance the risk following combined exposure and does so in a nonlinear fashion.

Figure A3-2. Mesothelioma in another asbestos cement pipe worker with no radiographic signs of asbestosis.

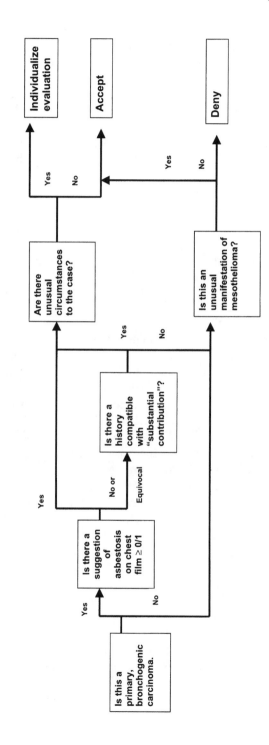

This means that it is not possible to trade off the effects of asbestos and smoking as if their contributions were additive or linear. Because the risks of lung cancer are nonlinear, simple regressions or calculations of relative risk associated with a given level of asbestos exposure and a given smoking history cannot resolve the problem. A much more complicated interactive regression, or curvilinear function, would be required to estimate the contribution of each factor. In practice, an attempt to apply such a complicated formula based on statistical patterns in a large population with large variance would appear arbitrary in the case of an individual and would be open to challenge based on the characteristics of the individual claimant.

One problem in dealing with this interaction is that past studies of lung cancer among smoking asbestos-exposed workers were based on much higher asbestos exposure levels than occur today and were documented in populations with a generally higher prevalence and intensity of smoking than occurs today. (Past studies also did not break down this observed interaction by age group, which would be helpful in thinking about apportionment.) The old rules of thumb may no longer apply in an era when asbestos exposure is far less, with concomitant reduction in cigarette smoking. As the magnitude of each exposure is reduced, it is likely that the interaction becomes less as well because it too is likely to be exposure-dependent. Thus one must conclude that although the apportionment by cause of a lung cancer to asbestos or cigarette smoking is not a simple linear tradeoff, it is probably no longer a tradeoff between steeply exponential curves either. Paradoxically, this reduces the influence of cigarette smoking as the dominant factor in the equation and makes it easier to conceptualize apportionment between the two factors.

The rules of rebuttable presumption remain useful in this application. The principle of presumption is that a risk attributed to exposure to a possible cause must be approximately double that without exposure in order to conclude that it is more likely than not, all other things being equal. While this magnitude of risk has been demonstrated in many studies, the degree of exposure may provide a rebuttable premise, for example, when the claimant or plaintiff had not accumulated sufficient exposure for one to expect a significant contribution.

At first, it might seem that because cigarette smoking accounts for most of the risk for developing lung cancer, the odds that a cancer was caused by cigarette smoking in a person who smoked but was not exposed to asbestos were 10 to 1, an overwhelming ratio corresponding to a 90% apportionment by cause on a population basis. This leads to a clearly justified presumption that in all cases of comparable smoking history, a lung cancer would have been caused by the cigarette smoking, not by one of the other factors contributing only 10%. Correspondingly, the odds that a cancer was caused by asbestos in a nonsmoking, asbestos-exposed person would be 5 to 1, clearly justifying the presumption in a nonsmoker. If the tradeoff were linear, it might be tempting to compare the

10-fold risk against the 5-fold risk and to conclude that cigarette smoking was twice as important a factor, for odds of 2 to 1.

This is not logical in a compensation context and does not take into account the interaction between cigarette smoking and asbestos. The preferred analysis would be to observe that risk is excessive *among smokers*. This is the only relevant comparison if one "takes the worker as he [or she] comes" and applies the "thin skull" rule, that unusual susceptibility in the injured party does not absolve the employer or manufacturer of liability. (In workers' compensation, of course, the employer is not held liable. The burden of liability is shifted to the system if the claim is accepted.) The odds that a cancer was associated with asbestos exposure in a cigarette smoker compared with a nonexposed cigarette smoker would then be around 5 or 10 to 1, more than enough to justify a presumption that in any smoker exposed to asbestos, the cancer in question was due to the asbestos exposure. Because the mechanism is interactive, the cigarette smoking contributed risk, "but for" the asbestos exposure, the probability of the individual smoker developing the lung cancer would have been much less. Given this analysis, the strength of the interaction between asbestos exposure and cigarette smoking does not have to be extremely high to justify a presumption on this basis alone, as long as the combined risk is at least double that of cigarette smoking alone.

There is evidence for an interaction between smoking and chrysotile exposure, but the critical issue is whether there is strong evidence for an effect of asbestos that doubles the risk of lung cancer among exposed smokers compared with unexposed smokers. Studies in the chrysotile asbestos manufacturing sector in China [47] do show an interaction consistent with that described in the classic insulation workers' studies of the past. The asbestos effect is on the order of a factor between 6 and 7 as a ratio of the risks of "medium" smokers who are exposed to asbestos to smokers who are not exposed to asbestos compared with a factor of 4 as a ratio of the risks of nonsmokers, exposed to unexposed. Thus, in this cohort, the risk conferred by exposure to chrysotile asbestos increases the risk of lung cancer among smokers by a factor greatly exceeding a simple doubling of risk.

Studies of Quebec chrysotile miners have not shown a positive interaction. They do demonstrate an asbestos effect that approaches but falls short of a doubling of risk among smokers of approximately 1.7 [13,48]. It is not known how the limitations that have already been discussed would affect this risk estimate. Given the statistical uncertainties and the wide confidence interval (which went up to 5.4 at the upper bound), 1.7 can be taken as consistent with a doubling.

Workers in an East End London factory showed an approximate doubling of risk among smokers exposed to asbestos compared with those who were not [48]. The authors briefly reviewed similar studies of insulation workers and showed that although risk estimates varied, the relative risk for exposed smokers compared with unexposed smokers was greatly in excess of doubling and in the case of insulation workers exceeded 5.

Given this analysis, it is clear that in either smokers or nonsmokers, the occurrence of a compatible bronchogenic carcinoma in a worker exposed to asbestos at a substantial level of exposure generally should be apportioned 100% to the asbestos exposure.

Mesothelioma

The worst outcome of asbestos exposure is mesothelioma, a cancer with a poor prognosis and an almost invariable association with asbestos exposure. Mesothelioma in the presence of a history of asbestos exposure must be presumed to have been caused by asbestos. Chrysotile asbestos generally is considered less likely to induce mesothelioma than amphibole forms [49]. However, even a history of exposure to chrysotile alone does not rule out an association because of the contamination or concomitant use of amphiboles. There are some risk factors for mesothelioma other than asbestos exposure, chiefly family history and possibly infection with the virus SV40, which is very common. However, mesothelioma without a history of exposure to asbestos is very rare, and these additional risk factors do not seem to be important in greatly increasing risk unless the individual is exposed to asbestos. Cigarette smoking does not increase the risk of mesothelioma, and there is no evidence that it modifies the clinical course or progression of the cancer. Thus any impairment associated with the cancer, including pain, chest wall mechanical problems, respiratory insufficiency, and disabling symptoms, is apportioned entirely to asbestos.

Given the poor prognosis for recovery, the subjective symptoms that will accompany progressive impairment, and thus a reduced capacity to work and to disability, it is only reasonable to apportion both cause and impairment to the asbestos as soon as the symptoms or signs of mesothelioma become manifest. Both the original impairment and the prognosis for permanent impairment are soon determined by the tumor, and the cause of the mesothelioma can be presumed in almost all cases to be the asbestos exposure.

Equity

Asbestos-related outcomes vary greatly in their suitability for apportionment. For mesothelioma and asbestosis, apportionment is not a meaningful process because development of the disease, by definition, implies asbestos-related causation. The only meaningful question is whether the diagnosis is correct. For airflow obstruction, it is a complex and technical but theoretically valid approach. For lung cancer, it is complicated by the positive interaction and its implications for presumption, but there are no markers or approaches that support apportionment in the individual case. This means that different asbestos-exposed workers with different outcomes are being judged differently by the current system of workers' compensation. In some cases, e.g., patients with asbestosis who have a predictably high cancer risk, the sequence of these outcomes is almost a matter of chance, and the injured worker may as easily have presented with lung cancer first as asbestosis.

Unlike apportionment of impairment, where there are consensus standards such as the *AMA Guides to the Evaluation of Permanent Impairment,* apportionment by cause has achieved no consensus, defies the imposition of rigid standards, and is not convertible (as is percentage impairment of the total person) from one disease category to another. Within this class of injured workers, is it reasonable to apportion in some cases and not others simply because apportionment is possible in those cases?

This raises an issue of equity. On the one hand, it is standard procedure for workers' compensation to evaluate hand injuries, occupational lung disease, noise-induced hearing loss, and brain injury by different criteria. The "apportioned" causation may be reflected in the apportioned impairment (in these cases always for aggravational injury) so that eventually these very different cases are evaluated on a comparable scale. However, asbestos-related diseases reflect different outcomes of a common exposure in a situation where the effect is not aggravational but simultaneously causal. Why should these related disorders be treated so differently?

Asbestos-related diseases are attractive models for the application of apportionment. However, a close and detailed examination of how apportionment applies to these diseases uncovers serious problems. With advances in biomarkers, epidemiology, and models derived from various disease entities, it may be possible to put apportionment on a more scientific basis. To validate the approach, however, more focused research into apportionment as an objective will be required.

References

1. Bégin R, Dufresne A, Plante F, Massé S. Asbestos related disorders. *Can Respir J* 1994;1:167–186.

2. Bedrossian CWM. Asbestos-related diseases: A historical and mineralogic perspective. *Semin Diagn Pathol* 1992;9:91–96.

3. Craighead JE, Abraham JL, Churg A, et al. The pathology of asbestos-associated diseases of the lungs and pleural cavities: Diagnostic grading criteria and proposed grading schema. *Arch Pathol Lab Med* 1982;106:644–696.

4. Nevitt C, Daniell W, Rosenstock L. Workers' compensation for non-malignant asbestos-related lung disease. *Am J Indust Med* 1994;26:821–830.

5. Finkelstein M. Analysis of mortality patterns and workers' compensation awards among asbestos insulation workers in Ontario. *Am J Indust Med* 1989;16:523–528.

6. Barroetavena MC, Teschke K, Bates DV. Unrecognized asbestos-induced disease. *Am J Indust Med* 1996;29:183–185.

7. Bignon J, Brochard P. Epidemiology of lung cancer in relation to asbestos exposure. In: Liddell D, Miller K (eds). *Mineral Fibers and Health*. Boca Raton, FL: CRC Press, 1991. Pp 197–210.

8. Liddell FD, McDonald AD, McDonald JC. Dust exposure and lung cancer in Quebec chrysotile miners and millers. *Ann Occup Hyg* 1998;42(1):7–20.

9. McDonald AD, Case BW, Churg A, et al. Mesothelioma in Quebec chrysotile miners and millers: Epidemiology and etiology. *Ann Occup Hyg* 1997;41(6):707–719.

10. Camus M, Siemiatycki J, Meek B. Nonoccupational exposure to chrysotile asbestos and the risk of lung cancer. *N Engl J Med* 1998;338(22):1565–1571.

11. Meyers J. Asbestos, cancer, and the environment: What do studies of mining regions tell us? *OEM Report* 1998;12(9):81–85.

12. Landrigan PJ. Asbestos: Still a carcinogen. *N Engl J Med* 1998;338(22): 1618–1619.

13. McDonald AD, Fry JS, Woolley AJ, McDonald J. Dust exposure and mortality in an American chrysotile textile plant. *Br J Indust Med* 1983;40(4):361–367.

14. Selikoff IJ, Hammond EC, Seidman H. Mortality experience of insulation workers in the United States and Canada, 1943–1976. *Ann NY Acad Sci* 1979;330:91–116.

15. McDonald JC, Liddell FDK, Dufresne A., McDonald A. The 1891–1920 birth cohort of Quebec chrysotile miners and millers: Mortality 1976–1988. *Br J Indust Med* 1993;50:1073–1081.

16. Hughes JM. Epidemiology of lung cancer in relation to asbestos exposure. In: Liddell D, Miller K (eds). *Mineral Fibers and Health*. Boca Raton, FL: CRC Press, 1991. Pp 136–145.

17. Woodard PK, McAdams HP, Outnam CE. Asbestos exposure and asbestosis: Clarifying terminology and avoiding confusion. *J R Soc Med* 1995;88:669–671.

18. Dujič, Tocilj J, Sarič M. Early detection of interstitial lung disease in asbestos exposed non-smoking workers by mid-expiratory flow rate and high-resolution computed tomography. *Br J Indust Med* 1991;48:663–664.

19. Bégin R, Ostiguy, Filion R, et al. Computed tomography in the early detection of asbestosis. *Br J Indust Med* 1993;50:689–698.

20. Roggli VL, Pratt PC, Brody AR. Asbestos content of lung tissue in asbestos associated diseases: A study of 110 cases. *Br J Indust Med* 1986;43:18–28.

21. Ohlson C-G, Rydman T, Sundell L, et al. Decreased lung function in long-term asbestos cement workers: A cross-sectional study. *Am J Indust Med* 1984;5:359–366.

22. Kilburn KH, Warshaw RH. Airways exposure from asbestos exposure: Effects of asbestosis and smoking. *Chest* 1994;106(4):1061–1070.

23. Kilburn KH, Warshaw RH. Airway obstruction in asbestos-exposed shipyard workers: With and without irregular opacities. *Respir Med* 1990;84(6):449–455.

24. Barnhart S, Hudson LD, Mason SE, et al. Total lung capacity: An insensitive measure of impairment in patients with asbestosis and chronic obstructive pulmonary disease? *Chest* 1988;93:299–302.

25. Kee ST, Gamsu G, Blanc P. Causes of pulmonary impairment in asbestos-exposed individuals with diffuse pleural thickening. *Am J Respir Crit Care Med* 1996;154: 789–793.

26. Schwartz DA, Fuortes LJ, Galvin JR, et al. Asbestos-induced pleural fibrosis and impaired lung function. *Am Rev Respir Dis* 1990;141:321–326.

27. Rosenstock L, Barnhart S, Heyer NJ, et al. The relation among pulmonary function, chest roentgenographic abnormalities, and smoking status in an asbestos-exposed cohort. *Am Rev Respir Dis* 1988;138:272–277.

28. Samet JM, Epler GR, Gaensler EA, Rosner B. Absence of synergism between exposure to asbestos and cigarette smoking in asbestosis. *Am Rev Respir Dis* 1979;120:75–82.

29. Neri S, Boraschi P, Antonelli A, et al. Pulmonary function, smoking habits, and high resolution computed tomography (HRCT) early abnormalities of lung and pleural fibrosis in shipyard workers exposed to asbestos. *Am J Indust Med* 1996;30:588–595.

30. Becklake MR. Asbestos-related diseases of the lung and other organs: Their epidemiology and implications for clinical practice. *Am Rev Respir Dis* 1976;114:187–227.

31. Schwartz DA, Davis CS, Merchant JA, et al. Longitudinal changes in lung function among asbestos-exposed workers. *Am J Respir Crit Care Med* 1994;150:1243–1249.

32. Kennedy SM, Wedal S, Müller N, et al. Lung function and chest radiograph abnormalities among construction insulators. *Am J Indust Med* 1991;20:673–684.

33. Siracusa A, Forcina A, Mollichella E, et al. An 11-year longitudinal study of the occupational dust exposure and lung function of polyvinyl chloride, cement and asbestos cement factory workers. *Scand J Work Environ Health* 1988;14:181–188.

34. Mohsenifar Z, Jasper AJ, Mahrer T, Koerner SK. Asbestos and airflow limitation. *J Occup Med* 1986;28:817–820.

35. Ohlson C-G, Bodin L, Rydman T, Hogstedt C. Ventilatory decrements in former asbestos cement workers: A four year follow-up. *Br J Indust Med* 1985;42:612–616.

36. McDermott M, Bevan MM, Elmes PC, et al. Lung function and radiographic change in chrysotile workers in Swaziland. *Br J Indust Med* 1982;39:338–343.

37. Nakadate T. Decline in annual lung function in workers exposed to asbestos with and without pre-existing fibrotic changes on chest radiography. *Occup Environ Med* 1995;52:368–373.

38. Brodkin CA, Barnhart S, Anderson G, et al. Correlation between respiratory symptoms and pulmonary function in asbestos-exposed workers. *Am Rev Respir Dis* 1993;148:32–37.

39. Wright JL, Tron V, Wiggs B, Churg A. Cigarette smoke potentiates asbestos-induced airflow abnormalities. *Exp Lung Res* 1988;14:537–548.

40. Griffith DE, Garcia GN, Dodson RF, et al. Airflow obstruction in nonsmoking, asbestos- and mixed dust-exposed workers. *Lung* 1993;171:213–224.

41. Rom WN. Accelerated loss of lung function and alveolitis in a longitudinal study of non-smoking individuals with occupational exposure to asbestos. *Am J Indust Med* 1992;21(6):835–844.

42. Grimson RC. Apportionment of risk among environmental exposures: Application to asbestos exposure and cigarette smoking. *J Occup Med* 1987;29:253–255.

43. Kilburn KH, Warshaw RH, Einstein K, Bernstein J. Airway disease in non-smoking asbestos workers. *Arch Environ Health* 1985;40(6):293–295.

44. Churg A, Stevens B. Enhanced retention of asbestos fibers in the airways of human smokers. *Am J Respir Crit Care Med* 1995;151:1409–1413.

45. Brodkin CA, McCullough J, Sooyer B, et al. Lobe of origin and histologic type of lung cancer associated with asbestos exposure in the beta-carotene and retinol efficacy trial. *Am J Indust Med* 1997;32:582–591.

46. Hyers TM, Ohar JM, Crim C. Clinical controversies in asbestos-induced lung diseases. *Semin Diagn Pathol* 1992;9:97–101.

47. Zhu HL, Wang ZM. Study of occupational lung cancer in asbestos factories in China. *Br J Indust Med* 1993;50:1039–1042.

48. Berry G, Newhouse ML, Antonis P. Combined effect of asbestos and smoking on mortality from lung cancer and mesothelioma in factory workers. *Br J Indust Med* 1985;42:12–18.

49. McDonald JC, McDonald AD. Epidemiology of mesothelioma from estimated incidence. *Prevent Med* 1977;6:426–446.

Index